Learning Chess to Improve Math Ho Math Chess 何数棋谜 www.homathchess.com
Frank Ho, Amanda Ho © 1995 – 2021 All rights reserved.
Student name _____ Assignment date:_____

Learning Chess to Improve Math

数棋谜式
国际象棋

DO NOT COPY

Frank Ho   Amanda Ho

何数棋谜 培训

Ho Math Chess Learning Centre

Learning Chess to Improve Math   数棋谜式健脑国际象棋
 Math Chess 何数棋谜 www.homathchess.com
Frank Ho, Amanda Ho © 1995 – 2021   All rights reserved.

Student name _____ Assignment date:_____

Table of Contents

Preface 7
Ho's other publications 11
Part 1 Introducing to chess pieces and chessboard 12
Chessboard 13
Chessboard setup using traditional chess pieces 14
Chessboard setup 16
    Flat Chinese chess set and Ho Math Chess teaching set 17
Chess pieces and their mathematical values 19
Match chess pieces and spatial movements 20
    Symbolic Chess Language (SCL) for a flat chess set 21
Chess pieces' names and moves 24
Chessboard setup using traditional chess pieces 25
Cutting chessboard into equal parts 26
Notations of chess pieces 27
Sorting Symbol chess symbols attributes 28
Review of values of chess pieces (Points) 32
    Which side has more points? 33
    Advantages of using Ho Math Chess teaching set 37
    Characteristics of SCL 39
    Samples of SCL integrated into math 40
Part 2 Quickstart for beginners on chess moves 50
How the pawn moves 51
How the rook moves 56
How the bishop moves 61
How the king moves 64
How the queen moves 66
How the knight moves 69
Part 3 More chess moves and their connections to arithmetic 77
Chessboard and arithmetic problems 78

Learning Chess to Improve Math 数棋谜式健脑国际象棋
Ho Math Chess 何数棋谜 www.homathchess.com
Frank Ho, Amanda Ho © 1995 – 2021 All rights reserved.

Student name _____ Assignment date:_____

Using chessboard to create math problems – different sized squares 78
Chessboard and matchsticks 81
Chessboard and coordinates 82
Travelling across the chessboard 83
Travelling across the chessboard 84
Counting Paths using the chessboard 85

How does the pawn move? **86**
How pawns move and take 88
Pawn promotion 89
Types of pawns 91
En Passant 92

How does the rook move? **96**
No rooks attacking each other 98
Where can the rook move safely? 99
Rook travelling in chess notations 100
Rook Path 102
Perpendicular line and right angle 103
Parallel line and geometric shape 104

How does the king move? **105**
King's shortest path 107

How does the queen move? **108**
Placing 2 queens 109
Eight queens' problem 110

How does the bishop move? **113**
Bishop moving in Pascal triangle path 114
Bishop moving either on the white or black square 115
Bishop moving in odd dimension chessboard 116
Bishop moving in even dimension chessboard 117
Tracing graph with one stroke 118
Tracing graph with one stroke 119
Summary of bishop moving in odd or even dimension chessboard 120
Bishop moving on a mini-chessboard 121

How does the knight move? **122**

Learning Chess to Improve Math 数棋谜式健脑国际象棋
Ho Math Chess 何数棋谜 www.homathchess.com
Frank Ho, Amanda Ho © 1995 – 2021   All rights reserved.

Student name _____ Assignment date:_____

    Knight travelling is not a real distance **125**

    Knight's mini-tour **126**

    Knight's grand tour **127**

    Knight's move used in solving math problems **128**

    Knight tour and a magic square **131**

    Connecting knight **132**

Mixed chess moves problems **133**

Intersecting squares and set theory **136**

Part 4 Check, checkmate, or stalemate **137**

    Check or Checkmate **137**

The shortest moves of checkmate (2-move mate) **143**

Scholar's mate (4-move mate) **144**

Checkmate with the king at the corner **146**

Checkmate with the king on the side **147**

Checkmate with knight **148**

Checkmate with bishop **149**

Checkmate with rook **150**

Checkmate with queen **152**

Stalemate **154**

Check, checkmate, stalemate, or none of the above **157**

Under promotion **162**

Alternative moves **163**

When to attack? **164**

Attacking and Defending **167**

Order of exchanges **170**

Visualization and think ahead **171**

Zugzwang **172**

Overworked piece **173**

Part 5 Castling **174**

Castling **178**

Part 6 Tactics - Fork, Pin, Skewer, and Discovered Check **179**

How does the fork work? **180**

Learning Chess to Improve Math	数棋谜式健脑国际象棋
Ho Math Chess 何数棋谜 www.homathchess.com	
Frank Ho, Amanda Ho © 1995 – 2021 All rights reserved.	

Student name _____ Assignment date: _____

How does the pin work? **186**

   Using a pin to win a piece **187**

   Does White's pin win? **189**

How does the discovered check work? **190**

How does the skewer work? **194**

Part 7 Mathematical Chess Puzzles **197**

Pattern and logic **198**

Pattern and relation (Tabulation) **247**

Pattern and relation (Tabulation in $ax + by + ... = c,$ where a, b, c are constant.) **249**

Path and geometry **251**

Chess Pieces and geometry **259**

Chess and geometry **260**

Logic **262**

Tree diagram **269**

Fraction **271**

Venn diagram **273**

Probability **276**

Palindrome **278**

Chess and computations integrated problems **279**

   Chess math **280**

   Making mathematical sentence true **282**

   Computation using chess pieces values **283**

   Making ten **284**

   Reversed calculation of 5 .... **286**

   Doubling **287**

   Multiplication **288**

   Multiplication and addition **292**

   Multiplication and subtraction **294**

   Equation **297**

Arrangement **298**

Magic square **303**

If then Equation **304**

Learning Chess to Improve Math 数棋谜式健脑国际象棋
Ho Math Chess 何数棋谜 www.homathchess.com
Frank Ho, Amanda Ho © 1995 – 2021   All rights reserved.

Student name _____ Assignment date:_____

Counting Paths 307
Part 8 Chess and Math Connection 308
Math and Chess Contests 308
Appendix A Connection of Magic Chess and Math Puzzles 314
A free Paper Set of Ho Math Chess 345
Introducing Ho Math Chess in Chinese 介紹何数棋谜 348
Introducing Ho Math Chess™ 349

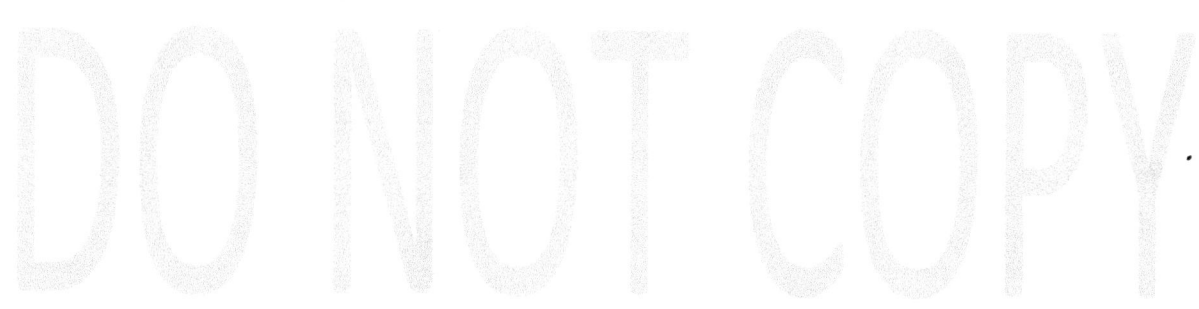

| Learning Chess to Improve Math 数棋谜式健脑国际象棋 |
| Ho Math Chess 何数棋谜 www.homathchess.com |
| Frank Ho, Amanda Ho © 1995 – 2021   All rights reserved. |

Student name _____ Assignment date:_____

Preface

How did I start to write this *Learning Chess to Improve Math* workbook?

I started to teach my son chess when he was five years old. At that time, a lot of information I had read indicated a strong relationship between mathematics and chess. My son was interested in chess, so what would happen if he had the same interest in chess on a subject requiring him to use his chess knowledge? What could chess offer in mathematics education? These kinds of questions sparked my interest in studying the relationship between chess and math. I found that there had been many chess or math puzzles published, but I could not find a collection of mathematical chess problems created explicitly for youngsters.

In 1995, I was involved in teaching math and chess simultaneously, and I started to seriously look into the possibility of creating some math and chess hybrid problems. This is how my son and I began to create the first generation of Math and Chess integrated workbook titled *Mathematical Chess Puzzles for Juniors* ISBN 0-9683967-0-4. It was archived at the National Library of Canada. It is designed and written to learn all kinds of problem-solving skills through over 100 mind-provoking and sometimes mind-boggling mathematical chess puzzles. The uniqueness of this book is that only basic chess knowledge and elementary math ability are needed to solve most of these puzzles.

I have been refining the contents ever since, and after almost 20 years of working on the first math and chess workbook, I have incorporated many math concepts. Today's version is the fourth generation. This workbook integrating chess and math puzzles could be used as supplemental or enriched material to supplement the math curriculum.

World's first and copyrighted *Mathematical Chess Puzzles for Juniors* workbook

The first edition of the workbook *Mathematical Chess Puzzles for Juniors,* created in 1995, was the world's first. I did a thorough literature and library catalogues searches and publicized my workbook on the internet (including rec.games.chess.misc) resulted in nothing similar to my workbook that had ever been published. There was no integrated chess and math workbook ever published for the elementary students when I published my workbook in 1995. Also, I have updated the workbook since I published the first one 20 years ago with many new and innovative ideas; still, my workbook is the only one on the market. It would be devastating for me if some copycats just copied my ideas and formats of worksheets and started to commercialize them. To protect my intellectual property, I am the world's first on the following ideas and concepts, and I am the original creator of unique formats of worksheets:

- 1995, I used chess pieces' symbols and incorporated chess pieces' values into math worksheets. (The value system is the one used by the Chess Federation of Canada.).
- In July 2004, I created a two-column format on each page, one column is for chess questions, and the other side is for math puzzles. These two columns show the logical relationship between chess and math. This is the second-generation version.
- In February 2005, I used symbols of chess pieces in the math puzzles to instil the concept of variables. This is the third generation of the workbook.

| Learning Chess to Improve Math 数棋谜式健脑国际象棋 |
|  Math Chess 何数棋谜 www.homathchess.com |
| Frank Ho, Amanda Ho © 1995 – 2021   All rights reserved. |

Student name _____ Assignment date:_____

- December 11, 2007, was the date when the world's first flat-surfaced, all-squared, uniform looks chess teacher set was made available to the world. This chess teacher set has become a collector's item since not only it is the world's first, but it also creates a new dimension on how math can be taught by combining chess and math through Frankho Symbolic Chess Language (Trademark Canada TMA771400). The theoretical background on this chess set was published in Vector (Fall 2007, Volume 48, Issue 3), the official Journal of the British Columbia Association of Mathematics Teachers in Canada.
- In August 2015, we republished the workbook with a new title *Learning Chess to Improve Math*, to highlight our idea of using chess to improve math.
- In May 2017, a new and revised workbook was published.

I found that, in real life, students do not just sequentially learn four operations. For example, when a child is taking one apple out of a basket with four apples, it is an operation of addition (getting one apple) and subtraction (3 apples left). So I thought it would be a good idea that students could learn multi-operation and multi-concept at the same time to reflect the real-life experience.

We initially created all problems and worksheet formats presented in this work, so no part of these worksheets formats or problems may be reproduced without our written permission.

This unique workbook, *Learning Chess to Improve Math,* has now been publicly published with input from Amanda Ho. We sincerely hope our readers will enjoy it as much as we have been in the past. Frank also invented a new flat chess set using geometry chess symbols. This innovative idea of using geometry chess symbols allows the student to work on integrated math and chess workbooks. One of the classic examples is the *Frankho ChessDoku,* which is also publicly published. This workbook integrates Sudoku, chess, and math all in one workbook to allow children to work on chess, math, and Sudoku simultaneously. Details about this workbook, *Frankho ChessDoku,* can be found at www.amazon.com.

Who should use this workbook?

This book is written for children age four and above.

Learning Chess to Improve Math is an ideal resource for parents, coaches, teachers, tutors, or students who are interested in the idea of using math and chess puzzles to enhance problem-solving ability. The chess moves, chess pieces, and chessboard are full of math concepts. A few examples are listed below:

- The ranks and files are related to coordinates.
- The ranks, files, diagonals and the colours of squares are related to patterns and geometry.
- The checkmate positions are the intersections of ranks or/and files related to geometry and probability.
- When a piece is being attacked or defended, it requires some arithmetic calculations regarding the number of attacking or defending pieces.

Learning Chess to Improve Math 数棋谜式健脑国际象棋
 Math Chess 何数棋谜 www.homathchess.com
Frank Ho, Amanda Ho © 1995 – 2021   All rights reserved.
Student name _____Assignment date:_____

This book offers fascinating opportunities to explore and discover how some math concepts are related to chess in a fun way. These puzzles can be used as supplemental material for problem-solving in math class or as an excellent enrichment while students are learning chess. They can also be used alone after students have learned the basic rules of playing chess.

What chess knowledge is required to do mathematical chess puzzles?

The chess knowledge required to do the mathematical puzzles is listed as follows:

- How to move the chess pieces, and how to write moves in algebraic notation.
- The values of chess pieces.
- How to castle.

What is the math knowledge required to do the mathematical chess puzzles?

Some math concepts integrated into this workbook are substantial, so instructors are asked to teach children according to their abilities using selective and appropriate problems.

What is the relation between chess and math?

This current workbook is the continuation of creating mathematical chess puzzles after my first workbook was published. So, what is the relation between mathematics and chess?

My belief is most board games are related to mathematics, and a chess game that had been refined in the past several thousands of years is no exception.

The chessboard and chess pieces themselves are geometry. The chessboard is symmetric in main diagonals in terms of its colours. The chessboard is made of 4 identical small boards divided by one horizontal line and one vertical line going through the centre. The set-up positions of chess pieces are symmetric between Black and White. The chess piece's set-up position on either side is palindrome except for the king and queen.

Rook's move is a slide motion (left/right, up/down) in geometry. The between moves of rook before reaching the destination is using the concept of the commutative property. For example, before Ra1 to Rh1,
Rook could move from a1 to c1 (4 squares), then from c1 to h1 (3 squares) or from a1 to d1 (3 squares), then from d1 to h1 (4 squares). The complication is that the player has to watch what would happen if the different choices are made, and this is much more complicated than adding the commutative property $3 + 4 = 4 + 3 = 7$. These complications involve the calculations of different paths and the opponent's possible responses. The deeper the player could calculate the chess paths, the higher is the possibility of playing better. The calculation of path requires logical thinking, which is very similar to using a factor tree to find out, for example, the prime factors of 64. Still, chess is more complicated in a way. The opponent's moves also have to be thought in advance. For example, find the product of primes for 32. The prime number tree could be as follows:

Learning Chess to Improve Math   数棋谜式健脑国际象棋

Ho Math Chess 何数棋谜 www.homathchess.com

Frank Ho, Amanda Ho © 1995 – 2021   All rights reserved.

Student name _____ Assignment date:_____

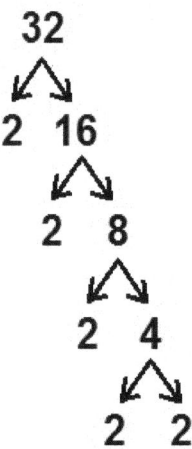

If the rook is at a1 and is free to make moves along file a and rank 1, what has to be considered before moving? The most important is to see any opponent's pieces that could intersect with the rook. Thinking mathematically would be to see what is y when $x = 1$ and what would be x when $y = 1$, we will be looking for intersections. The idea of coordinates would be more straightforward for chess players to learn if they already have acquired the practical experience of intersections coming from different chess pieces.

The idea of one-to-one cancellation of chess pieces left on the board is similar to the subtraction property of the equation.

One would think that chess perhaps has nothing to do with fractional numbers since all moves are all in whole numbers. Why is the queen the most powerful chess piece, and we usually move chess pieces toward the middle? They all have something to do with the ratio $\frac{a}{b}$ Where b is the 64 squares and a is the squares under control. Perhaps I could give one example to demonstrate how math concept and chess knowledge are integrated as follows:

Replace the ? by a number.

More details and examples can be found in Appendix A in this workbook.

Frank Ho

May 2017

| Learning Chess to Improve Math 数棋谜式健脑国际象棋 |
| Ho Math Chess 何数棋谜 www.homathchess.com |
| Frank Ho, Amanda Ho © 1995 – 2021   All rights reserved. |

Student name _____ Assignment date:_____

Ho's other publications

The following publications will be helpful if used together with Learning Chess to Improve Math together.

Junior Kindergarten Math (For pre-k and Junior Kindergarten)
Math Chess and Puzzles for Primary Grades
Primary Grades Math (Grades 4 and Under)
Elementary Grades Math (Grades 4 and Up)
Math Chess Sudoku Puzzles
Frankho ChessDoku 4 by 4
Frankho ChessDoku 5 by 5
Mom! I Learn Addition Using Math-Chess-Puzzles Connection
Mom! I Learn Subtraction Using Math-Chess-Puzzles Connection
Mom! I Learn Multiplication Using Math-Chess-Puzzles Connection
Mom! I Learn Division Using Math-Chess-Puzzles Connection
Math Contest Preparation, Problem Solving Strategies, and Math IQ puzzles for Grades 1 and 2
Math Contest Preparation, Problem Solving Strategies, and Math IQ puzzles for Grades 2 and 3
Math Contest Preparation, Problem Solving Strategies, and Math IQ puzzles for Grades 3 and 4
Math Contest Preparation, Problem Solving Strategies, and Math IQ puzzles for Grades 4 and 5
Math Contest Preparation, Problem Solving Strategies, and Math IQ puzzles for Grades 5 and 6
Math Contest Preparation, Problem Solving Strategies, and Math IQ puzzles for Grades 6 and 7

For details on the above publications, please contact Frank Ho at fho1928@gmail.com.

| Learning Chess to Improve Math   数棋谜式健脑国际象棋 |
| Ho Math Chess 何数棋谜 www.homathchess.com |
| Frank Ho, Amanda Ho © 1995 – 2021   All rights reserved. |

Student name _____ Assignment date:_____

Part 1 Introducing to chess pieces and chessboard

This part gives a brief introduction to chessboard and chess pieces and how each piece moves. It also introduces how they become a command language called Symbolic Chess Language (SCL) to link math, chess and puzzles on the math worksheets.

Ho Math Chess Teaching set is introduced, and examples of using SCL are given.

The Chinese version of the video on how to teach children to play chess can be found on the following website.

如何教四岁小孩下国际象棋

http://v.youku.com/v_show/id_XMTY4NTM3NTE4OA==.html?from=s1.8-1-1.2

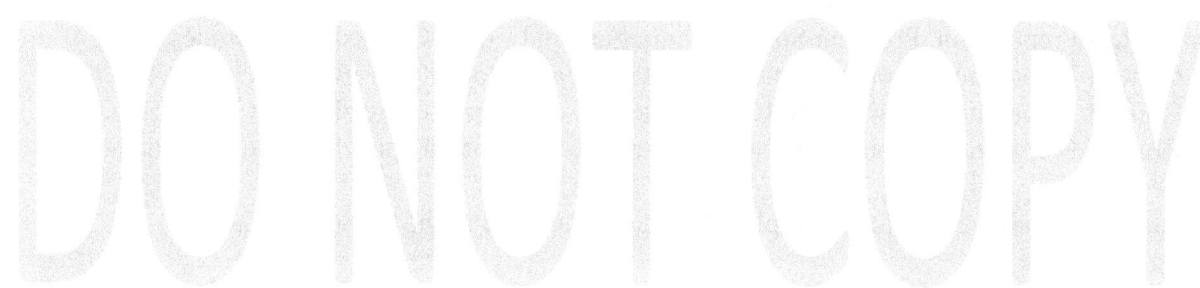

Learning Chess to Improve Math

Ho Math Chess 何数棋谜 www.homathchess.com

Frank Ho, Amanda Ho © 1995 – 2021   All rights reserved.

Student name _____ Assignment date:_____

Chessboard

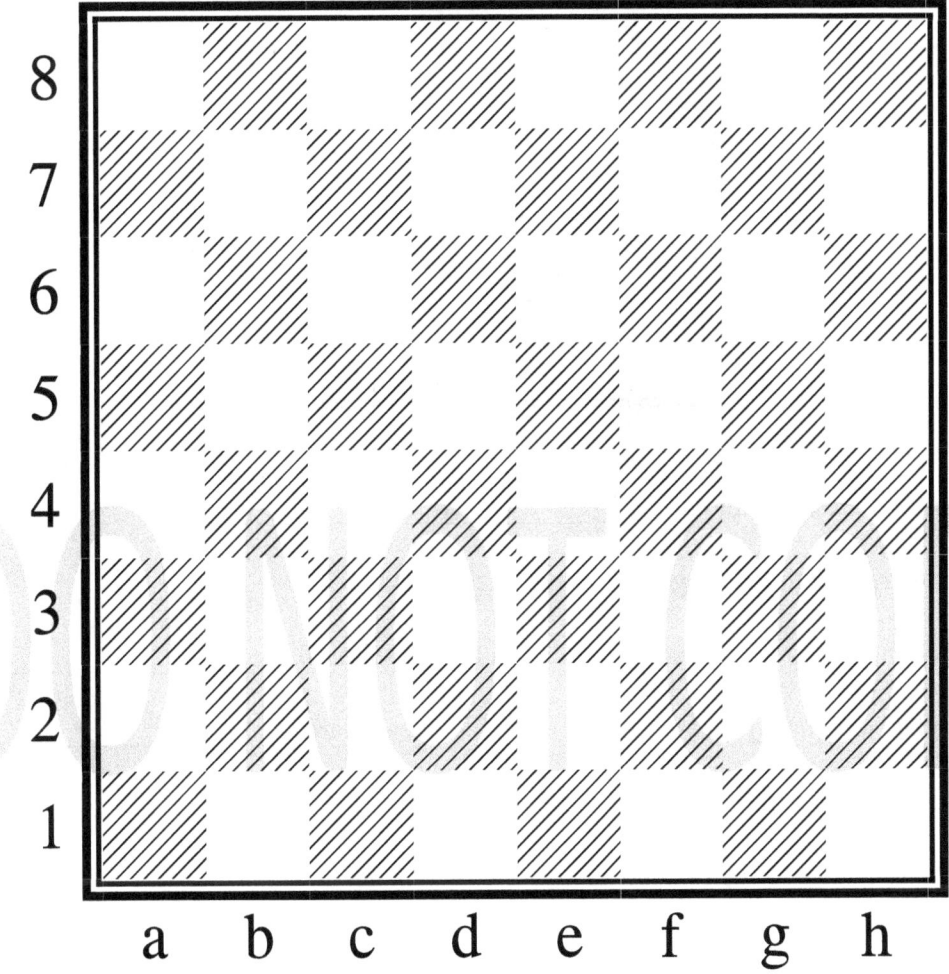

| Learning Chess to Improve Math   数棋谜式健脑国际象棋 |
| Ho Math Chess   何数棋谜   www.homathchess.com |
| Frank Ho, Amanda Ho © 1995 – 2021   All rights reserved. |

Student name _____ Assignment date:_____

Chessboard setup using traditional chess pieces

Look at the following chess diagram and answer the following questions.

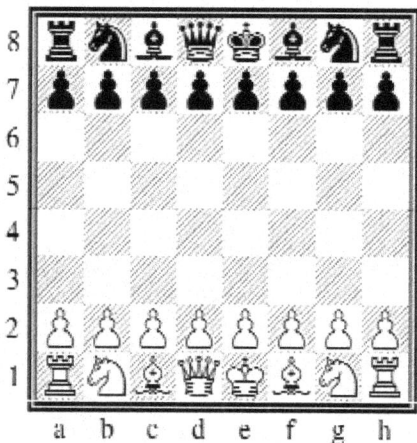

How many chess pieces are there altogether? _____

How many chess squares are there altogether on the chessboard? _____

How many White (light-coloured) squares are there on the chessboard? _____

How many Black (dark-coloured) squares are there on the chessboard? _____

The ratio of the White squares to the total chess squares is ____ to ____.

The ratio of the Black squares to the total chess squares is ____ to ____.

The ratio of the White squares to the Black squares is ____ to ____.

Learning Chess to Improve Math 数棋谜式健脑国际象棋
Ho Math Chess 何数棋谜 www.homathchess.com
Frank Ho, Amanda Ho © 1995 – 2021   All rights reserved.

Student name _____ Assignment date:_____

The following is a chessboard set-up to begin a game (each player's lower right-hand corner must be a white square.). White always makes the first move.

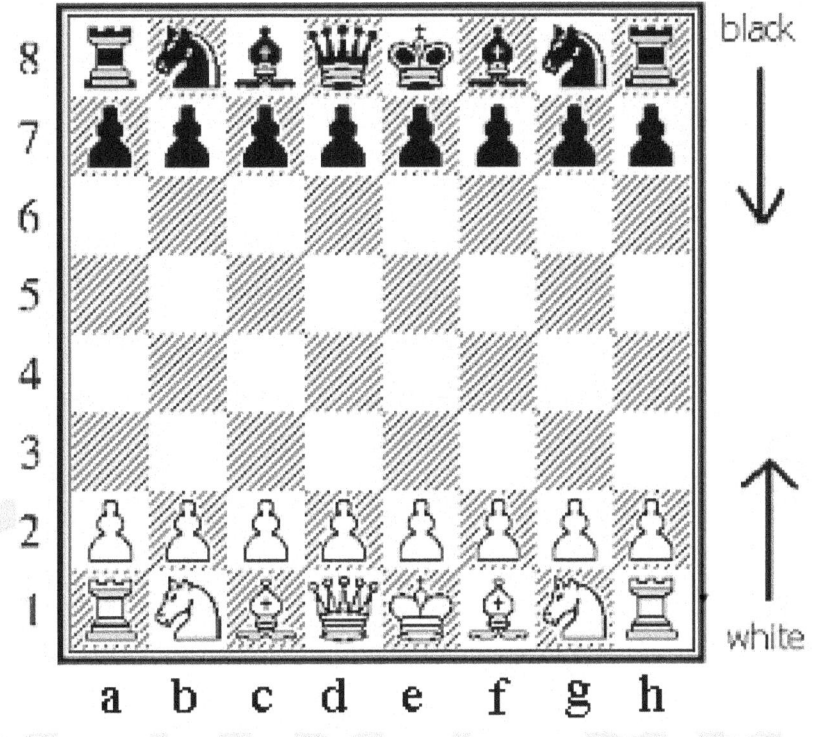

Student name _____ Assignment date:_____

Chessboard setup

- Both players must always have a White square in the right-hand corner.
- Queen is in its colour.

Circle the following incorrect board setups.

Learning Chess to Improve Math   数棋谜式健脑国际象棋
Ho Math Chess   何数棋谜   www.homathchess.com
Frank Ho, Amanda Ho © 1995 – 2021   All rights reserved.

Student name _____ Assignment date:_____

Flat Chinese chess set and Ho Math Chess teaching set

Chinese have been using the flat surface Chinese chess set with carved Chinese characters on chess pieces for more than thousands of years. Chinese uses Chinese characters to represent the meanings of chess pieces, and the Ho Math Chess set uses Geometry line and line segment symbols to represent chess moves. The flat surface chess set has many advantages over a traditional stand-up chess set.

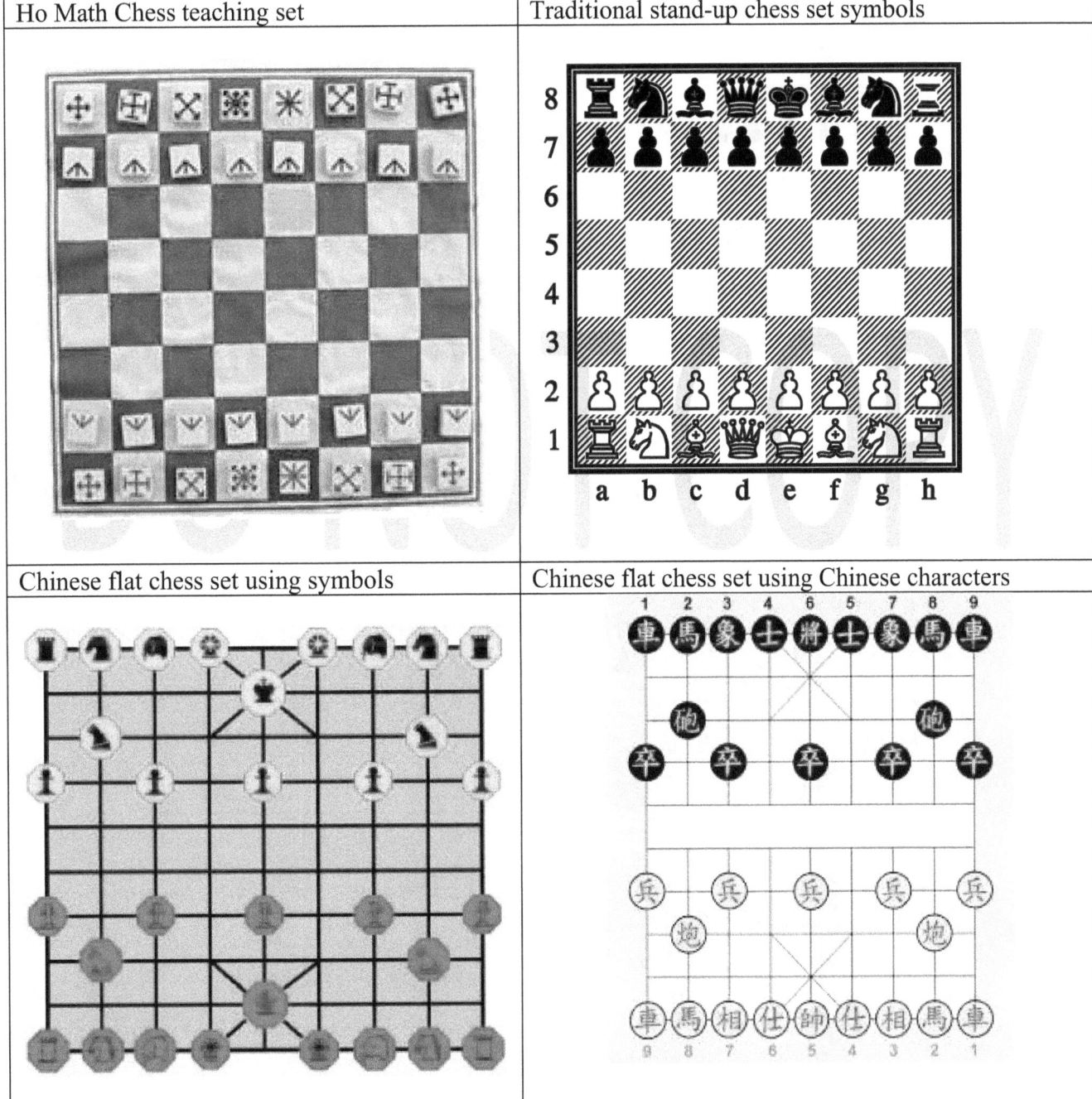

Learning Chess to Improve Math   数棋谜式健脑国际象棋
Ho Math Chess   何数棋谜   www.homathchess.com
Frank Ho, Amanda Ho © 1995 – 2021   All rights reserved.

Student name _____ Assignment date: _____

Ho Math Chess Teaching Set

The theory background on how this set was invented was published in Vector (Fall 2007, Volume 48, Issue 3), the official Journal of the British Columbia Association of Mathematics Teachers in Canada.

One-of-its-kind and unique Ho Math Chess Teaching Set is sold worldwide and carries Ho Math Chess reputable brand name. This Ho Math Chess teaching set is "out-of-this-world", a genius invention by using Frankho Geometry Chess Symbols (copyright and trademark applied).

More information on how to use Ho Math Chess Teaching Set can be found at www.mathandchess.com.

Ho Math Chess board set-up.
In real chess set, white is coloured as red.

How to Play Chess
The players sit facing each other with a white square of the board at each player's right. The diagram shows how the pieces are placed at the beginning of a game.

How the Pieces Move and Capture
The player who controls the white pieces - known simply as "White" - always makes the first move. "Black" responds and the game continues with the two players moving alternately. Only one piece may be moved during each turn, except during castling, which involves two pieces.
To capture, you move your piece onto a square occupied by one of your opponent's pieces. The opponent's piece is then removed from the board. In chess, you do not have to capture a piece just because it is possible to do so. You may never move a piece to a square occupied by one of your own pieces.

The Rook can move or capture any number of squares horizontally or vertically so long as its path is unobstructed.

ROOK

The Bishop may move or capture any number of squares diagonally in either direction, so long as the path is unobstructed.

BISHOP

The Knight can move in an "L" shape, as seen in the diagram, always moving from a light square to a dark square or vice-versa. The Knight is the only piece that may "jump over" other pieces on the board.

KNIGHT
  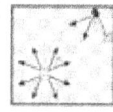

Castling
To castle, move your King two squares to the right or left, and then place the nearest unmoved Rook next to him, on the square over which the King has passed. Castling is only possible when no piece stands between the King and the Rook, and neither piece has already moved during the game, and the King is not under attack or will pass through a square that is under attack (meaning, a piece your opponent controls could be moved into that square next turn).

Long (0-0-0)

CASTLING

Short (0-0)

The King can move or capture one square in any direction.
KING

The Queen can move or capture across any number of squares, diagonal or horizontal or vertical, in any direction so long as her path is unobstructed.

QUEEN

PAWN

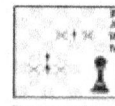 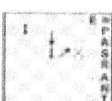

The pawn may move one square forward - never backwards - but may only capture one square diagonally. During the first turn that it moves, the pawn may move two squares forward, rather than the normal one square. If a pawn reaches the opposite end of the board, it must be promoted to another piece, except a King, of the same color (usually a Queen). Therefore, it is possible to have more than one Queen, or more than two Rooks, Knights, or Bishops of the same color on the board. The capture "en passant", when your opponent moves his pawn two spaces ahead, so that it sits next to your pawn, your pawn may move to the square over which the opponent's pawn had moved, and the opponent's pawn is removed, as if it had only moved one square. This option may only be exercised on the very next turn. Another way of looking at it is that you may capture an opponent's pawn that has just made its initial two square move, as if it had only made a one square move.

Check
Any move that attacks a King is called a "check". The object of chess is to attack the opponent's King in such a way that no matter how he replies, it will remain under attack. This is called a "checkmate" and wins the game. Your own King cannot be in check after you move. Therefore, you must remove any check your opponent makes against your King.

Stalemate
If a player, to move, is not in check but has no legal moves, the game is considered a draw. Neither player wins. This is called a stalemate. Another way to get a draw is if there are not enough pieces on the board to force a checkmate. For example, put a Knight and both Kings on the board. There is no checkmate possible, so the game is a draw.

Learning Chess to Improve Math 数棋谜式健脑国际象棋
Ho Math Chess 何数棋谜 www.homathchess.com
Frank Ho, Amanda Ho © 1995 – 2021   All rights reserved.

Student name _____ Assignment date:_____

Chess pieces and their mathematical values

There are only two prerequisites for students to work on chess puzzles in this workbook. They are basic chess moves and the values (points) assigned to each chess piece. There are many different point systems with different points assigned to chess pieces. To use a system suitable for elementary students, the point system used in this workbook is the same as the one used by the Teaching Manual published by the Chess Federation of Canada. All chess puzzles created in this workbook are related to some mathematics concepts; therefore, they are called mathematical chess puzzles. The mathematical chess puzzles in this workbook authored by Frank Ho, along with his previously published workbook *Mathematical Chess Puzzles for Juniors* (ISBN 0-9683967-0-4), are believed to be the world's first-ever published on the subject of mathematical chess puzzles for elementary students

Symbols of chess pieces	Names of chess pieces	Mathematical values
♛ symbols	Queen (major piece)	9
♜ symbols	Rook (major piece)	5
♝ symbols	Bishop (minor piece)	3
♞ symbols	kNnight (minor piece)	3
♟ symbols	Pawn	1
♚ symbols	King	0

Learning Chess to Improve Math 数棋谜式健脑国际象棋
Ho Math Chess 何数棋谜 www.homathchess.com
Frank Ho, Amanda Ho © 1995 – 2021   All rights reserved.

Student name _____ Assignment date:_____

Match chess pieces and spatial movements

Symbols of the traditional chess set	Draw lines to match	Symbols of Ho Math Chess flat chess set
♛ (Queen)		(8-directional arrow star)
♚ (King)		(8-point star)
♜ (Rook)		(4-directional arrow cross)
♞ (Knight)		(knight-move cross)
♝ (Bishop)		(X diagonal arrows)
♟ (Pawn)		(Y-shape)

Learning Chess to Improve Math 数棋谜式健脑国际象棋
Ho Math Chess 何数棋谜 www.homathchess.com
Frank Ho, Amanda Ho © 1995 – 2021   All rights reserved.
Student name _____ Assignment date:_____

Symbolic Chess Language (SCL) for a flat chess set

Frank Ho, the founder of Ho Math Chess Learning Centre, headquartered in Vancouver, Canada, invented a chess language called Symbolic Chess Language (SCL) to link math, chess and puzzles. Each chess symbol represents a corresponding physical chess piece (Figures 1 and 2). This set of chess symbols not only makes teaching chess easier for younger children as young as four years old, but it also serves as a set of command languages to link arithmetic and chess. The teaching idea of using this set of chess symbols is to create math and chess integrated problems or any variations of future problems as a result of using these symbols. This set of chess symbols and their teaching methods have been approved for intellectual property international copyright protection. Problems shown herein are merely exemplary and may be changed to suit different types of problems. Accordingly, it is the inventor's intent to embrace all such alternatives, modifications, and variations as fall within the spirit and broad scope of this invention.

As far as the training of playing chess itself is concerned, SCL symbols have many advantages over the regular chess fonts or traditional 3 D figurines in training children's critical thinking skills when integrating chess into math. The transformation concept in SCL symbols is self-explanatory, and it is easier for children to understand when each symbol direction is pointed by an arrow representing the actual movement direction of each chess piece. Children get hands-on experience in moving those pieces by simply following the directions displayed on each chess piece. The arrow represents a line in math, which means the chess piece can move as long as it is safe to do so. The line segment means the chess piece can only make one move.

The other advantage of using SCL is that they provide children with opportunities to learn important math concepts in patterns, sequence, symmetry, and transformation-related math problems. For example, a typical problem might involve how a 3D object such as a chess piece ♛ is transformed into a symbol (✳ or ♛) and then a symbol (✳ or ♛) is translated into a number (9), and finally, a numerical value is produced as an answer.

A mathematical symbol language using the set of SCL can be developed to create an array of innovative arithmetic problems since these symbolic chess symbols themselves representing the moving direction of chess figurines. For example, a black rook is represented by this symbol (↕↔ or ✦) and a highlighted arrow, such as ↔ indicating its direction of movement towards the right. In this rook case, the symbol not only can represent the chess piece itself, but it also has another attribute that has the four directions (up, down, left and right) of moving. The directions can be one way, two ways, three ways, or four ways, so altogether, there could be 15 ways of moving directions. A simple rook's move problem could become a very challenging problem when combined with arithmetic computation problems.

Learning Chess to Improve Math 数棋谜式健脑国际象棋
Ho Math Chess 何数棋谜 www.homathchess.com

Frank Ho, Amanda Ho © 1995 – 2021   All rights reserved.

Student name _____ Assignment date:_____

The effect is children feel thrilled and are more willing to work on chess and math combined problems since each problem requires children's creativity to create the questions by following a puzzle-like mini question and the requirement of having children write the questions reinforces the task of memorizing the basics facts of addition, subtraction, or multiplication without causing stress on children.

Ho Math Chess™ believes the invention of this SCL has brought integrated math and chess teaching to a new horizon, and we are very proud to be the leader in the continued research of math and chess integrated teaching.

Figure 1 SCL (Symbolic Chess Language) for black pieces

Points	1	5	3	3	0	9
Symbols of 3 D traditional chess pieces	♟	♜	♞	♝	♚	♛
English name	Pawn	Rook	Knight	Bishop	King	Queen
Symbols of flat chess pieces						
SCL handwriting symbol						

Figure 2 SCL (Symbolic Chess Language) for White pieces

Points	1	5	3	3	0	9
Symbols of 3 D traditional chess pieces	♙	♖	♘	♗	♔	♕
English name	Pawn	Rook	Knight	Bishop	King	Queen
Symbols of flat chess pieces						
SCL handwriting symbol						

The black and white colours of chess symbols, along with their black and white squares and their different font sizes, present the possibilities of creating a variety of pattern problems.

Learning Chess to Improve Math   数棋谜式健脑国际象棋
Ho Math Chess   何数棋谜   www.homathchess.com
Frank Ho, Amanda Ho © 1995 – 2021   All rights reserved.

Student name _____ Assignment date:_____

SCL

The setup of a chessboard using real flat chess pieces is as follows:

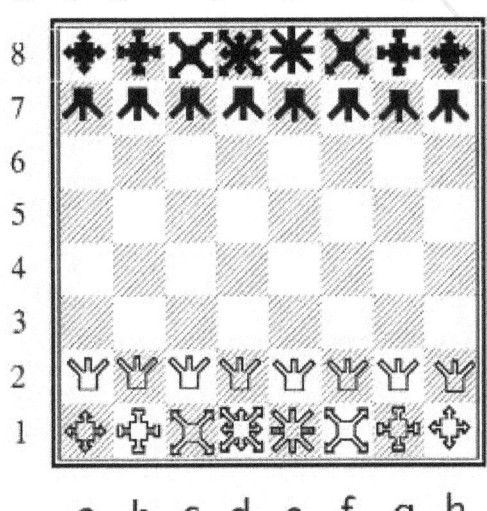

Learning Chess to Improve Math 数棋谜式健脑国际象棋
Ho Math Chess 何数棋谜 www.homathchess.com
Frank Ho, Amanda Ho © 1995 – 2021   All rights reserved.

Student name _____ Assignment date:_____

Chess pieces' names and moves

Symbol	Names of chess pieces	How does it move? (If it is not blocked and is safe to move.)
(Q)	Queen (major piece)	Up and down Left and right Diagonally Any number of squares
(K)	King	Up and down Left and right Diagonally one square at a time
(R)	Rook (major piece)	Up and down Left and right Any number of squares
(N)	kNight (minor piece)	L-shape or Y-shaped in 8 directions The only piece can jump over pieces.
(B)	Bishop (minor piece)	Diagonally Any number of squares
	Pawn	One or two squares forward on the first move and only one square forward after the first move. One square diagonally when taking the opponent's piece. When a pawn reaches the other end of the board, a pawn can be promoted to any piece other than a king or a pawn.

Learning Chess to Improve Math 数棋谜式健脑国际象棋
Ho Math Chess 何数棋谜 www.homathchess.com
Frank Ho, Amanda Ho © 1995 − 2021   All rights reserved.

Student name _____ Assignment date:_____

Chessboard setup using traditional chess pieces

Look at the following chess diagram and answer the following questions.

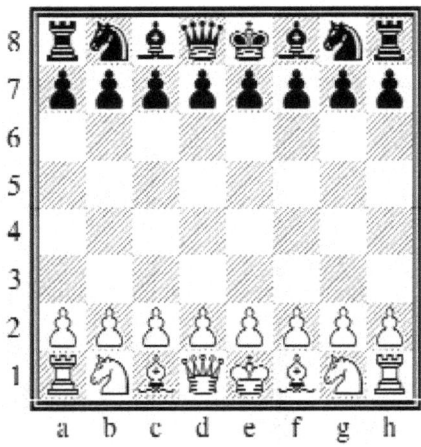

The middle line between ____ file and ____ file separates the chessboard into queenside and kingside. Are the kingside and the queenside symmetric in the colours of squares? _____
The middle line between ____ rank and ____ rank separates the chessboard into two equal parts.
The two main diagonals of the chessboard are $a1$ to ____ and $h1$ to ____.
Are those chess pieces symmetric in shapes when flipped from top to down in the middle line? _____
Are those chess pieces symmetric in shapes when flipped from left to right in the middle line? _____

Cutting chessboard into equal parts

Draw two straight lines to divide the following chessboard into four equal parts. Draw in more than one way, if possible.

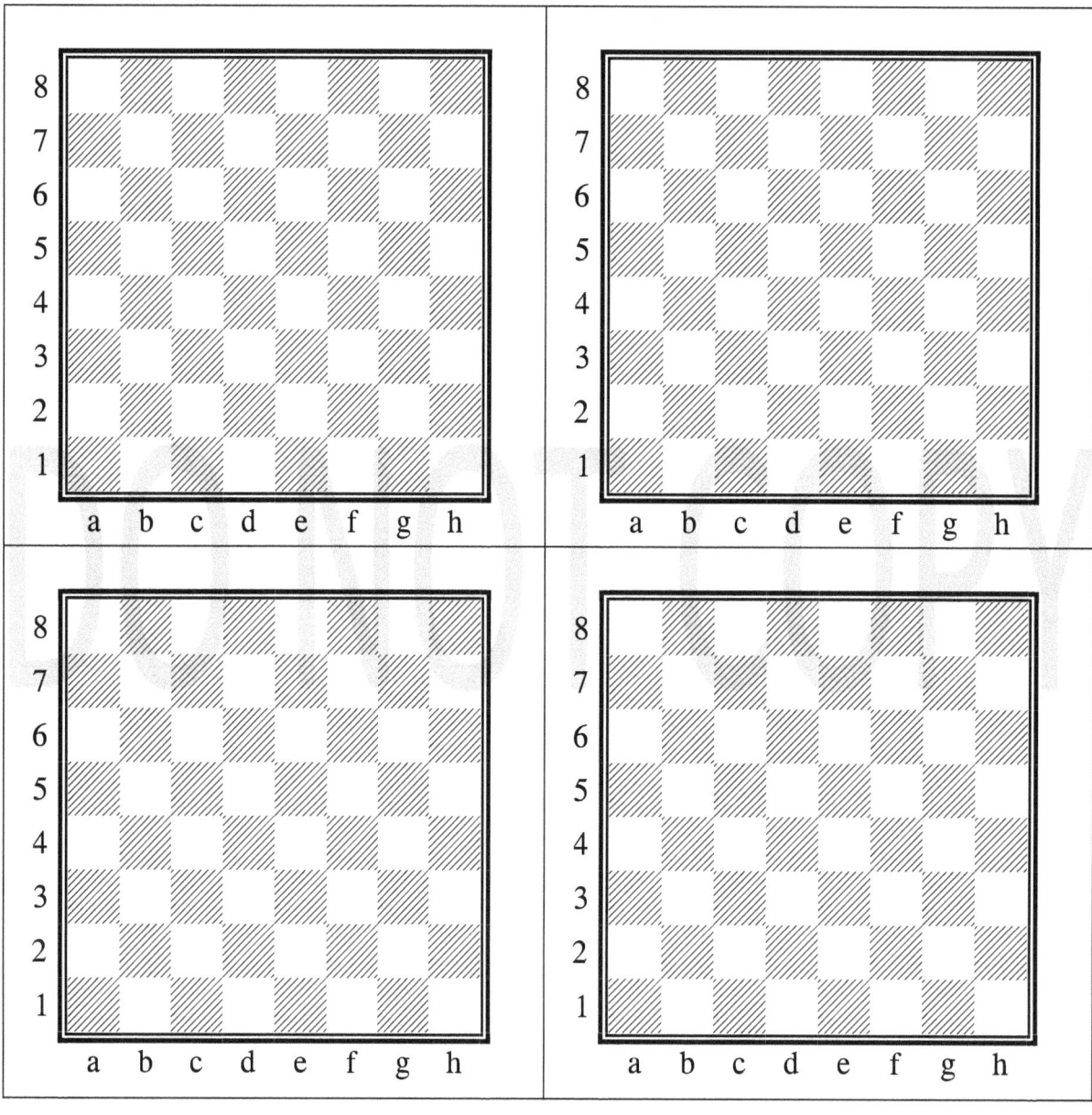

Learning Chess to Improve Math   数棋谜式健脑国际象棋
Ho Math Chess   何数棋谜   www.homathchess.com
Frank Ho, Amanda Ho © 1995 – 2021   All rights reserved.

Student name _____ Assignment date:_____

Notations of chess pieces

Symbol	Write names of chess pieces	Shorthand notation
♕	_____queen (major piece)	_____
♔	_____king	_____
♖	_____rook (major piece)	_____
♘	_____knight (minor piece)	_____
♗	_____bishop (minor piece)	_____
♙	_____pawn	_____ Not available

Learning Chess to Improve Math

Sorting Symbol chess symbols attributes

If students understand the colours of chess pieces and the colours of their occupied squares, it will also help them to understand how the chess piece moves. For example, a knight always moves to a different colour square. A black square bishop, sitting on a black square, always moves along black squares, so it can never take or protect any pieces sitting on the white squares. The queen or rook can travel either black or white square but must follow its directions.

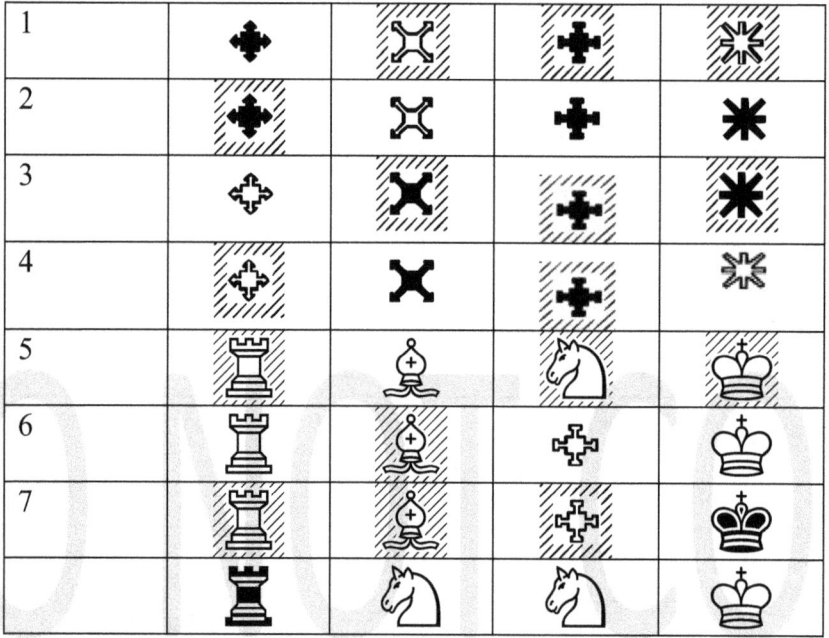

Replace 333each ? with a number.

Learning Chess to Improve Math 数棋谜式健脑国际象棋

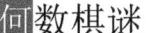 Math Chess 何数棋谜 www.homathchess.com

Frank Ho, Amanda Ho © 1995 – 2021   All rights reserved.

Student name _____ Assignment date: _____

Chess notation

Write chess notations besides squares marked by × or ✖.

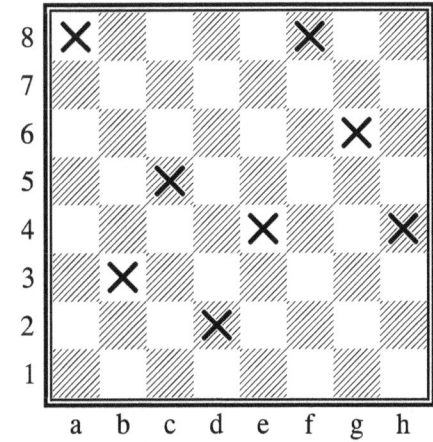

Write chess notations besides squares marked by × or ✖.

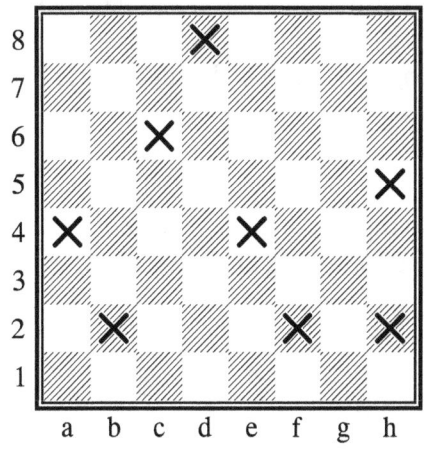

Write chess notations besides squares marked by × or ✖.

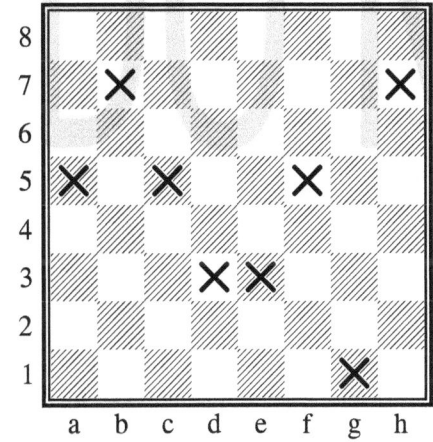

Write chess notations besides squares marked by × or ✖.

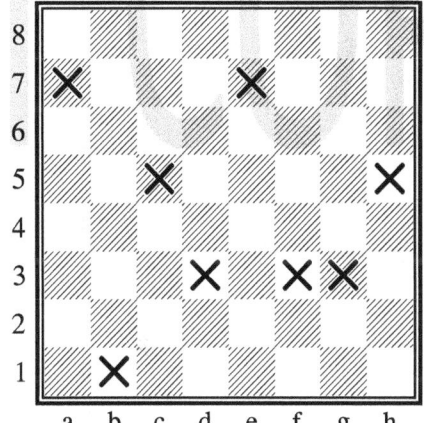

Learning Chess to Improve Math   数棋谜式健脑国际象棋
Ho Math Chess   何数棋谜   www.homathchess.com
Frank Ho, Amanda Ho © 1995 – 2021   All rights reserved.

Student name _____ Assignment date:_____

Chess notation

The letters and numbers located along the chessboard are used to identify the positions of chess pieces.

For example, Ra1 means there is an ♖ at the intersection of two crossed lines (horizontal squares are called ranks, and vertical squares are called files) a and 1.

Draw the following chess pieces located at h1, b7, and c8 of the following chess diagram.

Chess notation	Transformation
Draw the following chess pieces located at h1, b7, and c8 of the following chess diagram. h1 _____ b7 _____ c8 _____ d4 _____	Write the name of the square of Rh1 after moving left two squares and up to three squares. Answer _____ Write the name of the square of Kg5 after moving right 1 square and down two squares. Answer _____ Write the name of the square of Rh1 after moving the left two squares three times. Answer _____ Write the names of squares that Ne6 could move to: _____. Answer _____ How many ways can Rh1 move to the left? Answer _____

Chess notation

Chess notation	Coordinates
Write chess notations for the following chess pieces whose positions are shown in the diagram below. 	The concept of writing chess notation is entirely transferable to the concept of math coordinates. Draw ordered pairs of (1, 2), (2, 3), (3, 4) in the following diagram by using dots. 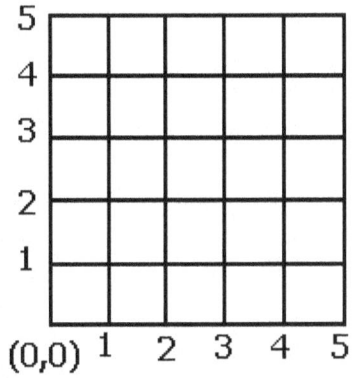
What is the chess piece on a5? _____ What is the chess piece on b3? _____ What is the chess piece on b6? _____ What is the chess piece on c7? _____ What is the chess piece on f1? _____ What is the chess piece on g2? _____	Draw ordered pairs of (2, 2), (3, 3), (4, 4) in the following diagram by using dots. 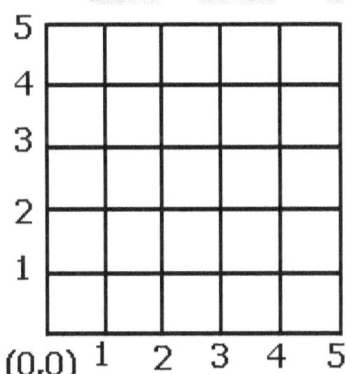
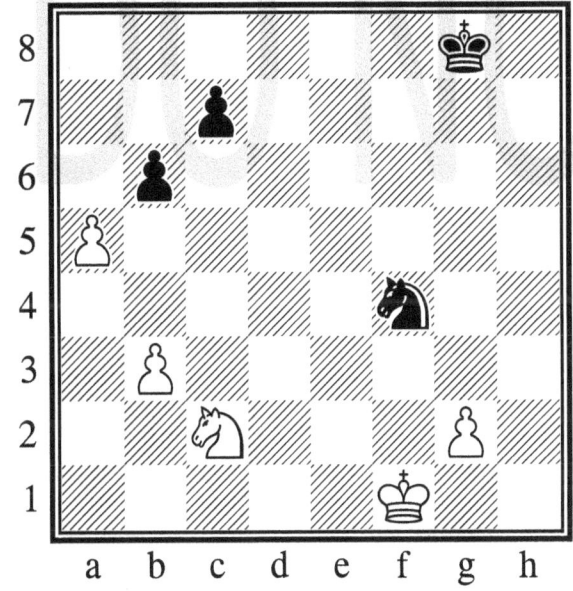	

Review of values of chess pieces (Points)

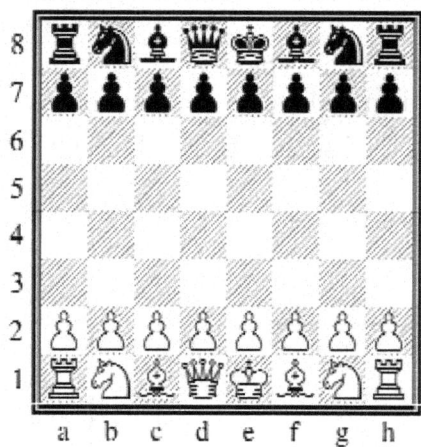

Quite often chess player assigns points to chess pieces to evaluate who has a better chance to win the game. Use the following points assigned to each Black or White chess piece to solve all the mathematical chess puzzles in this workbook.

 (king) = _____ point

 (pawn) = _____ point

 (knight) = _____ points

(bishop) = _____ points

(rook) = _____ points

(queen) = _____ points

Learning Chess to Improve Math   数棋谜式健脑国际象棋
 Math Chess   何数棋谜   www.homathchess.com

Frank Ho, Amanda Ho © 1995 – 2021   All rights reserved.

Student name _____ Assignment date:_____

Which side has more points?

Cancellation	Solve by addition or subtraction or cancellation
[chess board diagram]	$100 + 200 + 300 + 400 - 300 - 700 =$
	$200 + 200 - 400 + 1000 - 1000 =$
	$200 - 400 + 200 - 800 - 100 + 900 =$
The way to see which side has more points is not to add up all the total points of chess pieces on each side. Find out which side has more points by using "1 to 1 correspondence" cancellation. Cancel pawn with pawn and the same chess piece (or the same number of points) of each side. Which side has more points? _____ By how many? _____	$1\times 2\times 3\times 4\times 5\times 6\times 7\times 8\times 9\times 10\times 0 =$ ♛$+1 = 1+ x$ what is the value of x? (Hint: solve by the cancellation.)

Learning Chess to Improve Math   数棋谜式健脑国际象棋
 Math Chess 何数棋谜 www.homathchess.com

Frank Ho, Amanda Ho © 1995 – 2021   All rights reserved.

Student name _____ Assignment date:_____

Which side has more points?

Cancellation	Solve by addition or subtraction or cancellation
Which side has more points? _____ By how much? _____ The way to see which side has more points is not to add up all the total points of chess pieces on each side. Find out which side has more points by the cancellation. Cancel pawn with pawn and the same chess piece (or the same number of points) of each side. 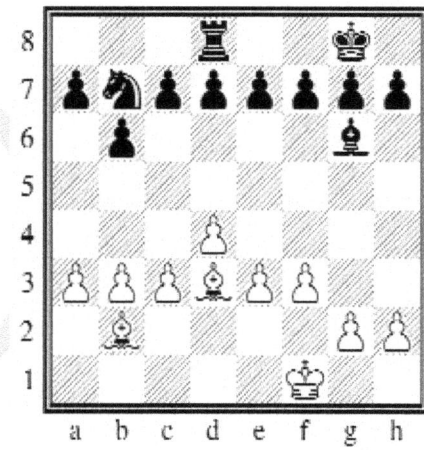	$9 - 8 + 7 - 6 + 5 - 4 + 3 - 2 + 2 - 1$ = $9 + 8 + 7 + 6 + 5 + 5 + 4 + 3 + 2 + 1$ = $19 - 9 + 18 - 8 + 17 - 7 + 16 - 6 + 15 - 5$ = $21 - 12 + 32 - 23 + 43 - 34 + 54 - 45$ =

Learning Chess to Improve Math   数棋谜式健脑国际象棋
 Math Chess   何数棋谜   www.homathchess.com

Frank Ho, Amanda Ho © 1995 – 2021   All rights reserved.

Student name _____ Assignment date:_____

Which side has more points?

Cancellation	Solve by addition or subtraction or cancellation
Which side has more points? _____ By how much? _____ The way to see which side has more points is not to add up all the total points of chess pieces on each side. Find out which side has more points by the cancellation. Cancel pawn with pawn and the same chess piece (or the same number of points) of each side. 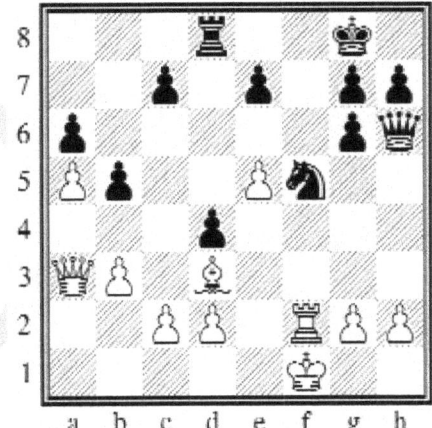	$100 + 200 + 300 + 400 - 300 - 700$ $=$ $1200 + 200 - 400 + 1000 - 1000$ $=$ $1 \times 100 + 2 \times 100 + 3 \times 100 \times 100 - 6 \times 100$ $=$ Evaluate the following. Do not multiply numbers together first. Cancel numbers whenever you can by having a pair of numerator and denominator divided by the same number. $\dfrac{1}{2} \times \dfrac{2}{4} \times \dfrac{4}{6} \times \dfrac{6}{8} \times \dfrac{8}{10} \times \dfrac{10}{12}$

Learning Chess to Improve Math   数棋谜式健脑国际象棋

 Ho Math Chess   何数棋谜   www.homathchess.com

Frank Ho, Amanda Ho © 1995 – 2021   All rights reserved.

Student name _____ Assignment date:_____

Which side has more points?

Cancellation	Solve by mixed operations or cancellation
Which side has more points? _____ By how much? _____ The way to see which side has more points is not to add up all the total points of chess pieces on each side. Find out which side has more points by the cancellation. Cancel pawn with pawn and the same chess piece (or the same number of points) of each side. 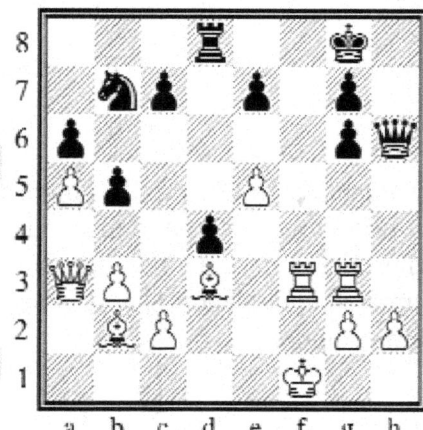	$422 - (211422 \times 2) + 123 - (246 \div 2)$ $=$ $1000000 \times 10000000000$ $=$ $100 - 1 + 200 - 1 + 300 - 1 + 400 - 1 + 500 - 1$ $=$ $8 \times \dfrac{2}{4} + \dfrac{4}{6} \times 12 + \dfrac{8}{10} \times 20$ $=$

Learning Chess to Improve Math   数棋谜式健脑国际象棋
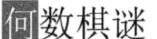 Math Chess   何数棋谜   www.homathchess.com

Frank Ho, Amanda Ho © 1995 – 2021   All rights reserved.

Student name _____ Assignment date:_____

Which side has more points?

Cancellation	Solve by mixed operations or cancellation
Which side has more points? _____ By how much? _____ The way to see which side has more points is not to add up all the total points of chess pieces on each side. Find out which side has more points by the cancellation. Cancel pawn with pawn and the same chess piece (or the same number of points) of each side. [chess board diagram]	$9999 + 49 - 94 - 49 + 87 - 87 + 94$ = _____ If □ is + 3 and ♖ is + 5 and ♞ is – 3 and ♜ is – 5, evaluate the following. ♞ + □ + ♖ + ♜ + ♜ = _____

Advantages of using Ho Math Chess teaching set

- It is specially designed for children as young as 4-year old to learn chess easily.
- Multi-function capabilities for playing traditional chess games and blind or half-blind games to improve memory.
- It can be used to play puzzles, in addition to chess.
- Pocket-sized chess set for easy carrying. Children love it!
- What you see is what you move! So easy to play chess now!!!! It is an amazing invention!
- World's first flat-surfaced international chess set with copyrighted Geometry Chess Symbol marked on each chess piece.

More details on how the Ho Math Chess teaching set can be used as a puzzles tool to solve puzzles can be found at http://www.homathchess.com/chessset.html. The following is a chess setup for playing multiple styles of chess using the Ho Math Chess teaching set.

Regular Ho Math Chess setup	Bind chess setup (No need to close eyes)	Half-blind chess setup

Learning Chess to Improve Math 数棋谜式健脑国际象棋
Ho Math Chess 何数棋谜 www.homathchess.com
Frank Ho, Amanda Ho © 1995 – 2021   All rights reserved.

Student name _____ Assignment date:_____

 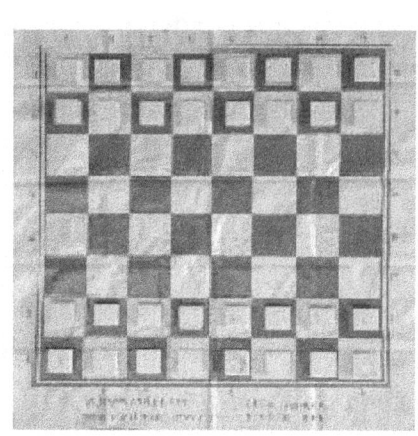 

Ho Math Chess teaching set is displayed in a pocket-sized box (The real box dimension is about 8 cm by 8 cm by 1 cm) as follows:

Characteristics of SCL

Each **flat chess set** symbol carries five attributes: value, direction, colour, background colour, and size.

Value

Each symbol has its own value. For example, the following gives corresponding points for each symbol for Black.

Points	1	5	3	3	0	9
Geometric chess symbols						

The static value of each symbol turns symbols into numerical values in a meaningful way. The transition and training of understanding abstract concepts into forming a concrete numeric value are considered a milestone in a child's mental development. A simple example such as

 = 3 + 3 = 6.

Direction

SCL also serves as a set of command language when its direction on the symbols is highlighted. For example, the following symbol instructs a queen to move in the northern direction.

When the above symbol is used in combination with a chessboard, a result can be achieved by asking the child to perform an arithmetic calculation.

The following examples demonstrate the concepts described above.

Learning Chess to Improve Math 数棋谜式健脑国际象棋
Ho Math Chess 何数棋谜 www.homathchess.com
Frank Ho, Amanda Ho © 1995 – 2021   All rights reserved.

Student name _____ Assignment date:_____

Samples of SCL integrated into math

Getting numbers by following chess moves

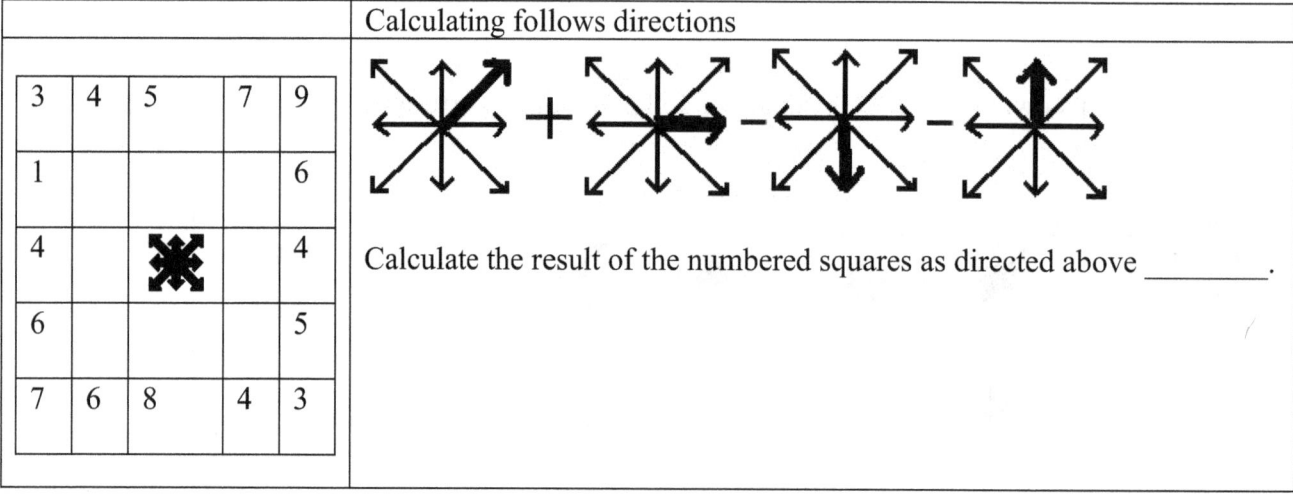

More complicated problems can be created by combining the direction with coordinates specified. The following example demonstrates the idea described.

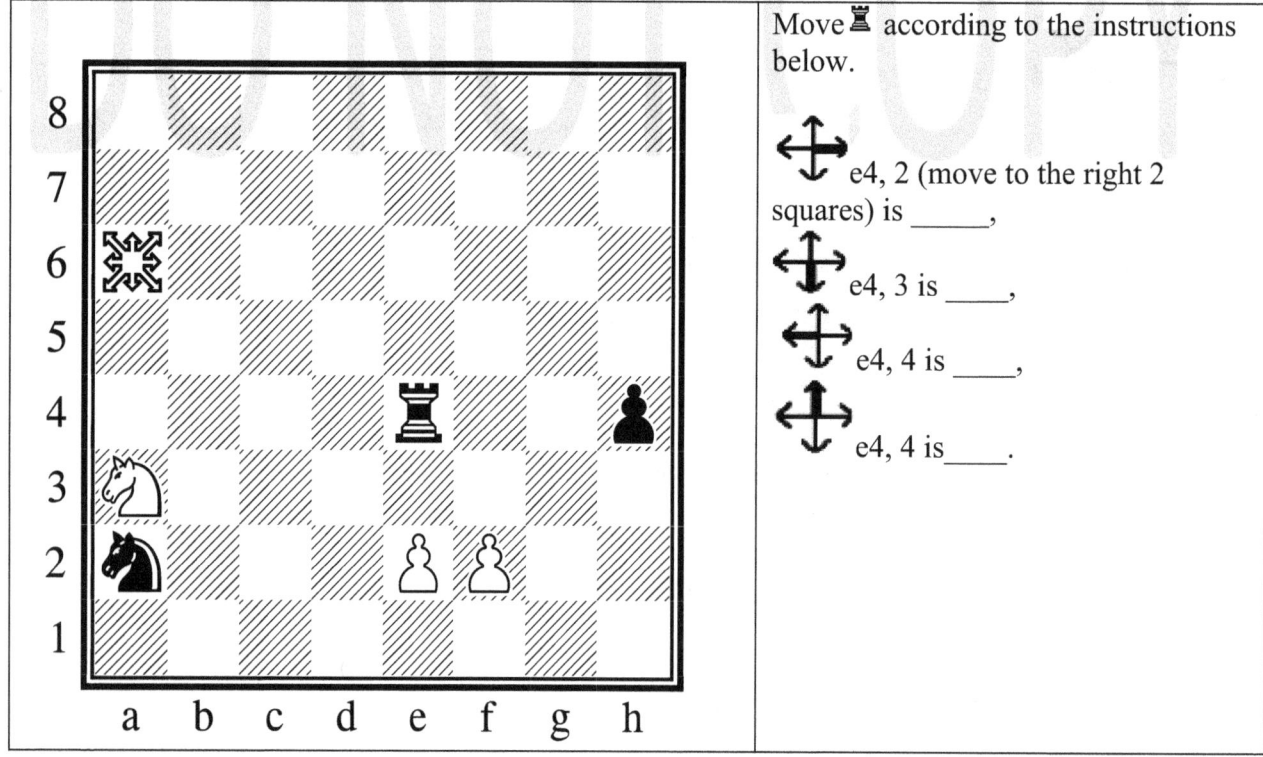

Reversing chess moves

A reverse problem of the above example requires a child to think backwards. The following example demonstrates the idea.

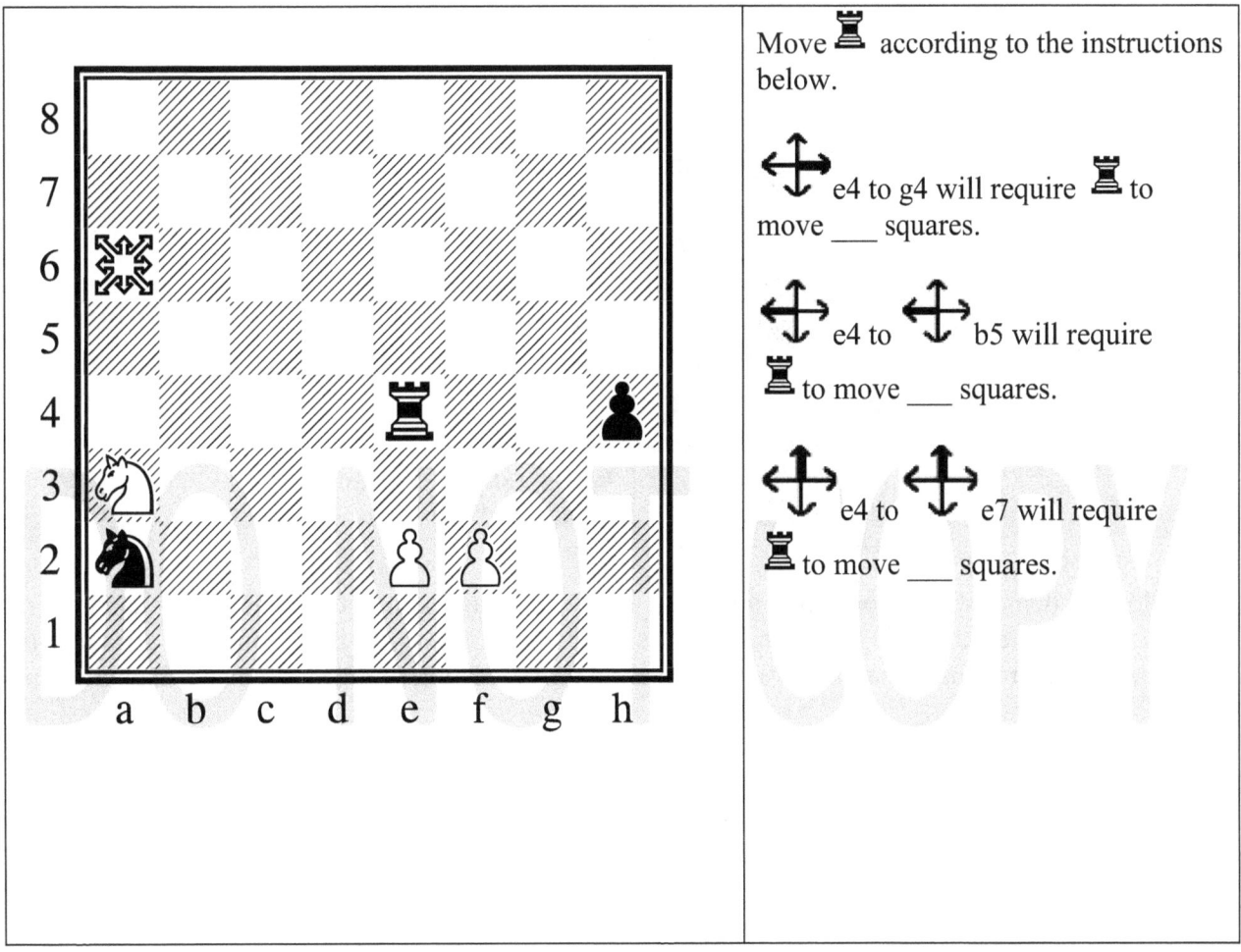

Learning Chess to Improve Math 数棋谜式健脑国际象棋
Ho Math Chess 何数棋谜 www.homathchess.com
Frank Ho, Amanda Ho © 1995 – 2021   All rights reserved.

Student name _____ Assignment date:_____

Using colour, background colour, and different sizes to create patterns

The black and white colours of chess symbols and their black or white squares, and their different font sizes present the possibilities of creating a variety of pattern problems. The following example demonstrates the concept.

Observe the following pattern and replace each ? with a chess piece.

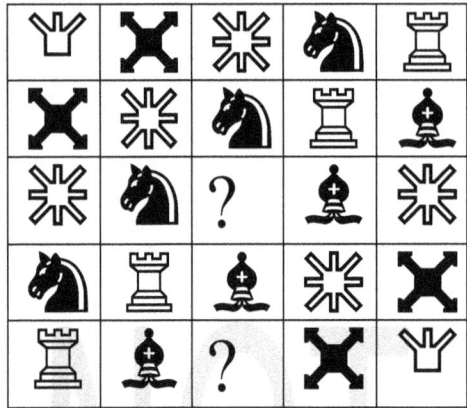

The following demonstrates how some repetitive and boring basic computation questions can be turned into puzzle-like questions using SCL and requires children's creativity to figure out each question. In addition, the requirement of having children write out each question reinforces the learning outcome.

Learning Chess to Improve Math

Ho Math Chess www.homathchess.com

Frank Ho, Amanda Ho © 1995 – 2021   All rights reserved.

Student name _____ Assignment date:_____

Addition

e	11	12	13	14	15
d	16	17	18	19	20
c	21	22	2	23	24
b	25	26	27	28	29
a	30	31	32	33	34
	1	2	3	4	5

Move by one square at a time from the original square.

The original square is at c3

C3 + ⬌ + ⬌ = ___ + ___ + ___ = ___

2 + 23 + 24 = 49

The original square is at c3

C3 + ⬌ + ⬌ = ___ + ___ + ___ = ___

The original square is at c3

C3 + ⬌ + ⬌ = ___ + ___ + ___ = ___

The original square is at c3

C3 + ⬌ + ⬌ = ___ + ___ + ___ = ___

Multiplication

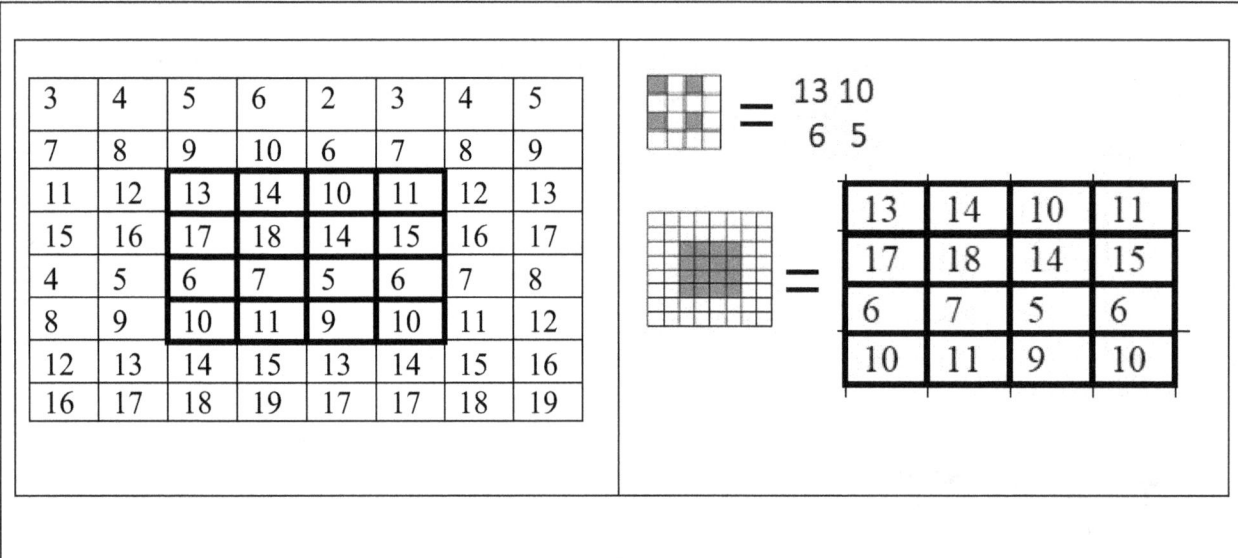

Learning Chess to Improve Math   数棋谜式健脑国际象棋
Ho Math Chess   何数棋谜   www.homathchess.com
Frank Ho, Amanda Ho © 1995 – 2021   All rights reserved.

Student name _____ Assignment date:_____

Multiplication using function concept and spatial relation

3	4	5	6	2	3	4	5
7	8	9	10	6	7	8	9
11	12	13	14	10	11	12	13
15	16	17	18	14	15	16	17
4	5	6	7	5	6	7	8
8	9	10	11	9	10	11	12
12	13	14	15	13	14	15	16
16	17	18	19	17	17	18	19

Row 1: Product of ⤢ ... of ▦ of ▦ = ___ × ___ = ___ (10 × 15 = 150)

Row 2: Product of ⤢ ... of ▦ of ▦ = ___ × ___ = ___

Row 3: Product of ↕ of ▦ of ▦ of ▦ = ___ × ___ = ___

Row 4: Product of ↔ of ▦ of ▦ of ▦ = ___ × ___ = ___

Row 5: Product of ↔ of ▦ of ▦ of ▦ = ___ × ___ = ___

Row 6: Product of ↔ of ▦ of ▦ of ▦ = ___ × ___ = ___

Multiplication using function concept and spatial relation

3	4	5	6	2	3	4	5
7	8	9	10	6	7	8	9
11	12	13	14	10	11	12	13
15	16	17	18	14	15	16	17
4	5	6	7	5	6	7	8
8	9	10	11	9	10	11	12
12	13	14	15	13	14	15	16
16	17	18	19	17	17	18	19

Product of ⤢ ... of [grid] of [grid] = ___ × ___ = ___
   2×7=14

Product of ⤢ ... of [grid] of [grid] = ___ × ___ = ___

Product of ↔ of [grid] of [grid] of [grid] = ___ × ___ = ___

Product of ↕↔ of [grid] of [grid] of [grid] = ___ × ___ = ___

Product of ↕↔ of [grid] of [grid] of [grid] = ___ × ___ = ___

Product of ↕↔ of [grid] of [grid] of [grid] = ___ × ___ = ___

Learning Chess to Improve Math 数棋谜式健脑国际象棋

Ho Math Chess 何数棋谜 www.homathchess.com

Frank Ho, Amanda Ho © 1995 – 2021   All rights reserved.

Student name _____ Assignment date:_____

Four operations

These are just some sample questions that use Ho Math Chess' invention of SCL (Symbolic Chess Language). These puzzle-like questions allow children to create the specific questions by following SCL commands using image processing with the comparison, spatial relation, logic, interactions, etc.

27 39 48 / 29 3 58 / 78 18 17	12 21 31 / 41 3 52 / 62 71 82	13 19 15 / 18 3 14 / 17 12 16	12 21 18 / 15 3 24 / 6 9 27
39 + 3 = 42	21 − 3 = 18	19 × 3 = 57	21 ÷ 3 = 7
___ + ___ = ___	___ − ___ = ___	___ × ___ = ___	___ ÷ ___ = ___
___ + ___ = ___	___ − ___ = ___	___ × ___ = ___	___ ÷ ___ = ___
___ + ___ = ___	___ − ___ = ___	___ × ___ = ___	___ ÷ ___ = ___
___ + ___ = ___	___ − ___ = ___	___ × ___ = ___	___ ÷ ___ = ___
___ + ___ = ___	___ − ___ = ___	___ × ___ = ___	___ ÷ ___ = ___
___ + ___ = ___	___ − ___ = ___	___ × ___ = ___	___ ÷ ___ = ___
___ + ___ = ___	___ − ___ = ___	___ × ___ = ___	___ ÷ ___ = ___

Rook path puzzle

How many ways can ♜ travel to ✥ bypassing each square only once? Mark the path by lines.

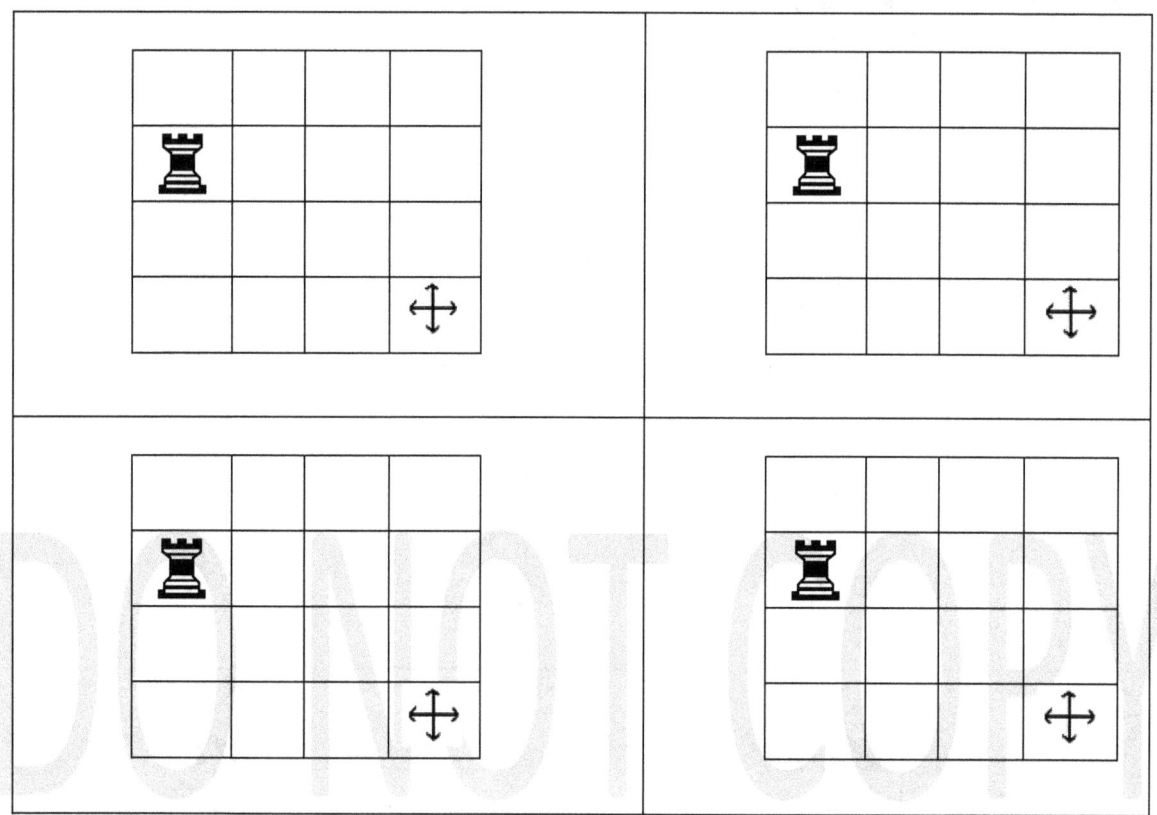

Spatial relation and directions

	Direction	Direction	Direction	Direction
(grid with ✹ marker)	(arrows, up bold) Colour red	(arrows, up-left bold) Colour green	(arrows, right bold) Colour blue	(arrows, down bold) Colour black
(grid with ✢ marker)	(cross shape) Colour red (small grid with x)	(cross shape) Colour green	(cross shape) Colour blue	(cross shape) Colour black

Part 2 Quickstart for beginners on chess moves

Many students like to play chess immediately after the first chess lesson or even after a half of hour lesson introducing moves of chess pieces. Our Ho Math Chess flat chess set could achieve this quickstart purpose. The reason students could play chess immediately using our chess set is that all possible moves are marked on each piece.

This section serves as a crash course on chess moves.

How the pawn moves

Symbol	Names of chess pieces	How does it move? (If it is not blocked and is safe to move.)
♙ ♟ ♙ ♟	Pawn	One or two squares forward on the first move and only one square forward after the first move. One square diagonally when taking an opponent's piece. When a pawn reaches the other end of the board, a pawn can be promoted to any piece other than a king or a pawn.

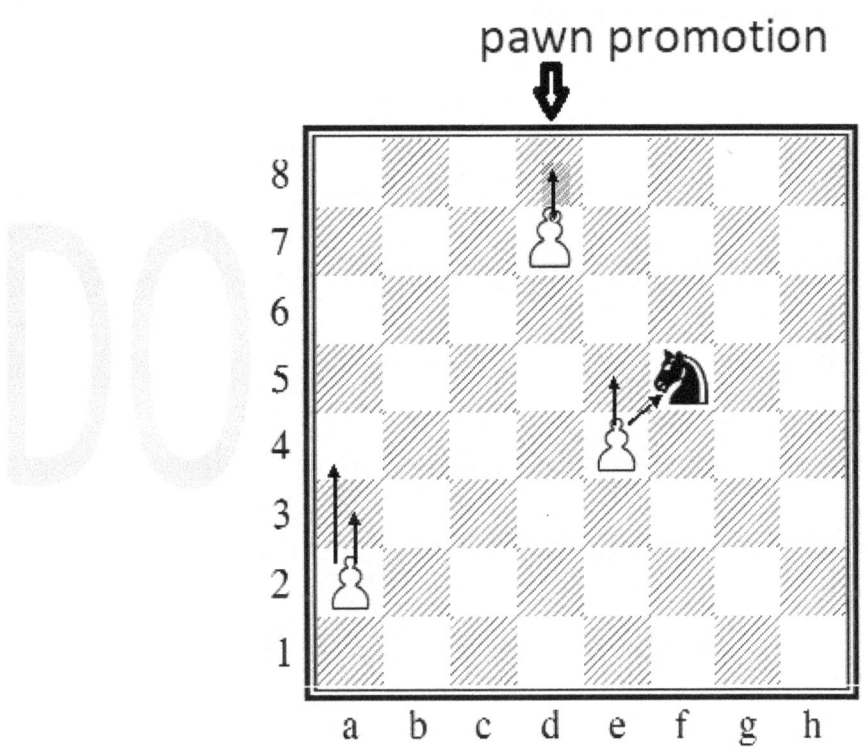

How the pawn moves

Draw lines to show all possible moves of each pawn

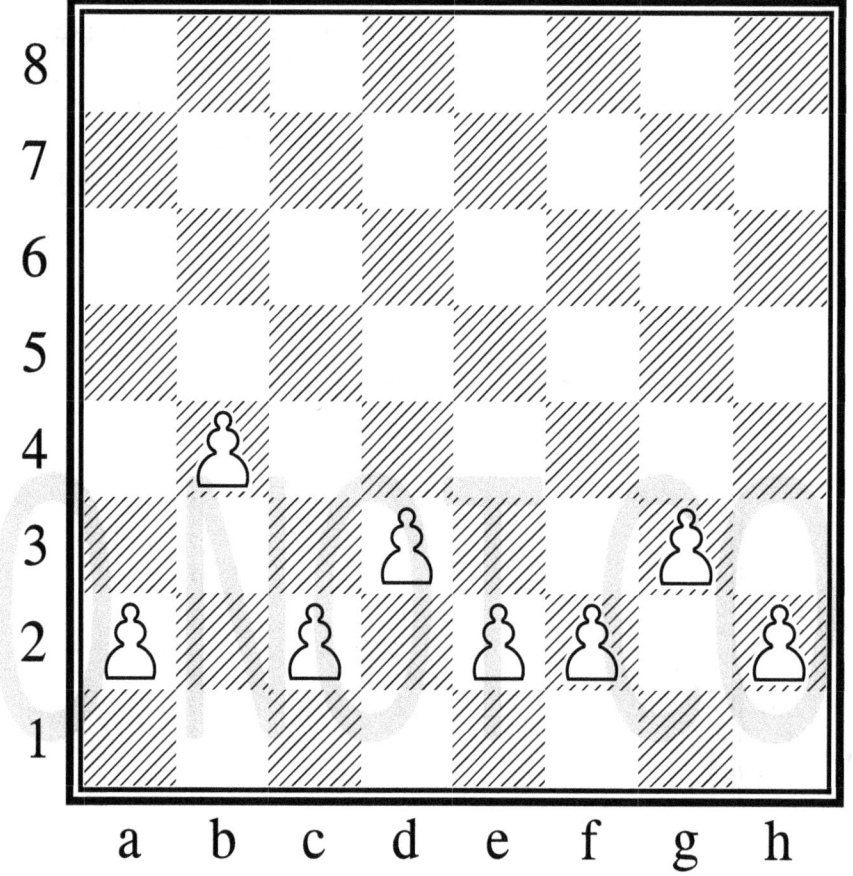

Learning Chess to Improve Math

Ho Math Chess   www.homathchess.com

Frank Ho, Amanda Ho © 1995 – 2021   All rights reserved.

Student name _____   Assignment date: _____

How the pawn moves

Show all the possible squares where White pawns can take or move to by drawing arrows.

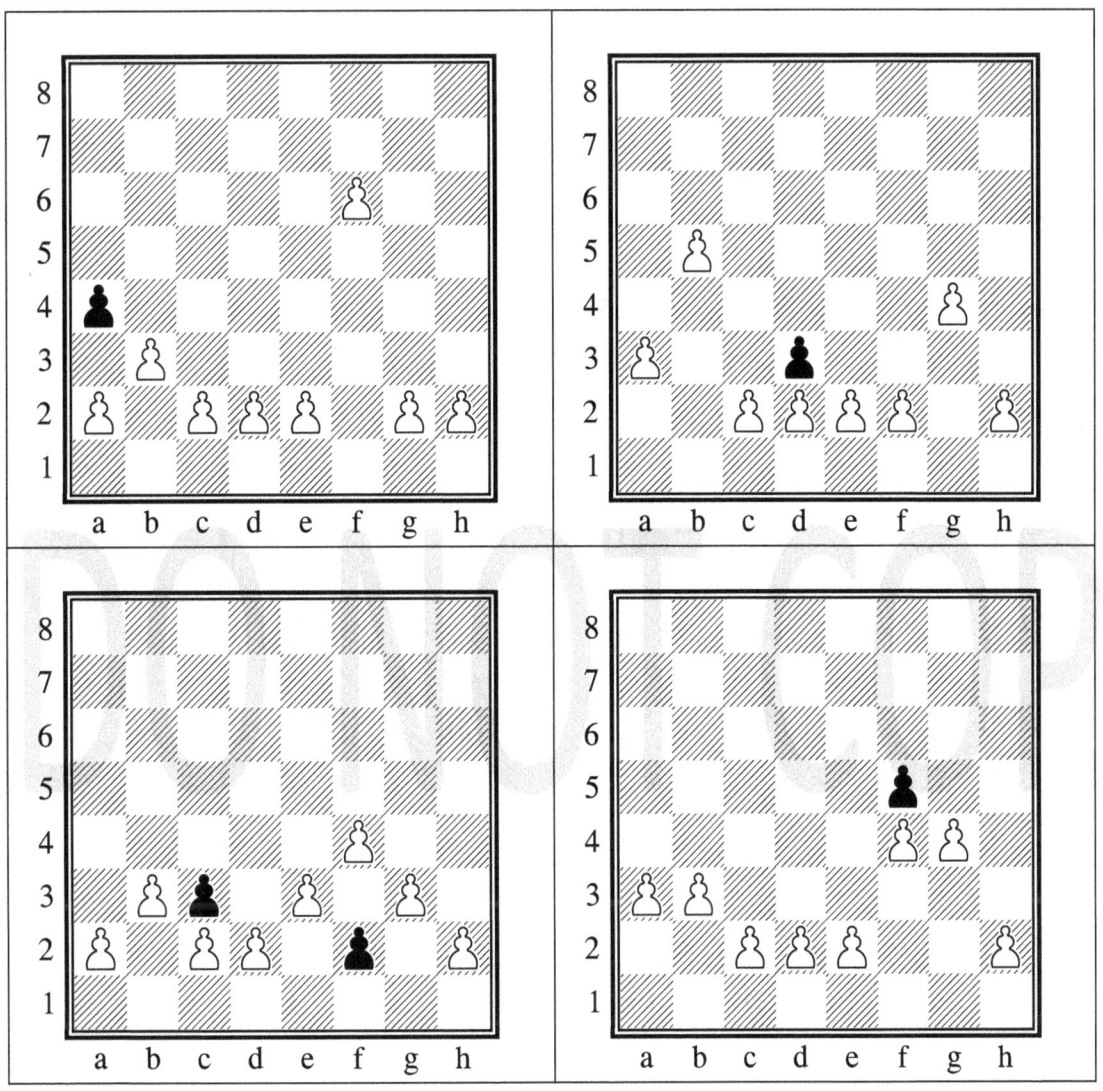

How the pawn moves

Draw lines to show all possible moves of each pawn. Do not move to the squares where the black knight can take a pawn.

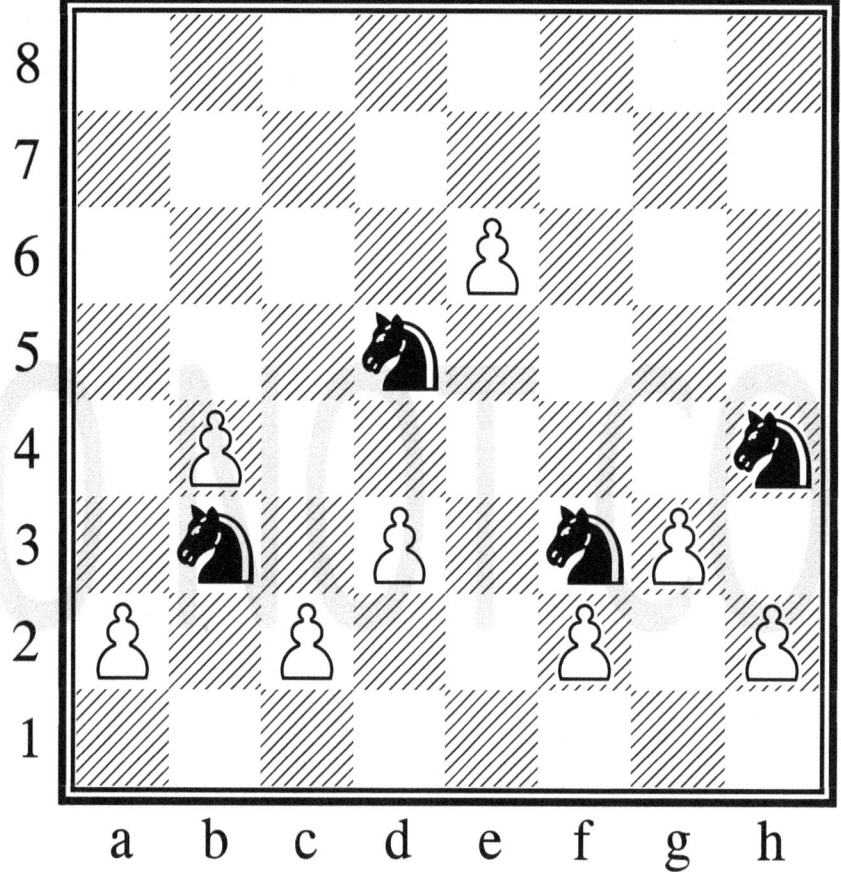

How the pawn moves

Show how pawn moves by drawing arrows. (Note that Black is moving toward the south.)

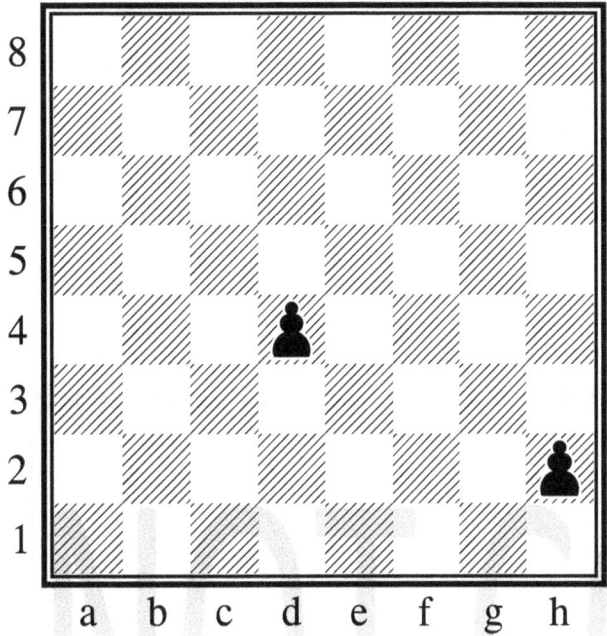

How the rook moves

Symbol	Names of chess pieces	How does it move? (If it is not blocked and is safe to move.)
♖ ♖ (R)	Rook (major piece)	Up and down Left and right Any number of squares

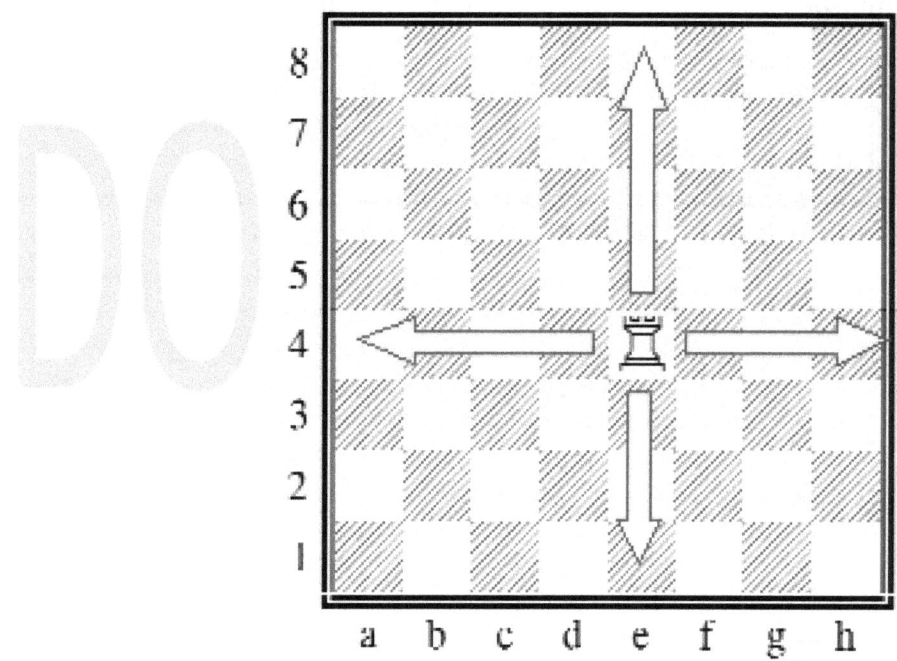

Show how the rook moves by drawing arrows.

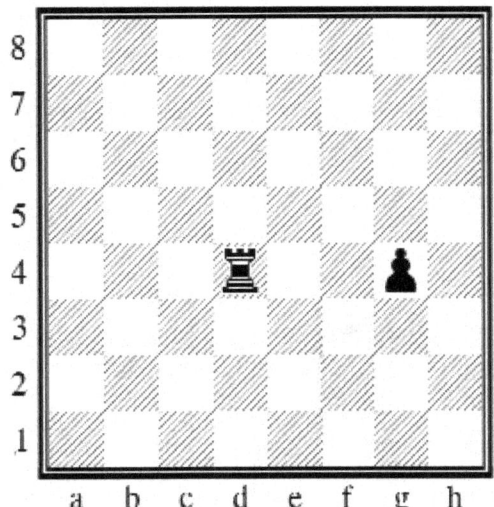

Rook moves

Show all the possible squares where White rook can take or move to by marking X.

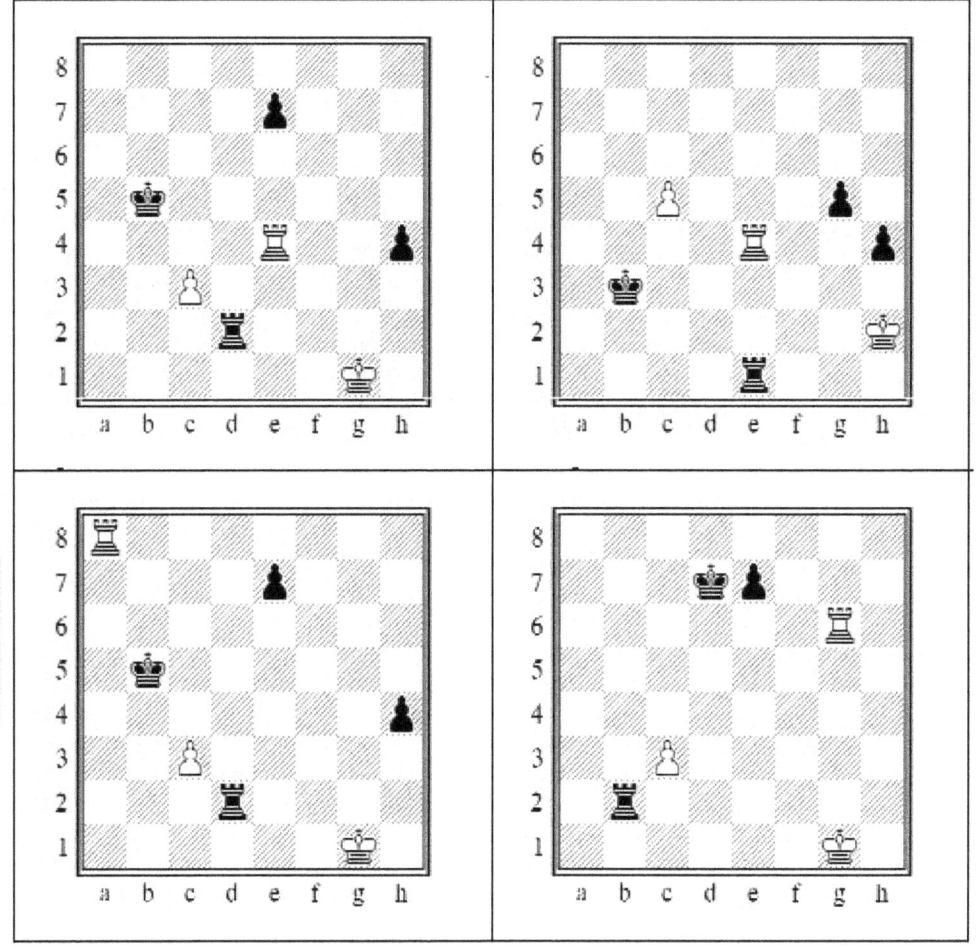

Learning Chess to Improve Math 数棋谜式健脑国际象棋
Ho Math Chess 何数棋谜 www.homathchess.com
Frank Ho, Amanda Ho © 1995 – 2021   All rights reserved.

Student name _____ Assignment date:_____

Rook Moves

Show rook's shortest path to the marked square by an arrow(s).

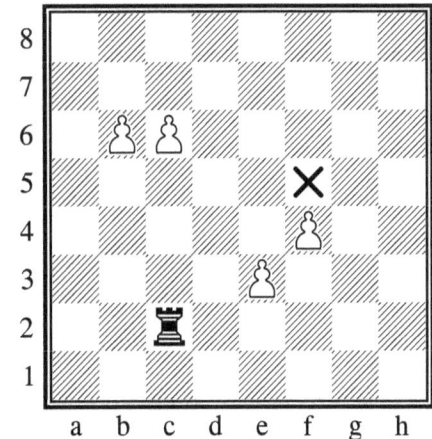

Show rook's shortest path to the marked square by an arrow(s).

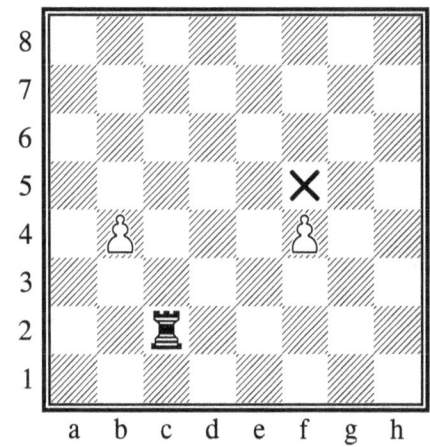

Show rook's shortest path to the marked square by an arrow(s).

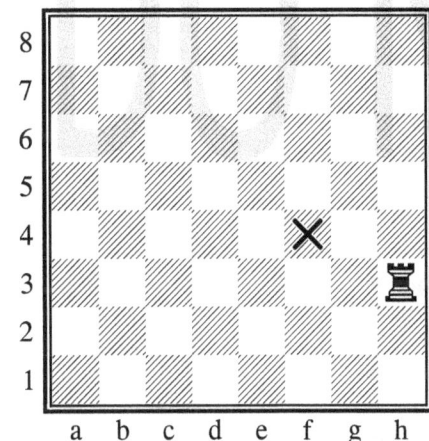

Show rook's shortest path to the marked square by an arrow(s).

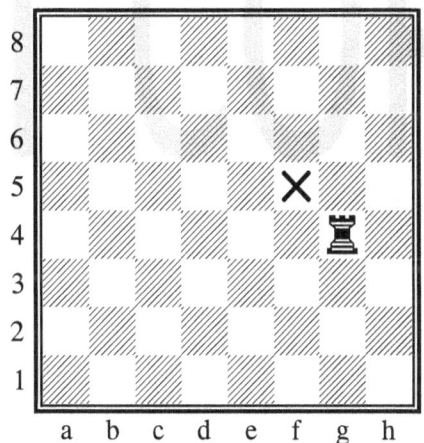

Learning Chess to Improve Math 数棋谜式健脑国际象棋
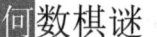 Math Chess 何数棋谜 www.homathchess.com

Frank Ho, Amanda Ho © 1995 – 2021   All rights reserved.

Student name _____ Assignment date:_____

Rook Moves and translation

Mark the square with an X after moving right three squares and upon two squares.

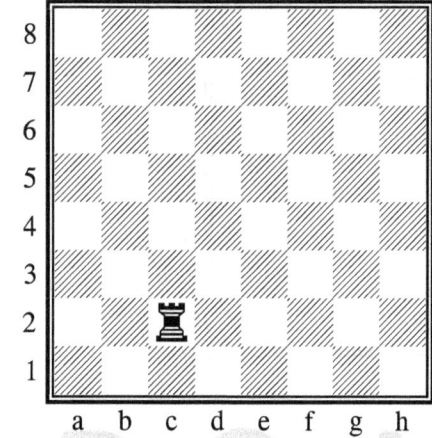

Mark the square with an X after moving (4, 5) (right four squares and up to five squares.).

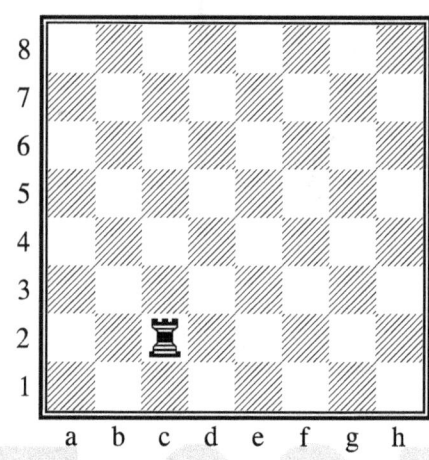

Mark the square with an X after moving (-4, 5). (left four squares and up to five squares)

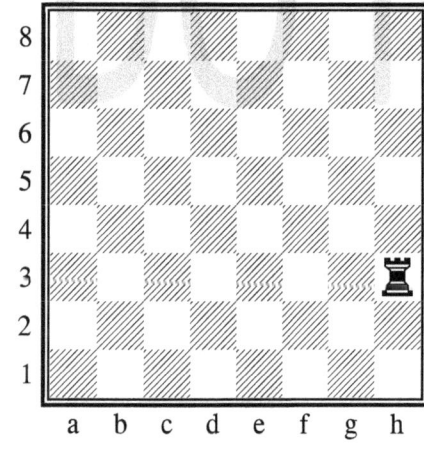

Mark the square with an X after moving (-2, -2). (left two squares and down two squares)

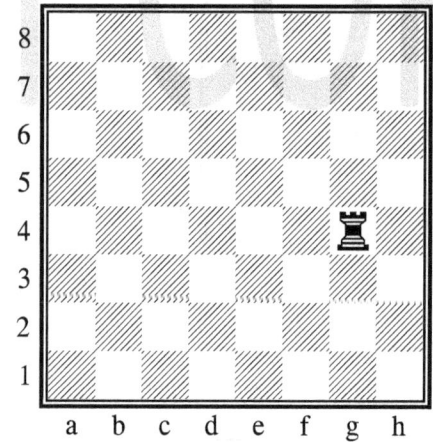

How the bishop moves

Symbol	Names of chess pieces	How does it move? (If it is not blocked and is safe to move.)
(B)	Bishop (minor piece)	Diagonally Any number of squares

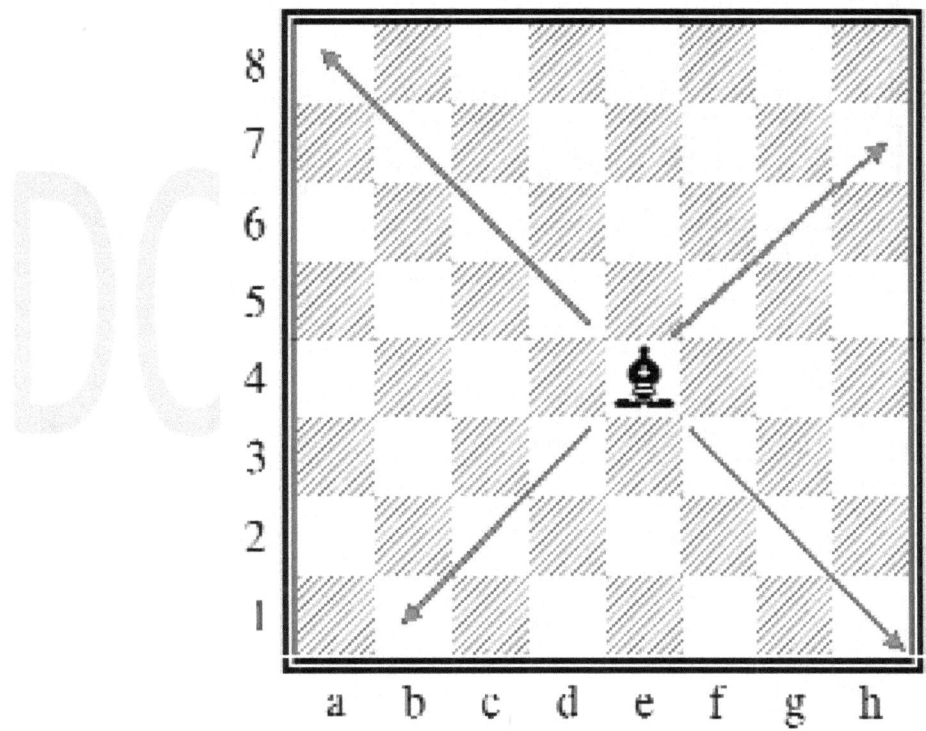

Show how the bishop moves by drawing arrows.

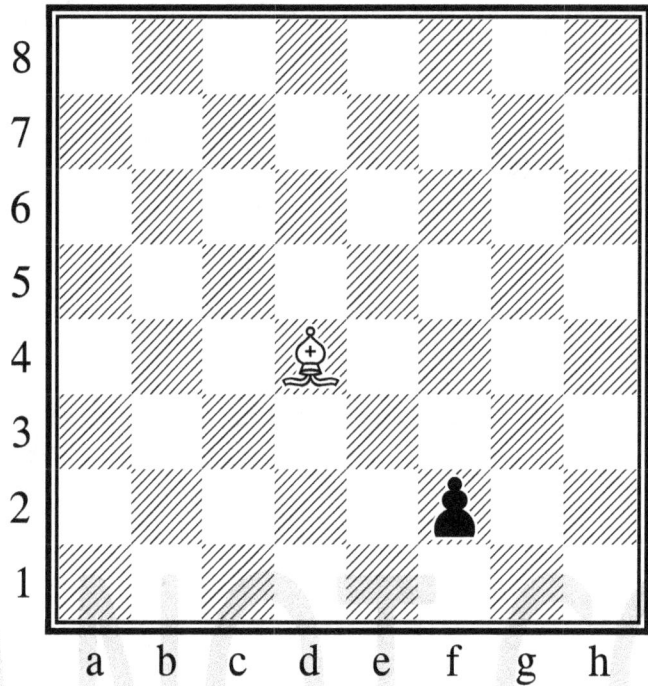

Bishop moves

Show all the possible squares where the White bishop can or move to by marking X.

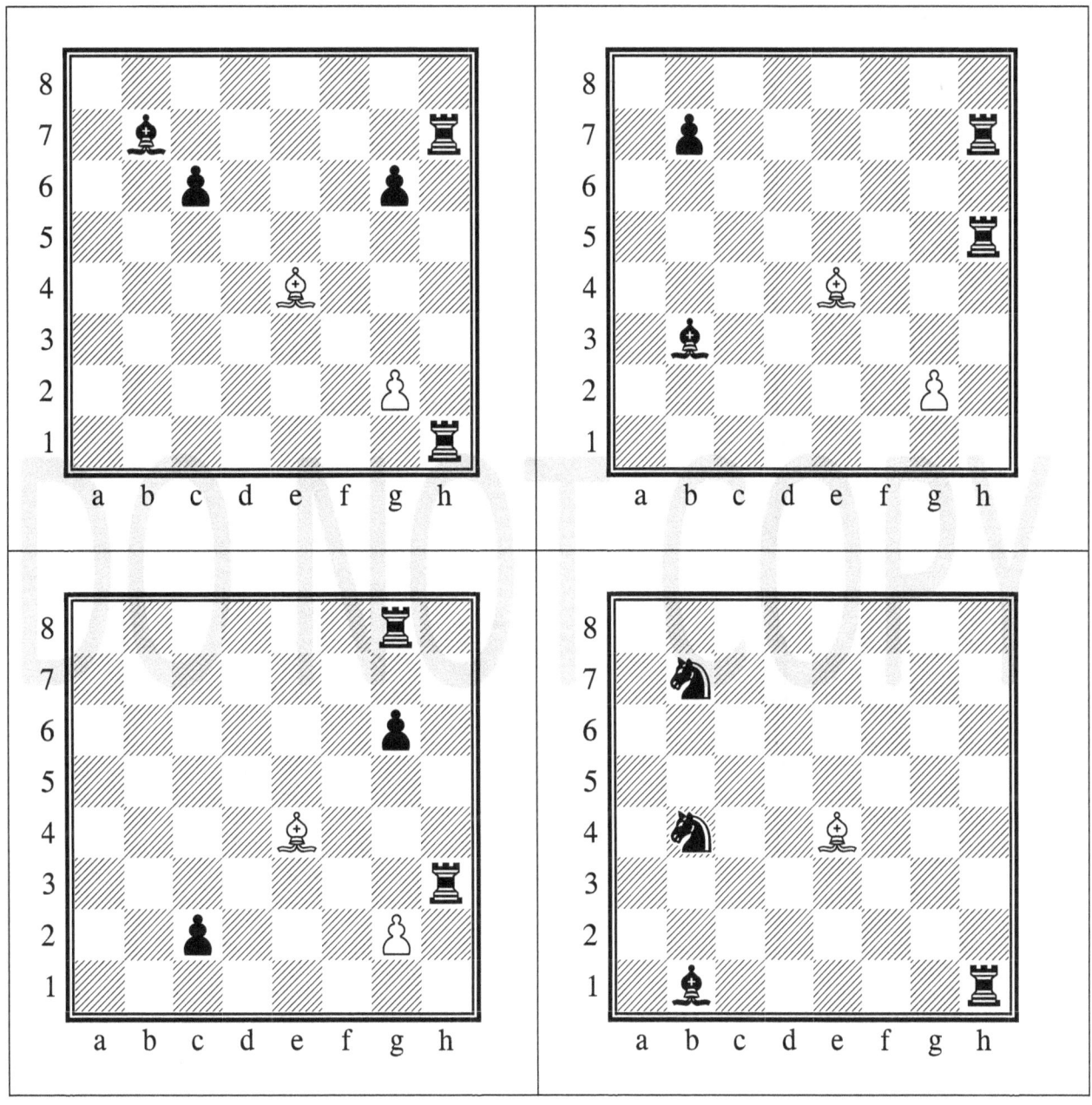

Learning Chess to Improve Math 数棋谜式健脑国际象棋
Ho Math Chess 何数棋谜 www.homathchess.com
Frank Ho, Amanda Ho © 1995 – 2021   All rights reserved.

Student name _____ Assignment date:_____

How the king moves

Symbol	Names of chess pieces	How does it move? (If it is not blocked and is safe to move.)
♔ ♚ (K) ✷ ✸	King	Up and down Left and right Diagonally one square at a time

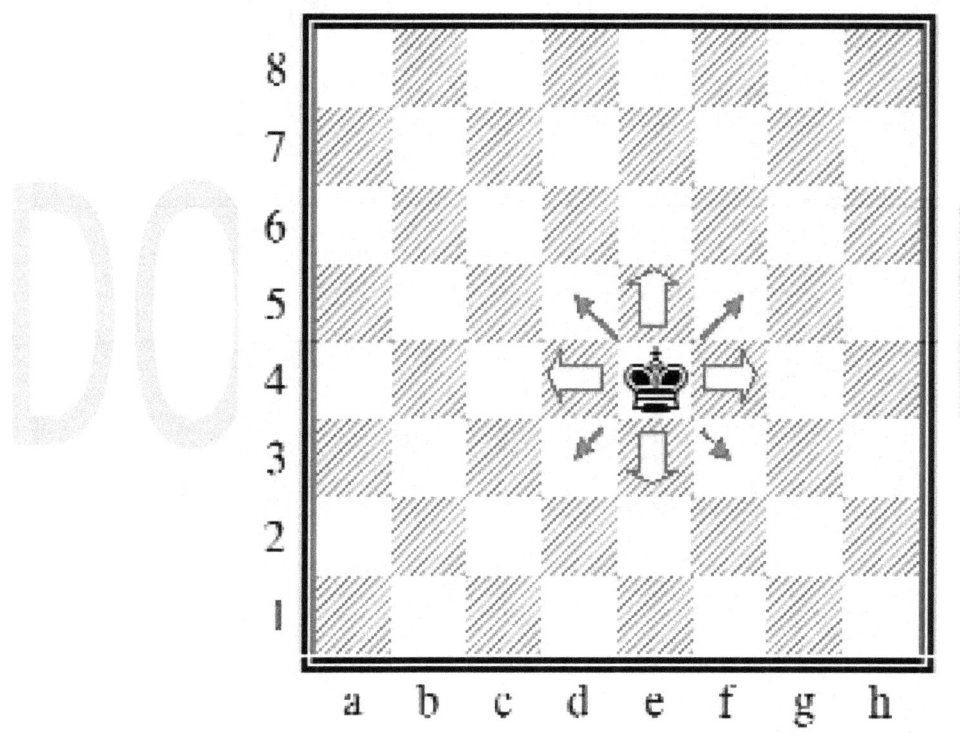

Show how the king moves by drawing arrows.

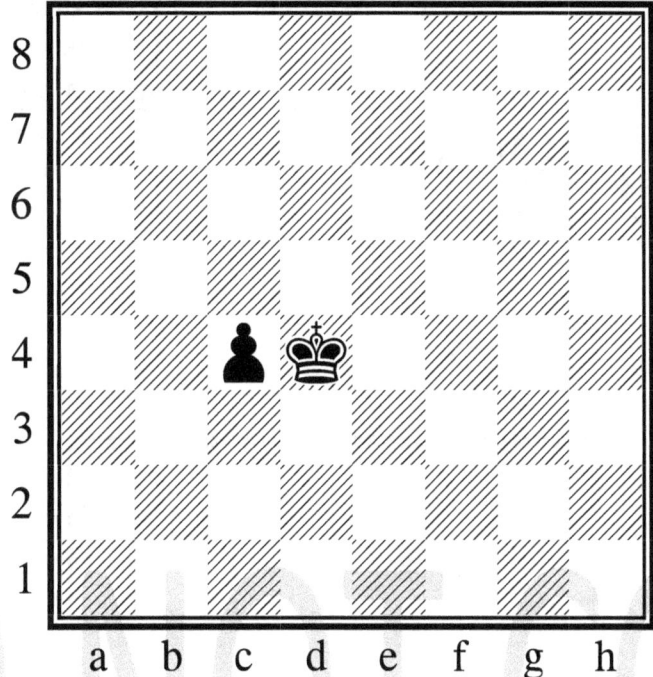

How the queen moves

Symbol	Names of chess pieces	How does it move? (If it is not blocked and is safe to move.)
♕♛ (Q) ✺✹	Queen (major piece)	Up and down Left and right Diagonally Any number of squares

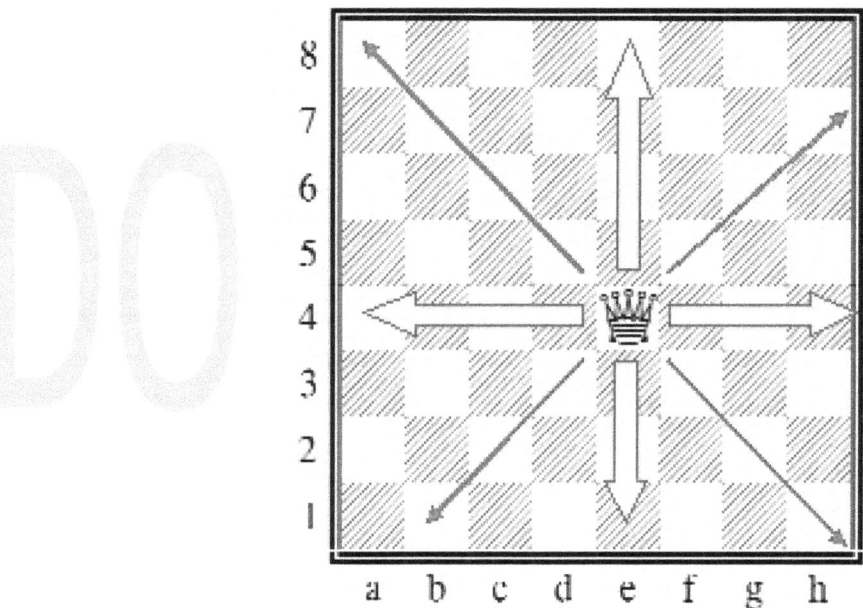

Show how the queen moves by drawing arrows.

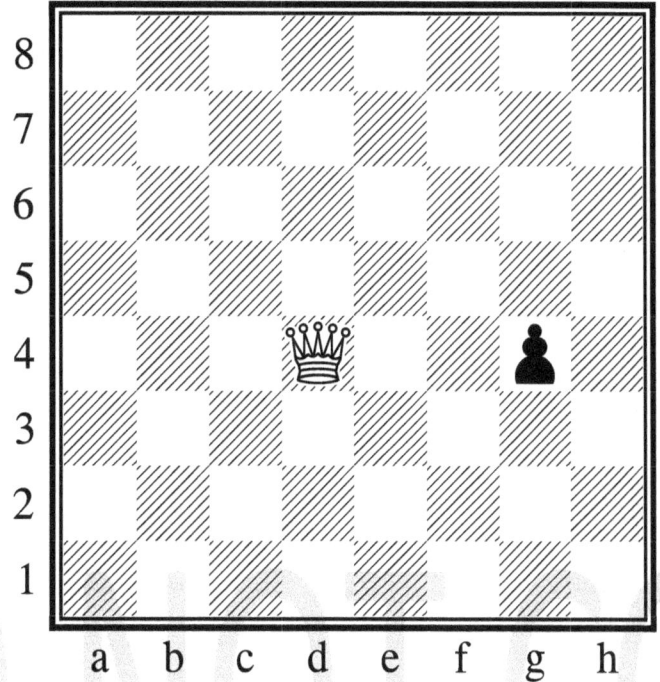

Queen moves

Show all the possible squares where the White queen can or move to by marking X.

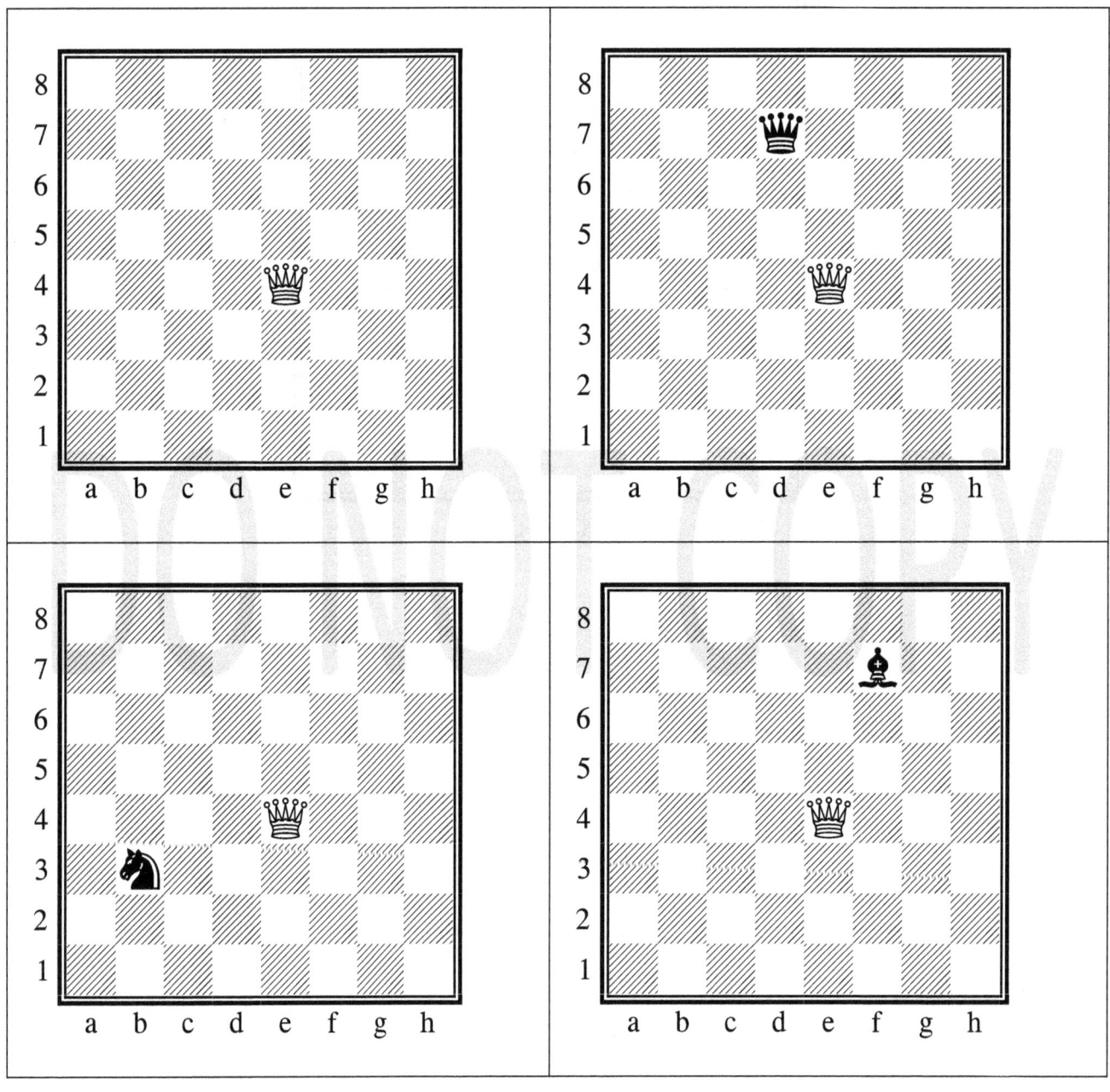

Learning Chess to Improve Math

How the knight moves

Symbol	Names of chess pieces	How does it move? (If it is not blocked and is safe to move.)
(N)	Knight (minor piece)	L-shape or Y-shape in 8 directions. Knight can also move along the diagonal in a rectangle. The only piece can jump over pieces.

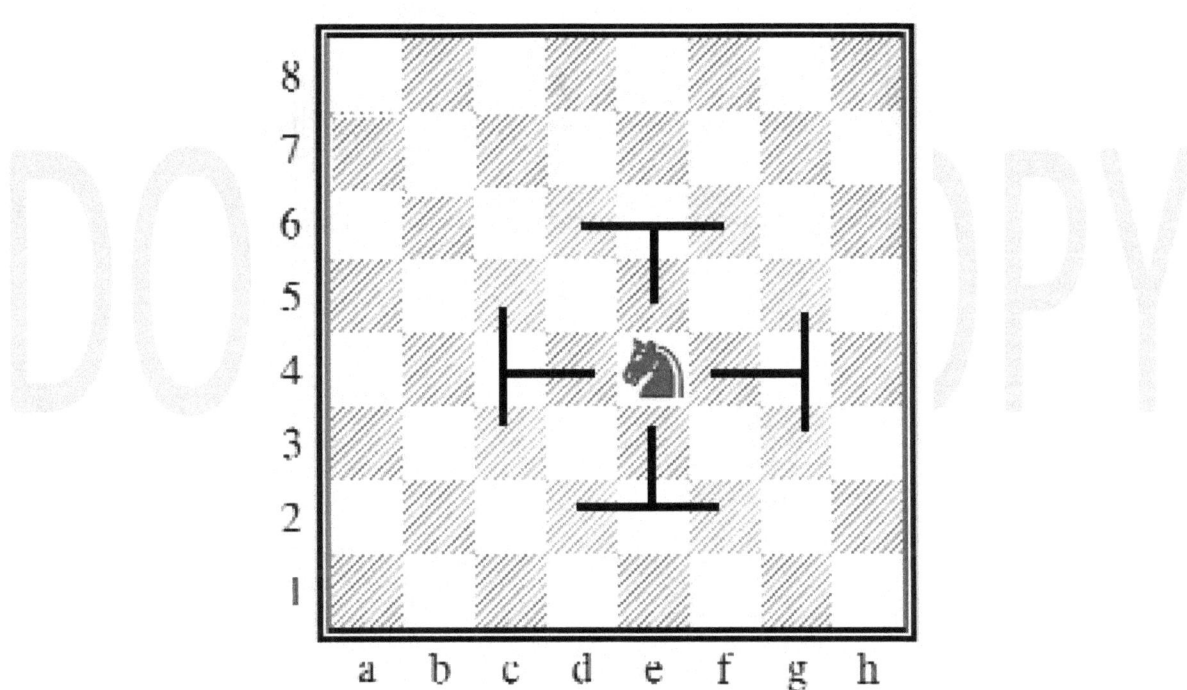

Show how the knight moves by marking ✗ or ☐ ▨,

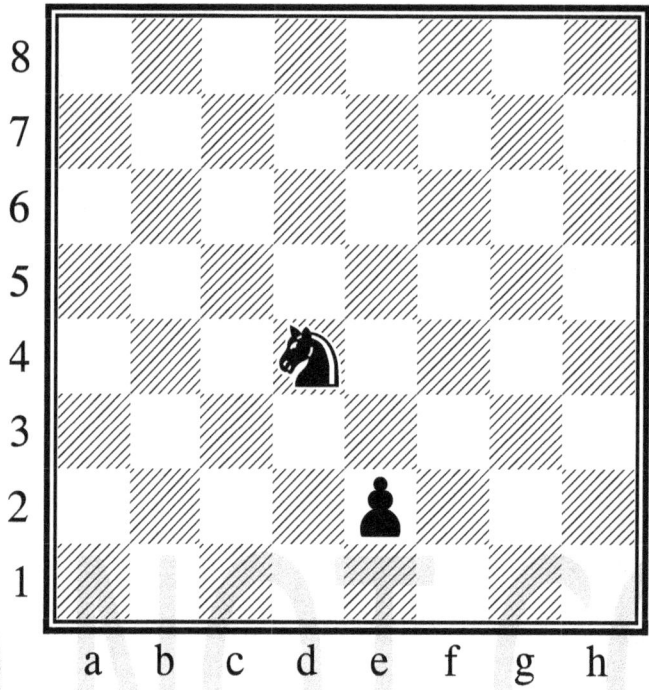

Knight Moves

Show all the possible squares where the White knight can take or move to by marking X.

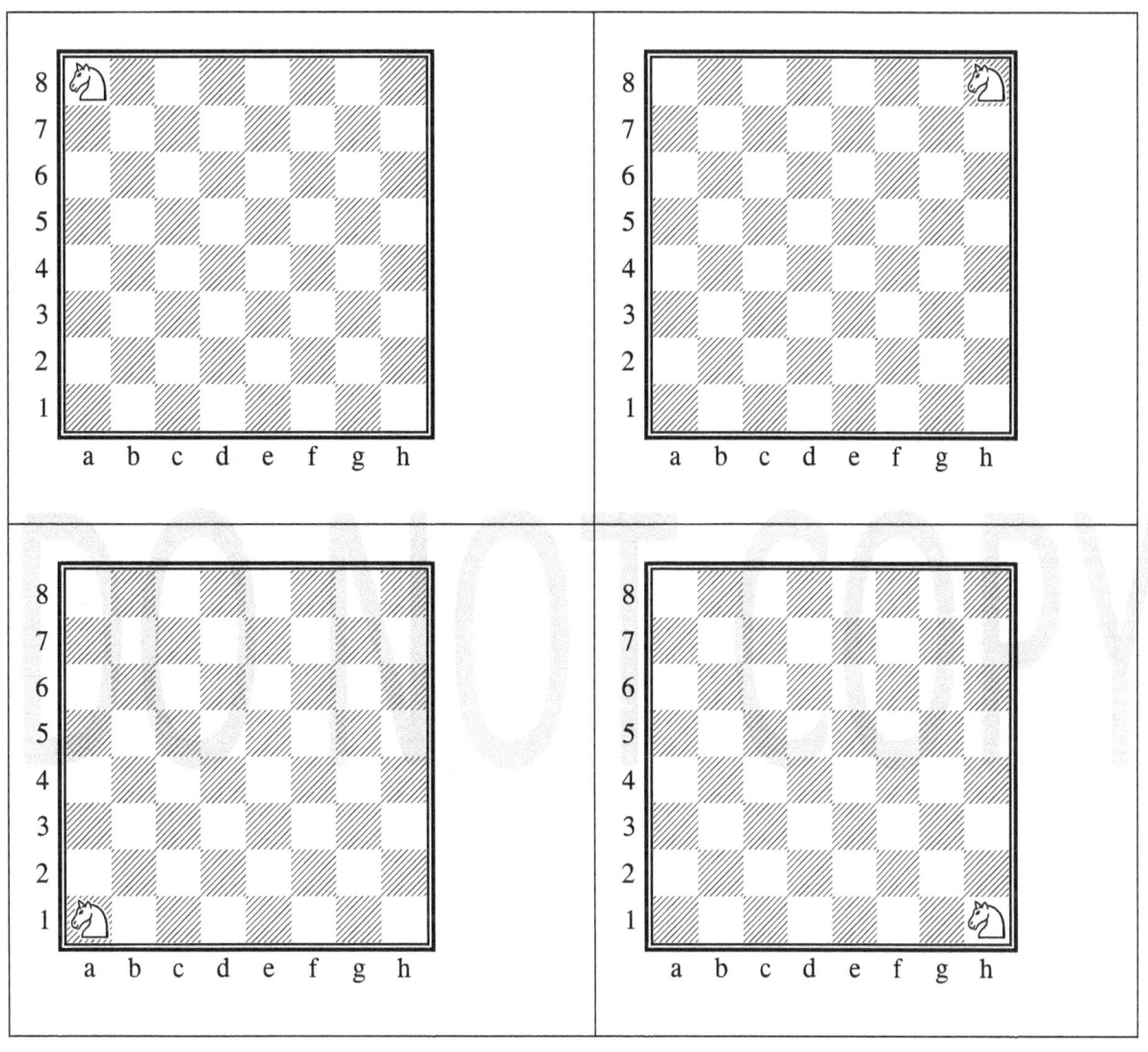

Knight Moves

Show all the possible squares where the White knight can take or move to by marking X.

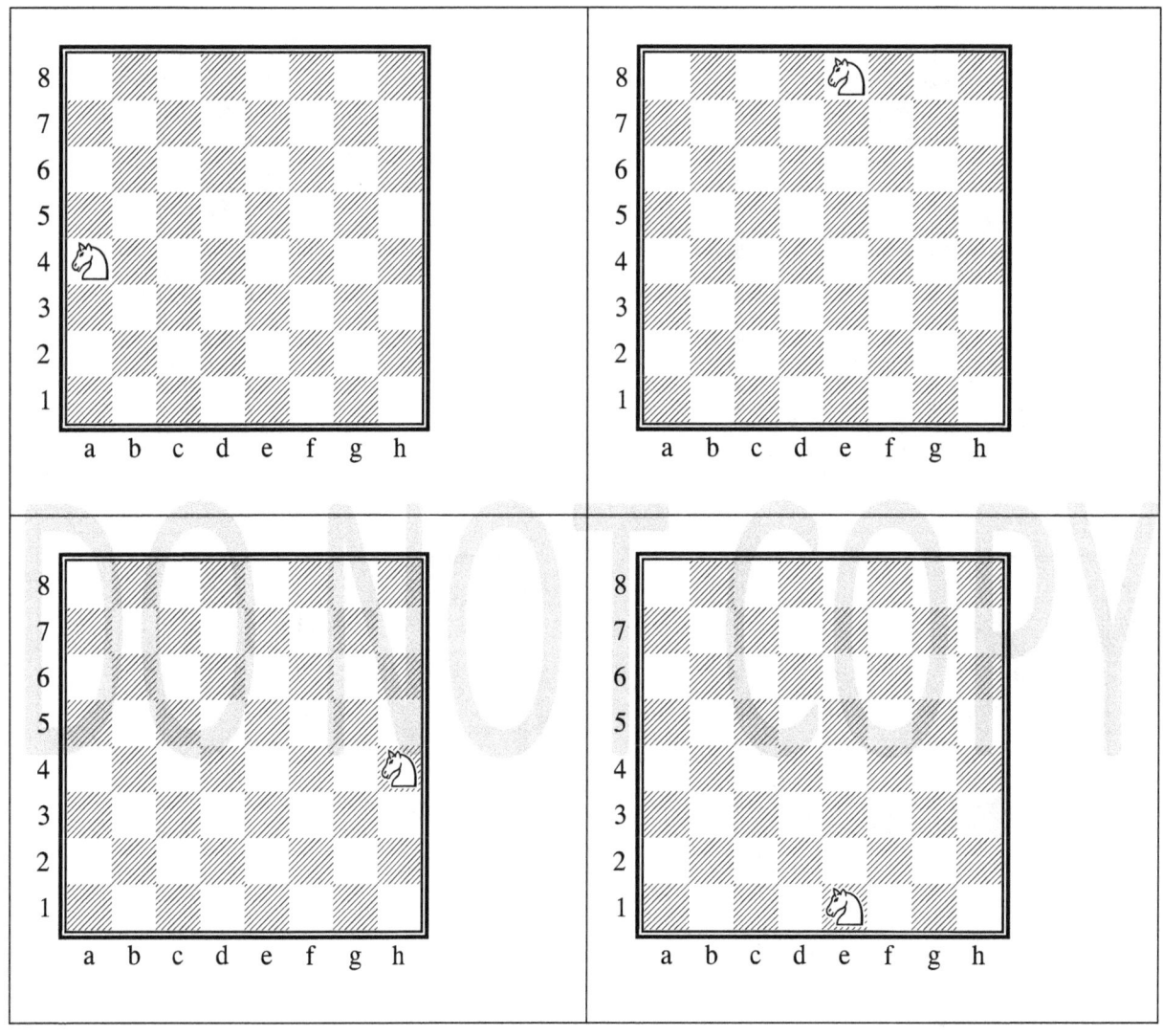

Knight Moves

Show all the possible squares where the White knight can take or move to by marking X.

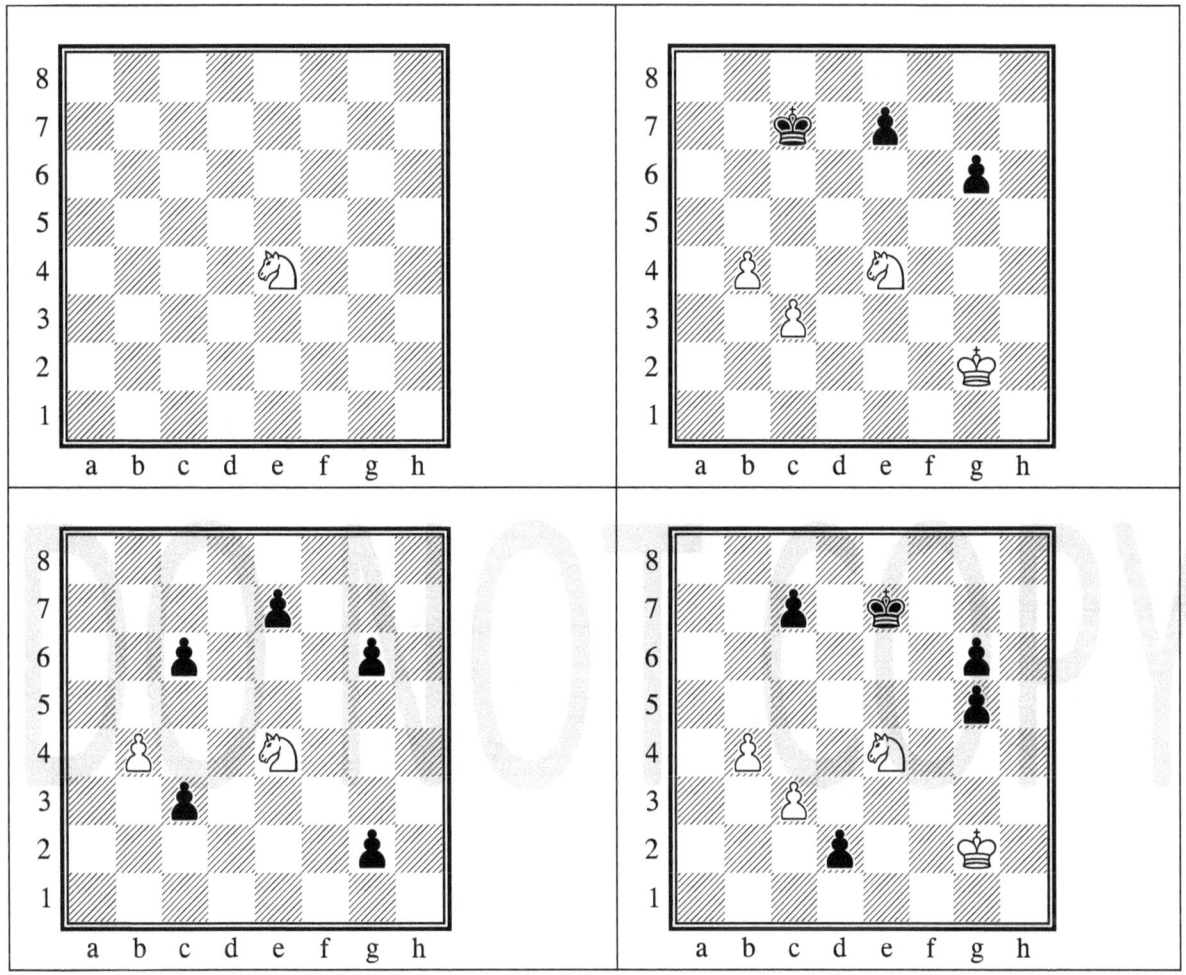

Learning Chess to Improve Math

Ho Math Chess 何数棋谜 www.homathchess.com

数棋谜式健脑国际象棋

Frank Ho, Amanda Ho © 1995 – 2021   All rights reserved.

Student name _____ Assignment date:_____

How knights move and take

Mark an "X" on every square where the knight can move to or take.

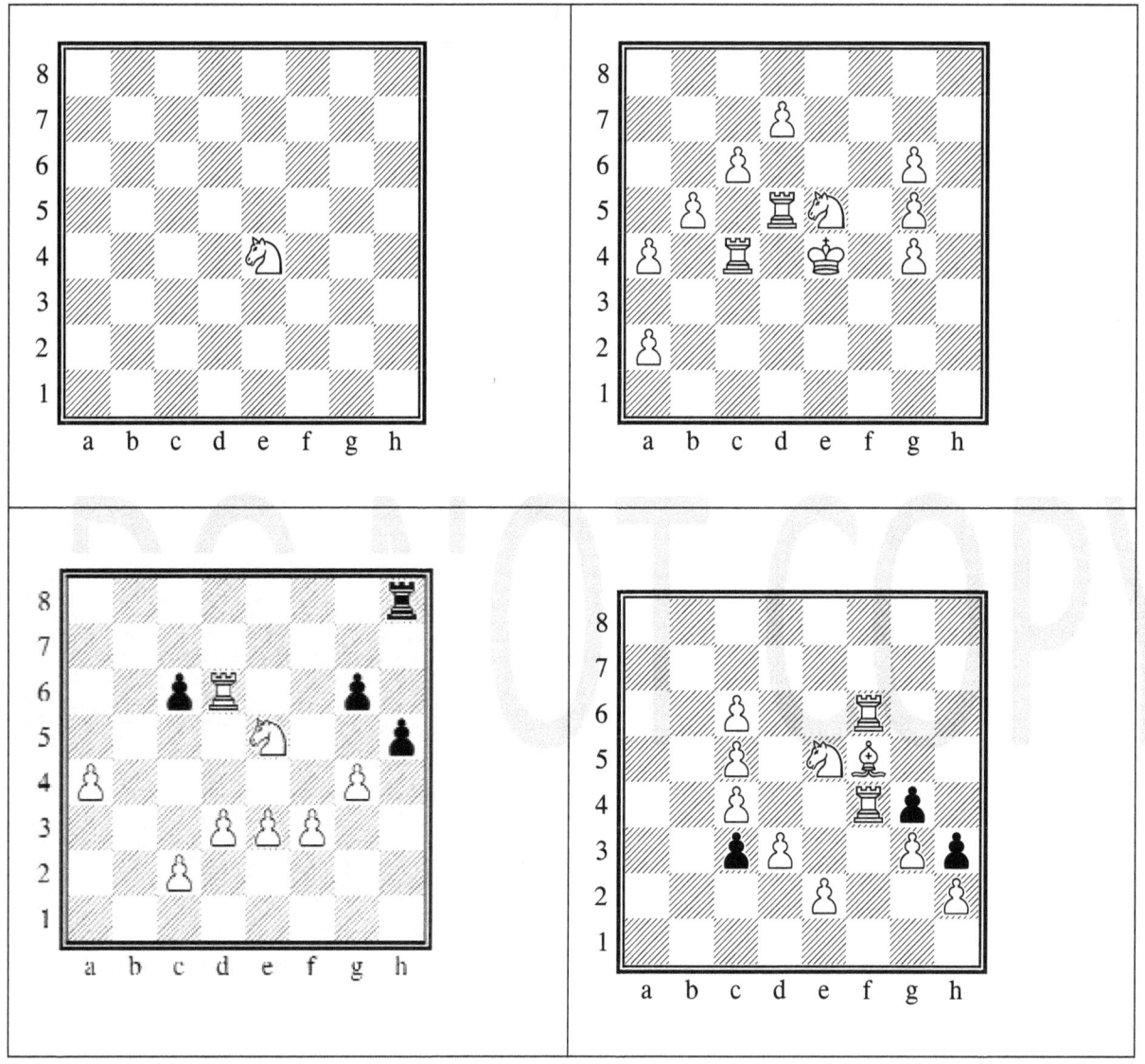

Learning Chess to Improve Math

How knights move and take

Mark an "X" on every square where the white knight can move to or take.

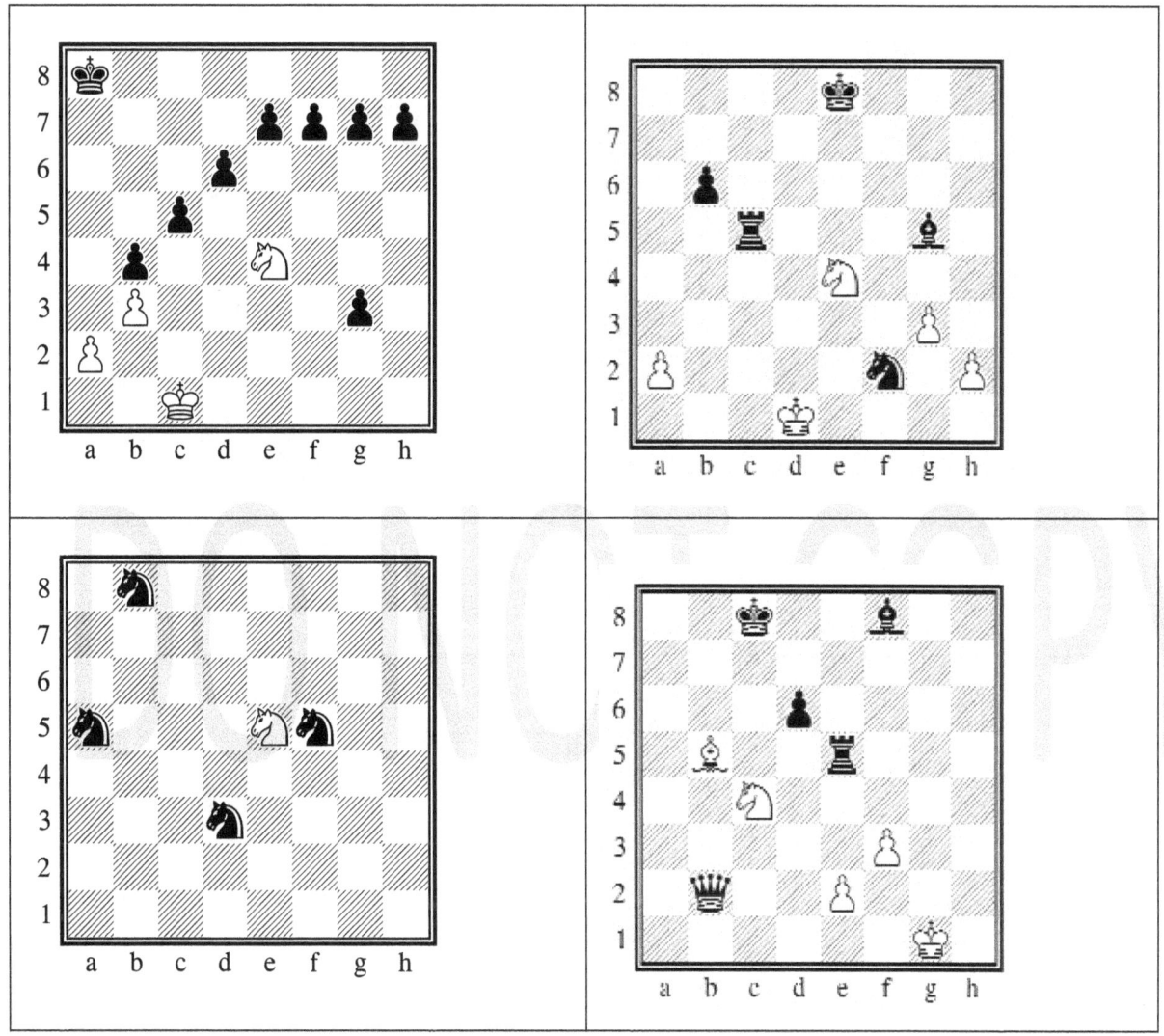

Learning Chess to Improve Math 数棋谜式健脑国际象棋
Ho Math Chess 何数棋谜 www.homathchess.com
Frank Ho, Amanda Ho © 1995 – 2021   All rights reserved.

Student name _____ Assignment date:_____

Knight Moves

Show all the possible squares where the White knight can take or move to by marking X.

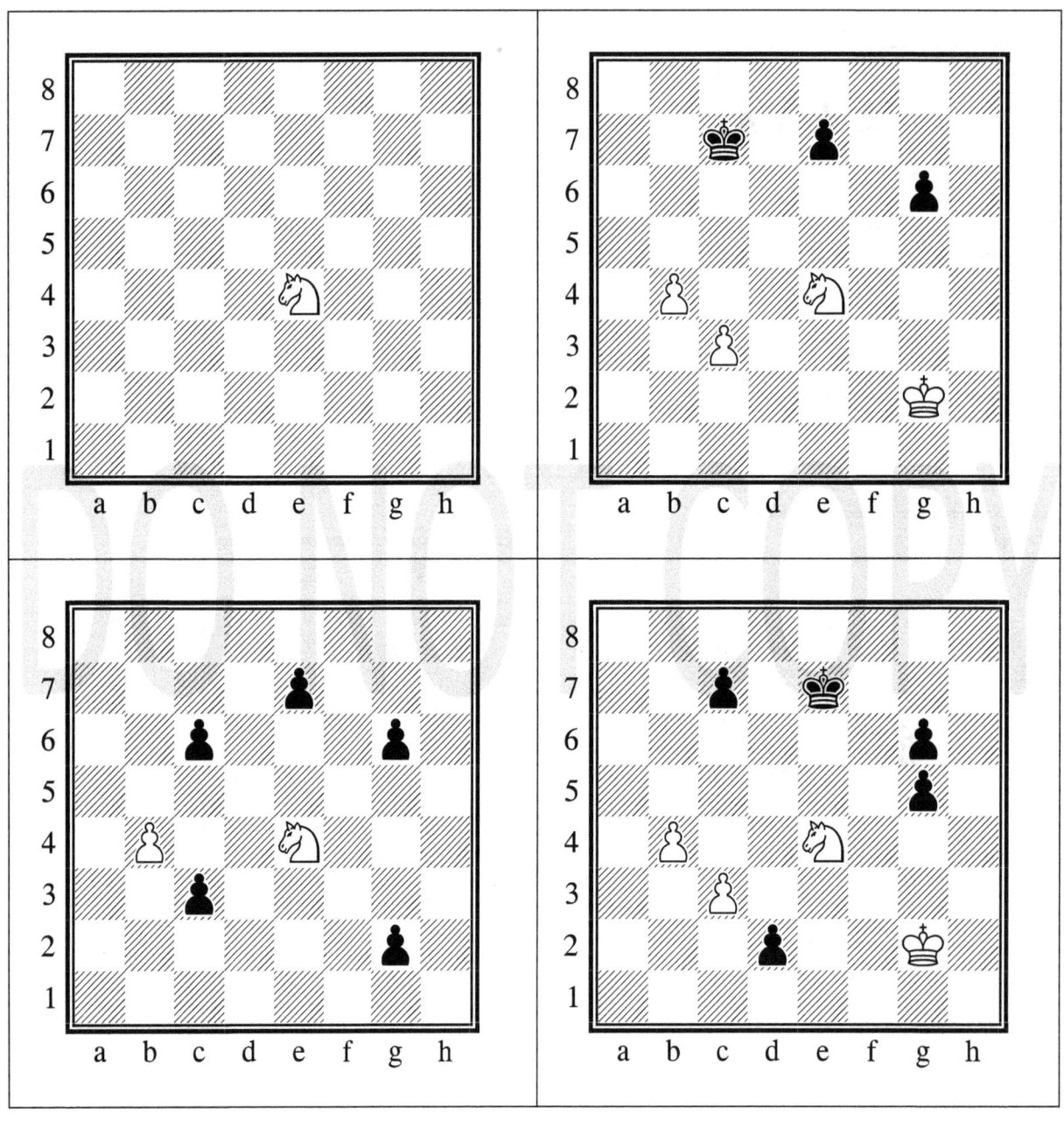

Part 3 More chess moves and their connections to arithmetic

Many students need more practice to be thoroughly familiar with chess moves, especially the knight moves.

This part teaches chess and its possible logical relations to the arithmetic concepts. Many chess problems have chess teaching on the left-hand side and related math problems on the right-hand side.

Teachers should pick up the appropriate math materials which match student's abilities.

Learning Chess to Improve Math 数棋谜式健脑国际象棋
Ho Math Chess 何数棋谜 www.homathchess.com
Frank Ho, Amanda Ho © 1995 – 2021   All rights reserved.

Student name _____ Assignment date:_____

Chessboard and arithmetic problems

Using chessboard to create math problems – different sized squares

What is the total of different-sized squares (The colour does not matter.) in the following five-by-five mini-chessboard?

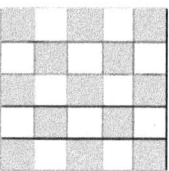

Students can count it, but it is very easy to come up with a wrong answer, so we observe its pattern and use the observed pattern rule to figure it out.

Different sized squares	Sum of squares
How many different sizes of squares are there on the following 1 by 1 square?	How many 1 × 1 squares are there? _____
How many different sizes of squares are there on the following 2 by 2 square?	How many 1 × 1 squares are there? _____ How many 2 × 2 squares are there? _____ So, the answer is _____
How many different sizes of squares are there on the following 3 by 3 square?	How many 1 × 1 squares are there? _____ How many 2 × 2 squares are there? _____ How many 3 × 3 squares are there? _____ 3 × 3 = 9 So, the answer is _____

Chessboard – different sized squares

Different sized squares	Sum of squares
How many different sizes of squares are there on the following 4 by 4 square?	How many 1 × 1 squares are there? _____ How many 2 × 2 squares are there? _____ How many 3 × 3 squares are there? _____ How many 4 × 4 squares are there? _____ So, the answer is _____
How many different sizes of squares are there on the following 5 by 5 square?	How many 1 × 1 squares are there? _____ How many 2 × 2 squares are there? _____ How many 3 × 3 squares are there? _____ How many 4 × 4 squares are there? _____ How many 5 × 5 squares are there? _____ So, the answer is _____

Chessboard – different sized squares

Squares on a chessboard	Sum of squares
How many different sizes of squares are there on a chessboard? 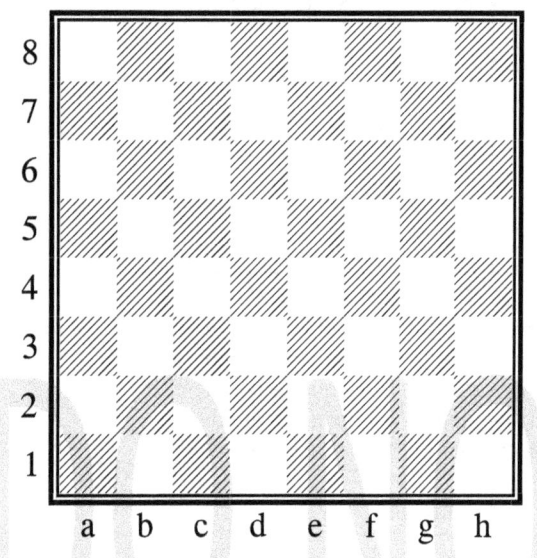 There are 64 of 1 by 1 square, but how about 2 by 2, 3 by 3, etc.? We need to calculate all the way up to 8 by 8 squares and add up all different sizes of squares as the answer.	How many 1 × 1 squares are there? _____ How many 2 × 2 squares are there? _____ How many 3 × 3 squares are there? _____ How many 4 × 4 squares are there? _____ **Do you see a pattern in the above results that could extend to 8 × 8 squares?** How many 5 × 5 squares are there? _____ How many 6 × 6 squares are there? _____ How many 7 × 7 squares are there? _____ How many 8 × 8 squares are there? _____ So, the answer is $8^2 + 7^2 +$ ___ + ___ + ___ + ___ + ___ + ___ = _____

Chessboard and matchsticks

Remove as few matchsticks (each line is considered a matchstick) as possible so that there are no different-sized squares.

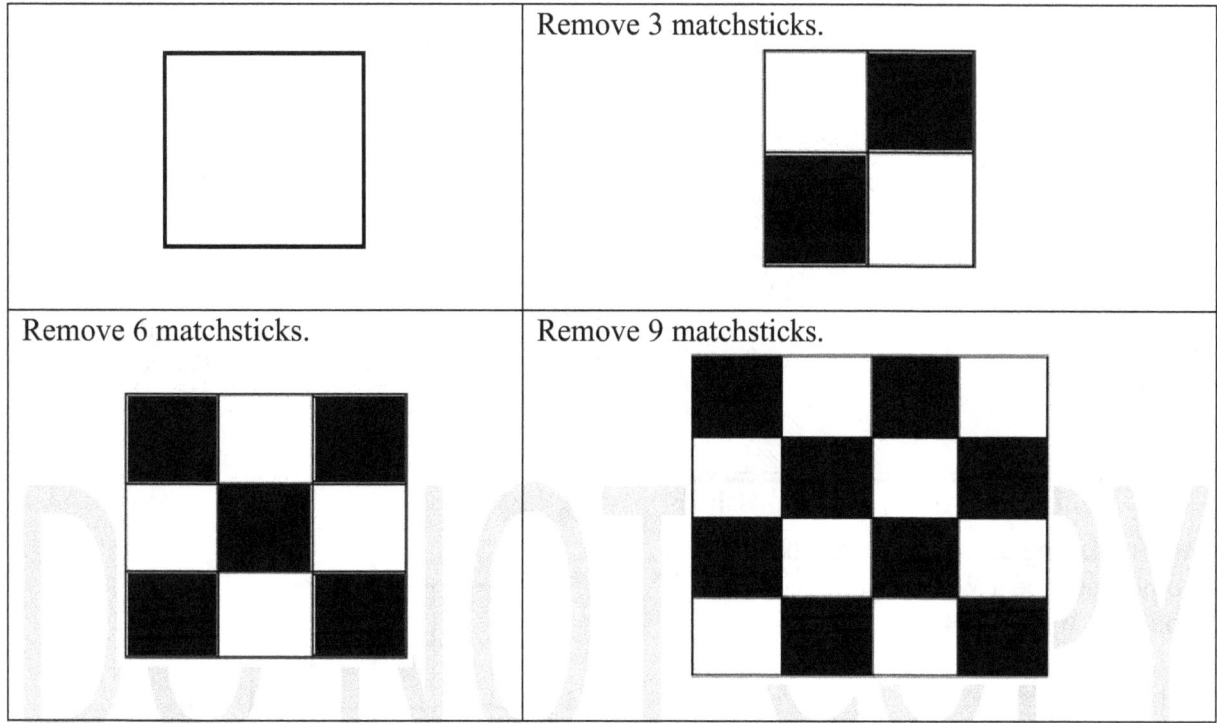

Learning Chess to Improve Math   数棋谜式健脑国际象棋
 Math Chess   何数棋谜   www.homathchess.com

Frank Ho, Amanda Ho © 1995 – 2021   All rights reserved.

Student name _____ Assignment date:_____

Chessboard and coordinates

Chessboard	Coordinate Problem
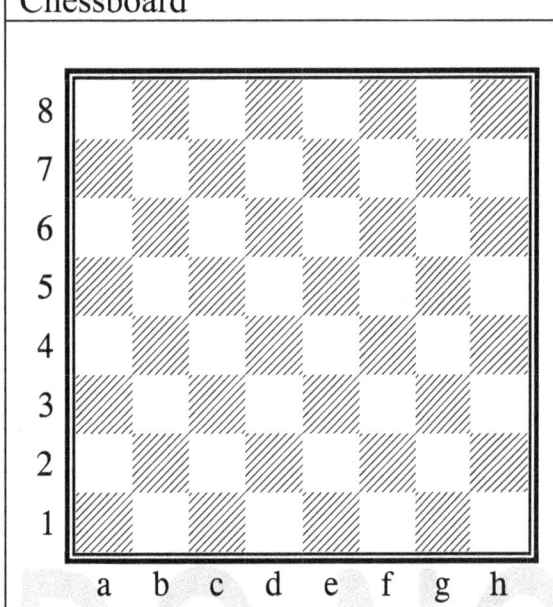 When playing chess, your right-hand lower corner must be a White square regardless if you play White or Black. What is king's side? _____ What is queen's side? _____ Where the queen should be placed? _____ What chess piece is the only piece, which can jump over other pieces? _____ Which chess piece can never move backward? _____ What is rank and file? _____ What are the main diagonals? _____ A chess game is divided into 3 stages and they are called _____ Why normally do chess players move the d or e pawn forward 2 squares in the opening? _____	The square a1 is Black, what would be the colour of g18? Can you solve it by figuring out a systematic way without counting the colour all the way one by one to g18? Answer: _____ What would be the colour of d1003? Answer: _____ If (1, 1) in the following is Black and (2, 1) is White, (1, 2) is White, (2, 2) is Black and (3, 3) is Black, what would be the colour of (1001, 2003)? Answer _____ 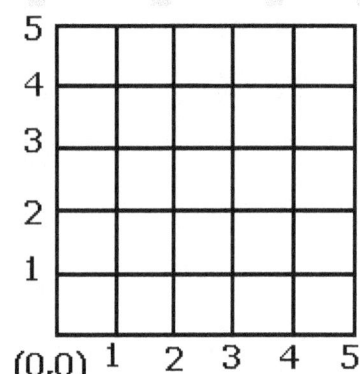 Hint: add the sum of coordinates.

Travelling across the chessboard

	If a queen travels across the 1 by 1 square diagonally, how many squares would have been travelled? _____	Can you find a pattern? $1 + 2 \times (1-1) = 1$
	If a queen travels across the 2 by 2 square diagonally, how many squares would have been travelled? _____	Can you find a pattern?
	If a queen travels across the 3 by 3 square diagonally, how many squares would have been travelled? _____	Can you find a pattern?
	If a queen travels across the 4 by 4 square diagonally, how many squares would have been travelled? _____	Can you find a pattern?

Travelling across the chessboard

	If a queen travels across the 5 by 5 square diagonally, how many squares would have been travelled? _____	Can you find a pattern?
	If a queen travels across the 8 by 8 square diagonally, how many squares would have been travelled? _____	

Counting Paths using the chessboard

How many ways are there when travelling from point A to point B (going right and down only)?

Learning Chess to Improve Math 数棋谜式健脑国际象棋

 Math Chess 何数棋谜 www.homathchess.com

Frank Ho, Amanda Ho © 1995 – 2021   All rights reserved.

Student name _____ Assignment date:_____

How does the pawn move?

How does the pawn move?	Pattern
Show all White pawns' next possible moves without being taken by marking an ✗ on each square.	Replace the following? with a number. (Hint: Observe the pawn's possible moves.) 4, 6, ?, 2
	Replace the following? with a number. 6, 9, ?, 3
	Replace the following? with a number. 12, 16, ?, 4

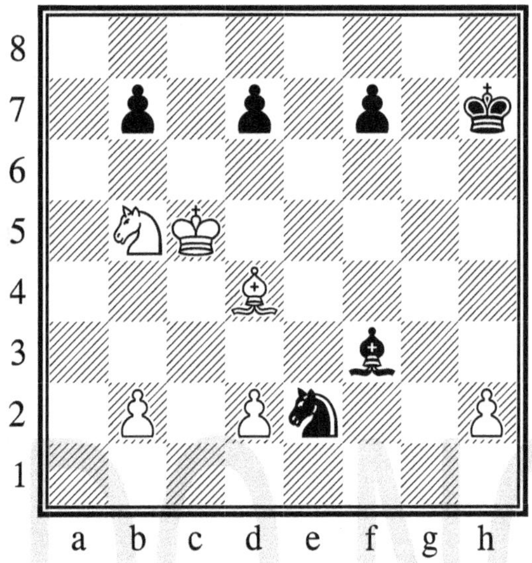

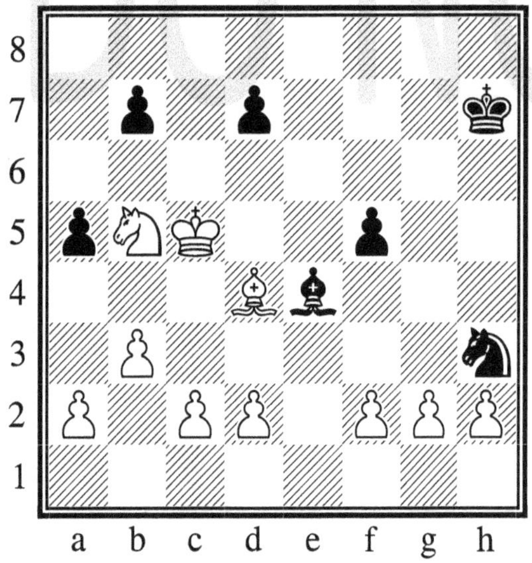

Learning Chess to Improve Math

How does the pawn move?

How does the pawn move?	Adding up to a comfortable number
Show all White pawns' next possible moves without being taken by marking an × on each square. 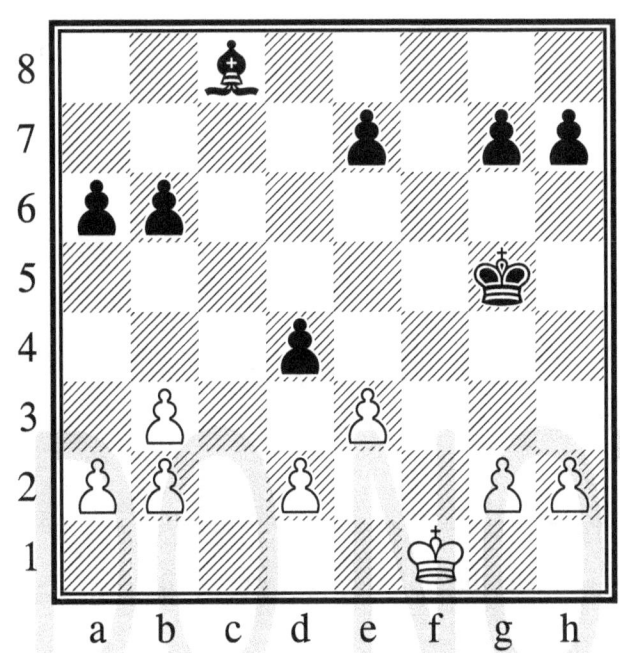 What happens if the pawn reaches the last rank (8th rank for White and 1st rank for Black)? _____ Pawn promotion is compulsory when it reaches the last rank, which means the pawn cannot remain as a pawn. A pawn can be promoted to be a Queen, Rook, Bishop, or Knight. The move of the pawn to the last rank and the promotion of physically changing pawn to a different piece are considered as one move. The promoted piece to a queen can be announced by saying, "I want a queen."	Even though the pawn only makes one move, sometimes the one move is very important, especially reaching the last rank. One (1) is a very important concept in math; quite often, it is used as a step stone of adding up to an important number. Calculate the following expressions. 1. ♕ + 1 + 8 + 2 + ♕ + 1 + ♕ + 1 + 8 + 2 + ♕ + 1 + 8 + 2 = 2. ♖ + ♖ + ♖ + ♖ + ♖ + 5 + 5 + 5 + 8 + 5 = 3. ♘ + ♘ + ♘ + ♘ + ♖ + 7 + 7 + 5 + 7 + 5 = 4. 11 − 1 + 12 − 2 + 14 − 3 + 13 − 4 + 15 − 6 + 16 − 5 = 5. 198 + 1 + 199 + 2 + 197 + 3 + 299 + 2 + 298 + 1 =

Learning Chess to Improve Math

How pawns move and take

Circle the white pawns, which made wrong moves.

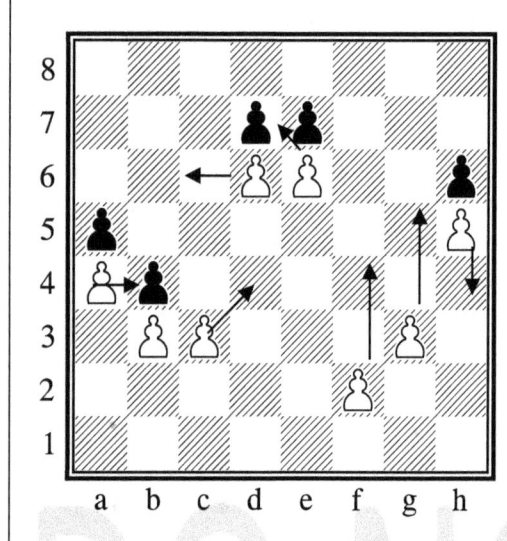

Replace the following ? with a number

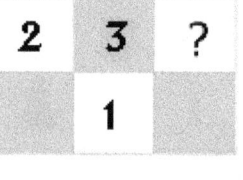

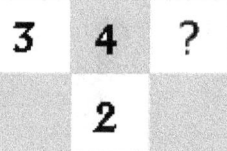

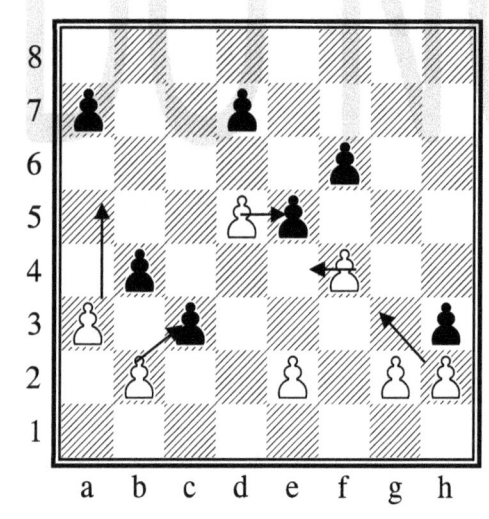

Replace the following ? with a number.

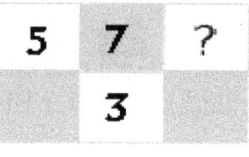

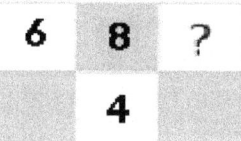

Learning Chess to Improve Math 数棋谜式健脑国际象棋
Ho Math Chess 何数棋谜 www.homathchess.com
Frank Ho, Amanda Ho © 1995 – 2021   All rights reserved.

Student name _____ Assignment date:_____

How pawns move and take

Circle the white pawns, which made wrong moves.

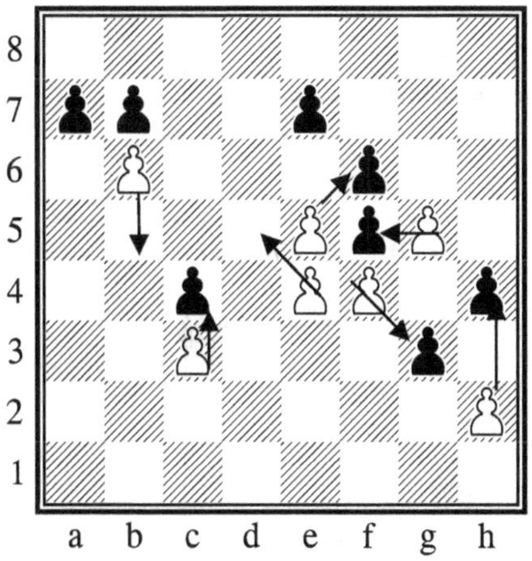

Replace the following ? with a number

4	6	?
	2	

9	12	?
	6	

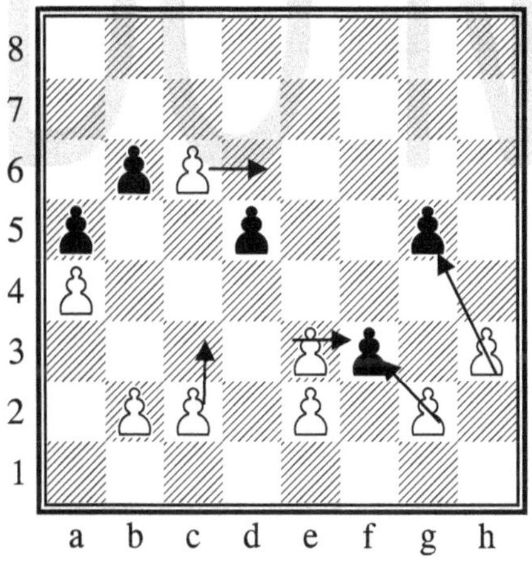

Replace the following ? with a number.

12	16	?
	8	

5	9	?
	1	

Pawn promotion

Show White's next move by an arrow.   Show White's next move by an arrow.

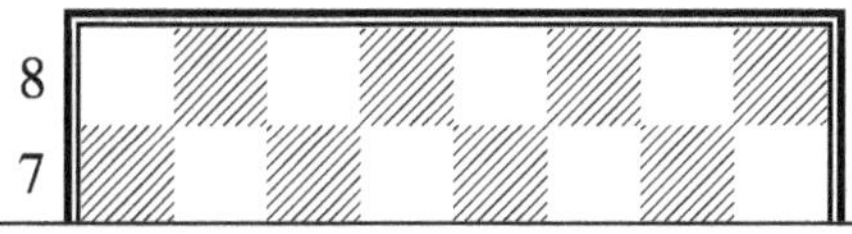

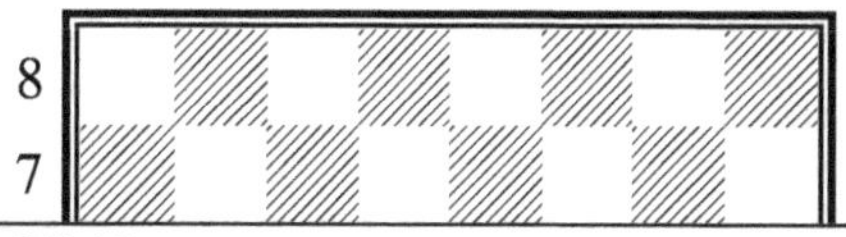

Learning Chess to Improve Math 数棋谜式健脑国际象棋
Ho Math Chess 何数棋谜 www.homathchess.com
Frank Ho, Amanda Ho © 1995 − 2021 All rights reserved.

Student name _____ Assignment date:_____

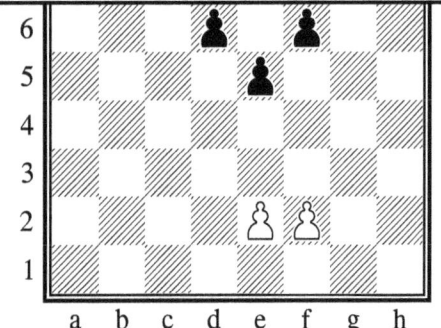

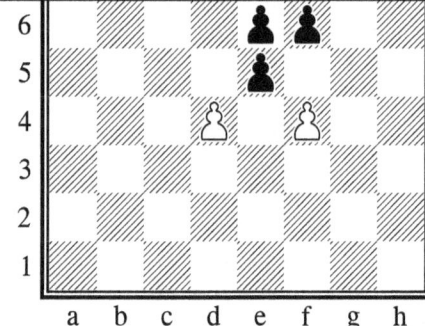

Show White's next move by an arrow.

Show White's next move by an arrow.

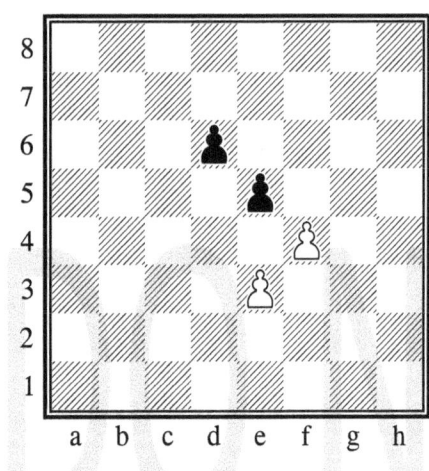

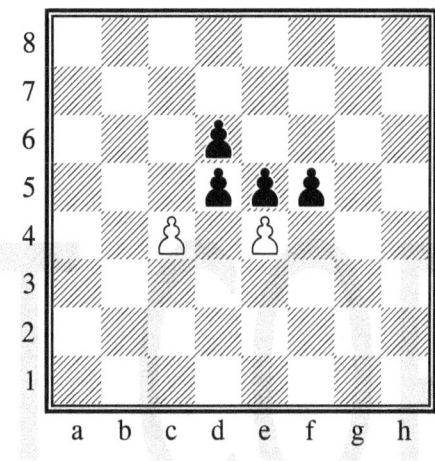

Types of pawns

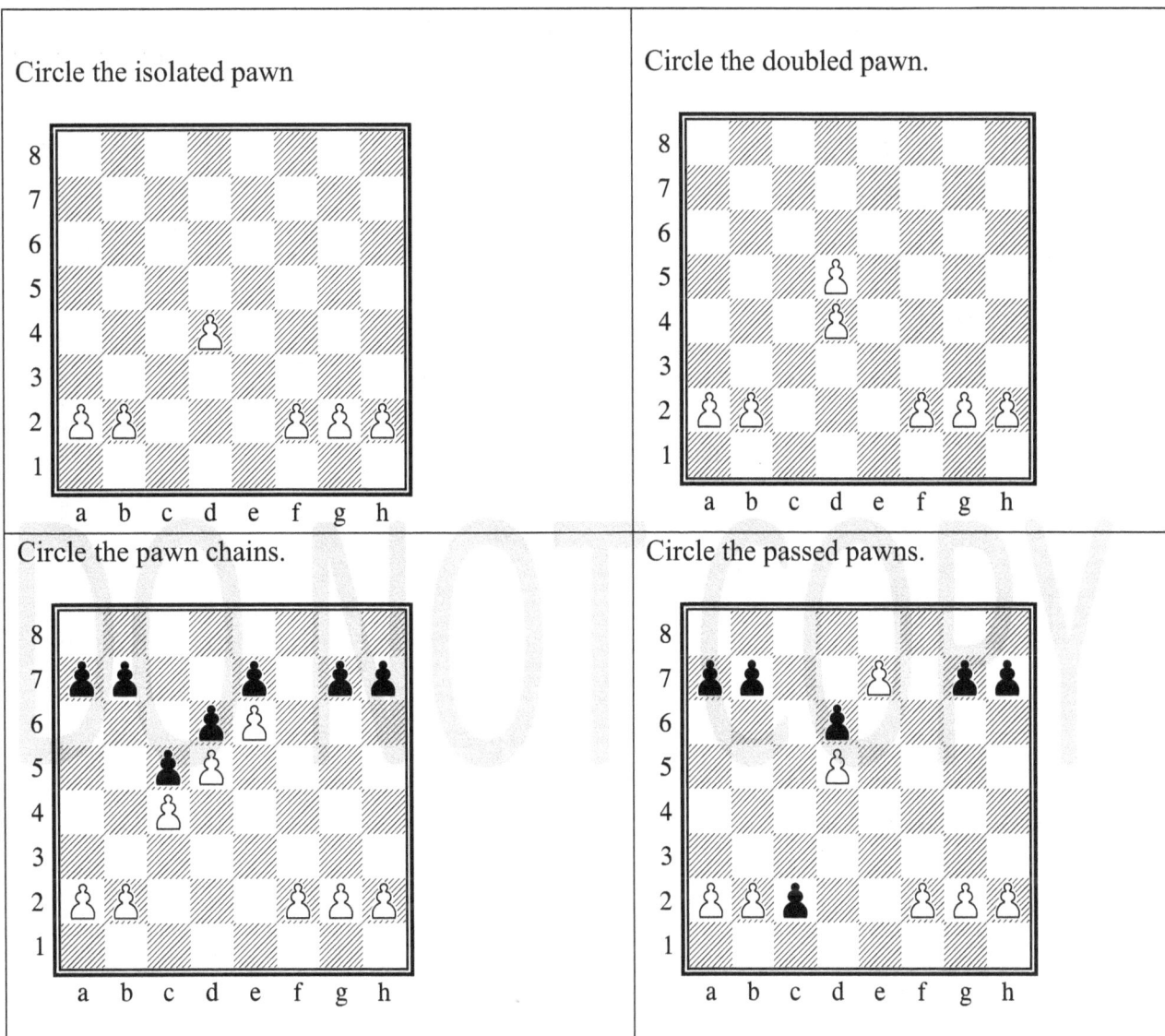

En Passant

En passant is a French word meaning "in passing". It is a special pawn capture that can only occur immediately after a pawn moves two squares forward from its starting position, and the opponent captures the just-moved pawn "as it passes" through the first square. Circle all the White pawns (move forward from the squares indicated by X's) that can be taken by the Black pawns.

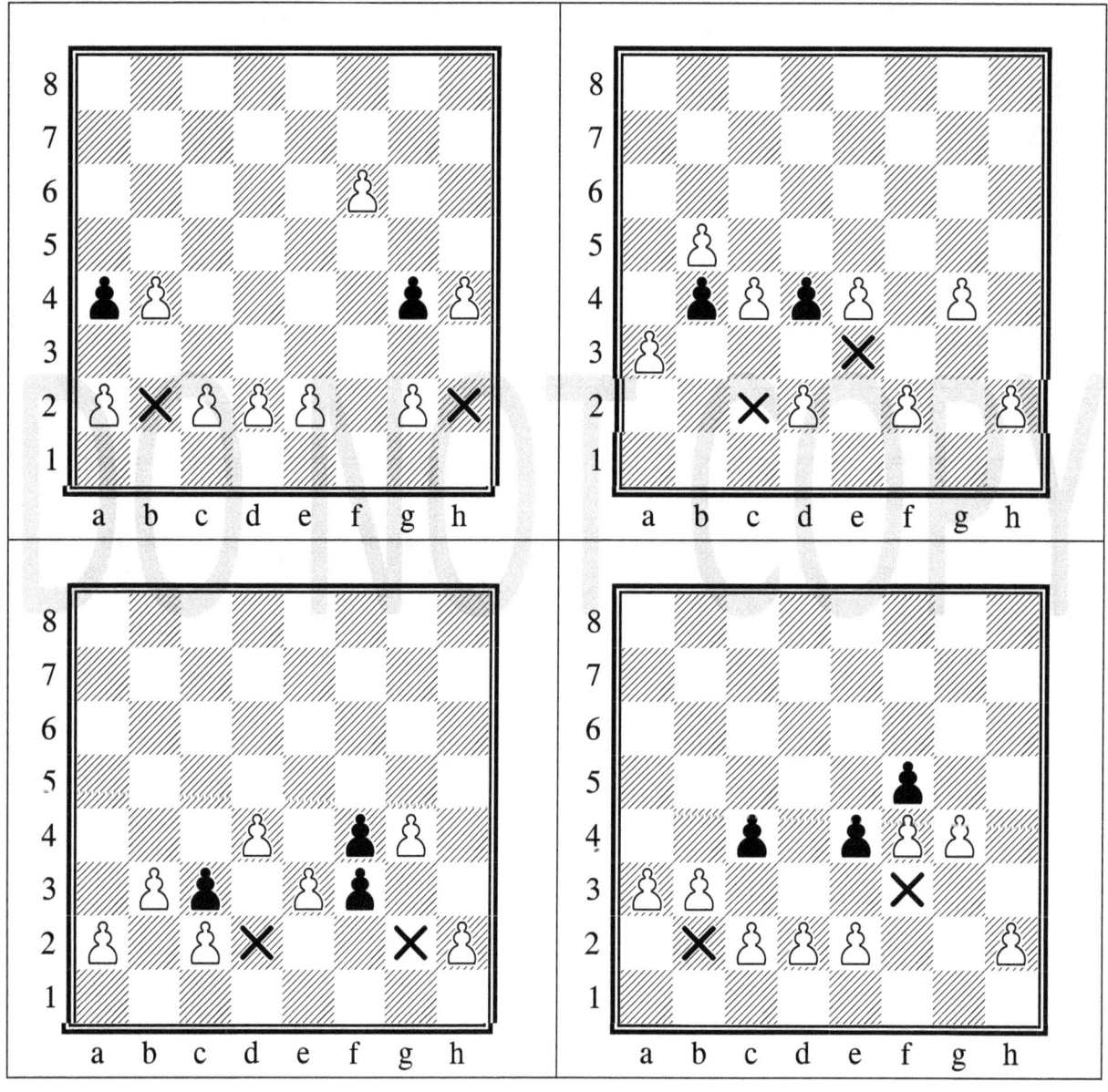

En Passant

Circle all black pawns that can "en passant" the just-moved white pawns.

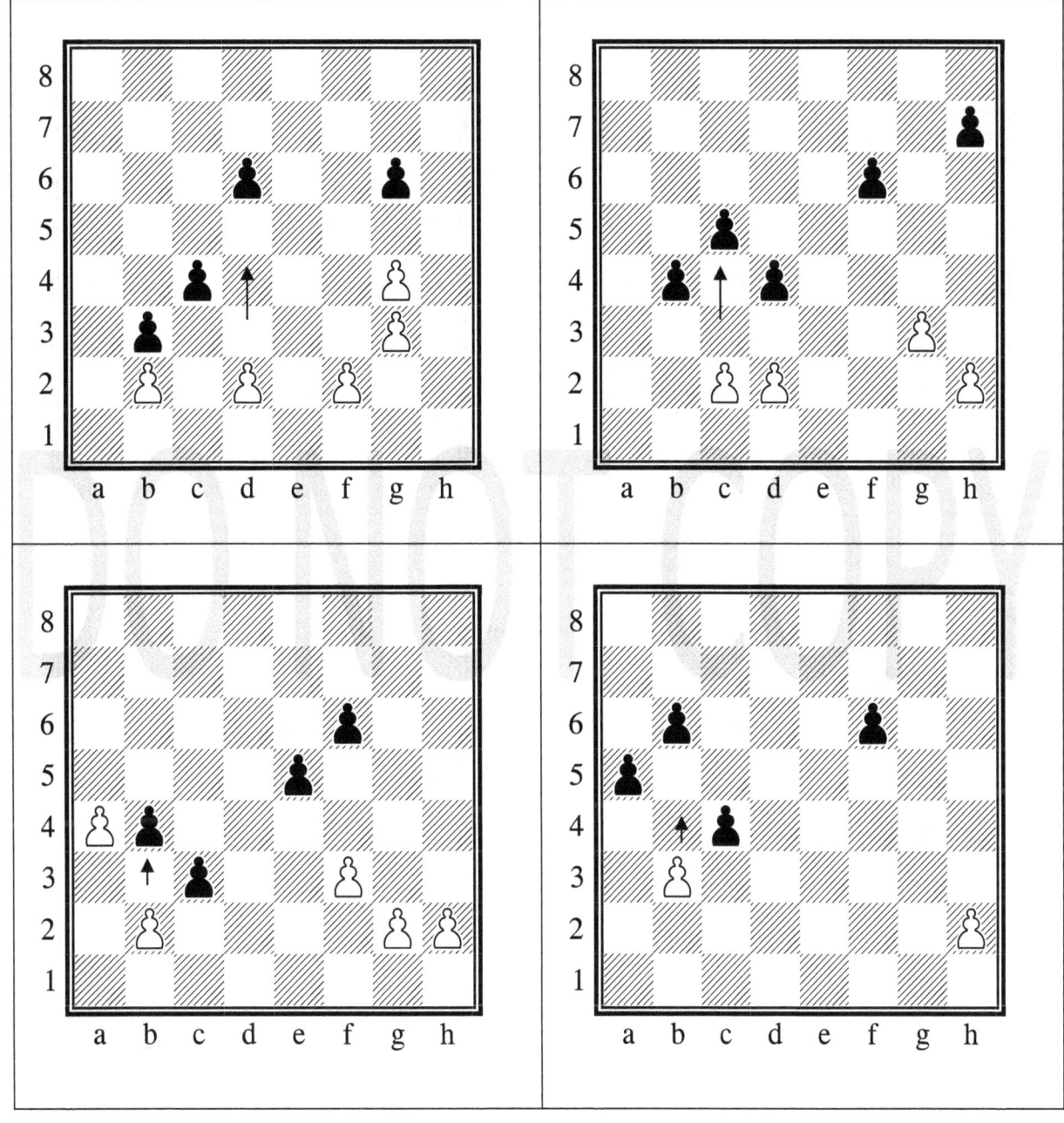

Learning Chess to Improve Math   数棋谜式健脑国际象棋
Ho Math Chess   何数棋谜   www.homathchess.com
Frank Ho, Amanda Ho © 1995 – 2021   All rights reserved.

Student name _____ Assignment date:_____

En Passant

Circle all black pawns that can "en passant" the white pawn that just moved.

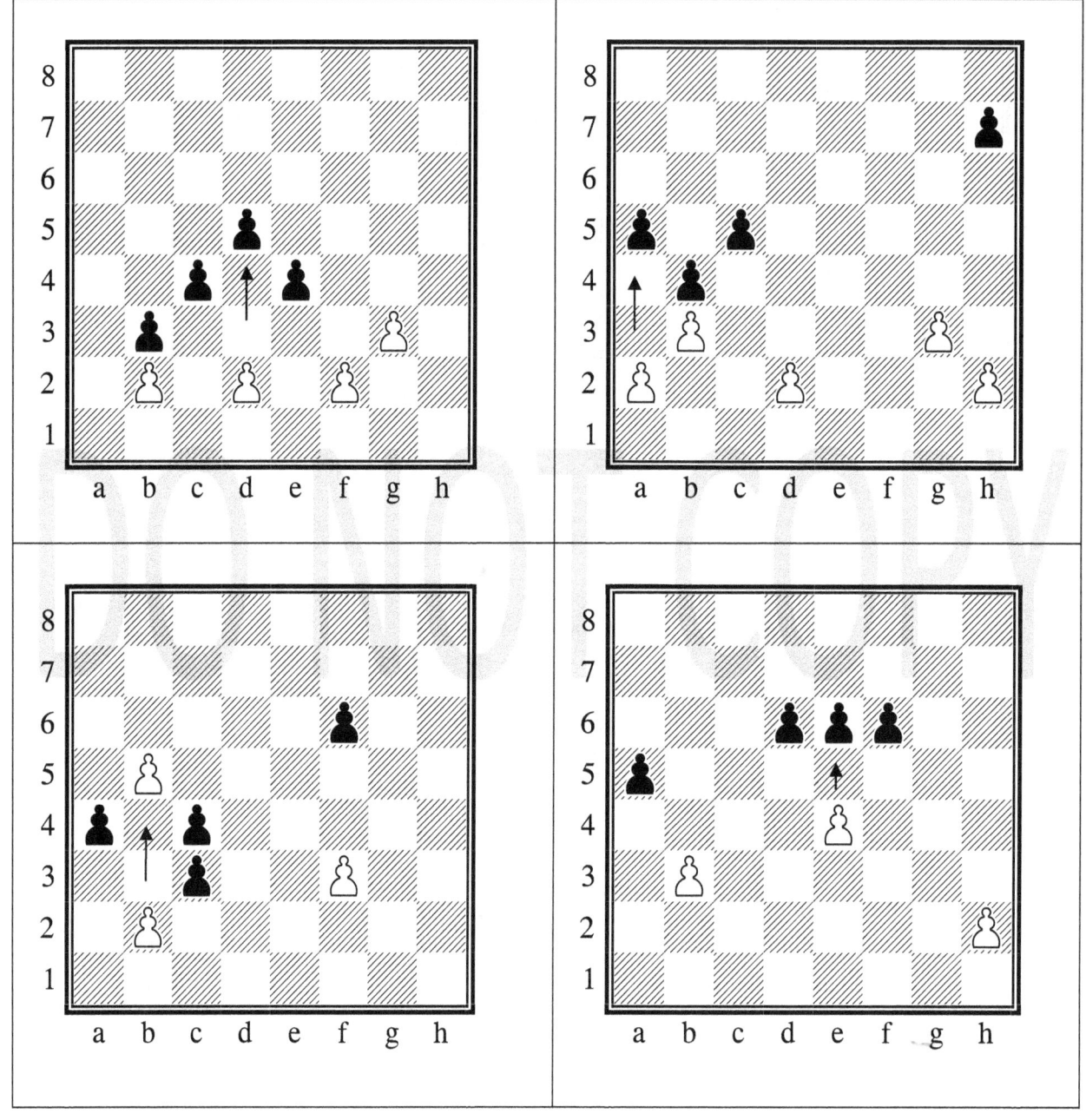

En Passant

Circle all the White pawns (move forward from the squares indicated by X's) that can be taken by the Black pawns.

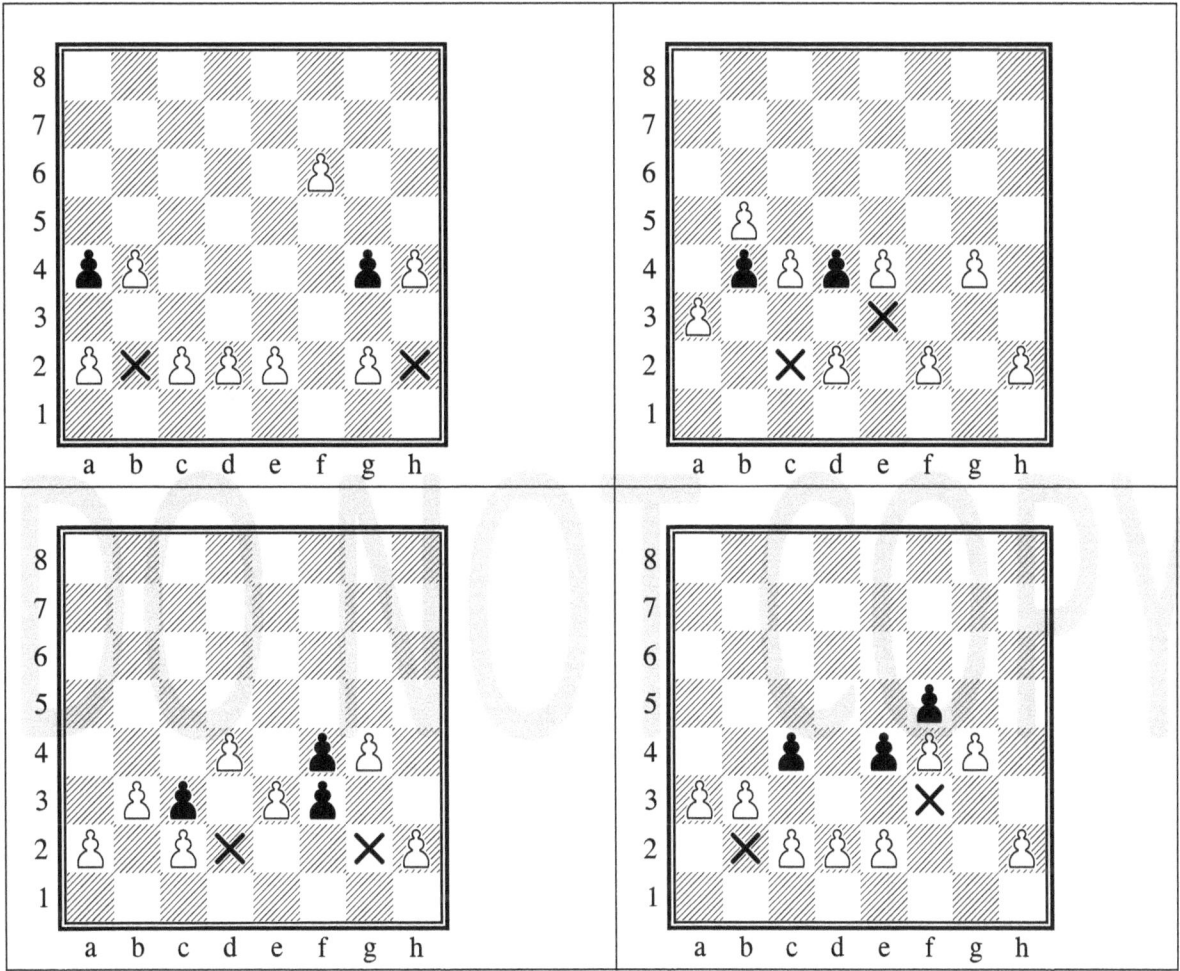

Learning Chess to Improve Math   数棋谜式健脑国际象棋
 Math Chess   何数棋谜   www.homathchess.com

Frank Ho, Amanda Ho © 1995 – 2021   All rights reserved.

Student name _____ Assignment date:_____

How does the rook move?

How does the rook move?	Solving by rook's move
Mark all White rooks' possible moves without being taken by an X in the following diagrams.	Replace each ? with a number.

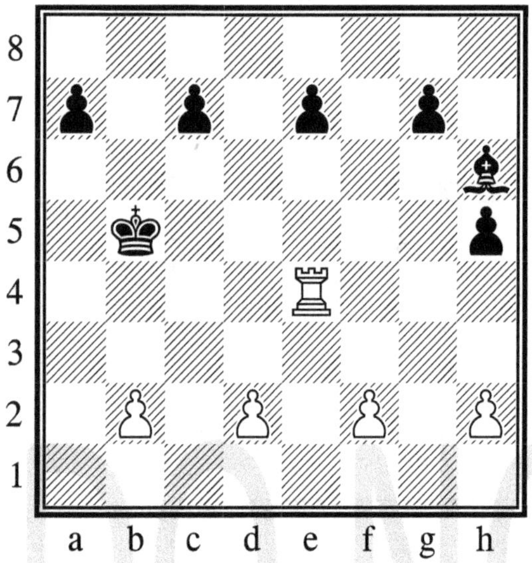

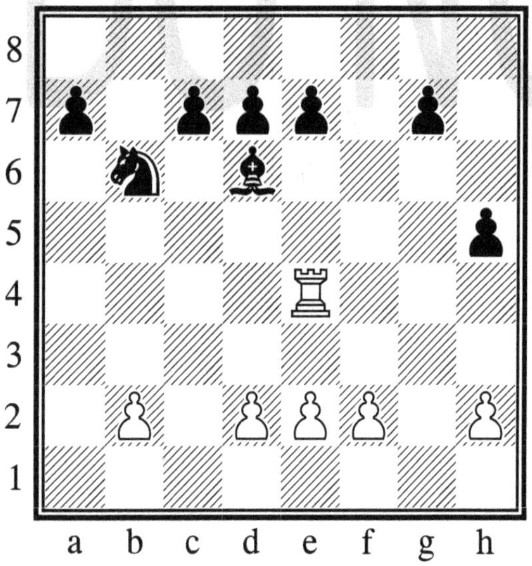

Learning Chess to Improve Math 数棋谜式健脑国际象棋
 Math Chess 何数棋谜 www.homathchess.com

Frank Ho, Amanda Ho © 1995 – 2021   All rights reserved.

Student name _____ Assignment date:_____

How does the rook move?

How does the rook move?	Solving by rook's move
Mark all White rooks' possible moves without being taken by an X in the following diagrams.	Find all possible answers of a and b as follows: _____
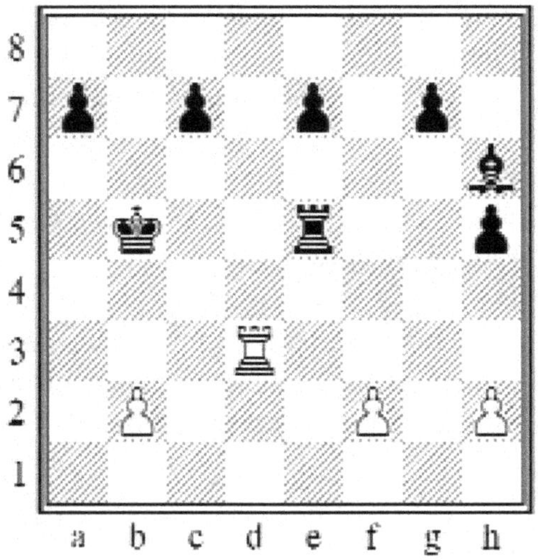	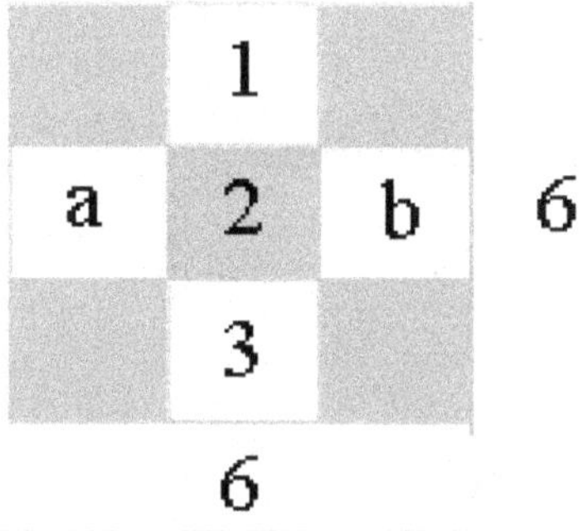 Grid: 1 (top), a 2 b = 6, 3 (bottom), total 6
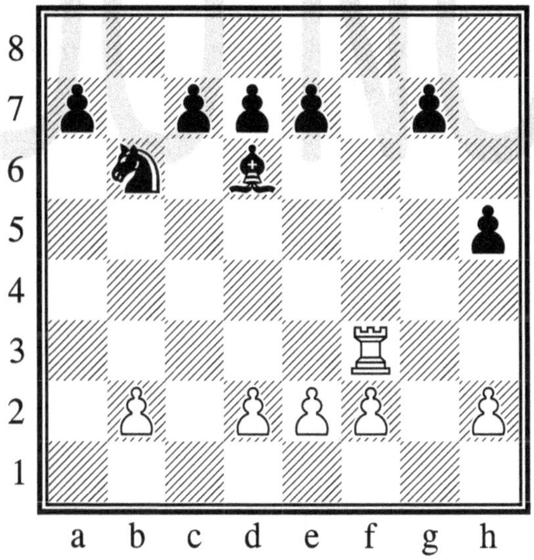	Find all possible answers of a and b as follows: 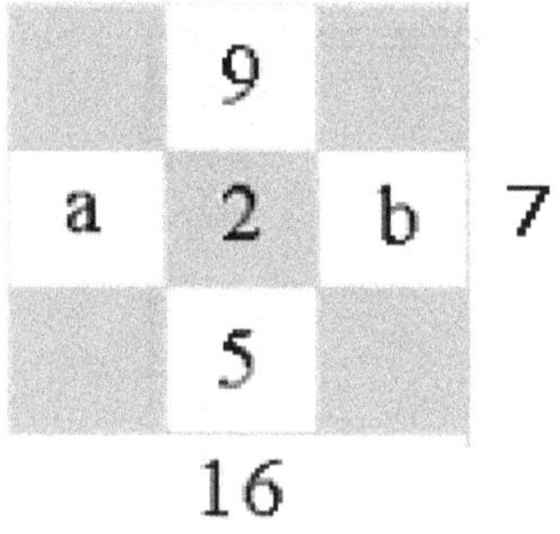 _____
	Grid: 9 (top), a 2 b = 7, 5 (bottom), total 16

Student name _____ Assignment date:_____

No rooks attacking each other

How does the rook move?	Solving by rook's move
There are four rooks. Place all four rooks on the following 4 by 4 chessboard such that none of the rooks can take each other. In other words, none of the rooks shall be placed in the same rank (row) or file (column). Write R (for "Rook) on each square for your answer. 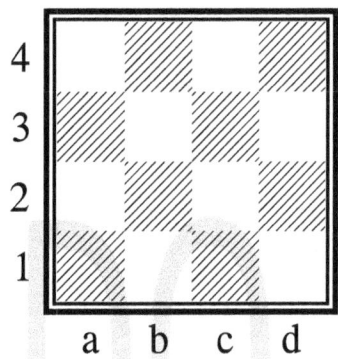 Use the following diagram to come up with a different position of rooks. 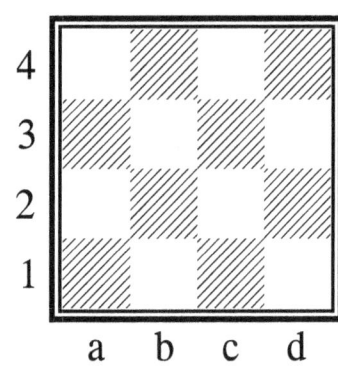	How many different positions can you have when placing four rooks on 4 by 4 chessboards? You can figure it out using mathematics. A. How many squares the first rook can be placed on the board? _____ B. How many squares can the second rook be placed on the board after the first rook has already been placed on the board? _____ C. How many squares can the third rook be placed on the board after the first rook and the second rook have already been placed on the board? _____ D. How many squares the fourth rook can be placed on the board after the first rook, second rook, and third rook have already been placed on the board? _____ **The answer is the product of answers of A, B, C and D.** _____

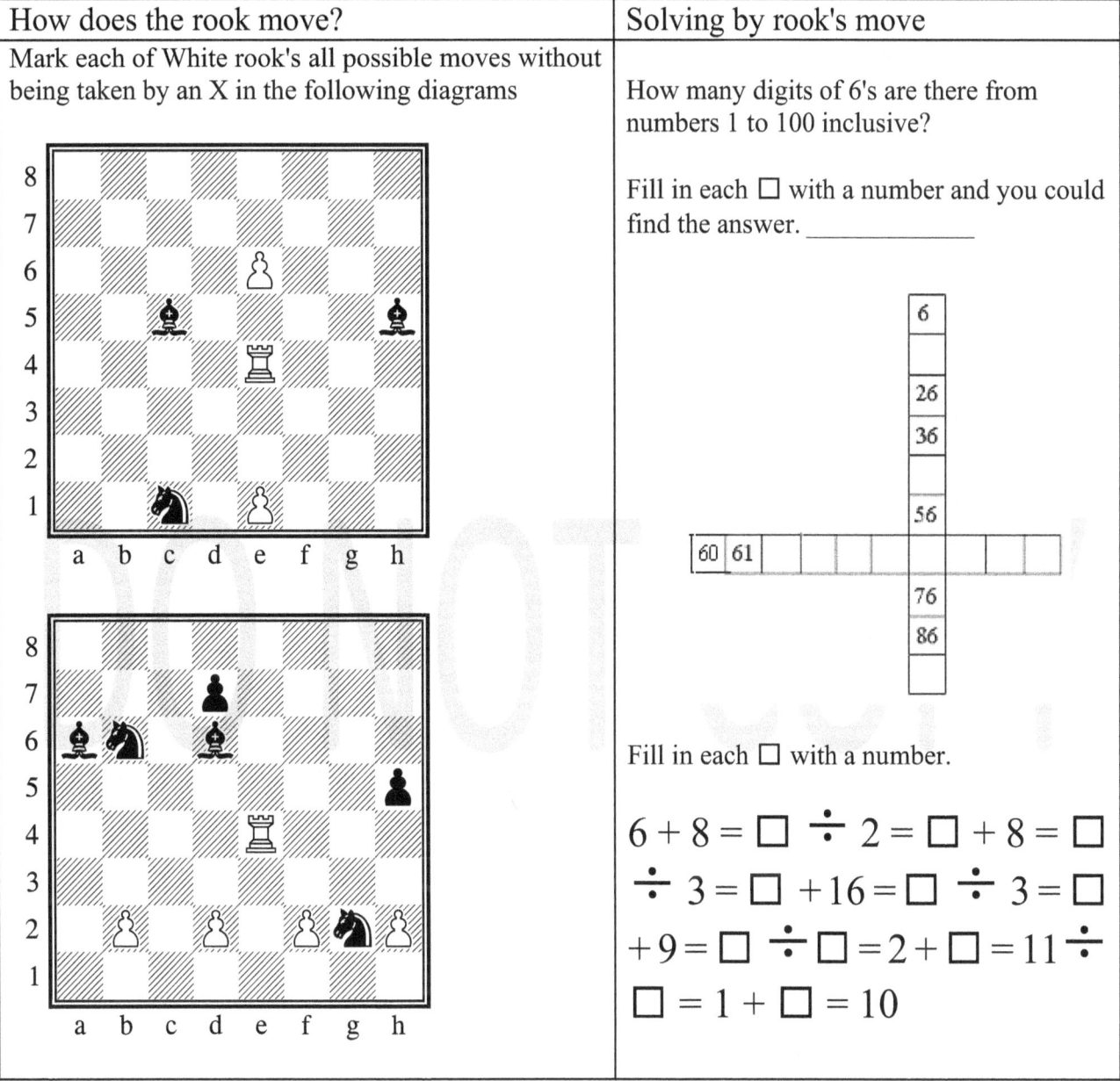

Rook travelling in chess notations

How does the rook move?	Clock arithmetic
Assume rook goes around the edge of the chessboard 28 squares in the direction of clockwise (h1 → a1 → a8 → h8 etc.). Which square does the rook finally land on? Write the name of the square in algebraic notation _____ 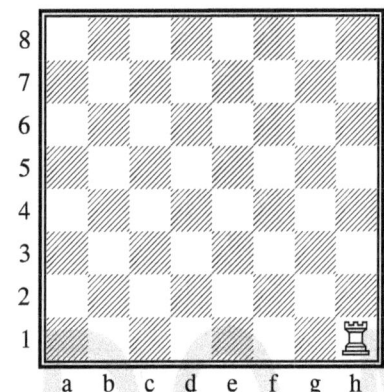 Assume rook goes around the edge of the chessboard 58 squares in the direction of clockwise. Which square does the rook finally land on? Write the name of the square in algebraic notation _____ 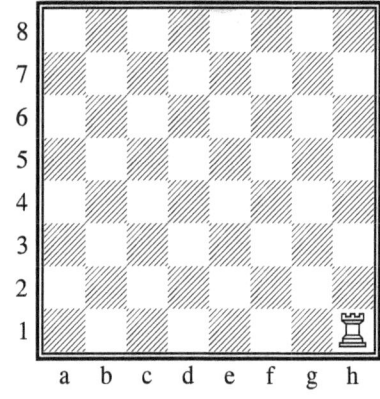	Look at the pattern of the following numbers, and the exponent is the remainder when divided by 4. $3^0=1$ $3^1=\underline{3}$ $3^2=\underline{9}$ $3^3=2\underline{7}$ $3^4=8\underline{1}$ $3^5=243$ $3^6=729$ What is the units digit of 3^{13}? The units digit of the exponential number with base three repeats in the pattern of 3, 9, 7, and 1. $3^{13} = 3^{4\times3=1} = 3^1$. So, the units digit is 3. What is the units digit of 3^{100}? $3^{100} = 3^{4\times25}$ The units digit is 1. What is the units digit of 3^{213}? ____ What is the units digit of 2^{203} ____ What is the units digit of 2^{2313} ____

Learning Chess to Improve Math 数棋谜式健脑国际象棋
Ho Math Chess 何数棋谜 www.homathchess.com
Frank Ho, Amanda Ho © 1995 – 2021   All rights reserved.

Student name _____ Assignment date: _____

How does the rook move?

Assume rook goes around the edge of the chessboard 128 squares in the direction of clockwise (h1 → a1 → a8 → h8 etc.). Which square does the rook finally land on? Write the name of the square in algebraic notation _____

Assume rook goes around the edge of the chessboard 356 squares in the direction of clockwise. Which square does the rook finally land on? Write the name of the square in algebraic notation _____

Clock arithmetic

If today is Thursday April 7th, what day is it on April 14th? _____

If today is Thursday April 7th, what day is it on April 21st? _____

Can you see that the day repeats itself every _____ days?

If today is Thursday April 7th, what day is it on June 7th? _____

Hint:
There are _____ days after April 7th (not including April 7th)
There are _____ days in May.
There are _____ days until June 7 (including June 7th)

There are _____ days in total after April 7th until June 7th.

The total days divided by seven should give an idea of how many times Thursday repeats itself.

The answer is _____.

Rook Path

Cross mark (✕) the square(s) where all rooks could meet by moving each rook in 3 moves.

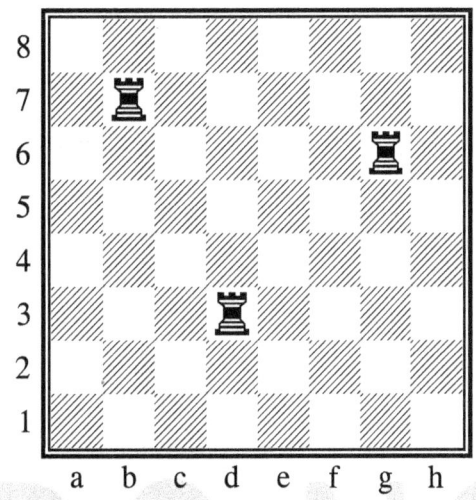

Cross mark (✕) the square(s) where all rooks could meet by moving each rook in 4 moves.

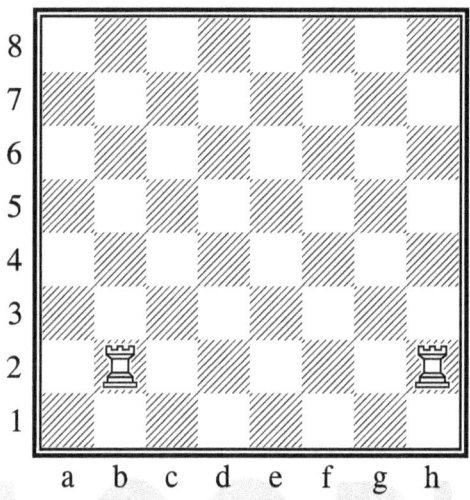

Cross mark (✕) the square(s) where all rooks could meet by moving each rook in 5 moves.

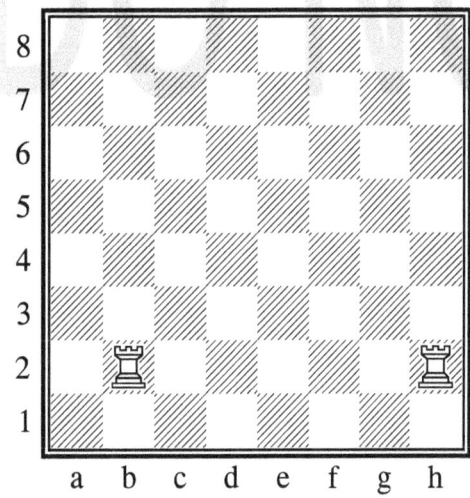

Cross mark (✕) the square(s) where all rooks could meet by moving each rook in 9 moves.

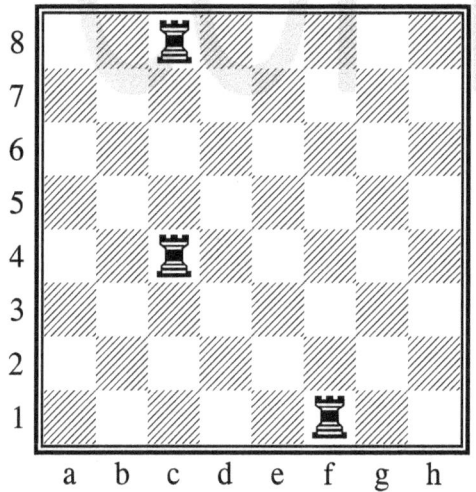

Perpendicular line and right angle

If the rook moves from b7 to h7 and the other rook moves from d3 to d8, then the paths of two rooks form two perpendicular lines. Mark these two lines. What is the smallest degree of the angle created by these two perpendicular lines? _____.

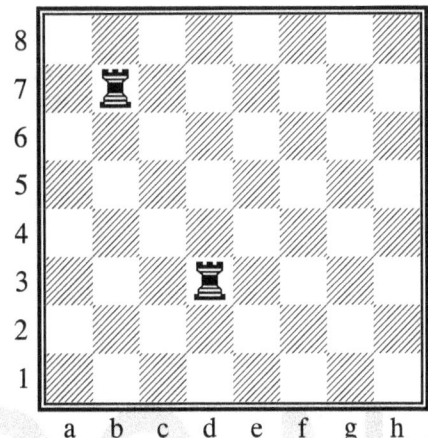

If the bishop moves from h1 to a8 and the other bishop moves from a1 to h8, then the paths of these two bishops form two perpendicular lines. Mark these two lines. What is the smallest degree of angles created by these two perpendicular lines? _____.

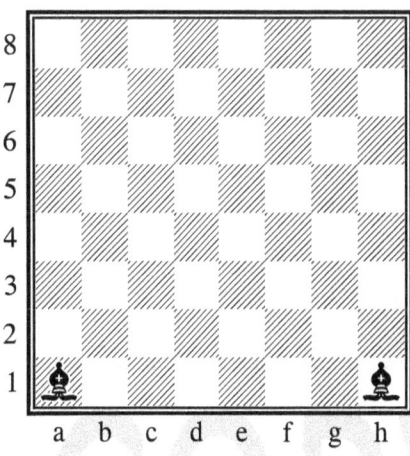

Mark the right angles intersected by the paths of the following two rooks.
_____

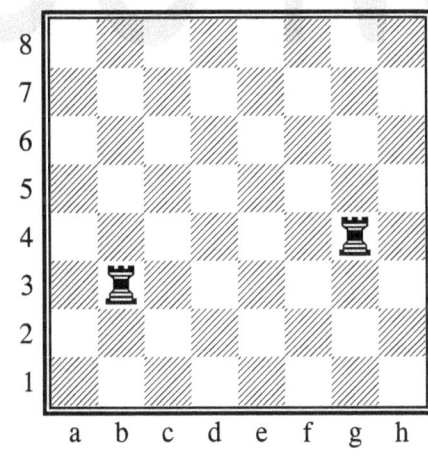

Mark the right angles intersected by the paths of the following two bishops.
_____

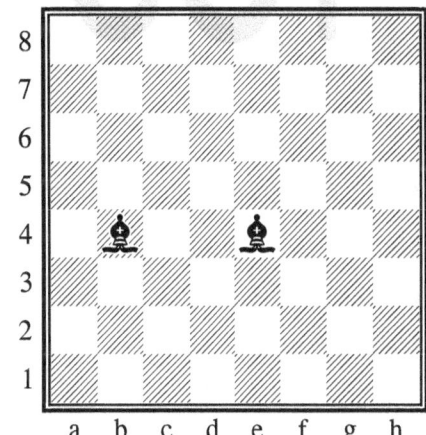

Parallel line and geometric shape

Draw all rooks' paths by connecting the central point of each square. Can you tell what kind of geometric shape is formed? _____

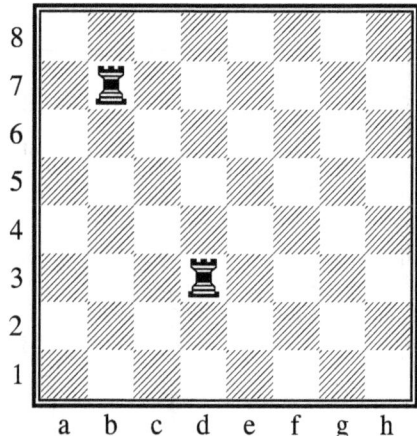

Draw all rooks' paths by connecting the central point of each square. Can you tell what kind of geometric shape is formed? _____

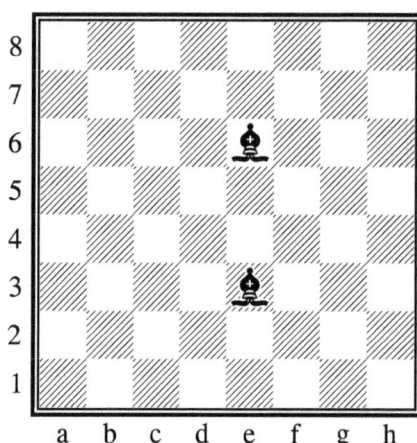

Draw all rooks' paths by connecting the central point of each square. Can you tell what kind of geometric shape is formed? _____

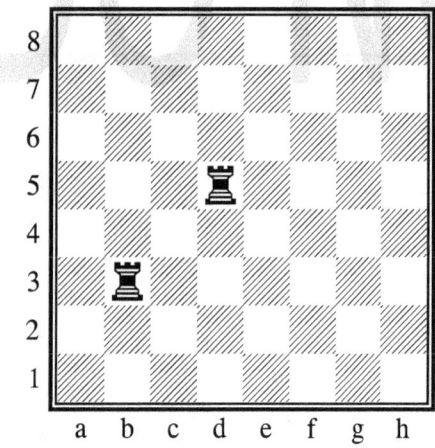

square

Draw all bishops' paths by connecting the central point of each square. Can you tell what kind of geometric shape is formed? _____

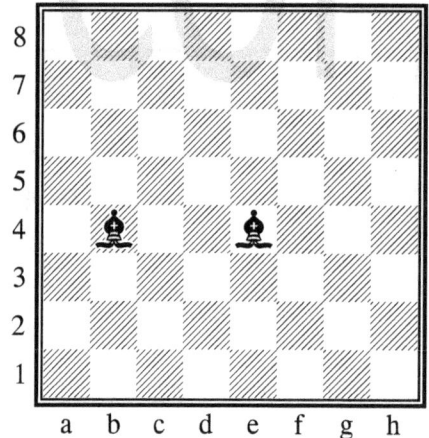

square

Learning Chess to Improve Math   数棋谜式健脑国际象棋
Ho Math Chess   何数棋谜   www.homathchess.com
Frank Ho, Amanda Ho © 1995 – 2021   All rights reserved.

Student name _____ Assignment date:_____

How does the king move?

Show all the possible squares where the White king can take or move to by marking X. Two kings cannot be next to each other (called in opposition). The king cannot move into a square where the king will be under attack.

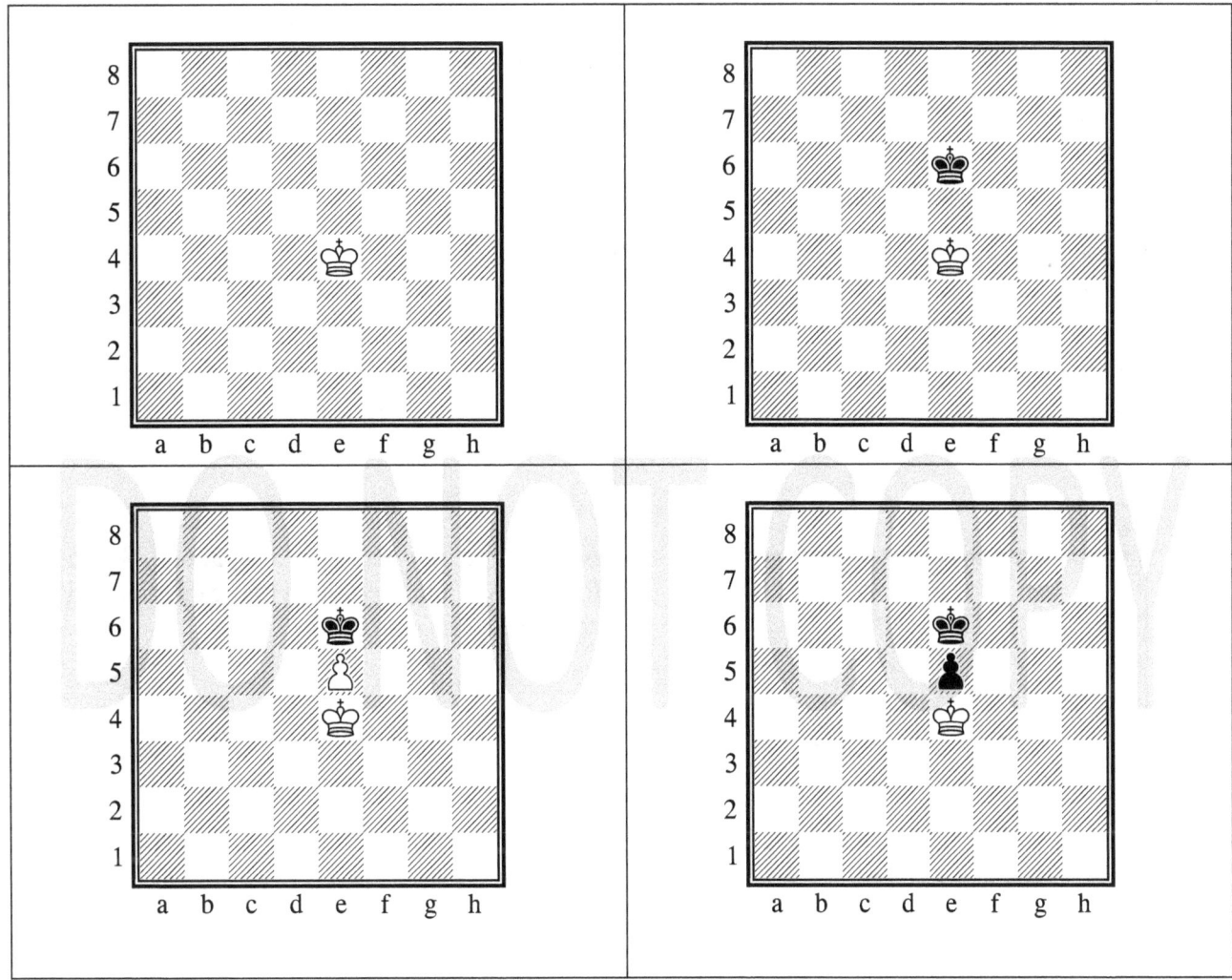

Learning Chess to Improve Math 数棋谜式健脑国际象棋

Ho Math Chess 何数棋谜 www.homathchess.com

Frank Ho, Amanda Ho © 1995 – 2021 All rights reserved.

Student name _____ Assignment date:_____

Show all the possible squares where the White king can take or move to by marking X. Two kings cannot be next to each other (called in opposition). The king cannot move into a square where the king will be under attack.

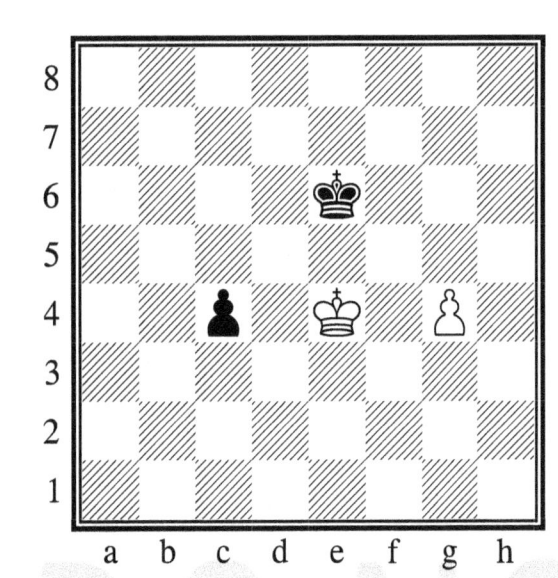

Assume the king is in the central square. Use king's moves (left-right and up-down) to place each of the numbers 1, 2, 3, 4, 5, 6, 7, 8 into one circle such that the sum of king's 2-move will add up to the same sum. If you do not know what to do, the hint is given in the next question below.

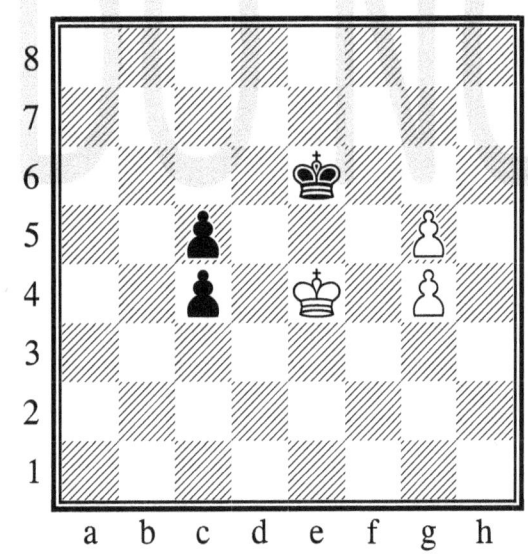

Arrange the numbers 1, 2, 3, 4, 5, 6, 7, 8 into four pairs of numbers such that each pair adds up to the same sum.

____ + ____ = ____

____ + ____ = ____

____ + ____ = ____

____ + ____ = ____

King's shortest path

Start at any square and draw the king's shortest path to travel every square once and only once in the following chessboard. No lines are allowed to cross each other.

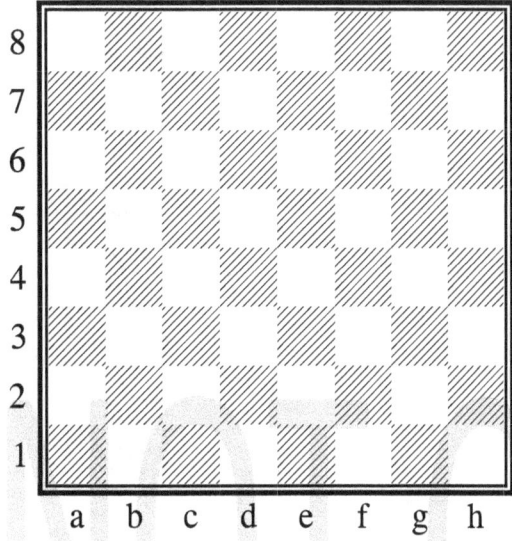

How does the queen move?

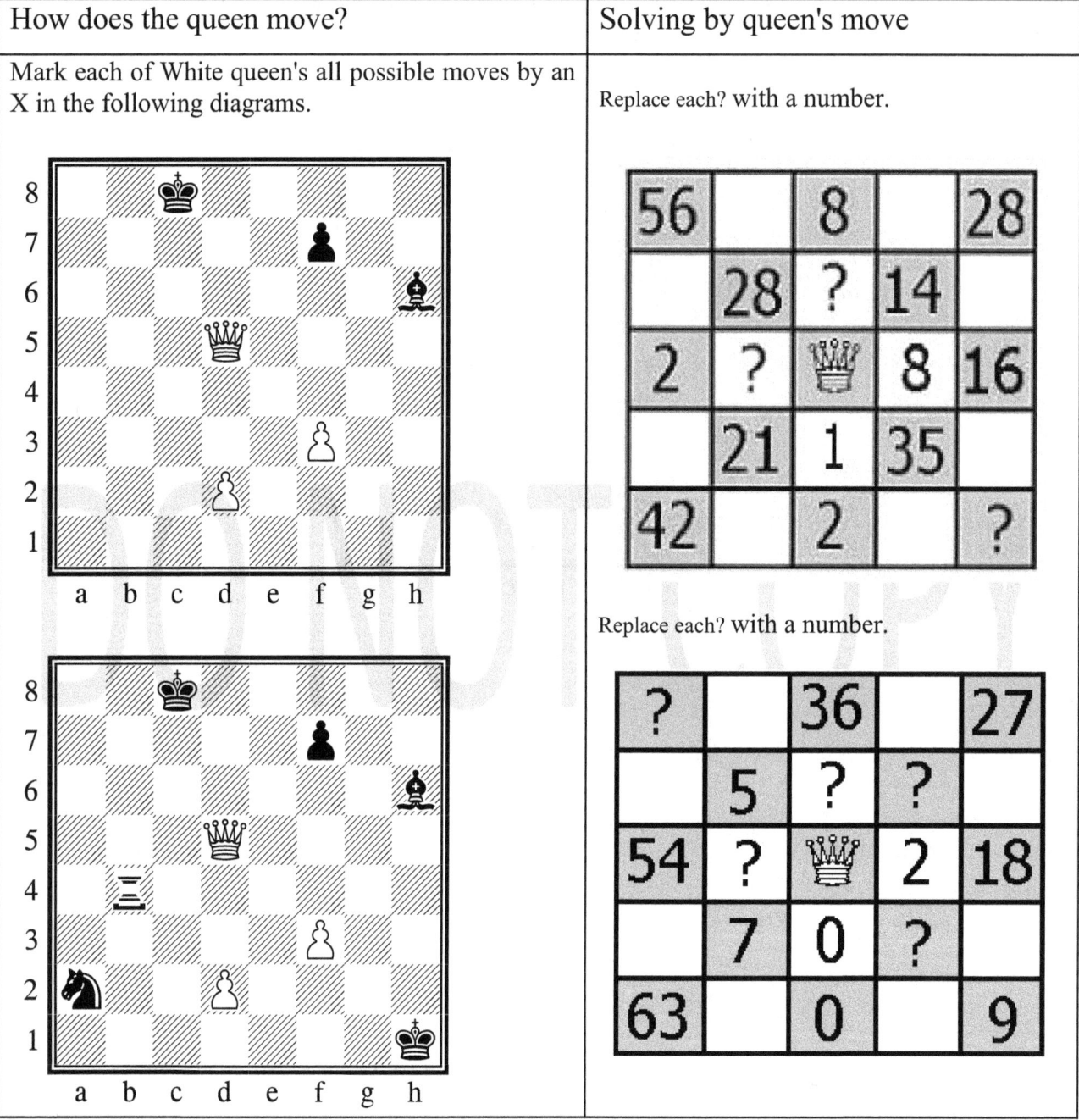

Learning Chess to Improve Math   数棋谜式健脑国际象棋
Ho Math Chess   何数棋谜   www.homathchess.com
Frank Ho, Amanda Ho © 1995 – 2021   All rights reserved.

Student name _____ Assignment date:_____

Placing two queens

How does the queen move?	Visualization of matchstick math
When a pawn advances to the last rank, the pawn could be promoted to any piece other than the king. So, you could have a maximum _____ queens when all pawns reach the last rank. Put two queens on the following chessboard, so the result is these two queens could control all squares. For example, the two queens have shown in the following diagram control all squares. Can you find three more solutions by drawing two queens on the following three empty diagrams? 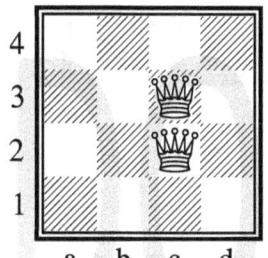 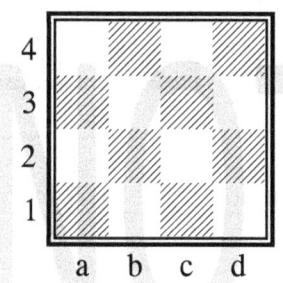 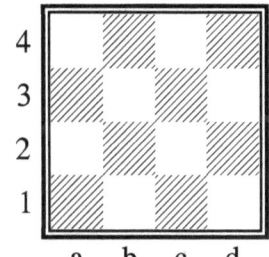 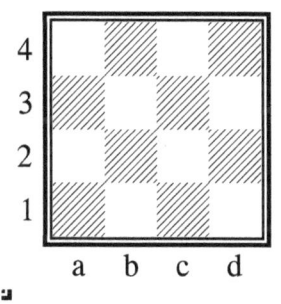	One benefit of playing chess is to develop a good visualization. In math, it helps if one has good visualization ability. Solve the following problems. 1. Take away one matchstick of the following expression such that the left-hand side will be equal to the right-hand side. 4 + 4 = ☐ 2. Change one matchstick of the following expression so that the left-hand side still equals the right-hand side. 7 + 4 − 1 = 10 3. Add one matchstick so that the left-hand side = the right-hand side. 4 + 4 + 4 = 448

Eight queens' problem

Place one more queen on each chessboard such that no queens can control each other.

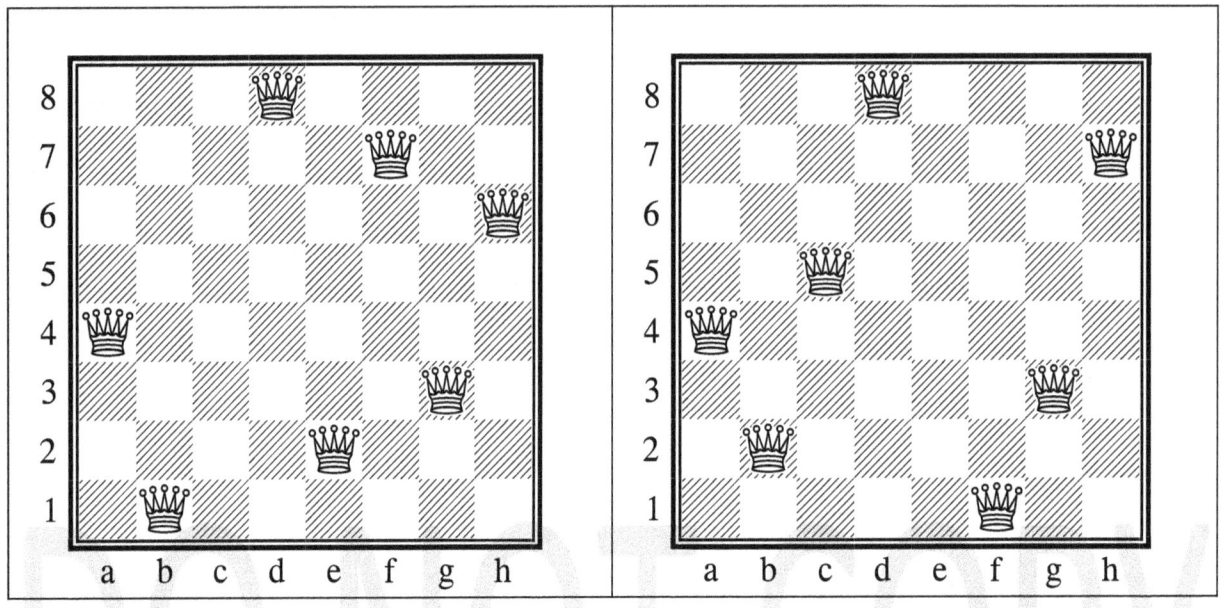

Place two more queens on each chessboard such that no queens can control each other.

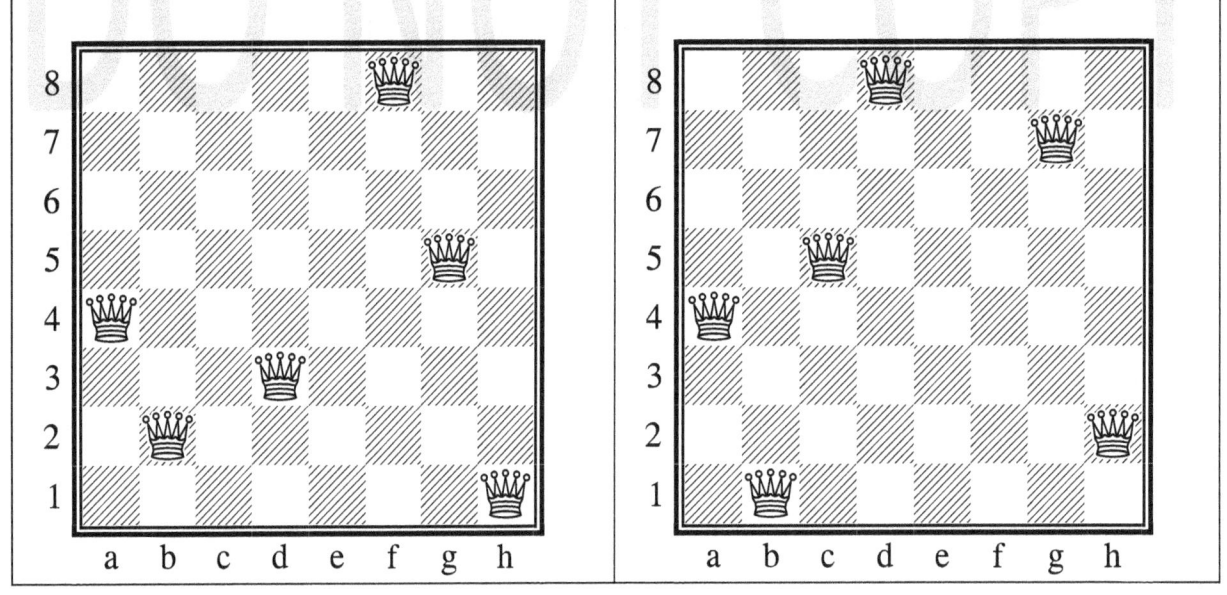

Eight queens' problem

Place three more queens on each chessboard such that no queens can control each other.

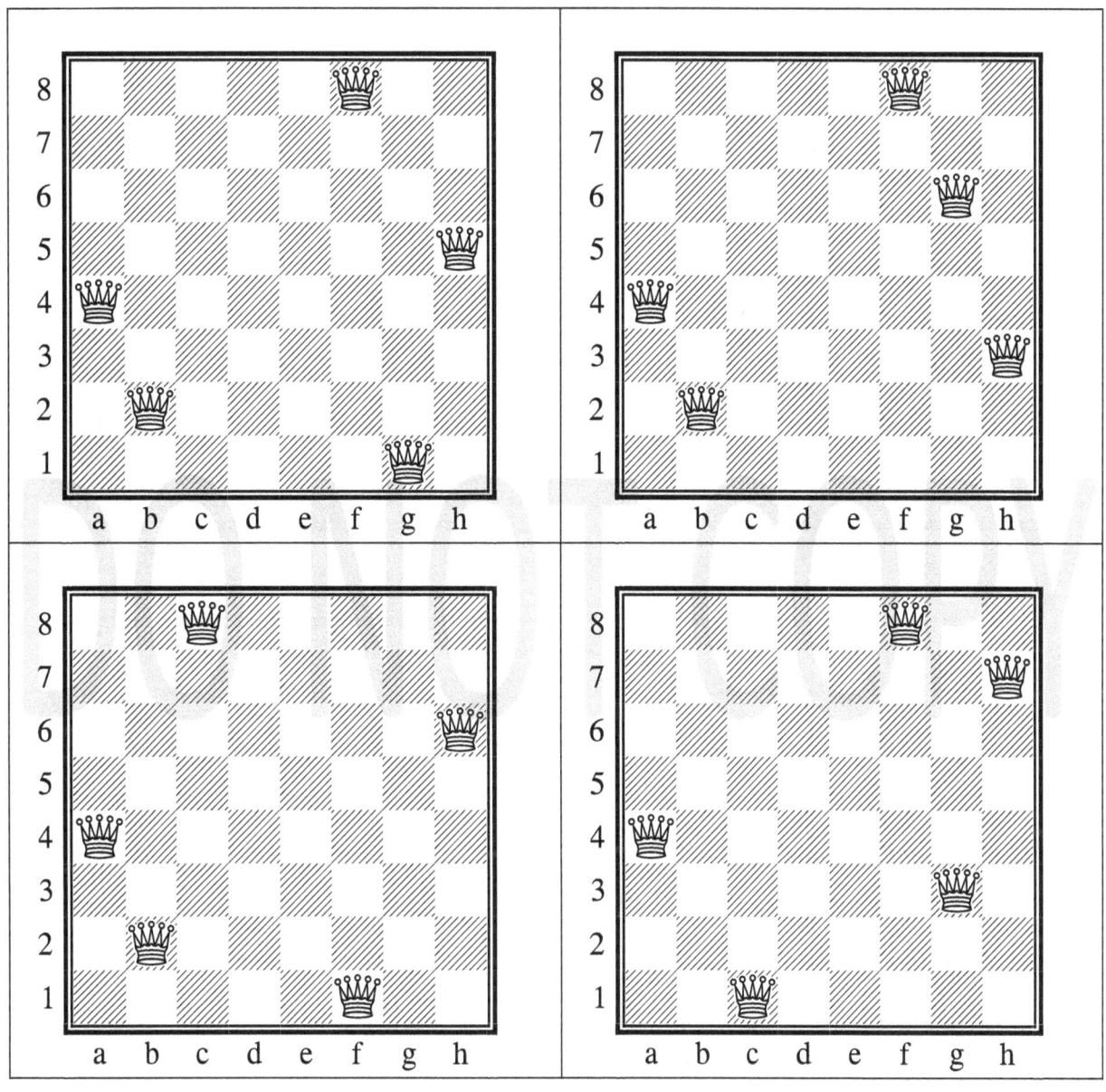

Eight queens' problem

Place four more queens on each chessboard such that no queens can control each other.

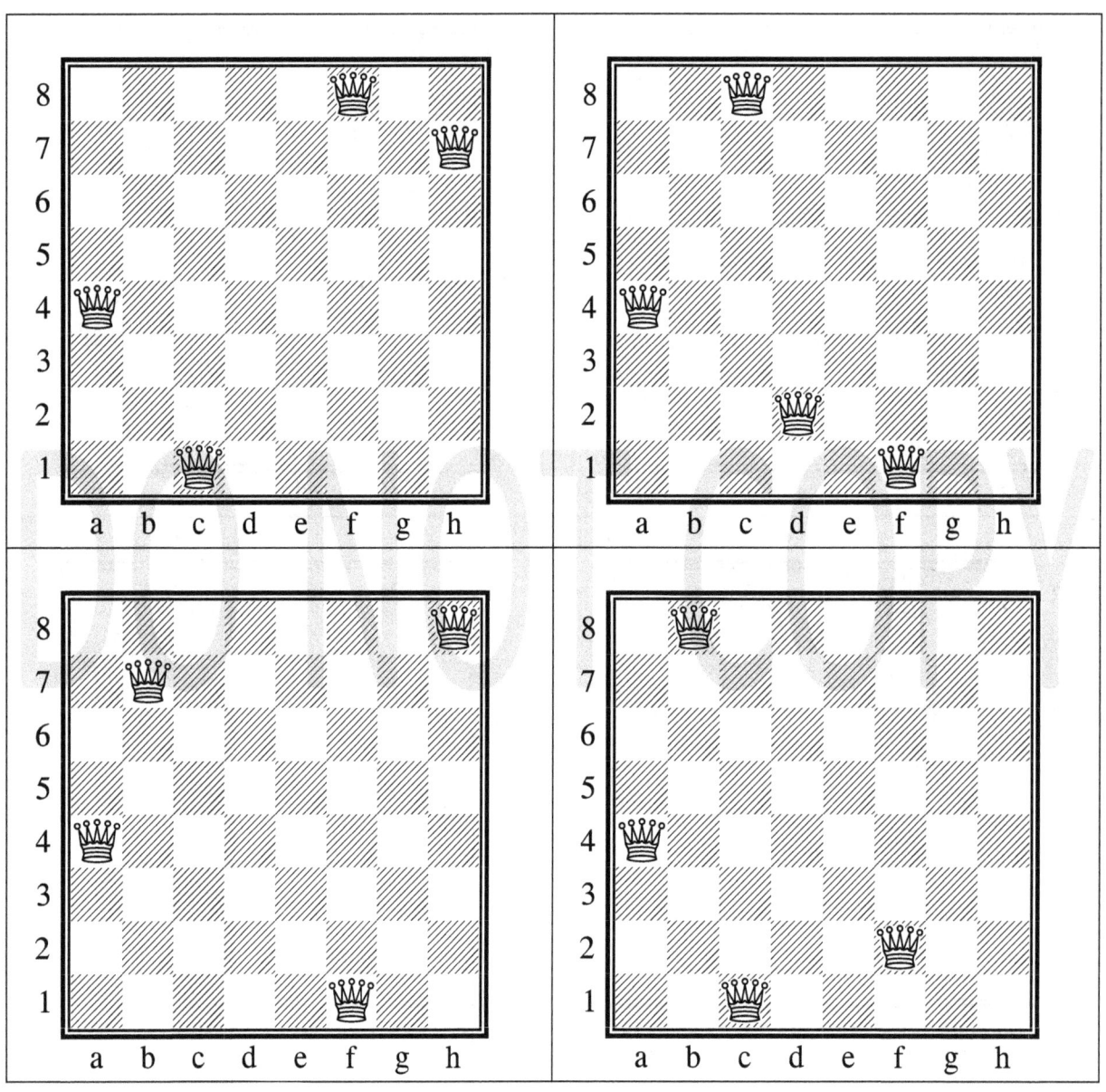

Learning Chess to Improve Math

Ho Math Chess 何数棋谜 www.homathchess.com

Frank Ho, Amanda Ho © 1995 – 2021   All rights reserved.

Student name _____ Assignment date: _____

How does the bishop move?

How does the bishop move?	Solving by bishop's move
Mark each of White bishop's all possible moves by an X in the following diagrams.	Replace each ? with a number.

(Chess board diagram: White bishop on e4, White king on d1, White pawns on b2, c2, f2; Black king on h8, Black pawns on b7, h7, Black knight on h1.)

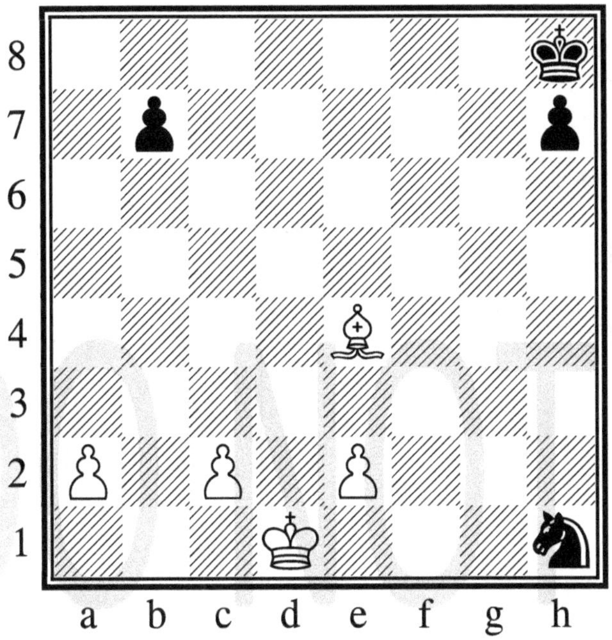

Right column puzzles:

Puzzle 1:
14		12
	8	
?		6

Replace each ? with a number.

Puzzle 2:
21		24
	8	
?		13

Replace each ? with a number.

Puzzle 3:
4		9
	8	
?		32

Bishop moving in Pascal triangle path

How does the bishop move?	Counting paths
How many ways are there for Be8 travelling to Be2?	How many paths are there to travel from top to down in such a way that each path consists of the words "HO MATH AND CHESS"? HHH O MM A TTTT H AAA N D CCC HHHH EE SSS

Learning Chess to Improve Math   数棋谜式健脑国际象棋
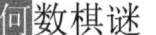 Math Chess   何数棋谜   www.homathchess.com
Frank Ho, Amanda Ho © 1995 – 2021   All rights reserved.

Student name _____ Assignment date: _____

Bishop moving either on the white or black square

How does the bishop move?	Visualization
Bishop moves diagonally either on Black squares or White squares. Start a bishop on any square of your choice and move to each square once and only once. Show your moves by drawing lines. How many squares (either white or black in colour) did you not visit when you finished? Answer _____ If you have only 3 squares left that you did not visit, then you are very good at finding the solution. 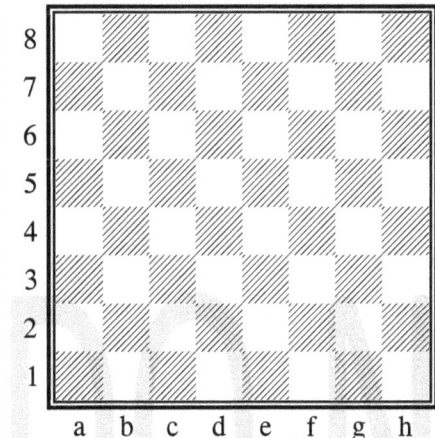 If you have more than 3 squares that you did not visit, then try the following diagram. Every time when you make a move, try to move as close to the board as possible and make a circular movement. Start at h4 and finish at f6. Do not visit squares indicated by . Show your moves by drawing lines. 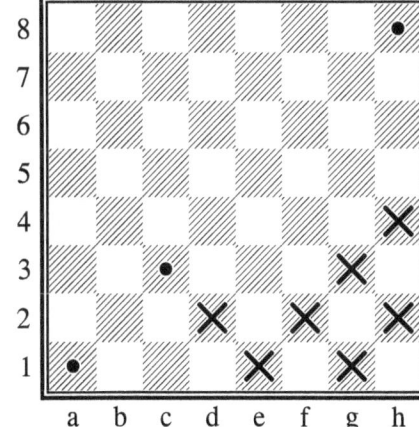	Observe the relationship of the following matchstick letters (all are the first letter of a chess piece.). Find an English letter to replace the "?".  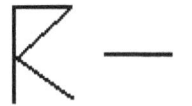

Learning Chess to Improve Math   数棋谜式健脑国际象棋

 Math Chess   何数棋谜   www.homathchess.com

Frank Ho, Amanda Ho © 1995 – 2021   All rights reserved.

Student name _____ Assignment date:_____

Bishop moving in odd dimension chessboard

How does the bishop move?	Tracing graph with one stroke
Can the bishop below travel all White squares once and only once? If yes, show the path by drawing lines. 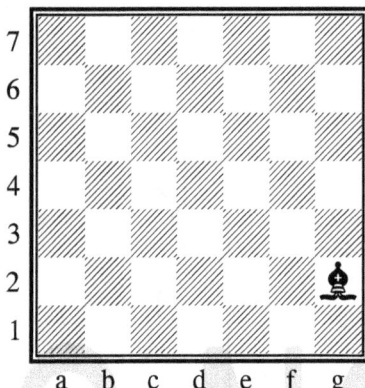 Can the bishop below travel all Black squares once and only once? If yes, show the path by drawing lines. 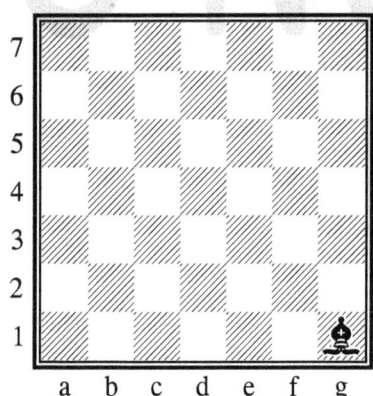	Trace the following diagram and circle the diagrams that you can trace each line once and only once without lifting your pencil off the paper. (If you think it is a traffic problem, then you only allow travelling each road once, but you are allowed to travel to each city more than once. Intersecting point is a city.)  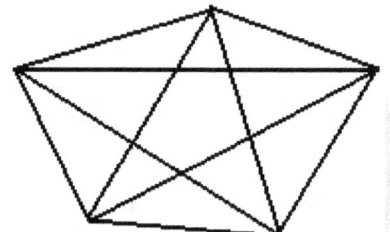 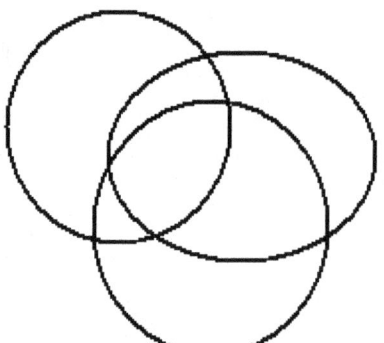

Bishop moving in even dimension chessboard

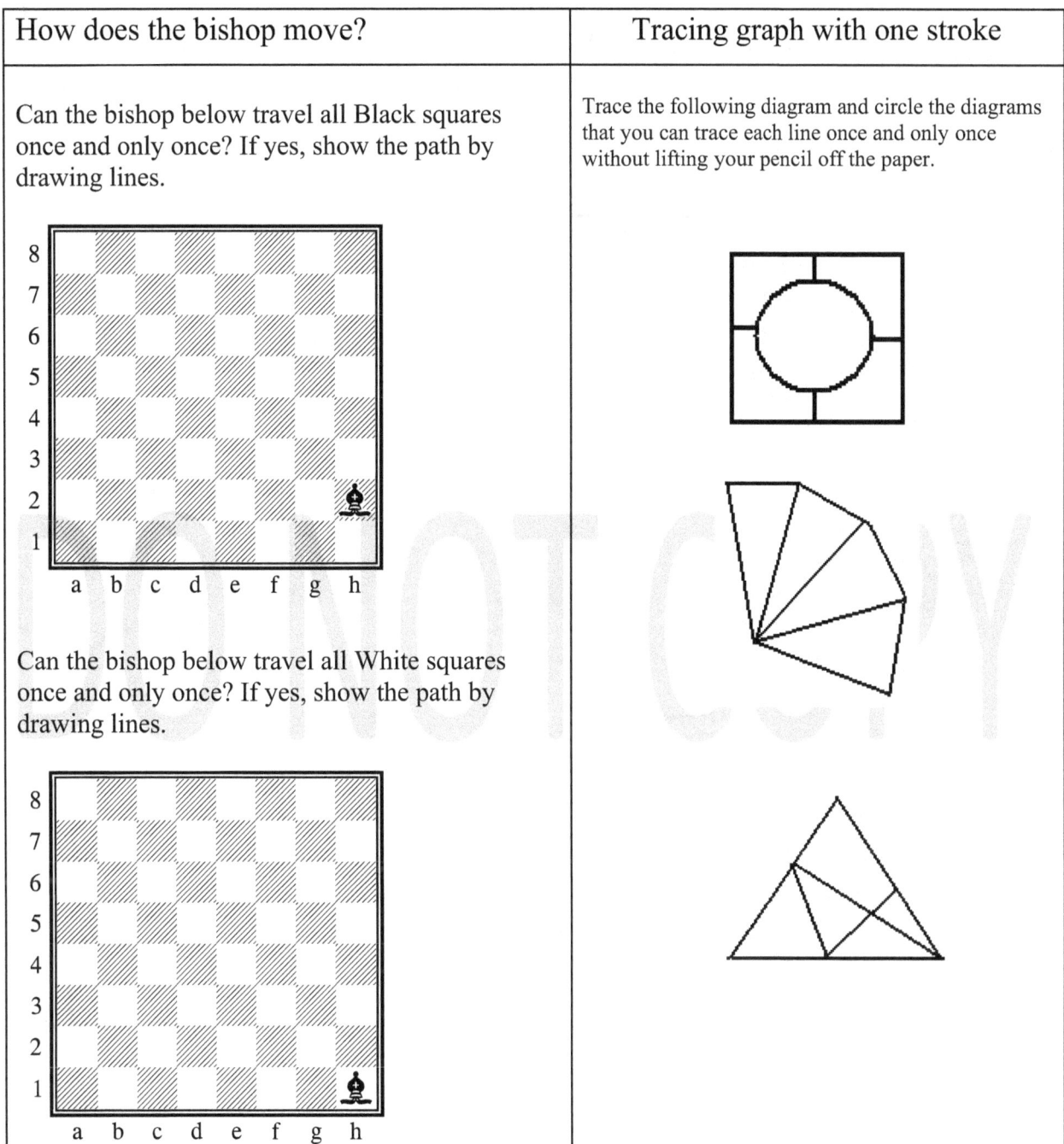

Student name ______________________Assignment date:_______________

Tracing graph with one stroke

Trace the following diagram and circle the diagrams that you can trace each line once and only once without lifting your pencil off the paper. (If thinking it as a traffic problem, then you only allow travelling each road once, but you are allowed to travel each city more than once. Intersecting point is a city.)

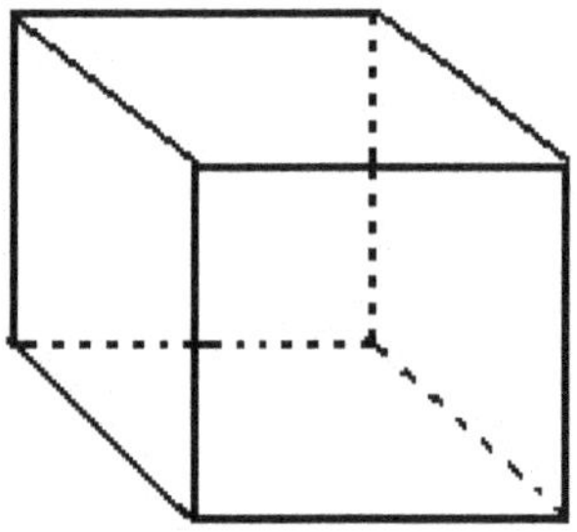

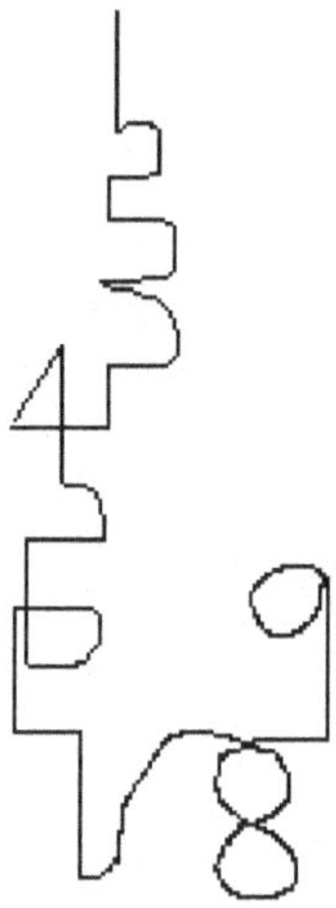

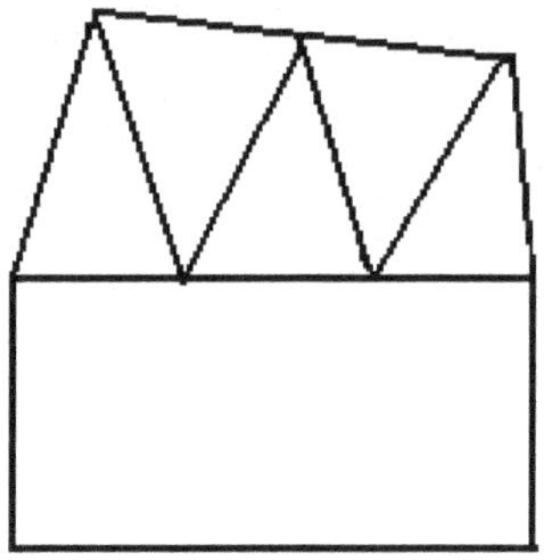

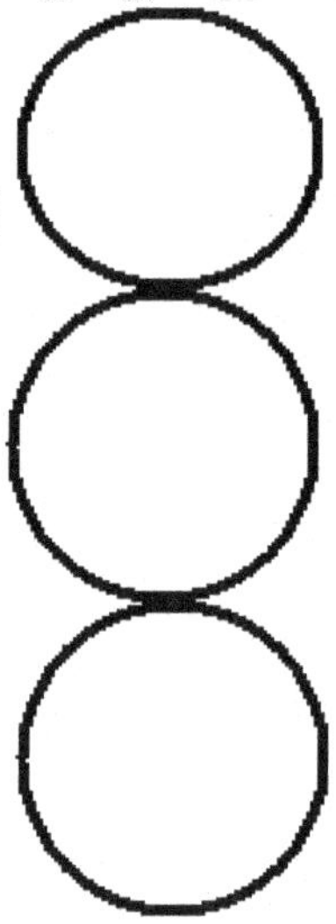

Tracing graph with one stroke

Trace the following diagram and circle the diagrams that you can trace each line once and only once without lifting your pencil off the paper. (If you think it is a traffic problem, then you only allow travelling each road once, but you are allowed to travel to each city more than once. Intersecting point is a city.)

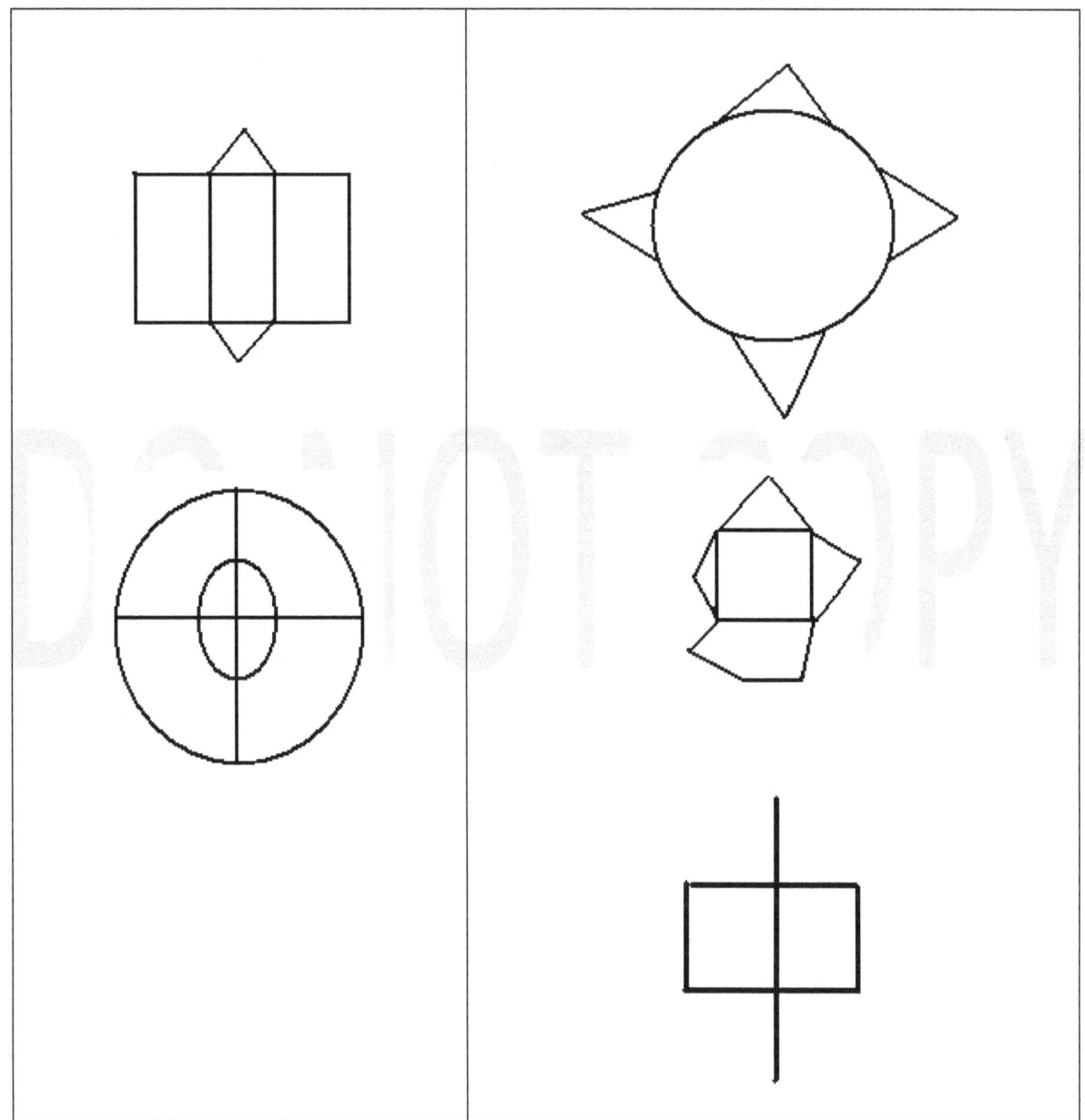

Summary of bishop moving in odd or even dimension chessboard

How does the bishop move?	Tracing graph with one stroke
By observing the previous two worksheets, can you draw a summary of how the bishop travels through each square once and only once? The dimension of a chessboard plays an important role in deciding if the bishop can travel every square or not. It also depends if the starting point is at the corner square or not. Can the bishop travel through each square once and only once? Fill in each of the following blank cells with YES or NO answer. 	Chessboard size	Start at corner	Does not start at a corner
---	---	---
Odd dimension		
Even dimension				A diagram can be traced once and only once (point itself can be traced more than once) without lifting the pen then the diagram has one of the following properties: 1. Points all have even paths. 2. Only 2 points with odd paths, one is a starting point, and the other is an endpoint. It cannot be traced once and only once if it has more than 2 points with odd paths.

Learning Chess to Improve Math 数棋谜式健脑国际象棋
Ho Math Chess 何数棋谜 www.homathchess.com
Frank Ho, Amanda Ho © 1995 – 2021   All rights reserved.

Student name _____ Assignment date:_____

Bishop moving on a mini-chessboard

How does the bishop move?	Tracing graph with one stroke
Why can't the following White bishop start at one corner square travel through all White squares once and only once? _____ _____ _____. 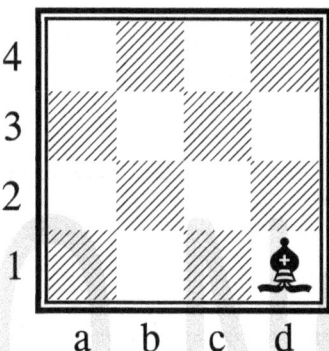 The above bishop path is translated into a mathematical model as follows. There are only 2 points with one path each, but neither of the points could be the end point of the other. This is the reason that bishop cannot visit every square regardless of the size of the chessboard. (In chess travelling problem, each city is allowed to be visited only once. Each dot below is a square or "city".) 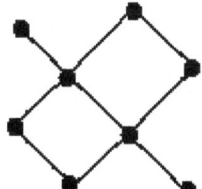	Trace the following diagram and circle the diagrams that you can trace each line once and only once without lifting your pencil off the paper. (If thinking it as a traffic problem, then you only allow travelling each road once, but you are allowed to travel each city more than once. Intersecting point is a city.)  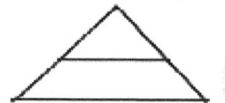 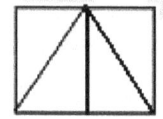 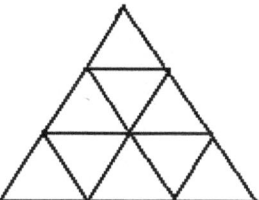

How does the knight move?

Show all the possible squares where the White knight can take or move to by marking X.
Answers may vary.

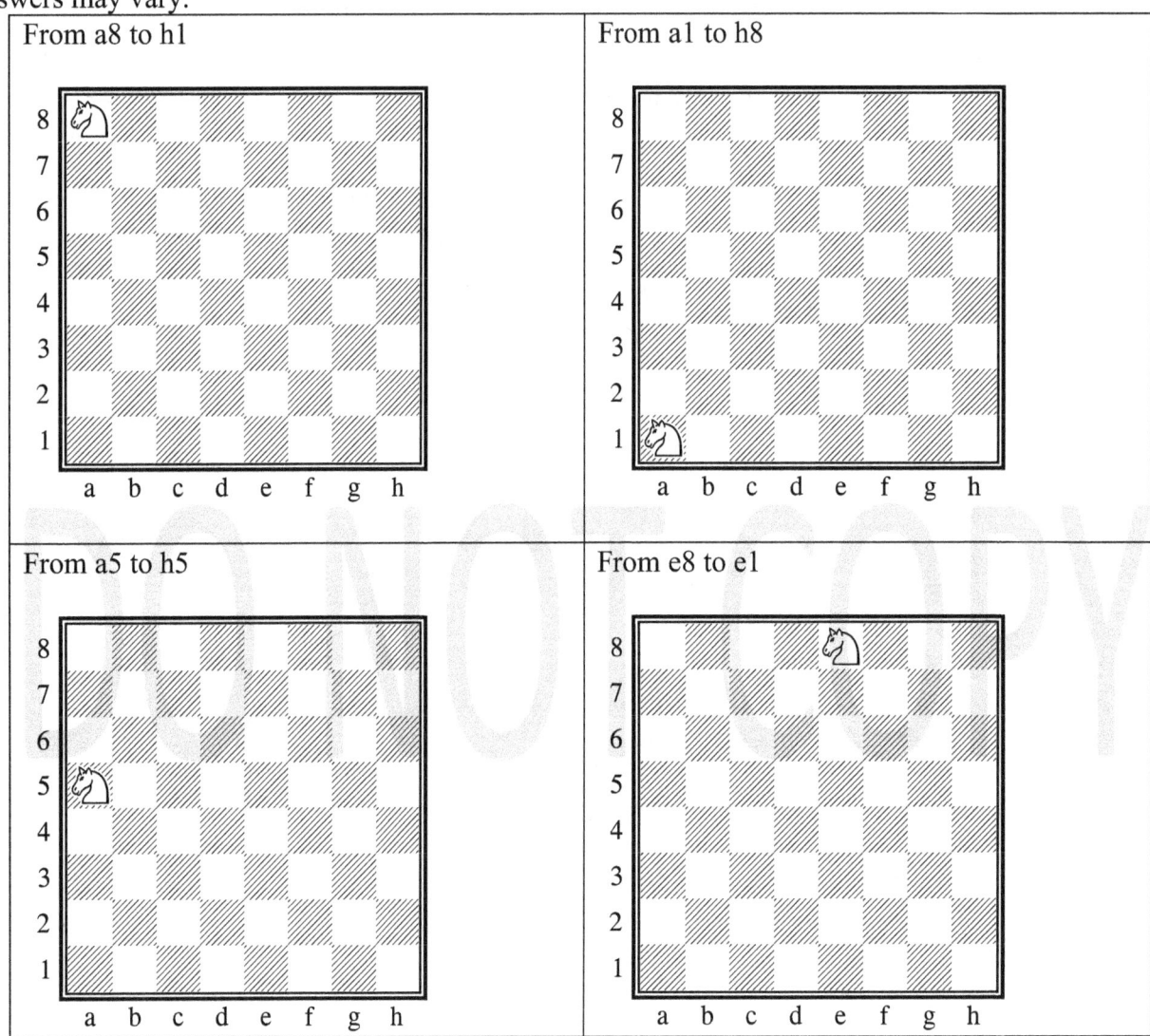

Learning Chess to Improve Math 数棋谜式健脑国际象棋

 Math Chess 何数棋谜 www.homathchess.com

Frank Ho, Amanda Ho © 1995 − 2021   All rights reserved.

Student name _____ Assignment date:_____

How does the knight move?

How does the knight move?	Solving by knight's move
Mark an X on each of the White knight's all possible moves without being taken in the following diagrams.	Place eight white knights such that each white knight is attacked by two black knights, and each black knight is attacked by two white knights.

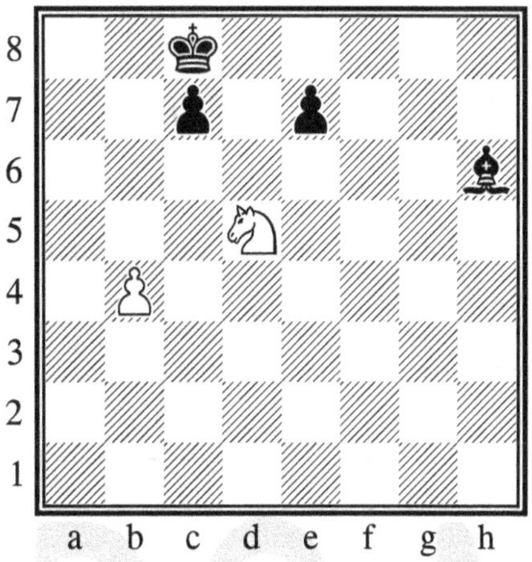

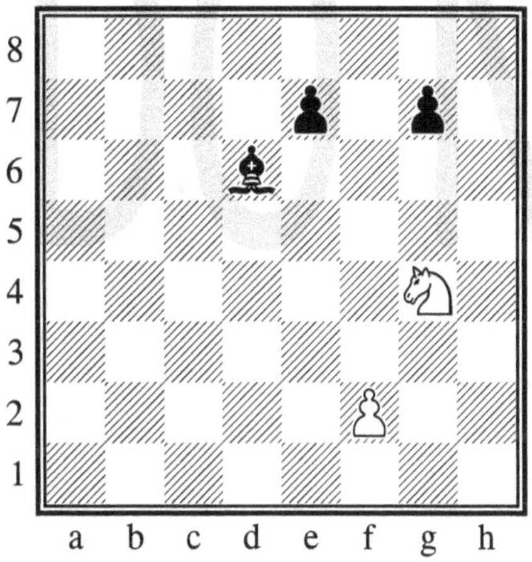

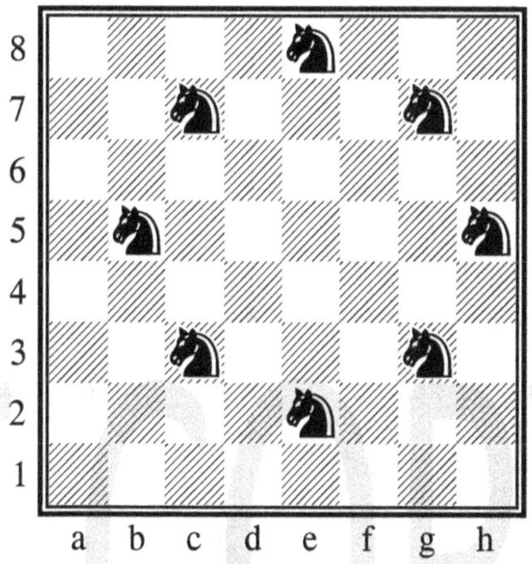

Learning Chess to Improve Math 数棋谜式健脑国际象棋
Ho Math Chess 何数棋谜 www.homathchess.com
Frank Ho, Amanda Ho © 1995 – 2021   All rights reserved.

Student name _____ Assignment date: _____

How does the knight move?

How does the knight move?	Solving by knight's move
Mark an X on each of the White knight's all possible moves without being taken in the following diagrams.	Replace each ? with a number.

(Top chessboard: White king absent; Black king on c8, Black pawns on c7 and e7, Black bishop on h6, White knight on d5, White pawn on b4.)

(Bottom chessboard: Black pawns on e7 and g7, Black bishop on d6, White knight on f4, White pawn on e2.)

Top grid (5×5) — Replace each ? with a number:

	30		9	
?				12
		♘		
24				15
	?		18	

Replace each ? with a number.

Bottom grid (5×5):

	60		14	
?				21
		♘		
?				28
	42		?	

Learning Chess to Improve Math 数棋谜式健脑国际象棋
Ho Math Chess 何数棋谜 www.homathchess.com
Frank Ho, Amanda Ho © 1995 – 2021   All rights reserved.

Student name _____ Assignment date:_____

Knight travelling is not a real distance

How does the knight move?	When 2 is not = 2?
Move the knight at d5 to each square identified by ⊡. For example, it will take two moves from d5 to move to b5. Nd5 – c7 – b5. Write the least number of moves required to reach each ⊡ from Nd5 on the squares of ⊡.	**Observe your results and see if all your answers are 2's?** Answer: _____. If each move is identified as 1 and 2-move is 2, then you would see that in chess, the meaning of "move" takes a different meaning since not all 2-move have an equal distance from d 5. For example, it takes knight two equal moves from d5 to b5 and from d5 to a4, yet physically a4 is farther away from d5 than b5. **How many moves does it take for the knight at d5 to move to the 5 White squares not identified ⊡ on the left side diagram?** Answer: _____

Knight's mini-tour

Many mathematicians have worked on the knight's tours, which means the knight can visit every square of an 8 by 8 chessboard once and only once. De Moivre's strategy is to move the knight in one direction as close to the border as possible.

Use De Moivre's strategy to create a knight tour by numbering every square once and only once.

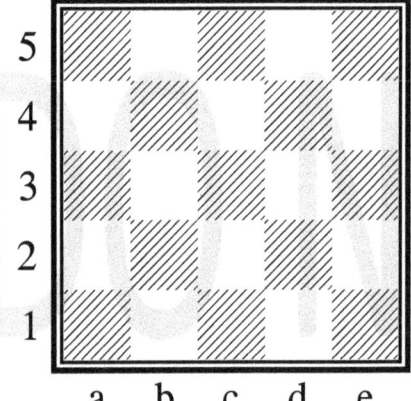

Write numbers: 1, 2, 3, 4 and 5 on the following squares such that each number is written only once in every row, column, and main diagonal. The L-shaped knight move could be used to solve this problem.

Knight's grand tour

Many mathematicians have worked on the knight's tour, which means the knight can visit every square of an 8 by 8 chessboard once and only once.

De Moivre's strategy is to move the knight in one direction as close to the border as possible. The solution is shown below on the right-hand side. Start at h8, then go to g6, h4, g2, e1, c2, a1, then go to b3, a5, b7, d8, f7, h6, g4.

Did you get the idea of how a knight should move? Start at square 1 and complete the entire tour by **numbering all the squares** the knight visited.

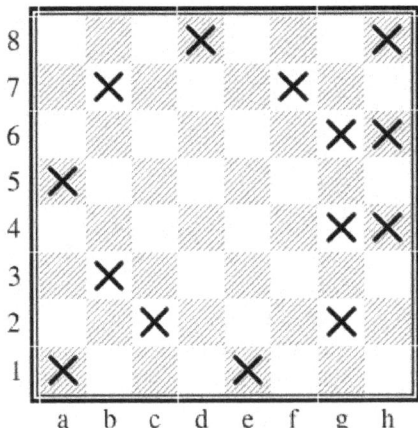

Knight's move used in solving math problems

Place numbers 1, 2, 3, 4, 5, 6, 7, 8, 9 in the following squares so that none of the rows, columns or main diagonals has the same total.	Place numbers 1, 2, 3, 4, 5, 6, 7, 8, 9 in the following squares so that all the rows, all the columns or main diagonals have the same total of 15.
(3×3 grid)	(3×3 grid)
Hint: Use the knight's move to place numbers.	Hint: Find out the sum of 1 to 9 and then divide by 3, which is 15. The middle square number is added four times so that five must be placed in the middle. The two extreme numbers: 1 and 9 must not be placed at four corners.

Frank Ho, Amanda Ho © 1995 – 2021 All rights reserved.
Student name ______________________ Assignment date: ________________

Knight's move used in solving math problems

This page is provided here for reference only, and there is no work to be done.
The knight move strategy does not work for 4 by 4 if we would like to place numbers 1 to 16 in each square such that the sums of all rows, columns and the main diagonals are all different.

The following are some examples.

11	1	4	8
2	6	9	12
5	10	14	16
15	3	7	13

15	1	4	7
2	11	8	5
10	14	16	12
13	3	6	9

DO NOT COPY

One strategy is as follows:

1. Place numbers 1, 5, 9, and 13 on each corner.
2. Place 2 in bishop's move starting from 1.
3. Place 3 in knight's move from the number 2.
4. Place 4 in long L move such as the following:

X	
	X

The final answer is as follows:

1	11	15	5
4	2	6	8
7	14	10	3
13	16	12	9

Learning Chess to Improve Math

Knight's move used in solving math problems

A spiral move strategy can be used to solve the odd dimension sum problem. For example, the followings are answers for 3 by 3 and 5 by 5 problems.

3	4	5
2	1	6
9	8	7

The sums for the above rows are 12, 9, and 24.
The sums for the above columns are 14, 13, and 18.
The sums for the above diagonals are 15, 11

Can you place whole numbers from 1 to 25 in each of the following squares such that each sum of rows, columns and the two main diagonals is all different?

Knight tour and a magic square

The following is another way of knight touring each square once and only once.

Add the sum of the first column numbers. _____
Add the sum of the second column numbers. _____

Add the sum of the third column numbers. _____

Add the sum of the fourth column numbers. _____

Add the sum of the first-row numbers. _____

Add the sum of the second-row numbers. _____

Add the sum of the third-row numbers. _____

Add the sum of the fourth-row numbers. _____

Add the sum of each diagonal numbers. _____

1	48	31	50	33	16	63	18
30	51	46	3	62	19	14	35
47	2	49	32	15	34	17	64
52	29	4	45	20	61	36	13
5	44	25	56	9	40	21	60
28	53	8	41	24	57	12	37
43	6	55	26	39	10	59	22
54	27	42	7	58	23	38	11

Connecting knight

This game's rule is the next move must be in knight's move, starting from the square where your previous move was. One player uses circle O, and the other player uses cross X to mark the moves.
Whoever first runs out of knight's move loses the game (Game created by Frank Ho.).

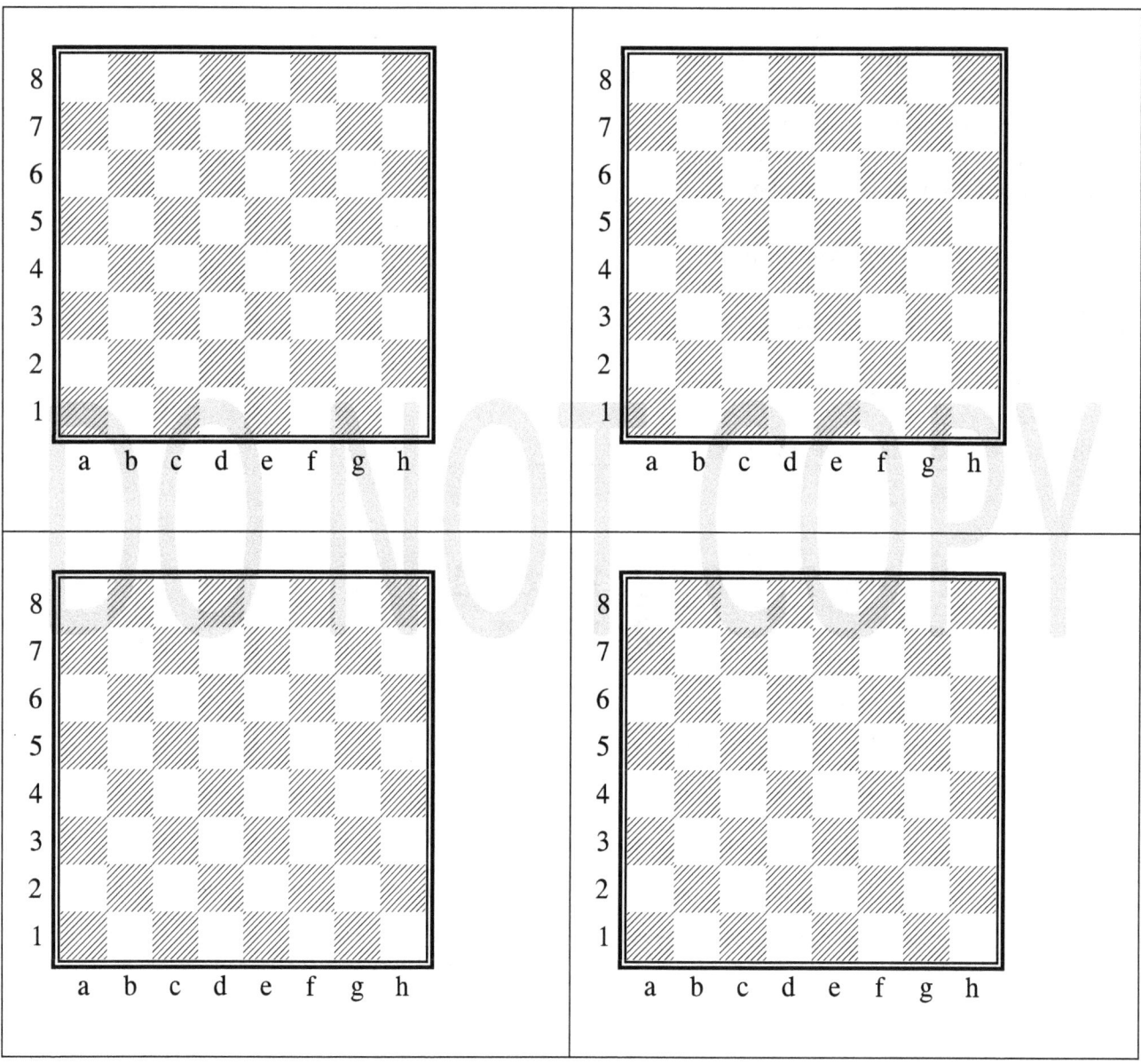

Learning Chess to Improve Math 数棋谜式健脑国际象棋
Ho Math Chess 何数棋谜 www.homathchess.com
Frank Ho, Amanda Ho © 1995 – 2021   All rights reserved.

Student name _____ Assignment date:_____

Mixed chess moves problems

How do chess pieces move?

Place the lowest number of White pawns (using the letter P) in such a way that each square numbered is attacked as many times as indicated on the square.

	a	b	c	d	e	f	g	h
8								
7	1	1	1	1	1	1	1	1
6								
5								
4								
3								
2								
1								

Place the lowest number of White knights (using the letter N) in such a way that each square numbered is attacked as many times as indicated on the square.

		1	1	1	1		
		1	1	1	1		
		1	1	1	1		
		1	1	1	1		

Learning Chess to Improve Math

Ho Math Chess   www.homathchess.com

Frank Ho, Amanda Ho © 1995 – 2021   All rights reserved.

Student name _____ Assignment date:_____

How do chess pieces move?

Place White knights (using the letter N) at the corners in such a way that each square numbered is attacked as many times as indicated on the square.

		1		1		
	1				1	
	1				1	
		1		1		

Place a White knight (using the letter N) in such a way that each square numbered is attacked as many times as indicated on the square.

		1		1		
	1				1	
	1				1	
		1		1		

How do chess pieces move?

Place the lowest number of White knights (using the letter N) on the right-hand side of the main diagonal in such a way that each number squared is attacked as many times as indicated on the square.

1							
1	1						
	1	1					
		1	1				
			1	1			
				1	1		
					1	1	
						1	1

Place the lowest number of White knights (using the letter N) in such a way that each square numbered is attacked as many times as indicated on the square.

		1		1			
		2		2			
		1		1			

Intersecting squares and set theory

Cross mark (X) the squares where both chess pieces can move to (intersect).

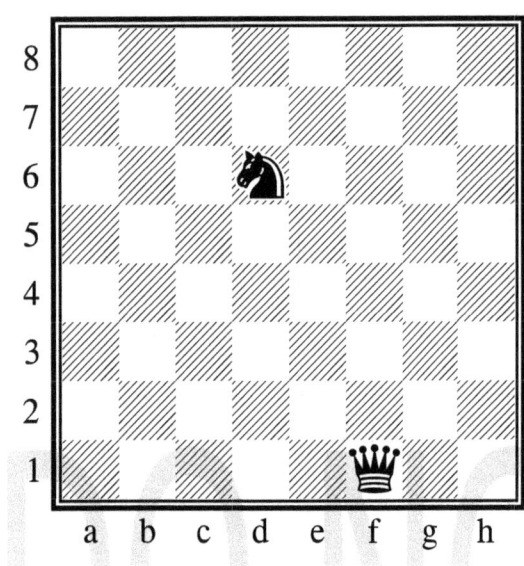

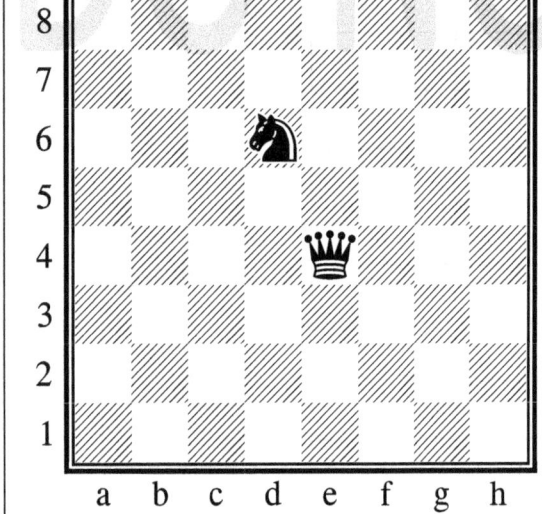

Find the elements that exist in both sets. ∩ means "intersect".

{A, B, C} ∩ {A,B}= _____
{1, 2, 3} ∩ {2, 3, 4, 5} = _____
{A, B, C} ∩ {A,B}= _____
{A, B, D} ∩ {A,E} = _____
{1, 2, 4} ∩ {2, 3, 4, 5} = _____
{1, 2, 3} ∩ {4, 5, 6, 7} = _____

What squares are both controlled by rook and knights?

Write the names of the squares in algebraic notations _____

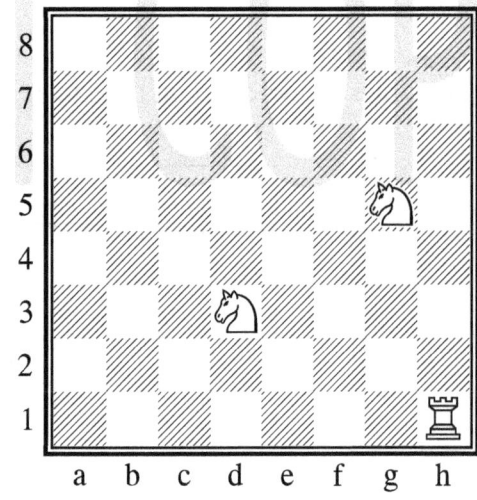

Learning Chess to Improve Math 数棋谜式健脑国际象棋
Ho Math Chess 何数棋谜 www.homathchess.com
Frank Ho, Amanda Ho © 1995 – 2021   All rights reserved.

Student name _____ Assignment date:_____

Part 4 Check, checkmate, or stalemate

Check or Checkmate

The objective of playing chess is to attack the opponent's king. When the king is being attacked, the king is said to be in "check" or being checked. The king cannot be put in check voluntarily. In other words, you cannot move the king to a square where it will be attacked. If a player puts the king in check by mistake, then the move must be allowed to be taken back, and another move should be allowed.

1. It is etiquette to say "check" when the king is under attack.
2. If the player decides to withdraw, then it is courtesy to put down the king and say, "I withdraw" before making a move, it means the game is finished, and the side withdrawing loses the game.
3. A player can offer a "draw" after making a move, and the opponent can accept or refuse before making a move. If a draw is acceptable, then it means it is a tie, so each side gets one-half point.

The king is checkmated, and the game is finished if all the following conditions are true.

1. King cannot get out of check by moving away.
2. The attacker cannot be taken away.
3. The attacker cannot be blocked (not possible for a knight.).

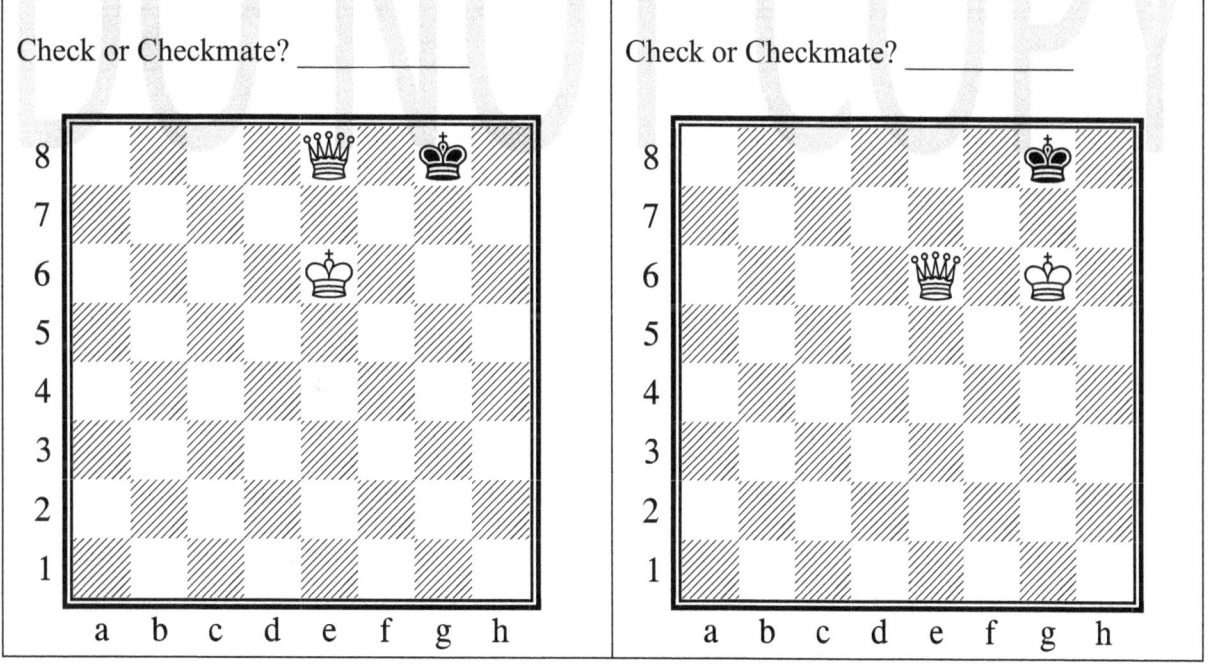

Learning Chess to Improve Math 数棋谜式健脑国际象棋

Ho Math Chess 何数棋谜 www.homathchess.com

Frank Ho, Amanda Ho © 1995 – 2021 All rights reserved.

Student name _____ Assignment date: _____

Check or Checkmate

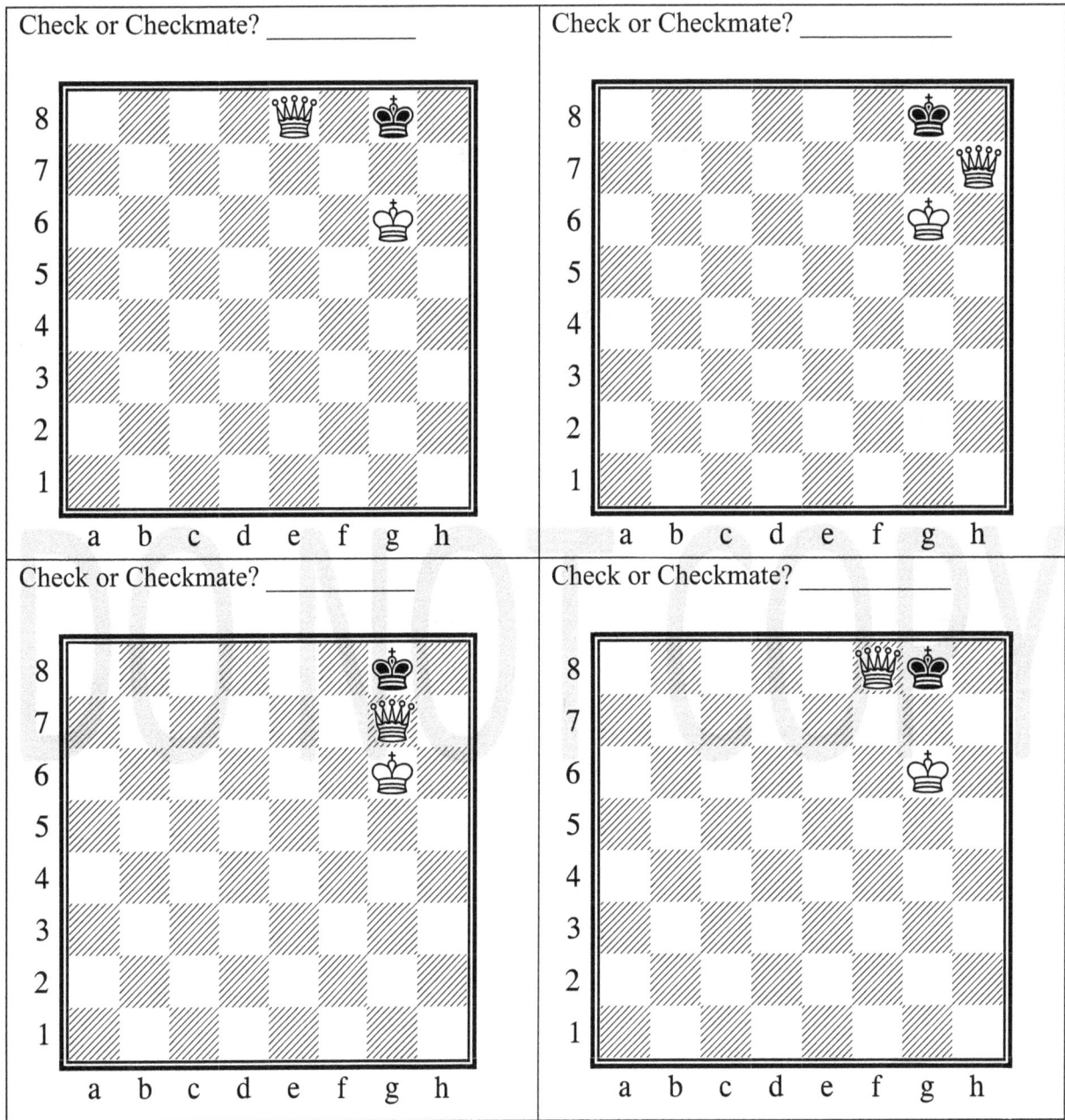

Check or Checkmate

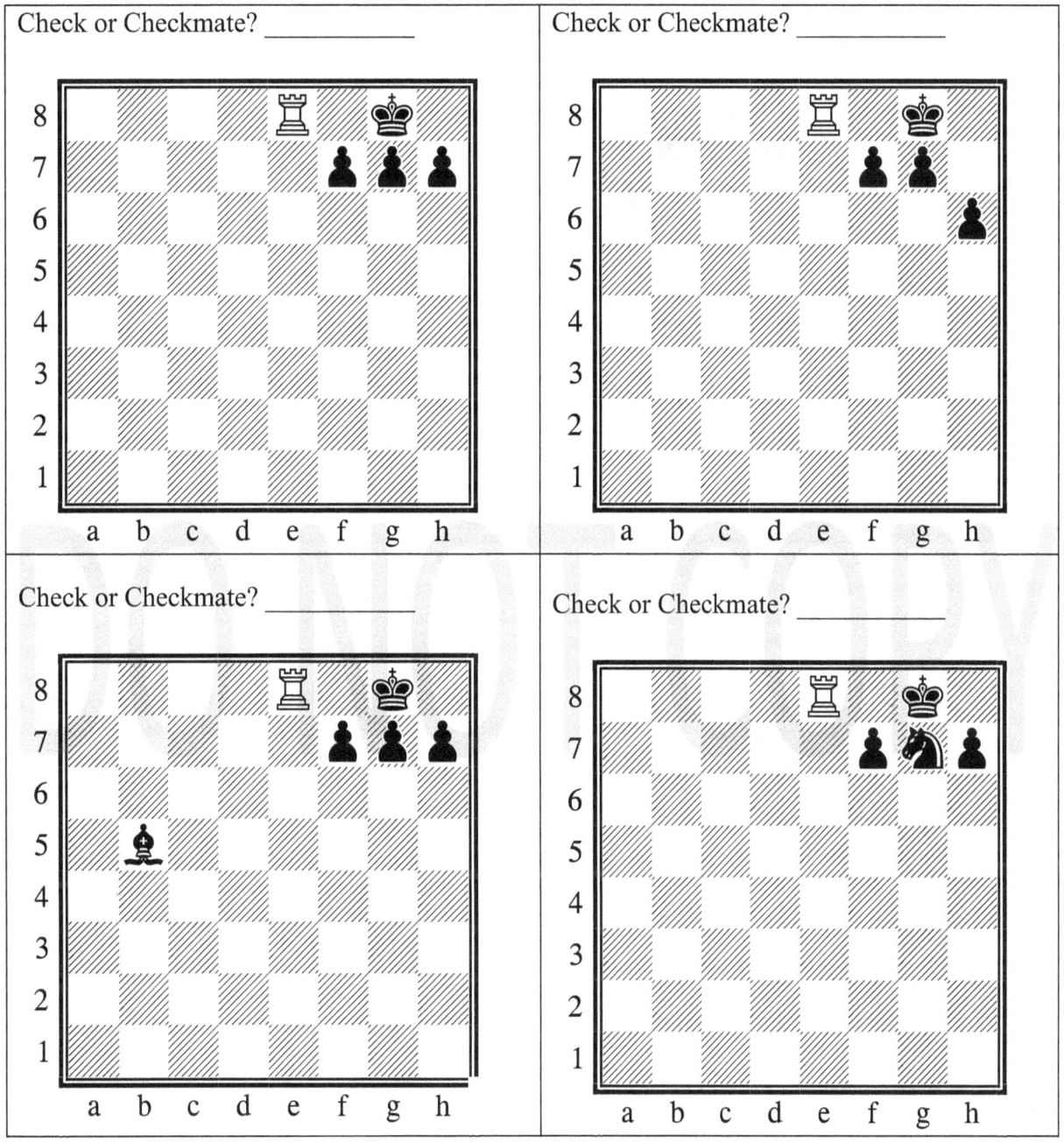

Check or Checkmate

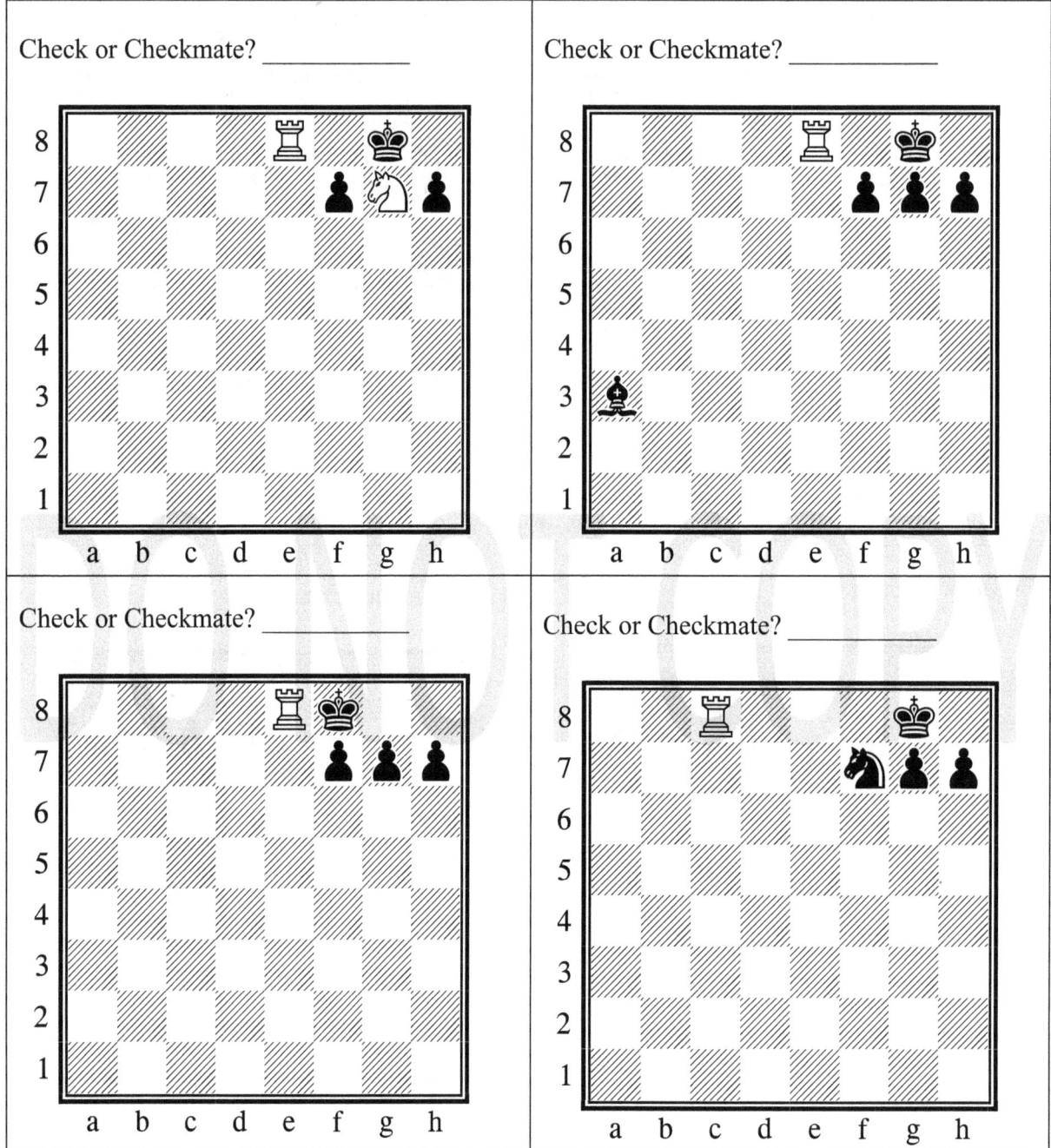

Learning Chess to Improve Math 数棋谜式健脑国际象棋
Ho Math Chess 何数棋谜 www.homathchess.com

Frank Ho, Amanda Ho © 1995 – 2021   All rights reserved.

Student name _____ Assignment date:_____

Check or checkmate

Is the black king in check or checkmate? Circle the answer.

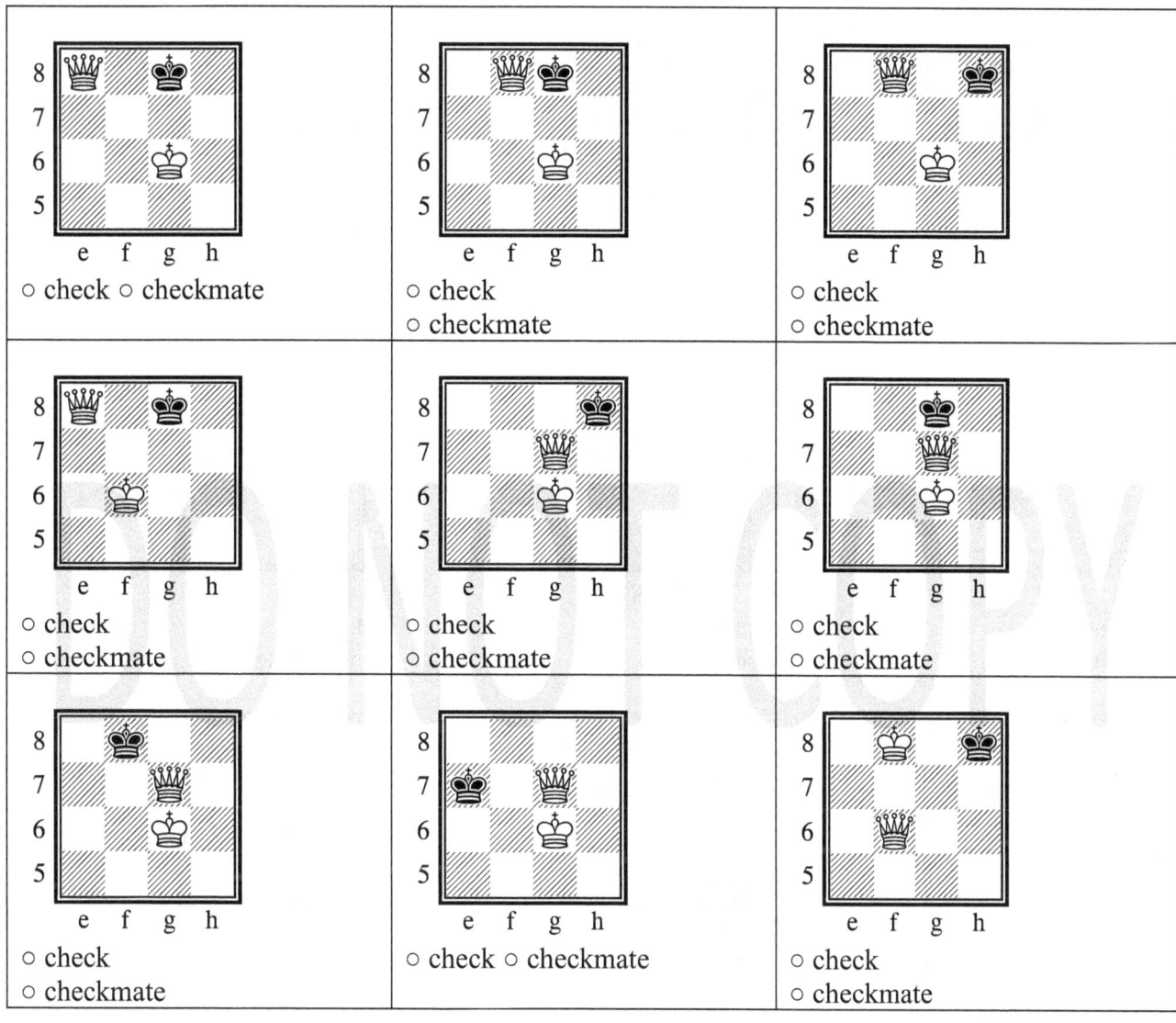

Check or checkmate

Is the black king in check or checkmate? Circle the answer.

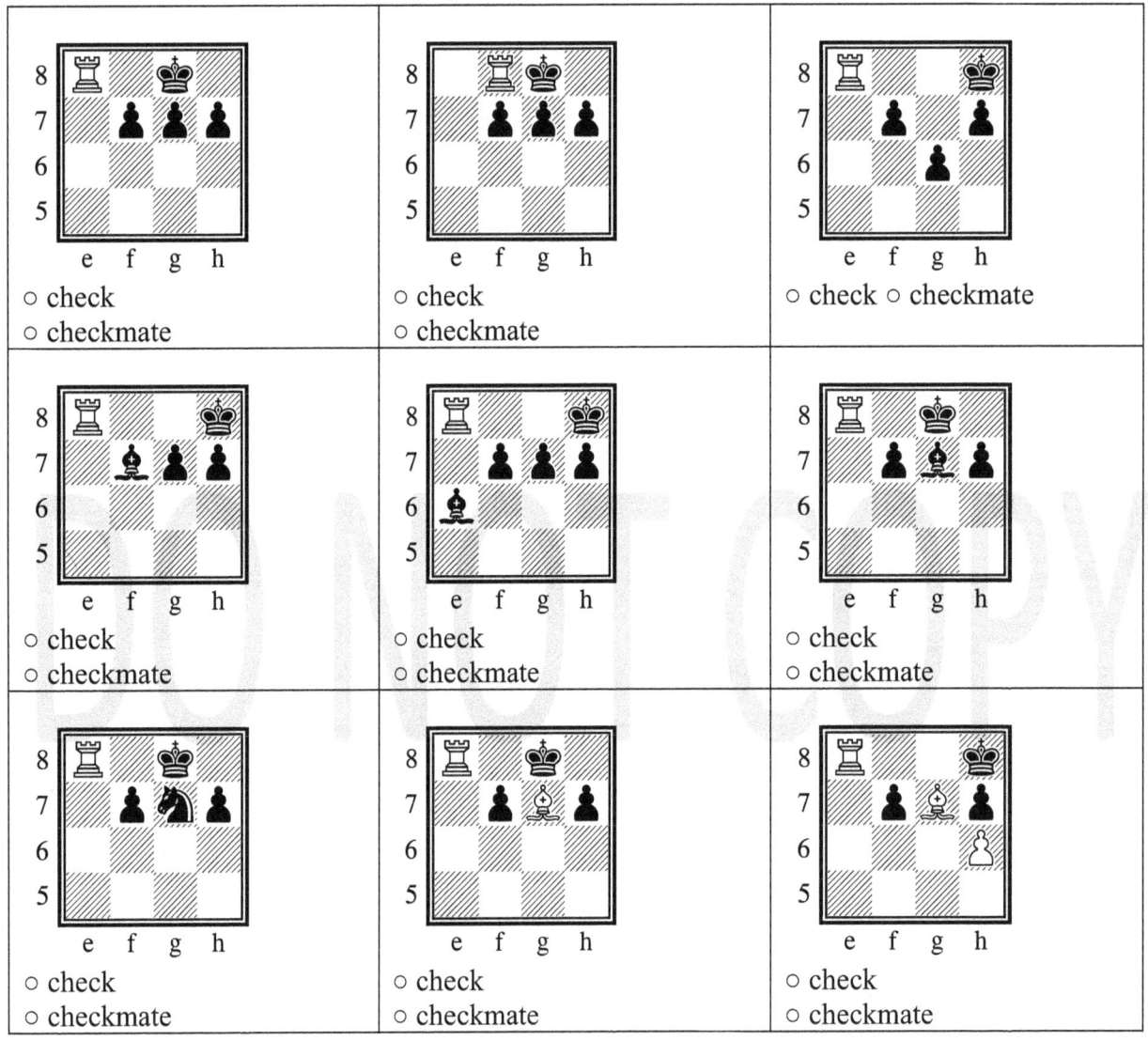

Learning Chess to Improve Math   数棋谜式健脑国际象棋

 Math Chess   何数棋谜   www.homathchess.com

Frank Ho, Amanda Ho © 1995 – 2021   All rights reserved.

Student name _____ Assignment date:_____

The shortest moves of checkmate (2-move mate)

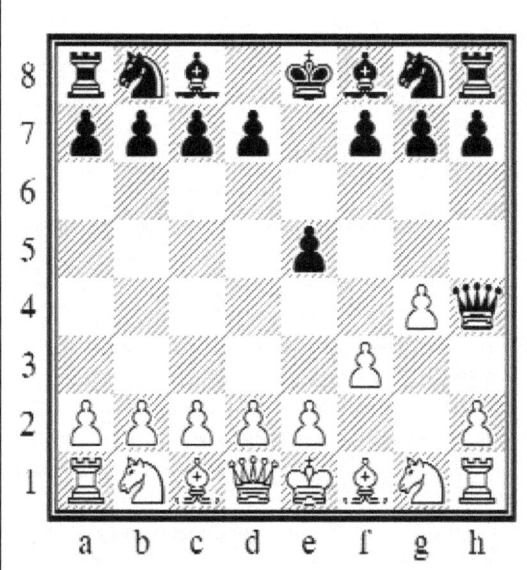

The shortest move of checkmate is two moves - checkmated by Black. Play the following moves.

1. f3 e5
2. g4, Qh4 # (# means checkmate)

This following mate is called a Fool's mate.

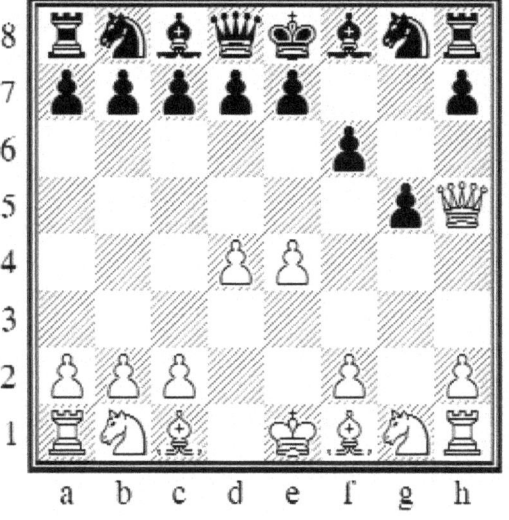

1. e4 f6
2. d4, g5
3. Qh4 # (# means checkmate)

What is the smallest prime number?
What is the smallest natural number?
What is the smallest whole number?
What is the largest one-digit integer?

Scholar's mate (4-move mate)

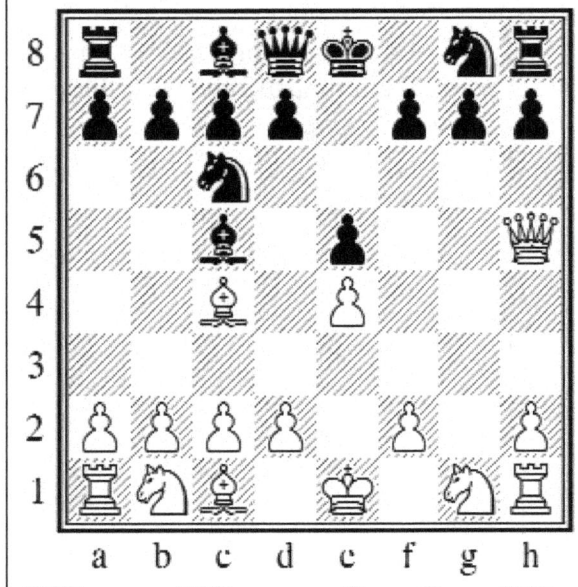

For Black, f7 is only guarded by the king. The scholar's mate involves e pawns and White bishop.

1. e4, e5,
2. Bc4, Bc5
3. Qh5, Nc6
4. _____# (means checkmate)

How to avoid Scholar's mate?

Black could play Nf6 to prevent the Scholar's mate.

1. e4, e5
2. Bc4, Nf6

The following is a mistake
1. e4, e5
2. Bc4, Bc5
3. Qh5, g6
4. Qxe5 +, _____
5. Qxh8,

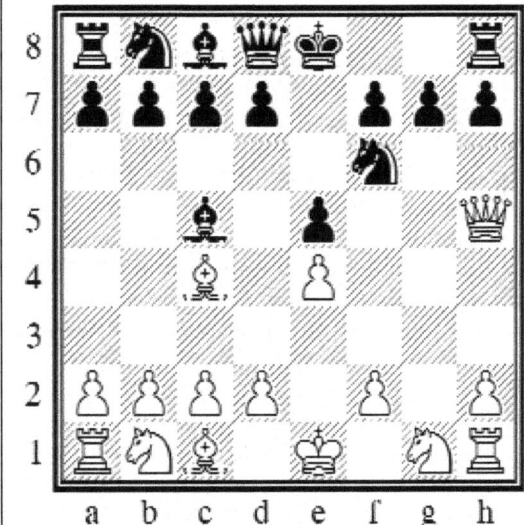

1. e4, e5,
2. Bc4, Bc5
3. Qh5, Nf6
4. _____# (means checkmate)

Black should have played 3. ... Qe7.

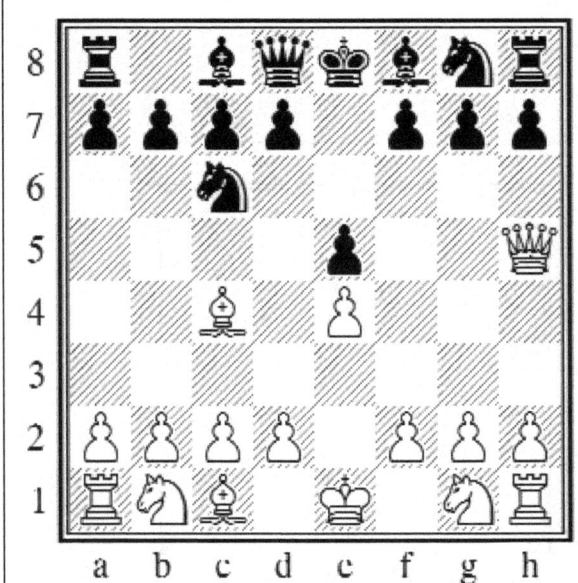

How to avoid Scholar's mate?

1. e4, e5
2. Qh5, Nc6
3. Bc4, Nf6
4. _____

Black should have played 3. ... g6

3. Bc4 g6
4. Qf5 Nf6
5. Qb3 Nd4 or Qe7

Checkmate with the king at the corner

White to mate in one move.

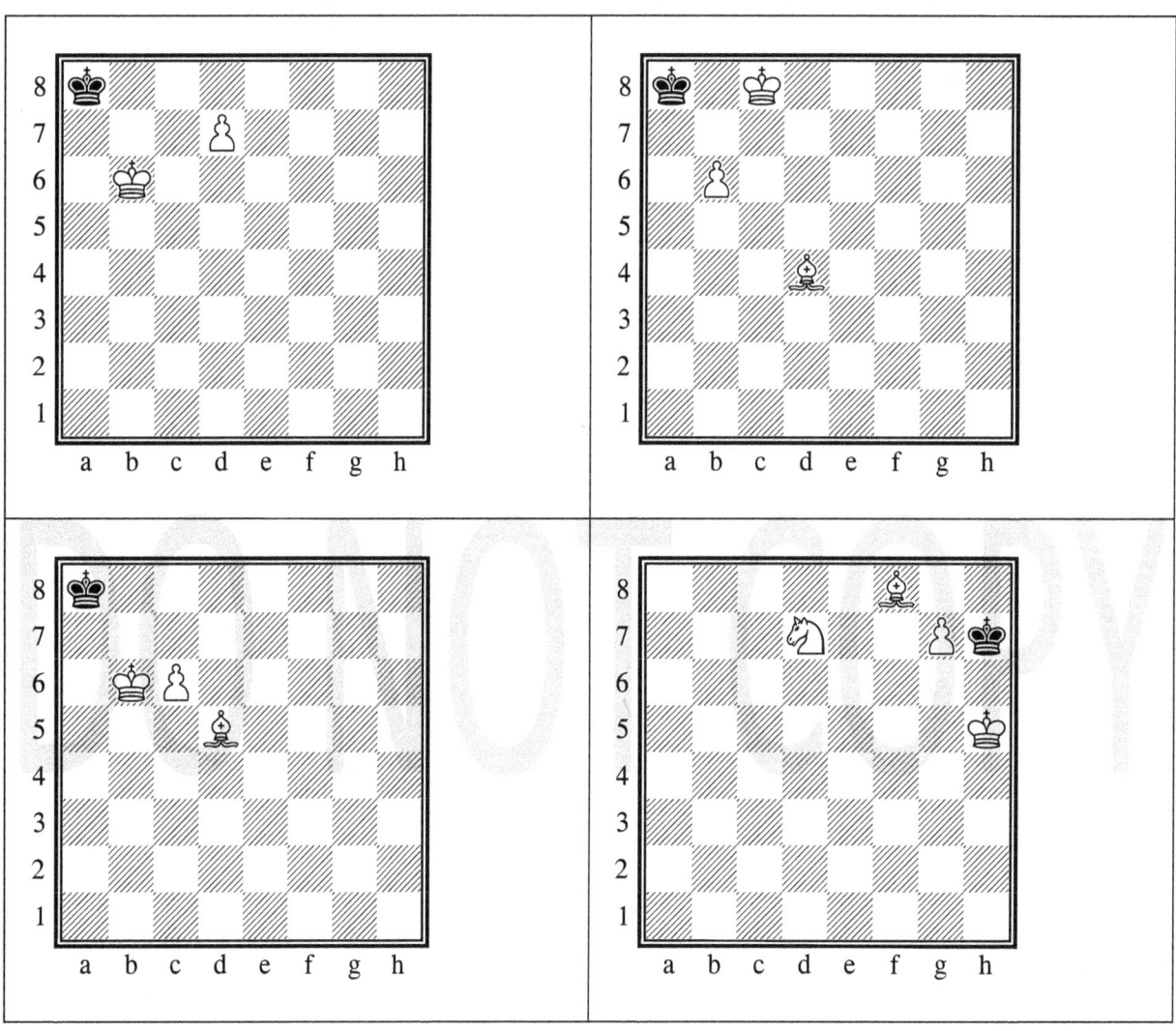

Learning Chess to Improve Math

Ho Math Chess　何数棋谜　www.homathchess.com

Frank Ho, Amanda Ho © 1995 – 2021　　All rights reserved.

Student name _____ Assignment date:_____

Checkmate with the king on the side

White to mate in one move.

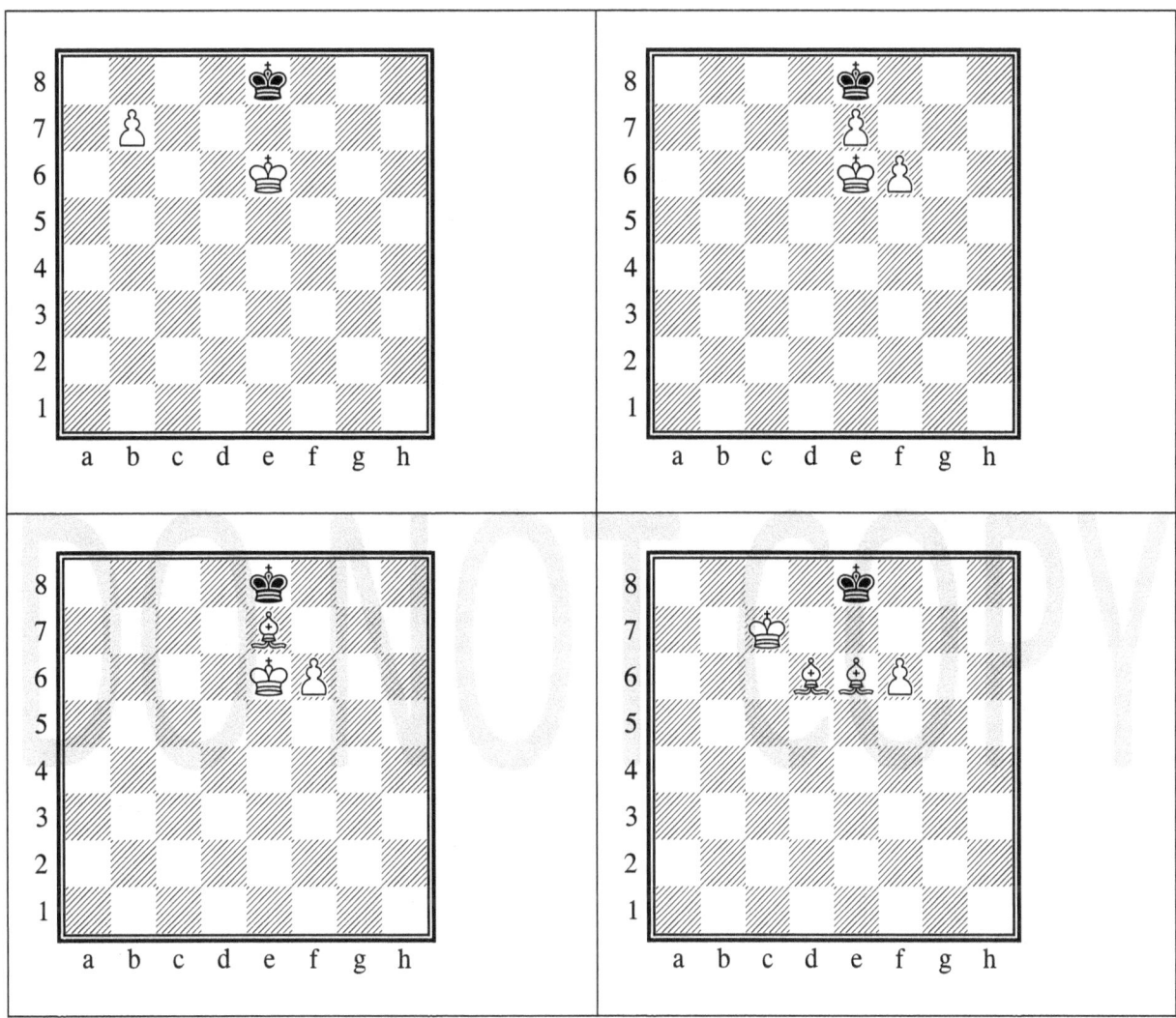

Checkmate with knight

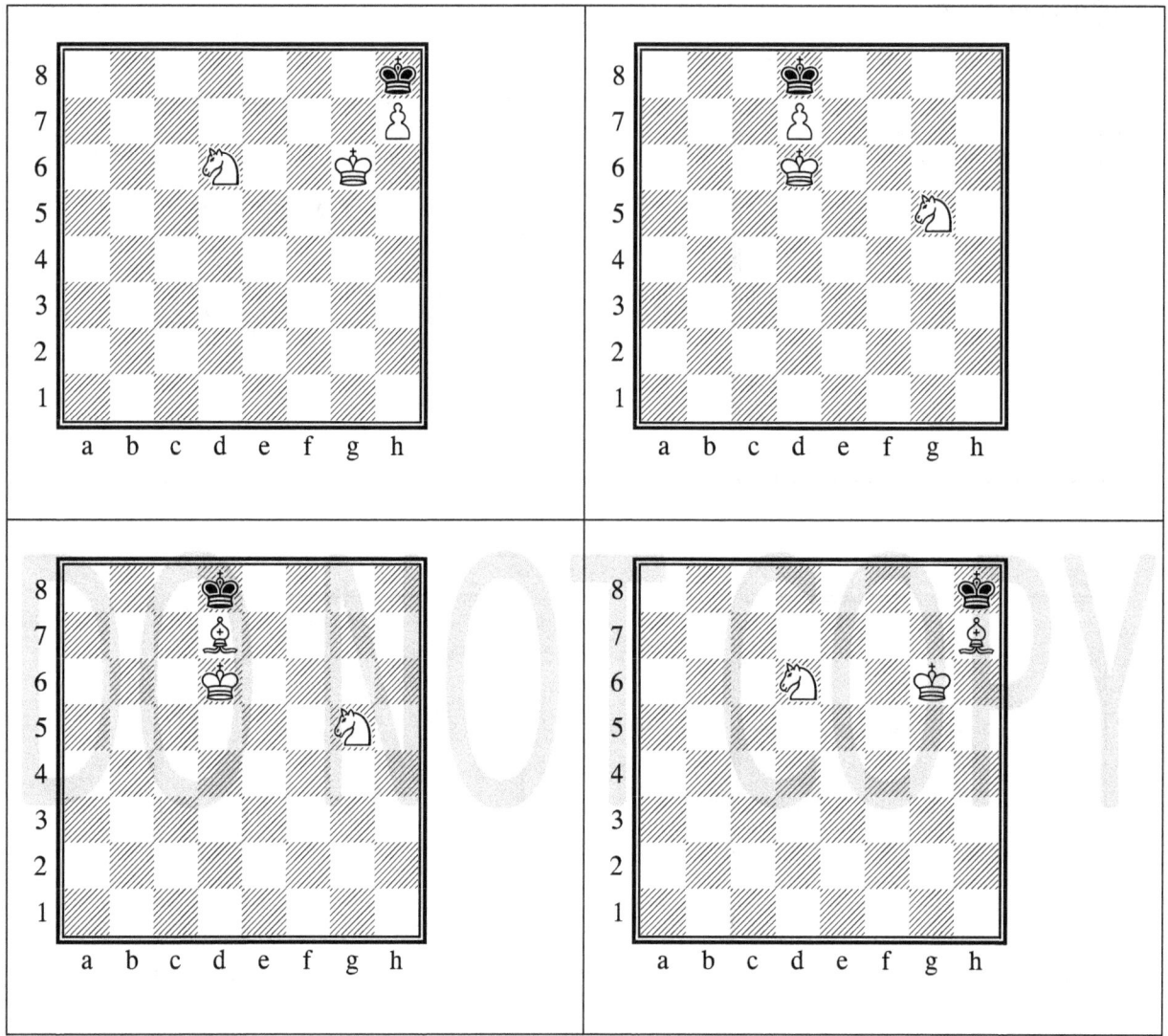

Learning Chess to Improve Math

Checkmate with bishop

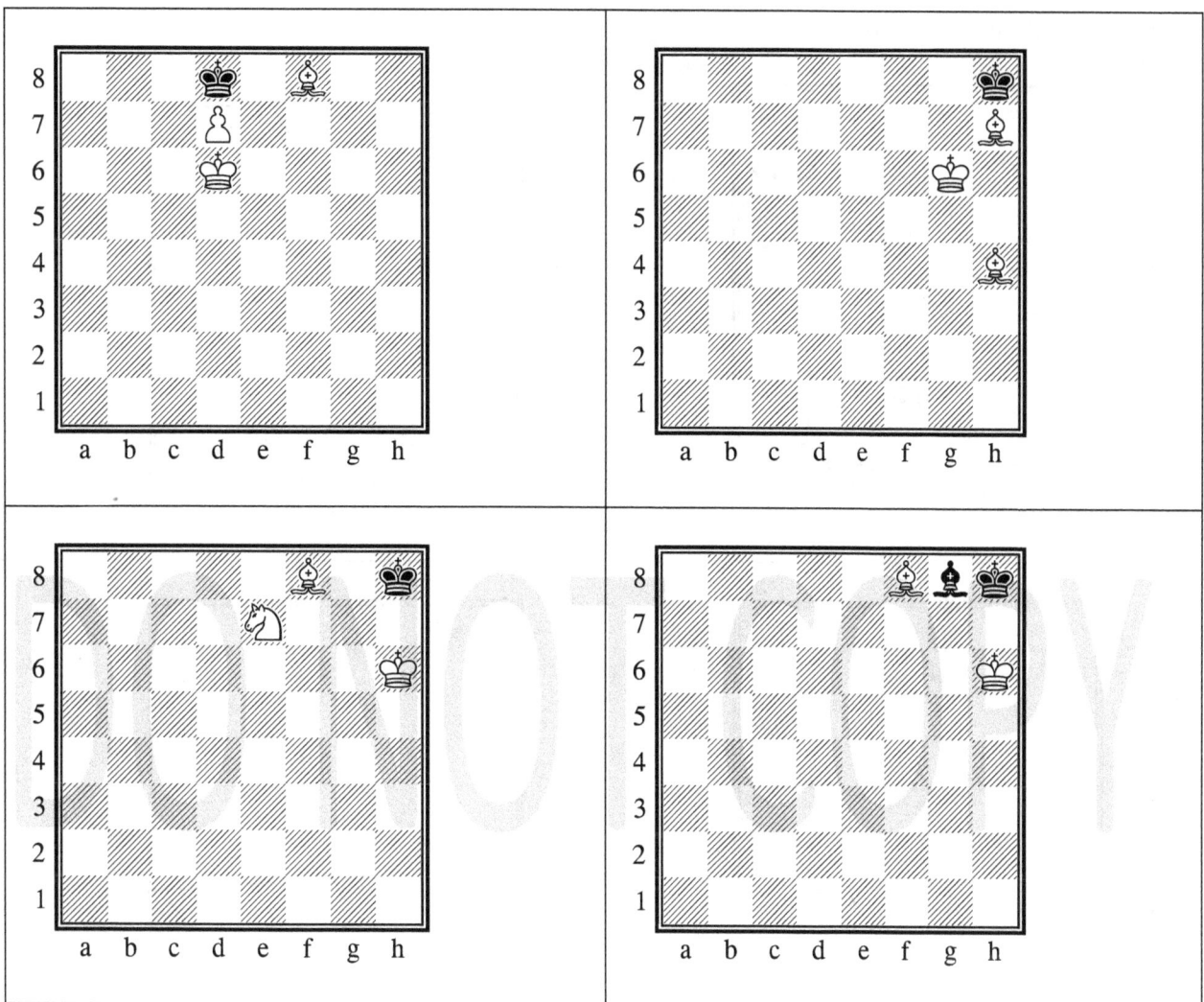

Checkmate with rook

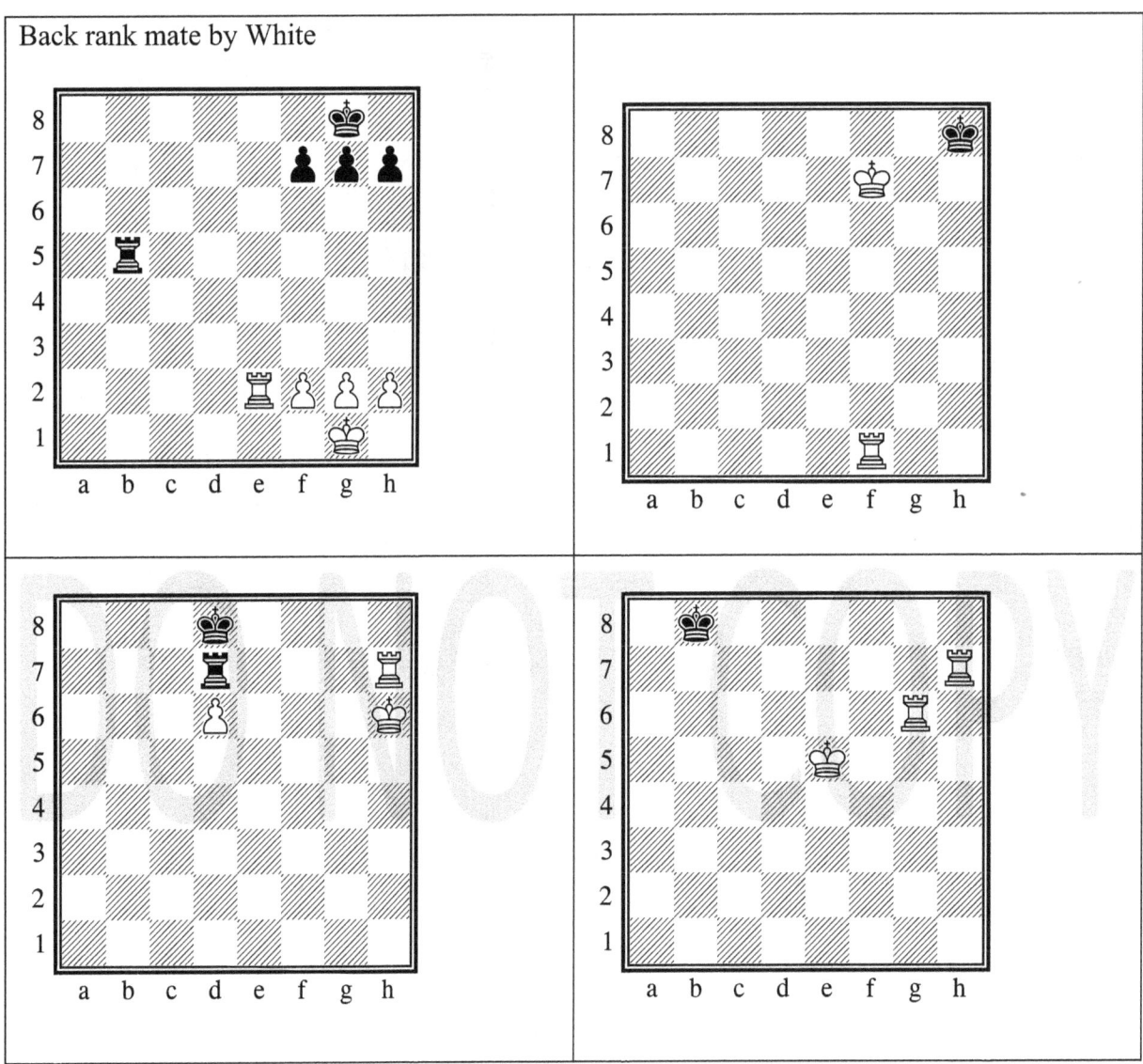

Checkmate with rook

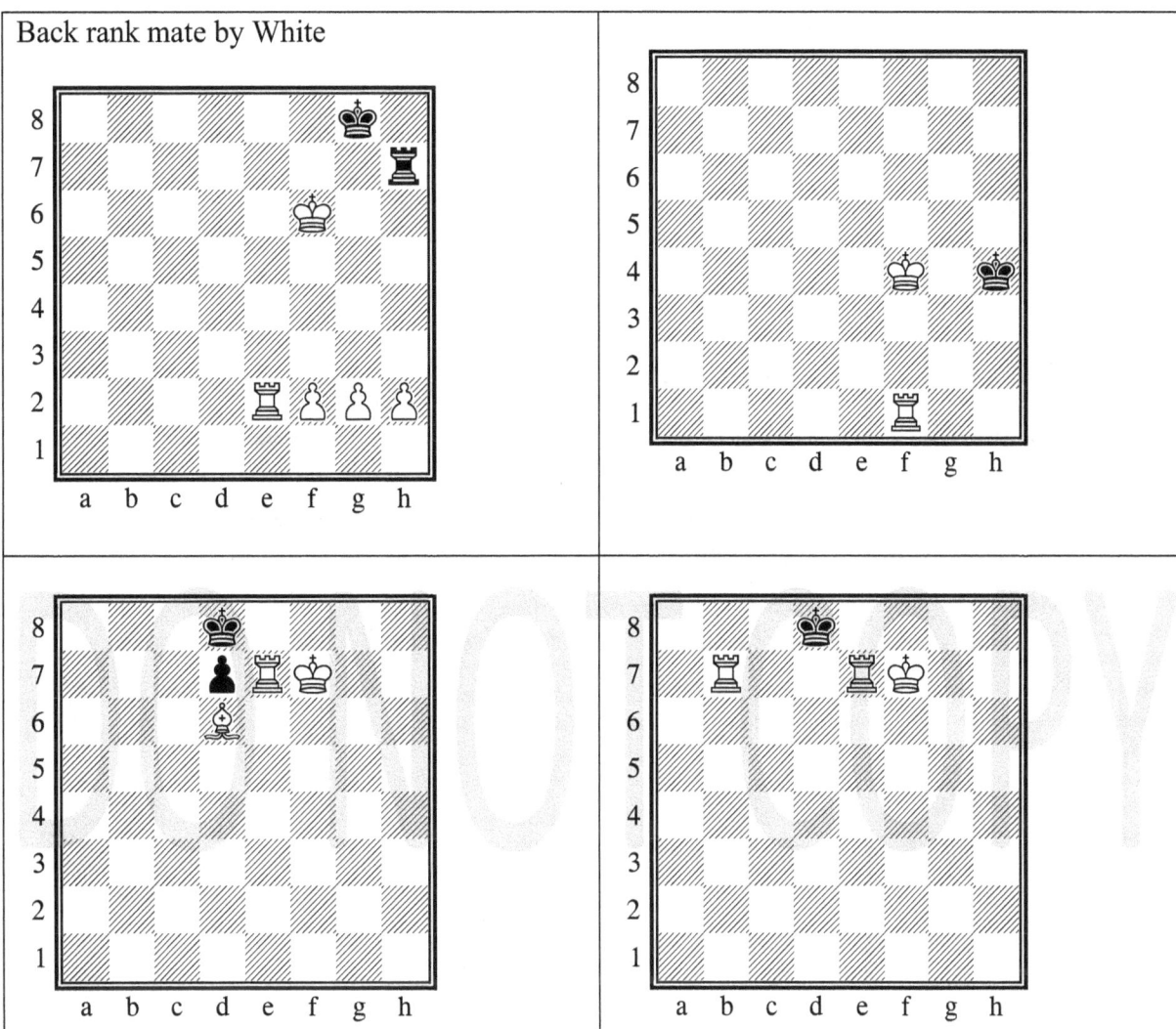

Checkmate with queen

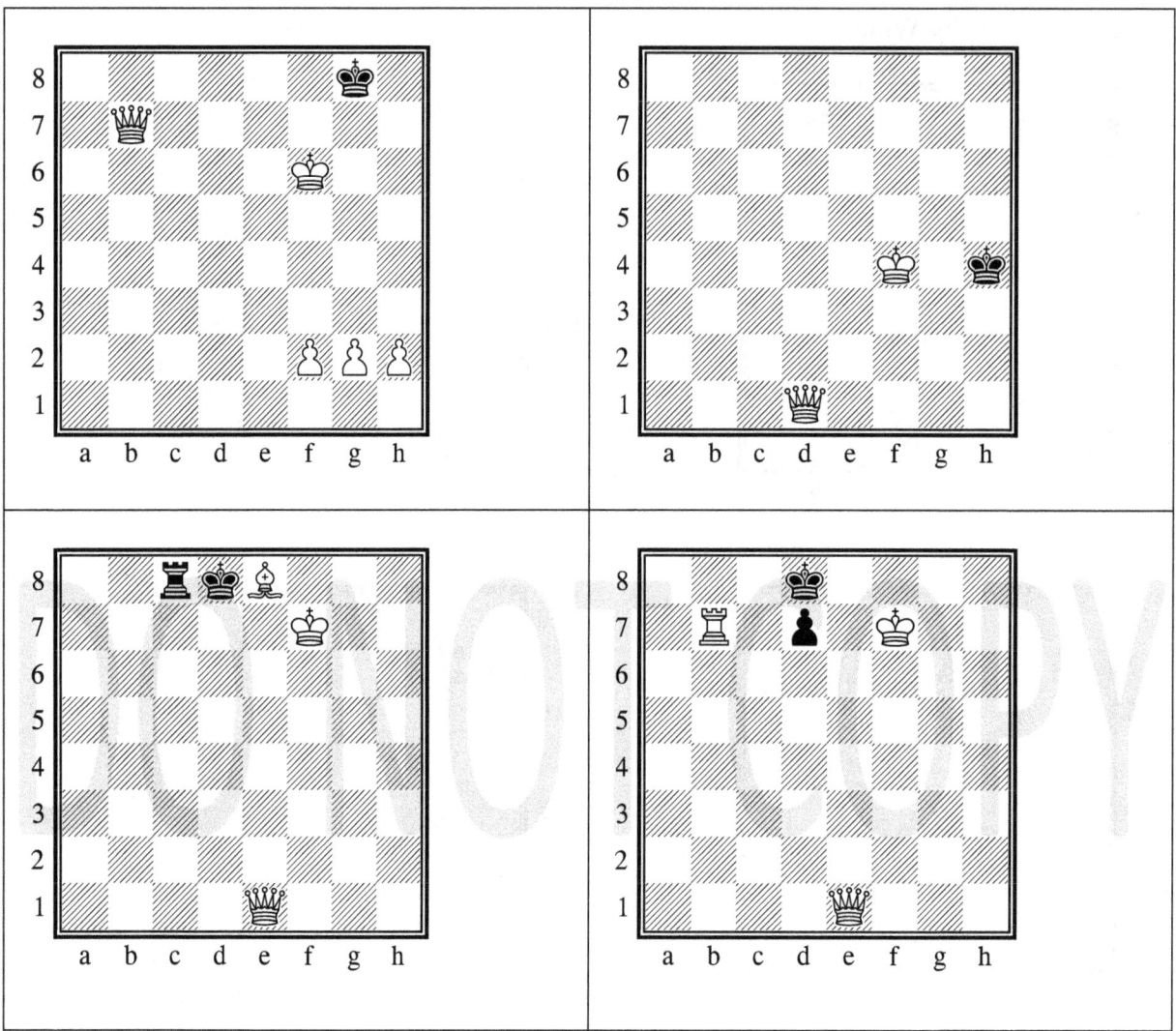

Checkmate with queen

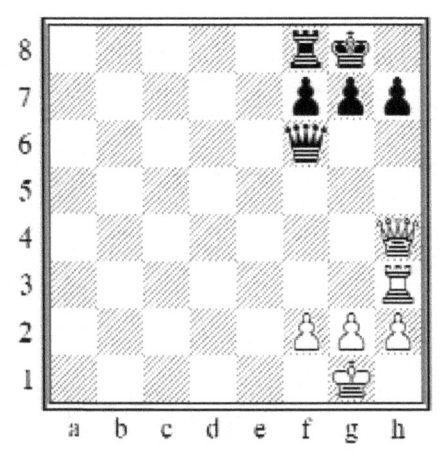
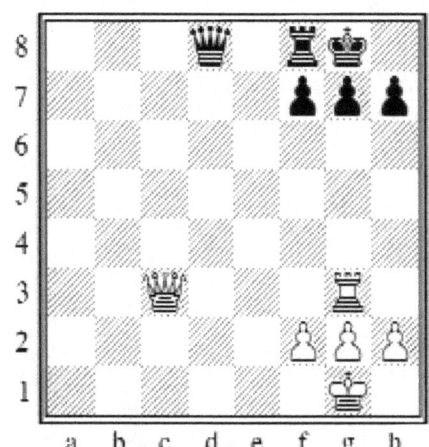
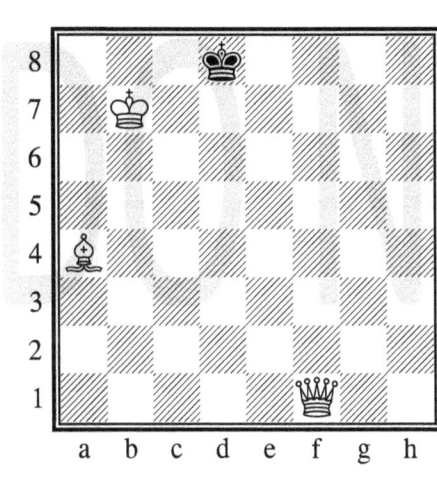
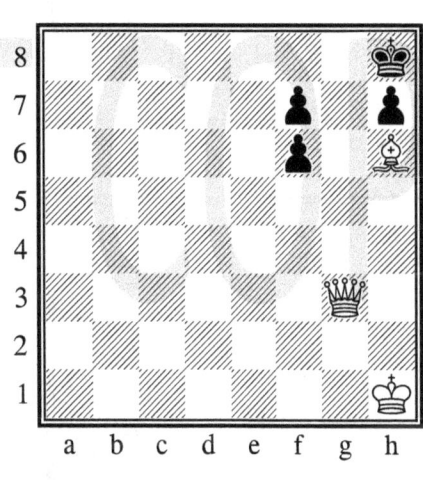

Stalemate

A stalemate happens when there is no check, but the side that is supposed to move does not have any legal move. The White is to move in the following diagrams.

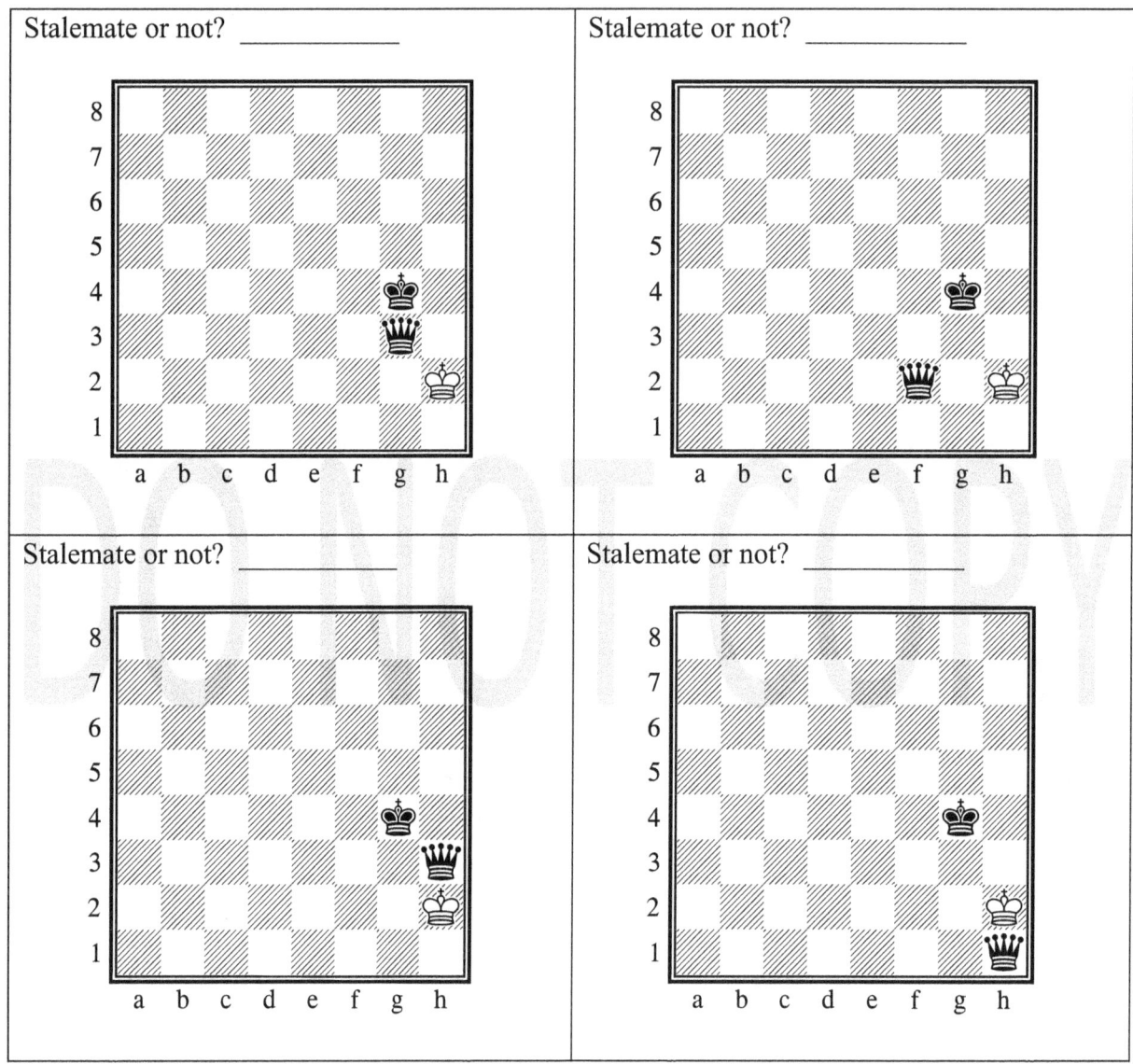

Stalemate

A stalemate happens when there is no check, but the side that is supposed to move does not have any legal move. The White is to move in the following diagrams.

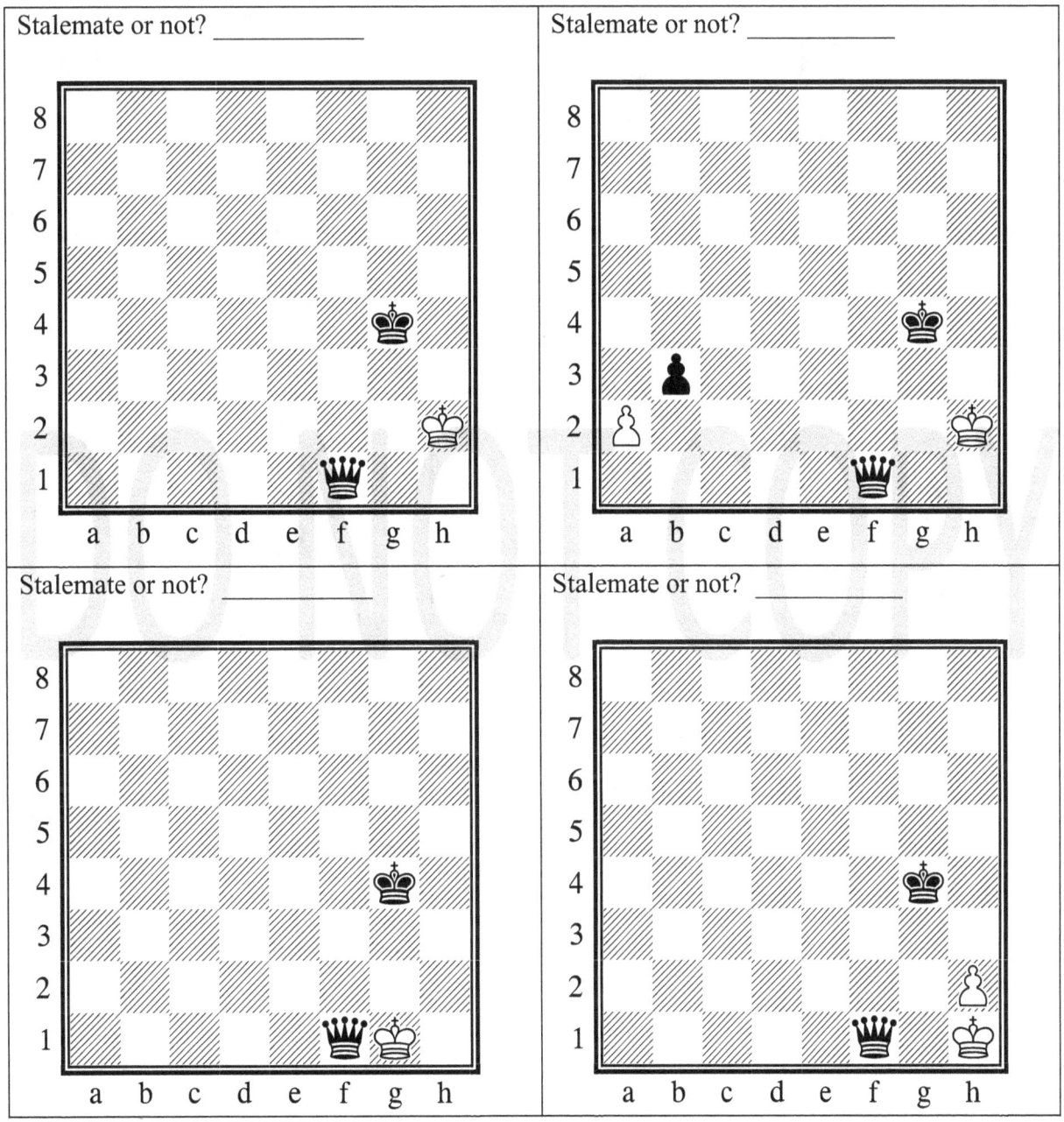

Learning Chess to Improve Math

Stalemate

Is the black king in a stalemate? Circle the answer.

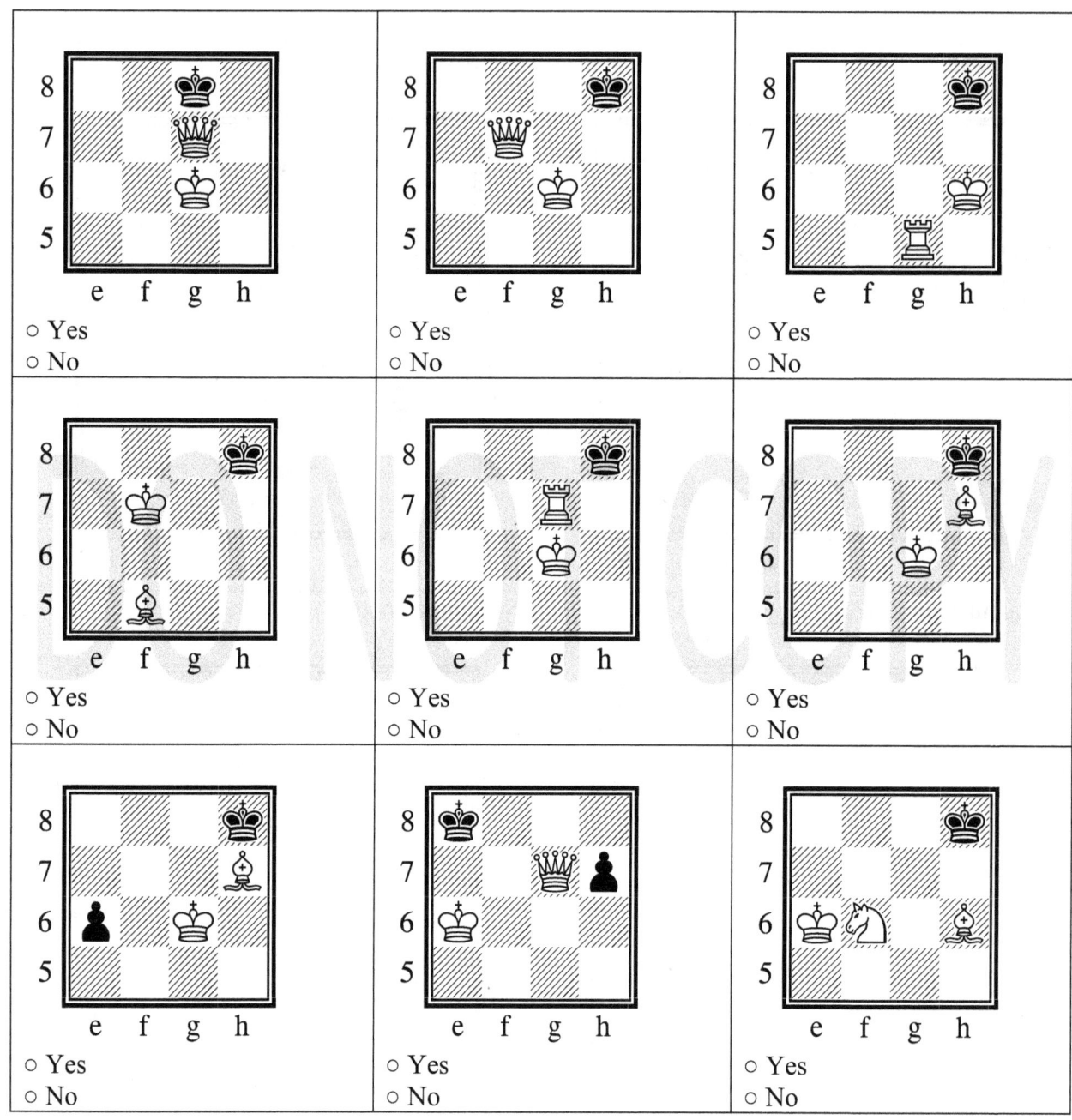

Learning Chess to Improve Math 数棋谜式健脑国际象棋
Ho Math Chess 何数棋谜 www.homathchess.com
Frank Ho, Amanda Ho © 1995 – 2021   All rights reserved.

Student name _____ Assignment date:_____

Check, checkmate, stalemate, or none of the above

Check, checkmate, stalemate, or none of the above? _____

Check, checkmate, stalemate, or none of the above? _____

Check, checkmate, stalemate, or none of the above? _____

Check, checkmate, stalemate, or none of the above? _____

Check, checkmate, stalemate, or none of the above

Check, checkmate, stalemate, or none of the above? _____

Check, checkmate, stalemate, or none of the above? _____

Learning Chess to Improve Math   数棋谜式健脑国际象棋
Ho Math Chess   何数棋谜   www.homathchess.com
Frank Ho, Amanda Ho © 1995 – 2021   All rights reserved.

Student name _____ Assignment date:_____

Check, checkmate, stalemate, or none of the above? _____

Check, checkmate, stalemate, or none of the above? _____

Check, checkmate, stalemate, or none of the above

Check, checkmate, stalemate, or none of the above? _____

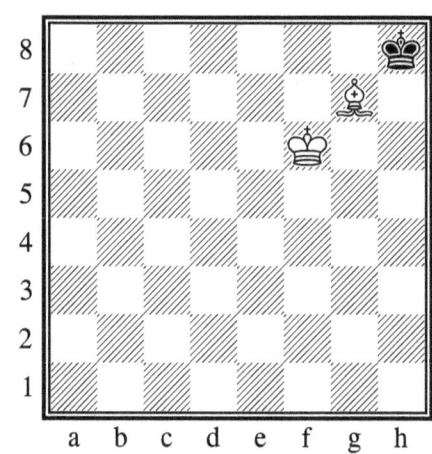

Check, checkmate, stalemate, or none of the above? _____

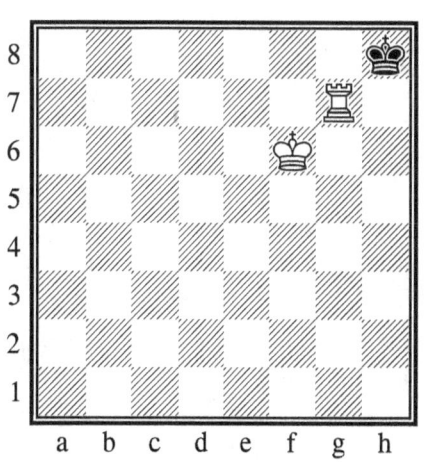

Check, checkmate, stalemate, or none of the above? _____

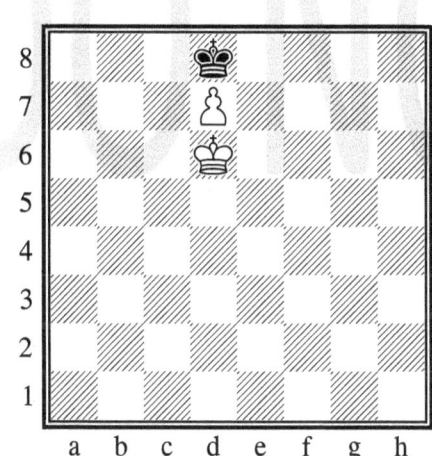

Check, checkmate, stalemate, or none of the above? _____

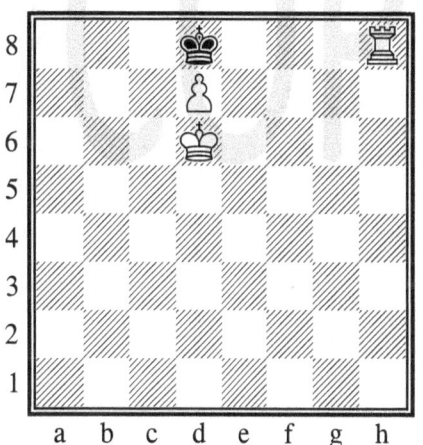

Check, checkmate, stalemate, or none of the above

Check, checkmate, stalemate, or none of the above? _____

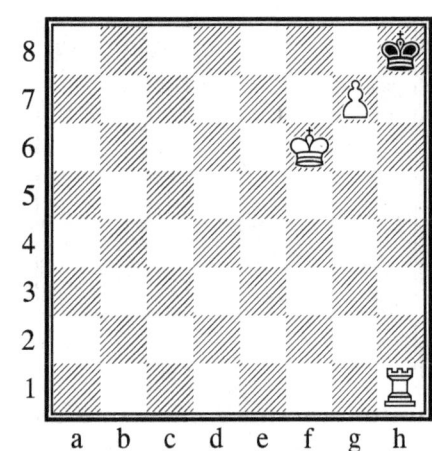

Check, checkmate, stalemate, or none of the above? _____

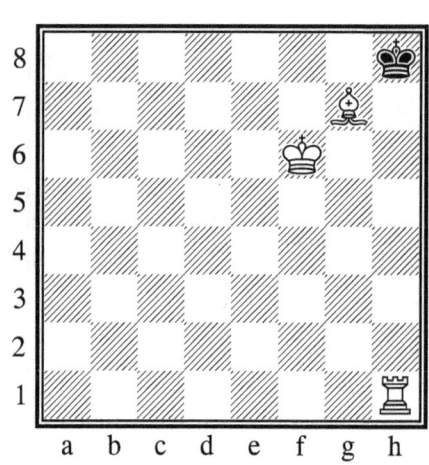

Check, checkmate, stalemate, or none of the above? _____

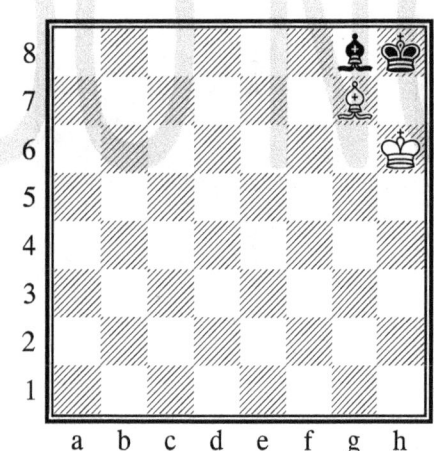

Check, checkmate, stalemate, or none of the above? _____

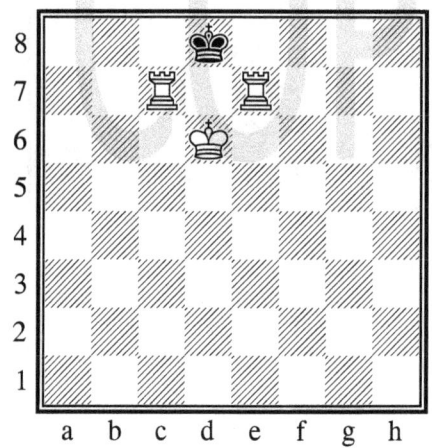

Learning Chess to Improve Math   数棋谜式健脑国际象棋
Ho Math Chess   何数棋谜   www.homathchess.com
Frank Ho, Amanda Ho © 1995 – 2021   All rights reserved.

Student name _____ Assignment date:_____

Check, checkmate, stalemate, or none of the above

Check, checkmate, stalemate, or none of the above? _____

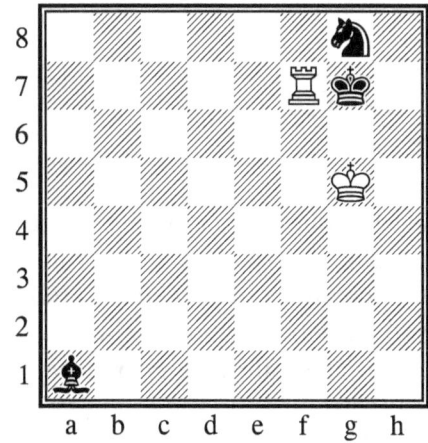

Check, checkmate, stalemate, or none of the above? _____

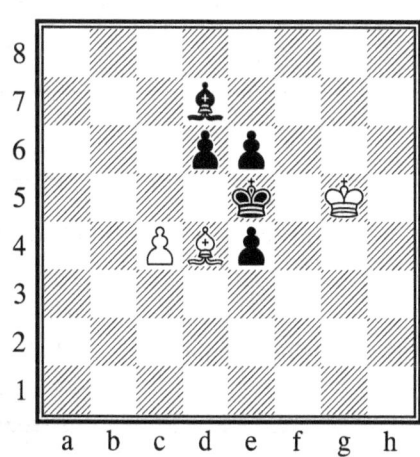

Check, checkmate, stalemate, or none of the above? _____

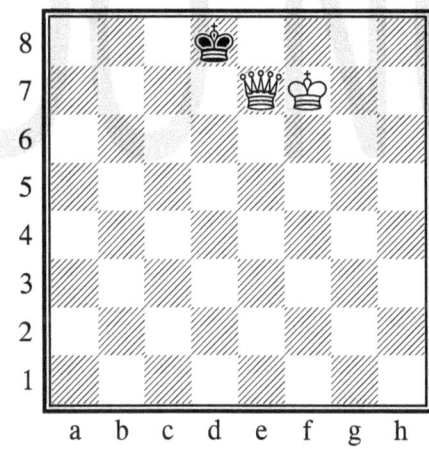

Check, checkmate, stalemate, or none of the above? _____

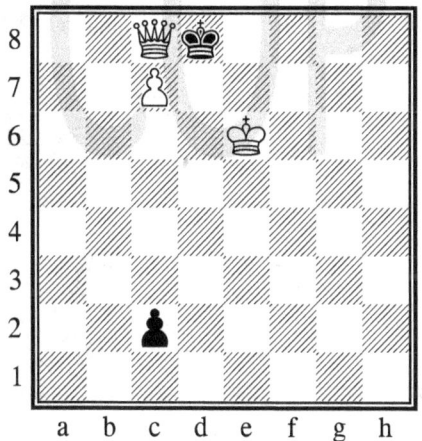

Learning Chess to Improve Math   数棋谜式健脑国际象棋
Ho Math Chess 何数棋谜 www.homathchess.com
Frank Ho, Amanda Ho © 1995 – 2021   All rights reserved.

Student name _____ Assignment date:_____

Under promotion

Normally we would like to promote a pawn to a queen but there are exceptions to this general guideline, as we would see from the following chess question. In math, there are also some "exceptions to the rules" conditions, as we will see these questions on the right-hand side.

Under promotion	Moving x to the right-hand side of the equation
White to move and win. Show White's move by an arrow. Do we always promote a pawn to a queen? _____ 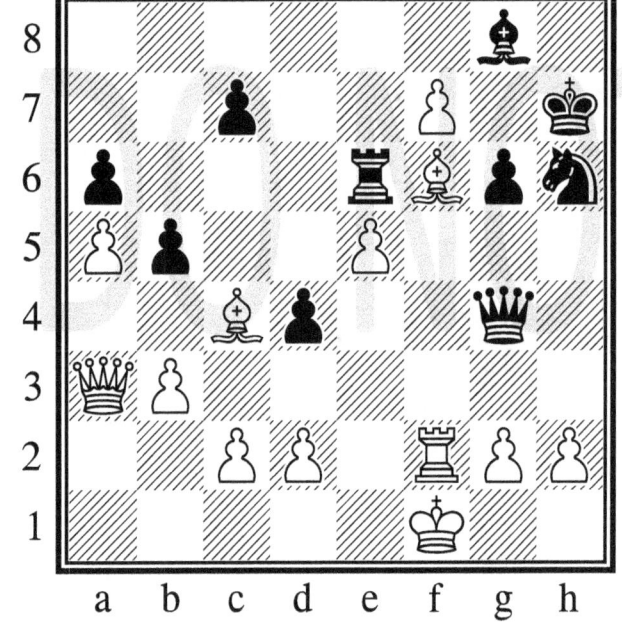	Under the promotion of pawn is one example of an exception to the rule; in math, there are some exceptions to the general guidelines when evaluating an equation. The following is one example. $3x+4=5x-6$ Normally, x is moved to the left, but if the move of x resulting a negative x, do we insist on moving x to the left? _____ The following question is more evidence that we do not always have to have x to the left-hand side. The less chance we have to deal with a negative sign, the less chance we would make a mistake in computation. $3x+4<5x-6$

Learning Chess to Improve Math   数棋谜式健脑国际象棋

Ho Math Chess   何数棋谜   www.homathchess.com

Frank Ho, Amanda Ho © 1995 – 2021   All rights reserved.

Student name _____ Assignment date:_____

Alternative moves

When a beginner chess player has presented an opportunity to take the opponent's piece, the response most of the time is the beginner chess will take the opponent's piece. This seems to be a natural and direct response; with better training, later on, most chess players would think of another alternative move before taking the piece. There are many analogies in math; one of them is the point on the line. Many students would just think a point is a point when it is given but, given more thought, one would discover the real use of a point. See the right-hand side for details.

When the real meaning may not be obvious.	Think of an "order pair" as "substitution."
Black pawn just moved from b7 to b6. What is White's move? Show White's move by an arrow.	An ordered pair (2,11) is on the line of $y = ax + 3$. Find the value of a.
	Just because (2,11) is called an ordered pair, it does not mean you have to think it is just a point. Think of it as an equivalent to a "substitution" problem, which means the point can always be substituted into the equation.

When to attack?

To win in chess, attacking and defending are unavoidable, and they are related to counting the number of chess pieces and analyzing their relative positions on the chessboard. When attacking, the number of attacking pieces and the opponent's defending pieces must be counted and analyzed.

From the number of chess pieces point of view, the condition of qualifying an attacking is the number of attacking pieces must be more than the defending pieces if all pieces are equal values.

The following three conditions are favourable to the attacker.

1. If the number of attacking pieces = the number of defending pieces and the attacker could win by exchanging pieces.

2. If the number of attacking pieces > the number of defending pieces and the attacker could win by exchanging pieces.

3. If the number of attacking pieces < the number of defending pieces but the attacker could win by exchanging pieces.

As mentioned above counting, the number of attacking and defending pieces is only one part of the analytical work one must do before making a move. The relative positions of pieces must also be analyzed to make the right and best move.

We have also presented here some geometric puzzles involving matchsticks which require you to remove sticks and then from a new shape or pattern. So, the goal is not simply just removing any sticks but the meaningful ones such that the results would be the shape we want.

These types of questions involve analyzing the conditions and then moving objects to achieve the results we want, whether it is a pure chess problem or a math puzzles problem. It requires similar counting, logical thinking, spatial relation and visualization skills.

Learning Chess to Improve Math 数棋谜式健脑国际象棋
Ho Math Chess 何数棋谜 www.homathchess.com
Frank Ho, Amanda Ho © 1995 – 2021   All rights reserved.

Student name _____ Assignment date:_____

Attacking and Defending

Attacking and Defending	Counting and spatial relation
the number of attacking pieces = the number of defending pieces Will White win material by c4 x d5? Answer: _____ Reason: _____ 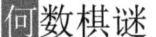	1. Take away two matchsticks in the following diagram to leave four equal-sized triangles. (Answer may vary.) 2. Take away 2 and rearrange the following matchsticks to leave two equal-sized triangles. (Answer may vary.)

Learning Chess to Improve Math

Ho Math Chess　www.homathchess.com

Frank Ho, Amanda Ho © 1995 – 2021　　All rights reserved.

Student name _____ Assignment date:_____

Attacking and Defending

Attacking and Defending	Counting
The number of attacking pieces = the number of defending pieces Will White win material by c4 x d5? Answer: _____ Reason: _____ 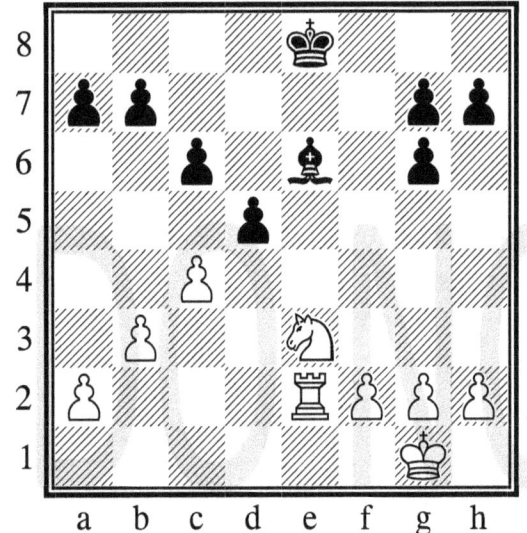	1. Rearrange matchsticks in the following diagram to leave eight equal-sized triangles. (Hint: tetrahedron, triangular pyramid)) (Answer may vary.) 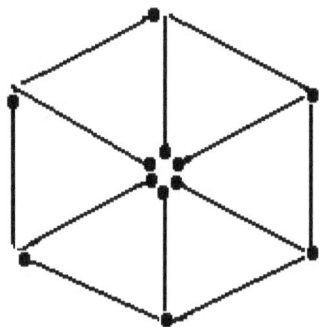 2. Take away four matchsticks in the following diagram to leave three equal-sized triangles. (Answer may vary.) 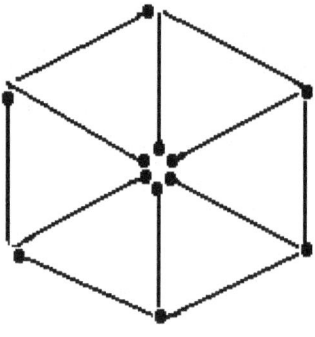

Learning Chess to Improve Math 数棋谜式健脑国际象棋

 Math Chess 何数棋谜 www.homathchess.com

Frank Ho, Amanda Ho © 1995 – 2021   All rights reserved.

Student name _____ Assignment date:_____

Attacking and Defending

Attacking and Defending	Counting
The number of attacking pieces > the number of defending pieces Shall White c4 attack Black d5? Answer: _____ Reason: _____ 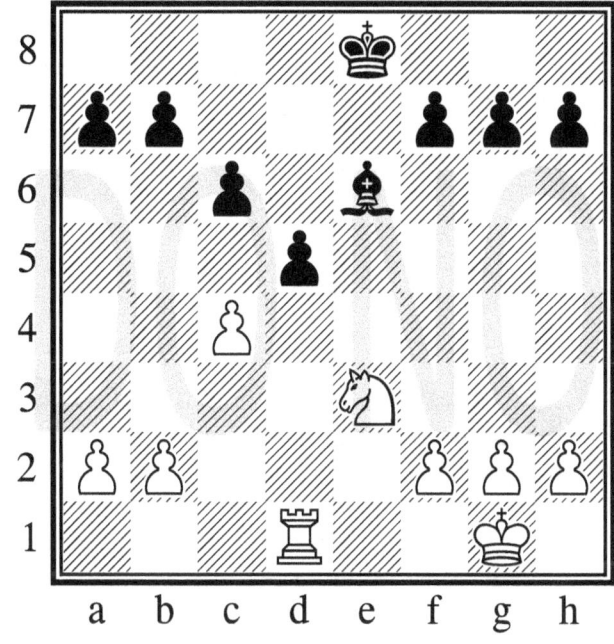	1. Take away 6 matchsticks in the following diagram to leave 2 squares. 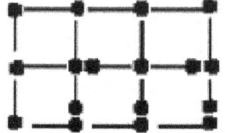 2. Take away three matchsticks in the following diagram to leave three squares. 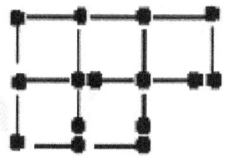 3. Take away two matchsticks in the following diagram to leave 2 squares. 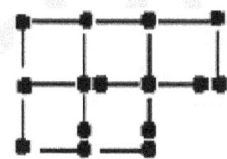

Learning Chess to Improve Math

Attacking and Defending

Attacking and Defending	Counting
The number of attacking pieces > the number of defending pieces but with unequal values of pieces Shall White Ne3  d5? Answer: _____ Reason: _____ 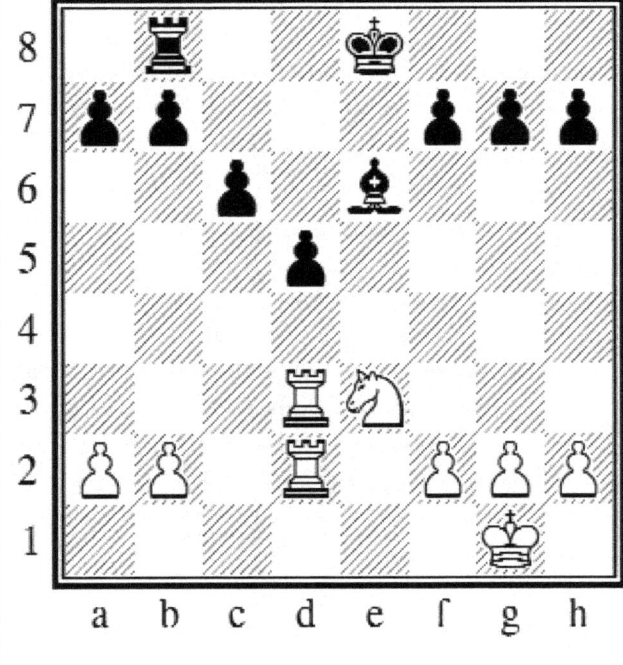	1. Take away four matchsticks in the following diagram to leave five squares only. 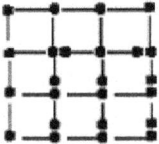 2. Take away 6 matchsticks in the following diagram to leave five squares. 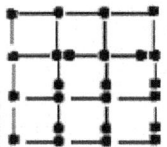 3. Take away 6 matchsticks in the following diagram to leave three squares (There is more than one solution). 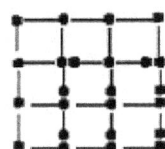

Learning Chess to Improve Math

Attacking and Defending

Attacking and Defending	Counting
The number of attacking pieces > the number of defending pieces, but shall White c4 attack d5? Answer: _____ Reason: _____	1. Carefulness is important in playing chess, so is working on math questions. Find all errors in the following computations and calculate the correct answers.

Circle the errors in computation	Correct computations
47 +28 615	47 +28
49 +94 1313	49 +94
412 −165 357	412 −165
417 −225 292	417 −225
35 ×23 915 70 985	35 ×23

Circle the errors in computation	Correct computations
406 4)16024 16 —— 24 24 —— 0	4)16024

Learning Chess to Improve Math   数棋谜式健脑国际象棋
 Math Chess   何数棋谜   www.homathchess.com

Frank Ho, Amanda Ho © 1995 – 2021   All rights reserved.

Student name _____ Assignment date:_____

Order of exchanges

Order of exchanges	Order of operations
The number of attacking pieces > the number of defending pieces but with unequal values of pieces Shall White c4 attack Black d5? Answer: _____ Reason: _____ 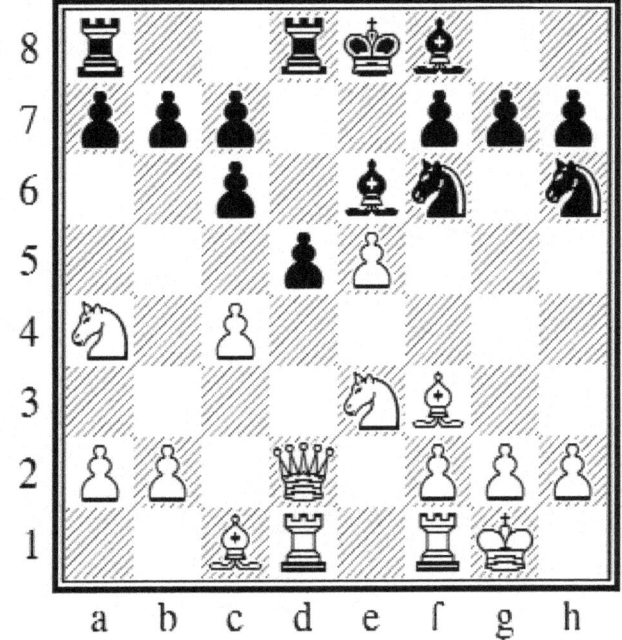	The left chess diagram shows how important the order of exchanged pieces is. In arithmetic, the order of how numbers are calculated is very important
	2 × 5 + 3 = _____ | 2 + 5 × 3 = _____
	4 × 25 = _____ | 25 × 4 = _____
	8 × 125 = _____ | 125 × 8 = _____
	25 − 5 × 2 = ___ | 20 × 5 − 4 − 25 = ___
	Sometimes, knowing how to calculate numbers in a particular order could get answers easily.
	2 × 17 × 5 = | 5 × 2317 × 2 =
	32 × 25 × 125 (Hint: 32 = 4 × 8) = | 125 × 13 × 8 (Hint: do 125 × 8 first) =
	32 × 25 = 32 × $\frac{100}{4}$ = | 32 × 125 = 32 × $\frac{1000}{8}$ =
	36 × 25 = 36 × $\frac{100}{4}$ = | 48 × 125 = 48 × $\frac{1000}{8}$ =

Visualization and think ahead

Visualization and think ahead	Observe and think
What is White's next move? Observe the diagram very carefully and think ahead. Show White's move by drawing an arrow. 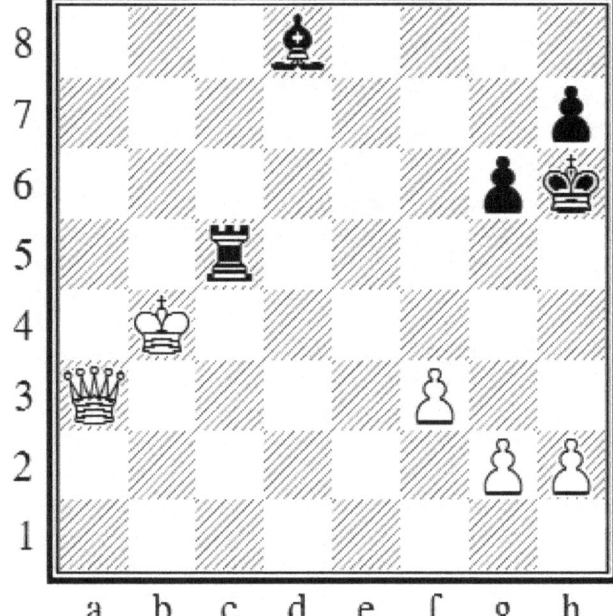	Doing math sometimes means one must observe the numbers' relations very carefully. Take your time and be patient to observe the following number pattern before you start to add the two numbers you happen to see from left to right. Calculate the sum of the following expression with no calculator. 100 − 98 + 99 − 97 + 98 − 96 + 94 = 81 + 118 + 9 + 5815 + 782 + 3185 + 9 = 1+2+3+4+5 = 11 + 12+13+ +14+15 − ___ Adam is 3 cm taller than Andrea and is 2 cm shorter than Andrew. Andrew is ___ cm ___ than Andrea. Brian weighs 5 kg more than Brighton and together they weigh 105kg. How much does Brian weigh? _____

Zugzwang

Zugzwang is a German word meaning "compulsion to move". In chess, zugzwang happens when it is one player's turn to move, but none of the moves is good. In other words, the fact that the player must make a move has forced them into a weakling position is called zugzwang.

Zugzwang	Doing unnecessary work
If it's a White move, what is White's next move? Mark each square with an X of all possible moves. What happens to White's pawn? _____ If it's Black move, what is Black's next move? Mark each square with an X of all possible moves. 4. What happens to Black's pawn? _____ The following case is zugzwang because whoever moves first loses a pawn. 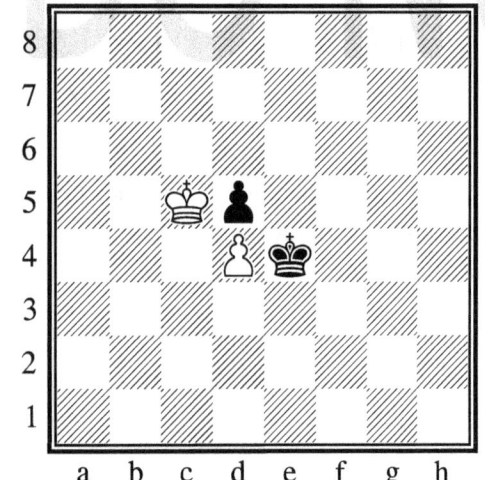	If making a move is considered a disadvantage in chess, then analogy in math is doing something that is not really necessary. In fact, it has a disadvantage in making wrong calculations in solving math problems. One rather wished they had not done anything. Circle the calculations (all are student's real work) that have been done wrong in the following questions. (1). $32 \times \frac{16}{25} = \frac{\cancel{32}\,4}{1} \times \frac{\cancel{16}\,2}{25} = \frac{8}{25}$ (2). $6 \times \frac{34}{34} = \frac{6}{1} \times \frac{34}{34} = \frac{\cancel{6}\,3}{1} \times \frac{\cancel{34}\,17}{34} = \frac{51}{34}$ (3). $4\frac{1}{3} + 1\frac{1}{2} = \frac{13}{3} + \frac{3}{2} = \frac{16}{5}$ (4). $4\frac{1}{3} - 1\frac{1}{2} = \frac{13}{3} - \frac{3}{2} = \frac{10}{1} = 10$

Overworked piece

Overworked piece	Overworked by skiprh4g steps
Show White's next best move by an arrow. 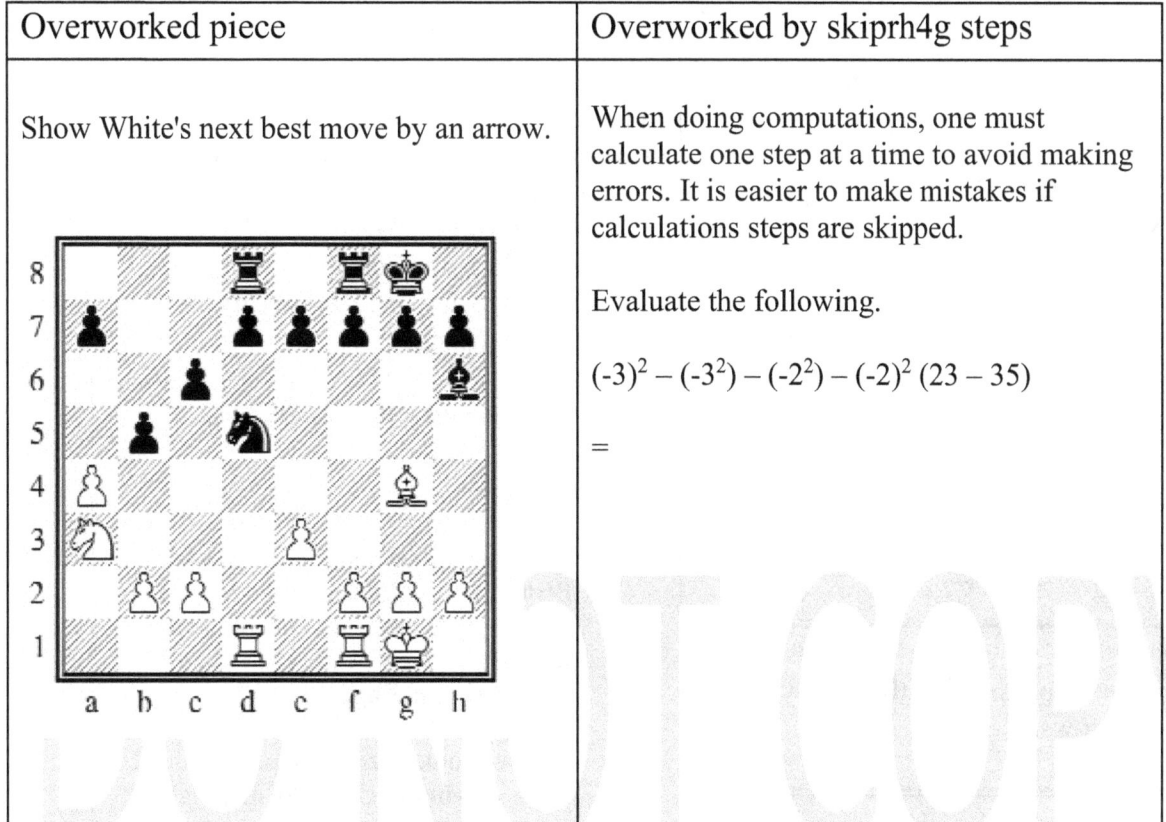	When doing computations, one must calculate one step at a time to avoid making errors. It is easier to make mistakes if calculations steps are skipped. Evaluate the following. $(-3)^2 - (-3^2) - (-2^2) - (-2)^2 (23 - 35)$ =

Part 5 Castling

Castling	Exchanging numbers
Show White's possible castling(s) by drawing 2 arrows. 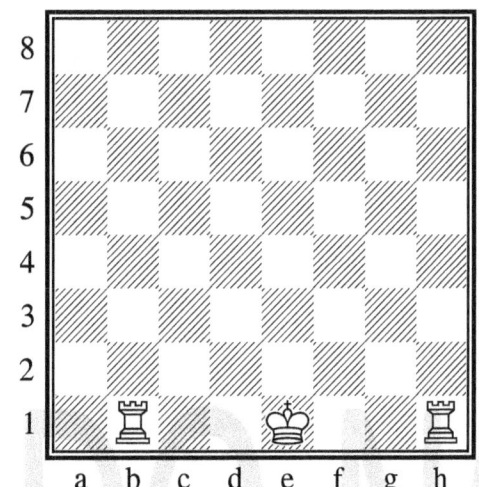 Show White's possible castling(s) by drawing arrows. 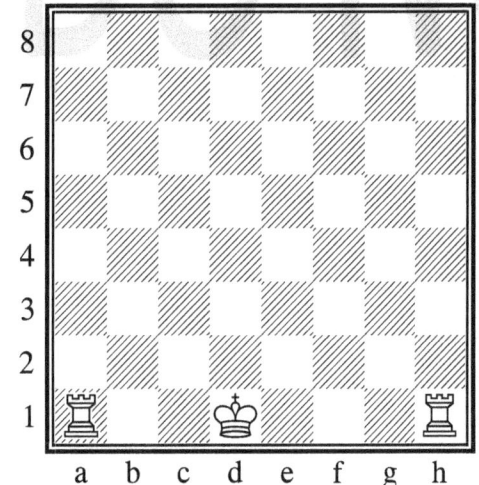 King has moved, so no castling.	In chess, king and rook can be moved at the same time when castling and the moves are considered as one move, but there are restrictions on when the castling can be done. In math, 2 numbers can exchange places but there are also restrictions on when they can be exchanged. **The restrictions of castling are:** 2 conditions: 1. The way to the castle must be clear. Bishop and knight must be moved on the kingside castling. Queen, bishop, the knight must be moved to queenside castling. 2. Neither rook nor king can be moved. Even moving back to the original squares still will make casting legal. 3 checks: 1. King cannot be in check 2. King cannot castle through check. 3. King cannot castle into check. Circle the following expressions if you think the exchanges of numbers are wrong. $3 + 2 = 2 + 3$ $4 \times 6 = 6 \times 4$

Castling

Castling	Exchanging numbers
Show White's possible castling(s) by drawing arrows.  Show White's possible castling(s) by drawing arrows. Note Rook just moved back to h1 from g1. 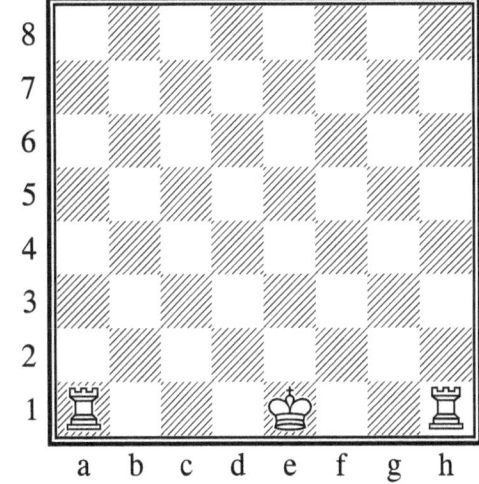	In chess, king and rook can be moved at the same time when castling and the moves are considered as one move, but there are restrictions on when the castling can be done. In math, 2 numbers can exchange places but there are also restrictions on when they can be exchanged. Circle the following expressions if you think the exchanges of numbers are wrong. $6 - 4 = 4 - 6$ $4 + 6 = 6 + 4$

Castling

Castling	Exchanging numbers
Show White's possible castling(s) by drawing arrows. 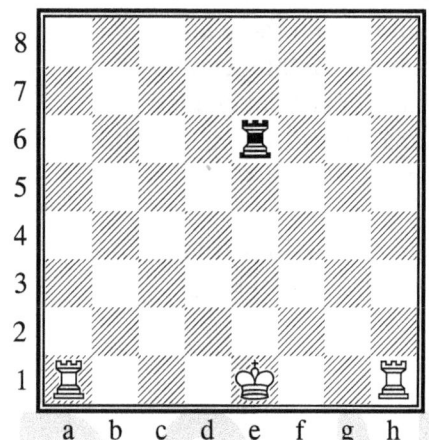 Show White's possible castling(s) by drawing arrows. 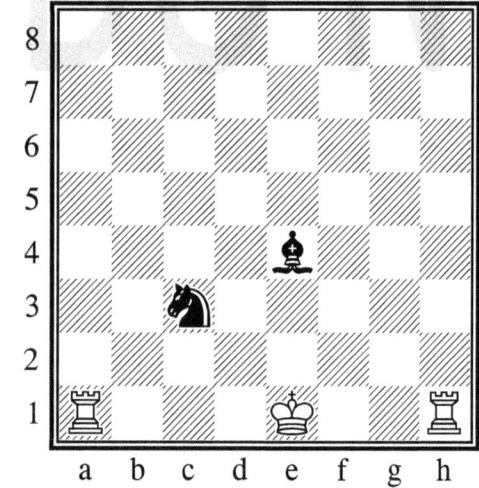	In chess, king and rook can be moved at the same time when castling and the moves are considered as one move, but there are restrictions on when the castling can be done. In math, 2 numbers can exchange places but there are also restrictions on when they can be exchanged. Circle the following expressions if you think the exchanges of numbers are wrong. $2 + 3 + 4 = 4 + 3 + 2$ $8 - 4 - 2 = 2 - 4 - 8$

Castling

Castling	Exchanging numbers
Show White's possible castling(s) by drawing arrows. 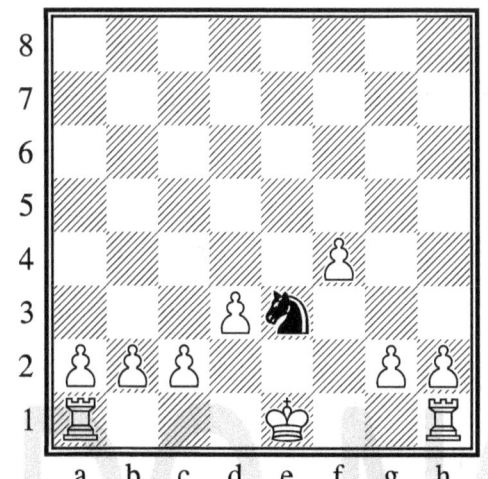 Show White's possible castling(s) by drawing arrows. **Note Rook just moved back to h1 from g1.** 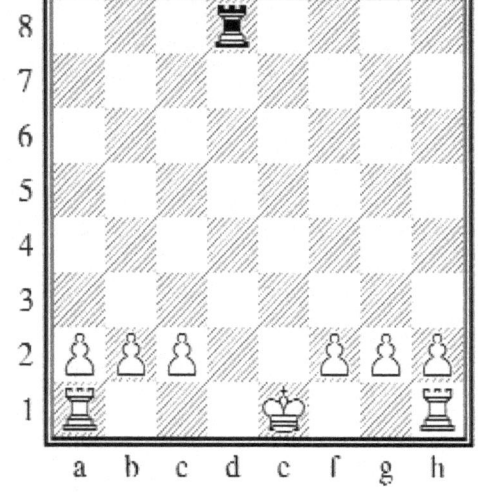	In chess, king and rook can be moved at the same time when castling and the moves are considered as one move, but there are restrictions on when the castling can be done. In math, 2 numbers can exchange places but there are also restrictions on when they can be exchanged. Circle the following expressions if you think the exchanges of numbers are wrong. $6 \div 4 = 4 \div 6$ $2 \times 3 + 2 = 3 \times 2 + 2$

Castling

Castling	Exchanging numbers
Show White's possible castling(s) by drawing arrows.  Show White's possible castling(s) by drawing arrows. 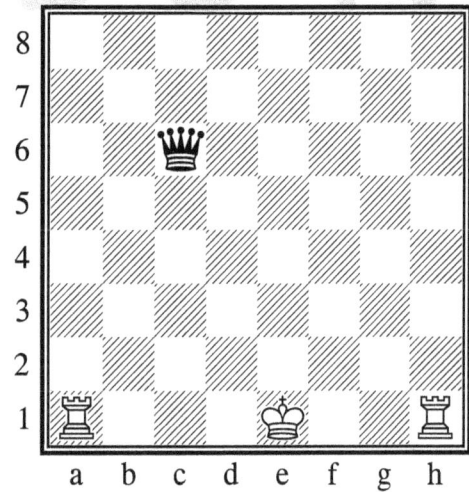	In chess, king and rook can be moved at the same time when castling and the moves are considered as one move, but there are restrictions on when the castling can be done. In math, 2 numbers can exchange places but there are also restrictions on when they can be exchanged. Circle the following expressions if you think the exchanges of numbers are wrong. $2 \times (3+2) = 2 \times (2+3)$ $6 \div 3 + 2 = 3 \div 6 + 2$

Learning Chess to Improve Math

Part 6 Tactics - Fork, Pin, Skewer, and Discovered Check

The four most important and common chess skills (tactics) are forks, pins, skewers, and discovered checks. The main difference between these chess tactics is how chess pieces are positioned.

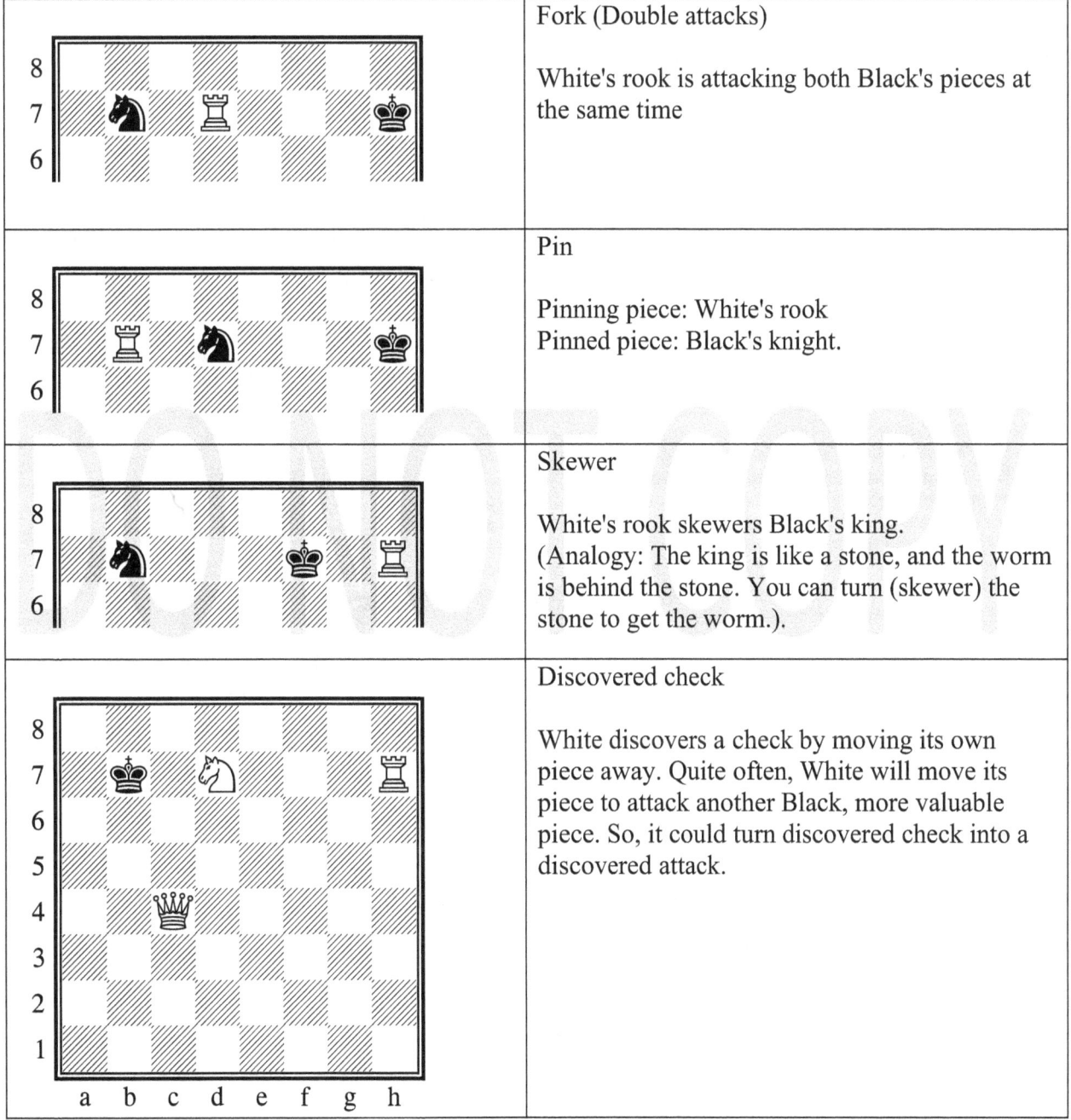

Fork (Double attacks)

White's rook is attacking both Black's pieces at the same time

Pin

Pinning piece: White's rook
Pinned piece: Black's knight.

Skewer

White's rook skewers Black's king.
(Analogy: The king is like a stone, and the worm is behind the stone. You can turn (skewer) the stone to get the worm.).

Discovered check

White discovers a check by moving its own piece away. Quite often, White will move its piece to attack another Black, more valuable piece. So, it could turn discovered check into a discovered attack.

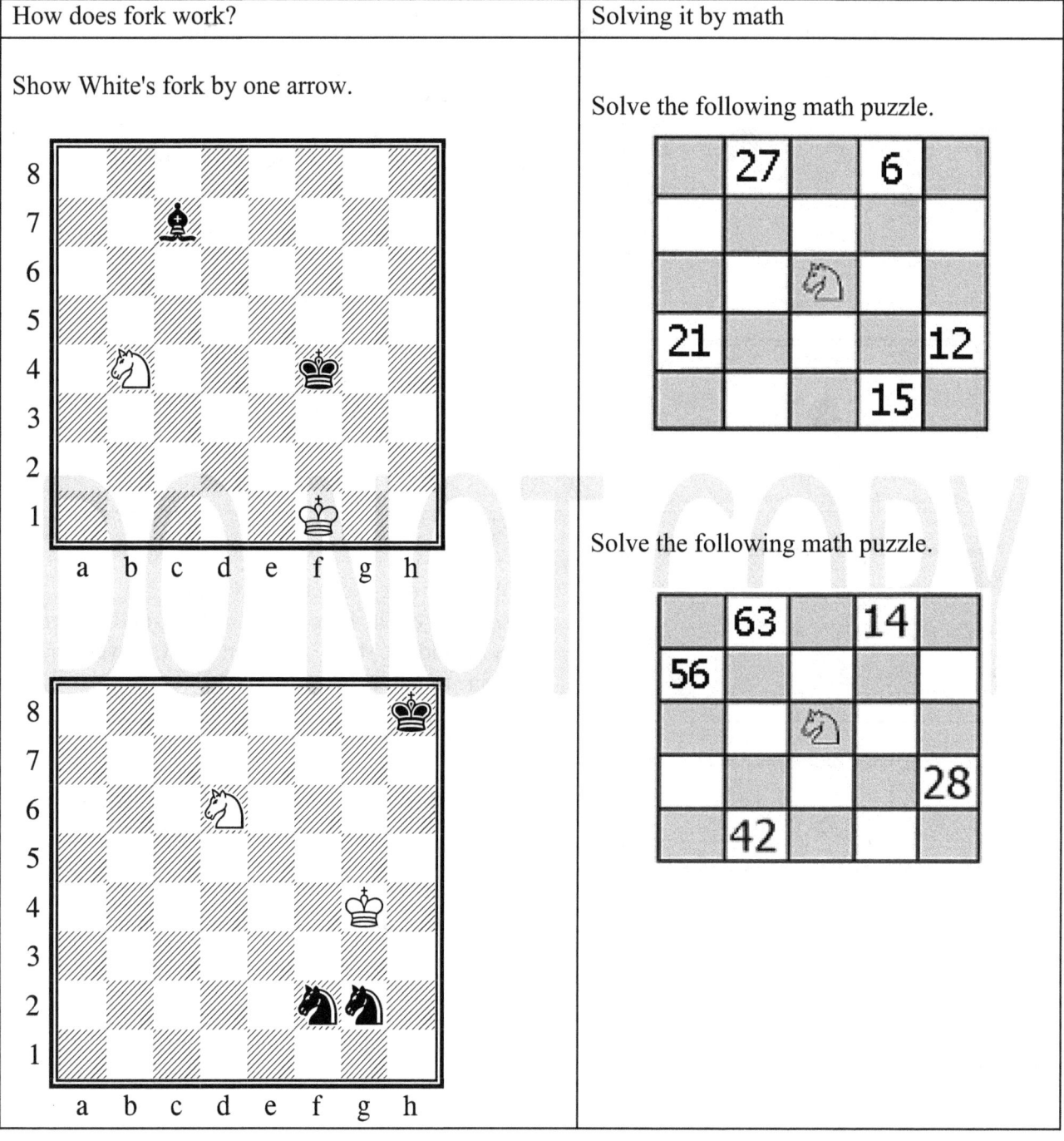

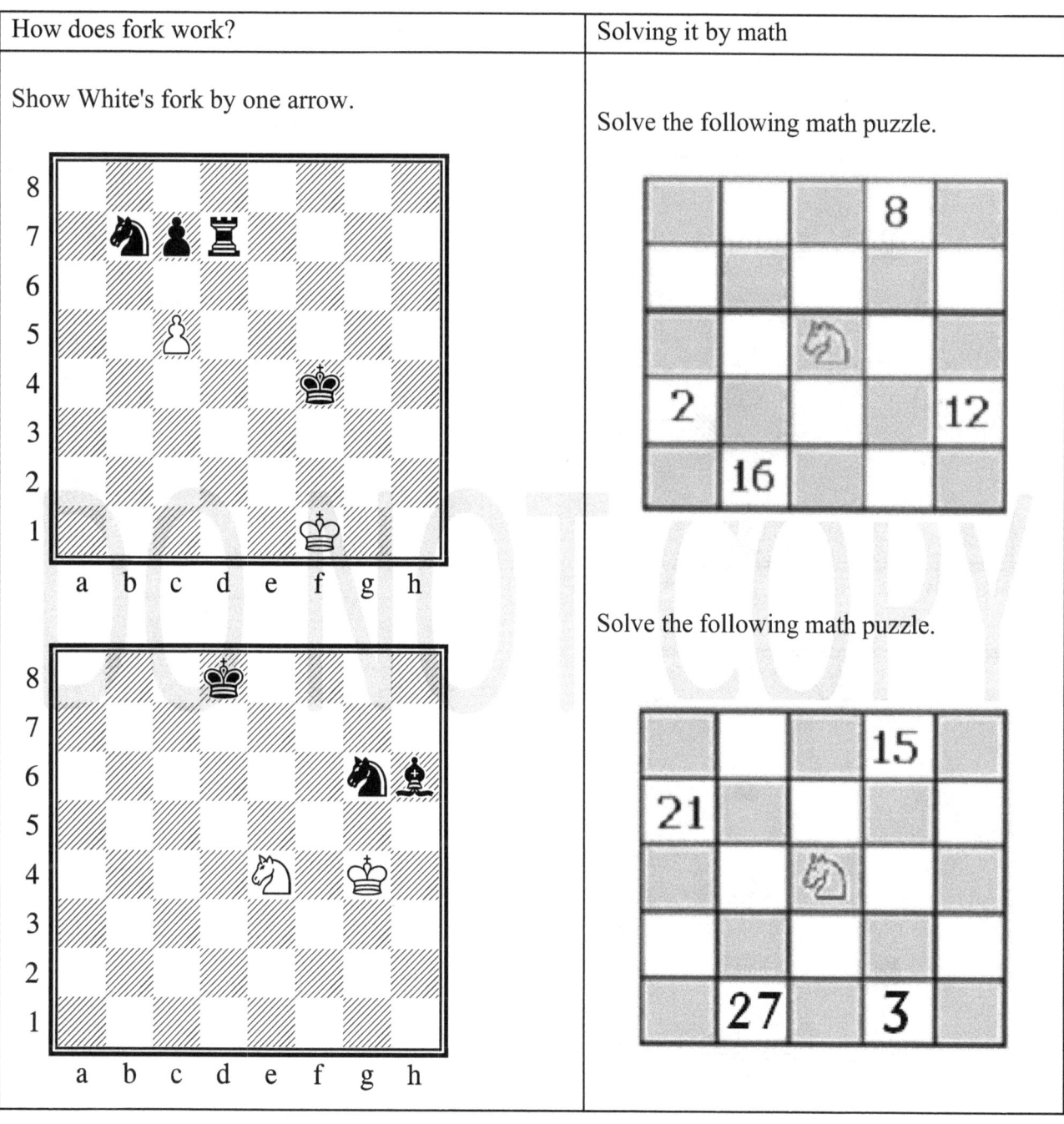

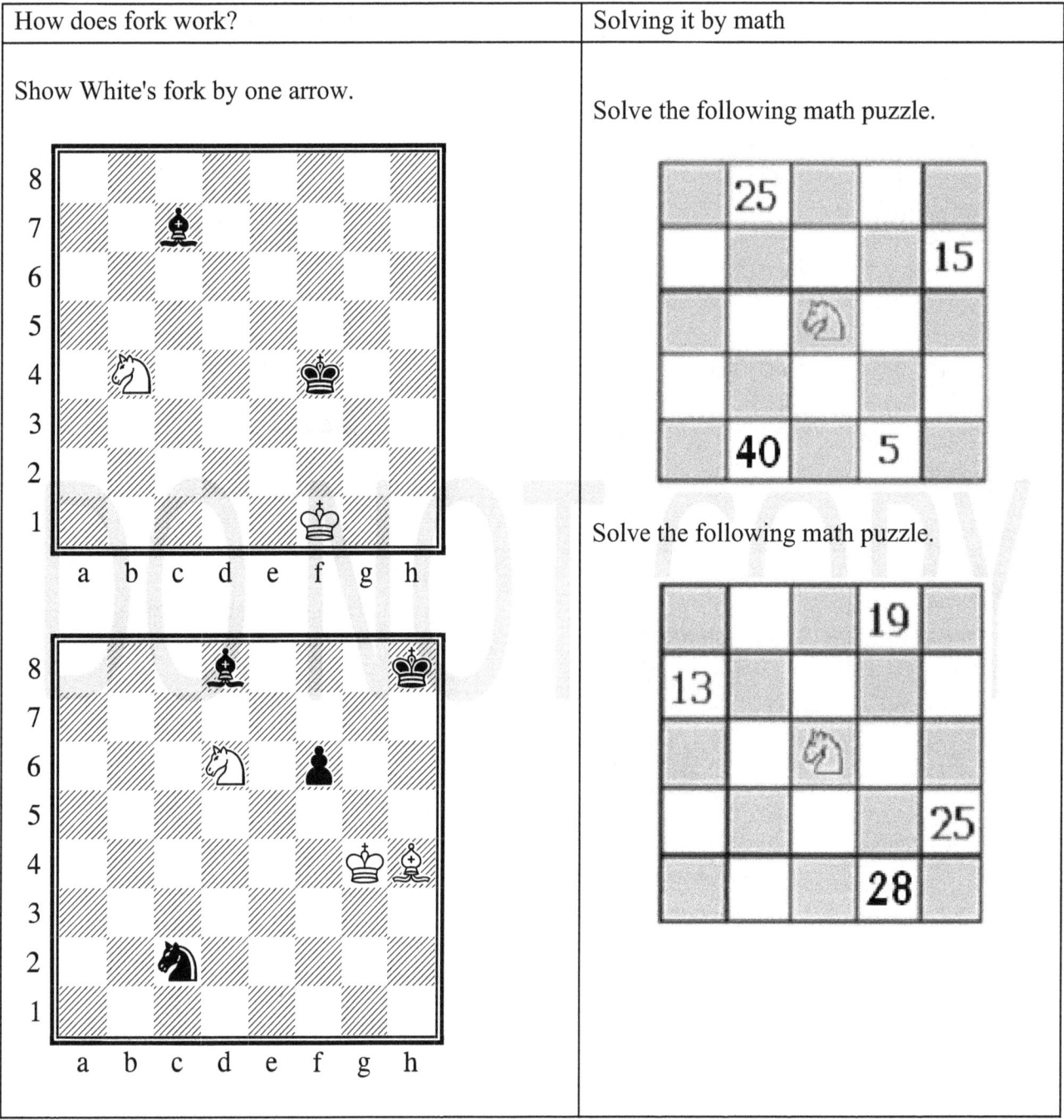

Learning Chess to Improve Math

Ho Math Chess www.homathchess.com

Frank Ho, Amanda Ho © 1995 – 2021   All rights reserved.

Student name _____ Assignment date:_____

How does the fork work?

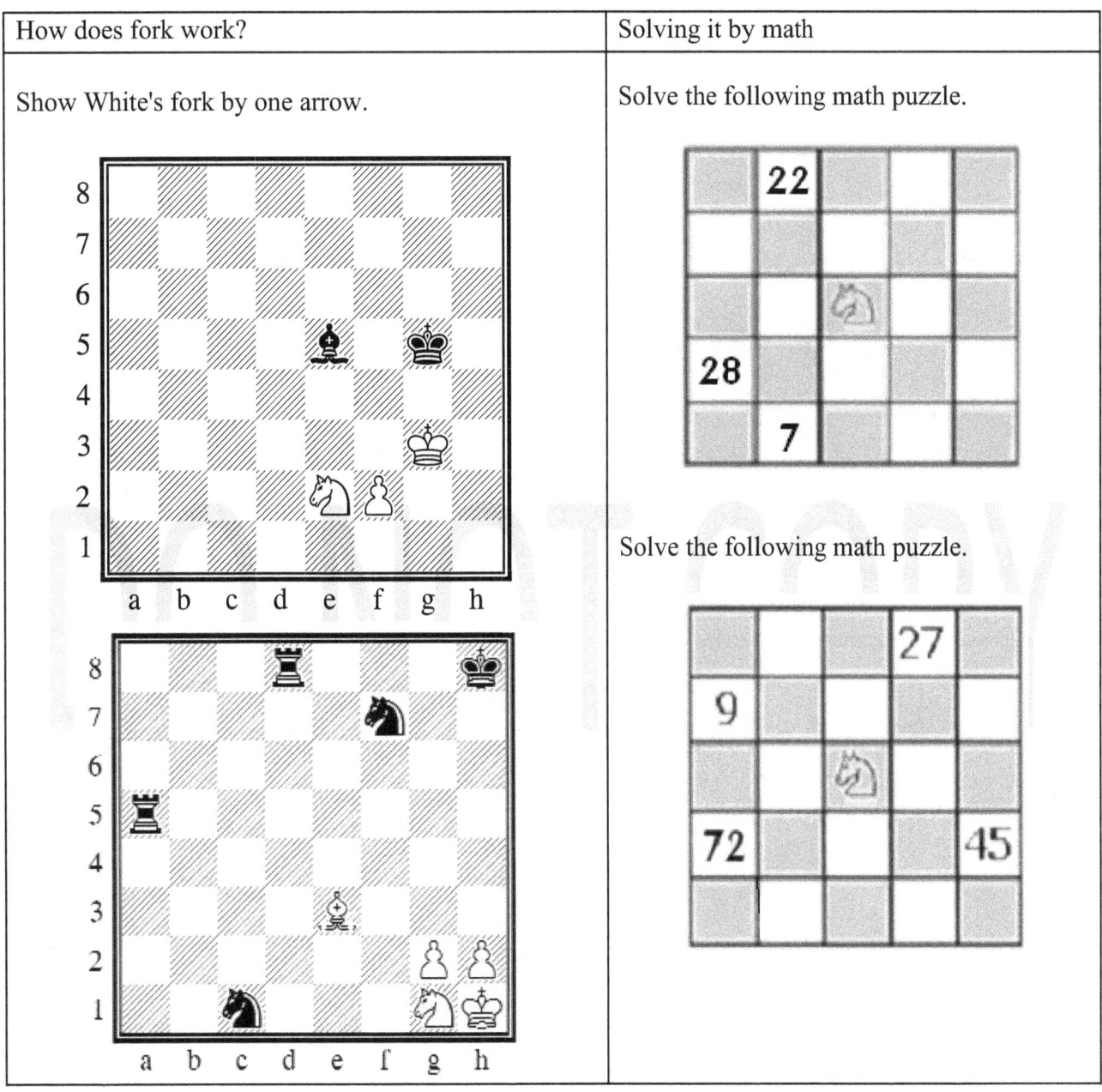

Learning Chess to Improve Math 数棋谜式健脑国际象棋

Ho Math Chess 何数棋谜 www.homathchess.com

Frank Ho, Amanda Ho © 1995 – 2021   All rights reserved.

Student name _____ Assignment date:_____

How does the pin work?

How does the pin work?	Magic numbers
Show White's pain by an arrow.  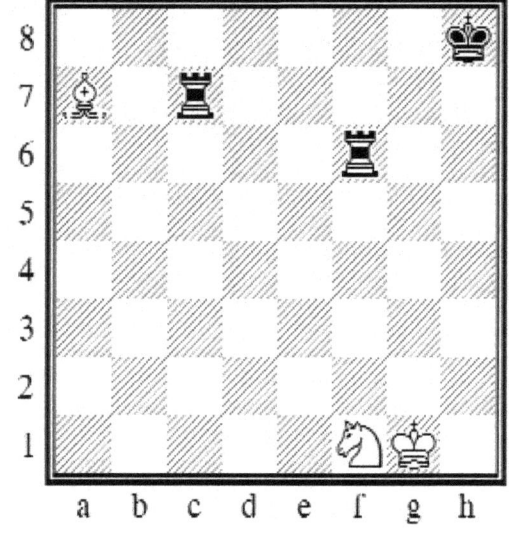	The visualization is important in playing good chess. Many math problems require good visualization skills. ## Magic Square A magic square is a square of numbers in which every row, column and main diagonal add up to the same sum. Replace each of the following ? by a number. | 7	?	3
---	---	---
?	6	?
?	?	5	 ## Magic triangle Place numbers 1, 2, 3, 4, 5, 6 in the following triangle so that the sum of numbers on each side of the triangle always adds to 10. (Hint: 3 × 10 = 30 − 1 − 2 − 3 − 4 − 5 − 6 = 9, What are the three corner numbers adding up to 9?) 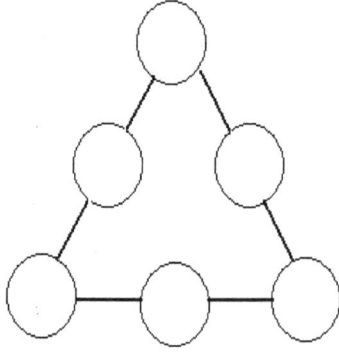

Learning Chess to Improve Math 数棋谜式健脑国际象棋

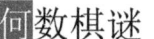 Math Chess 何数棋谜 www.homathchess.com

Frank Ho, Amanda Ho © 1995 – 2021   All rights reserved.

Student name _____ Assignment date:_____

How does the pin work?

How does the pin work?	Magic numbers
Show White's pin by an arrow. 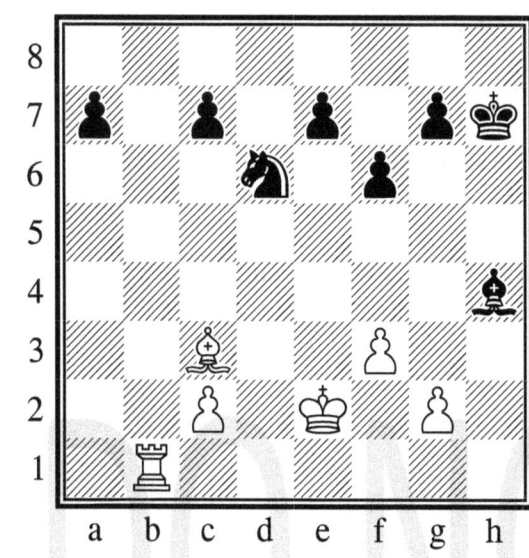 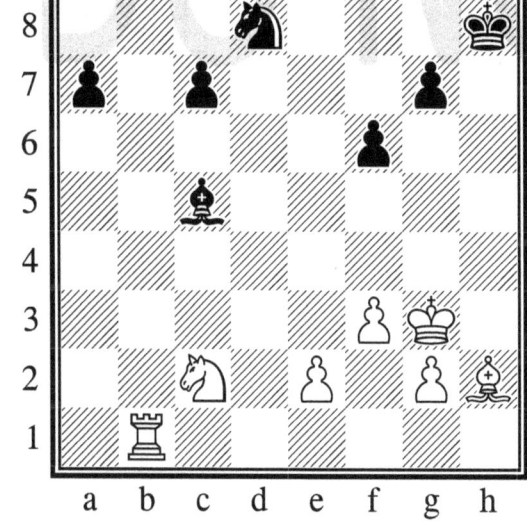	The visualization is important in playing good chess. Many math problems require good visualization skills. ### Magic Diamond A magic diamond is a diamond of numbers in which every line adds up to the same sum. Fill in each of the following ◯ by a number. 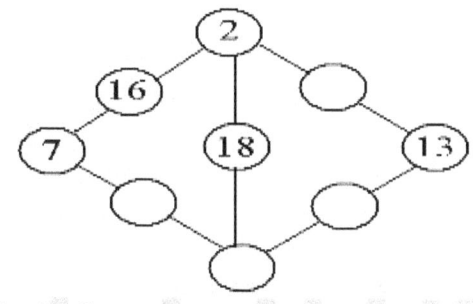 ### Magic Star A magic star is a star of numbers in which every line adds up to the same sum. Fill in each of the following ◯ by a number. 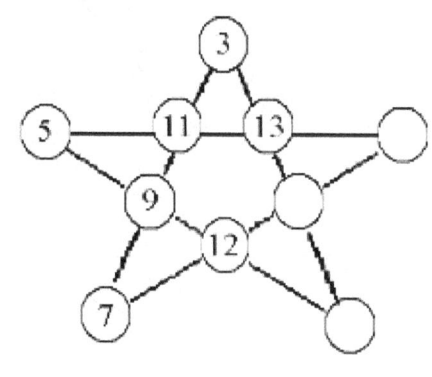

How does the pin work?

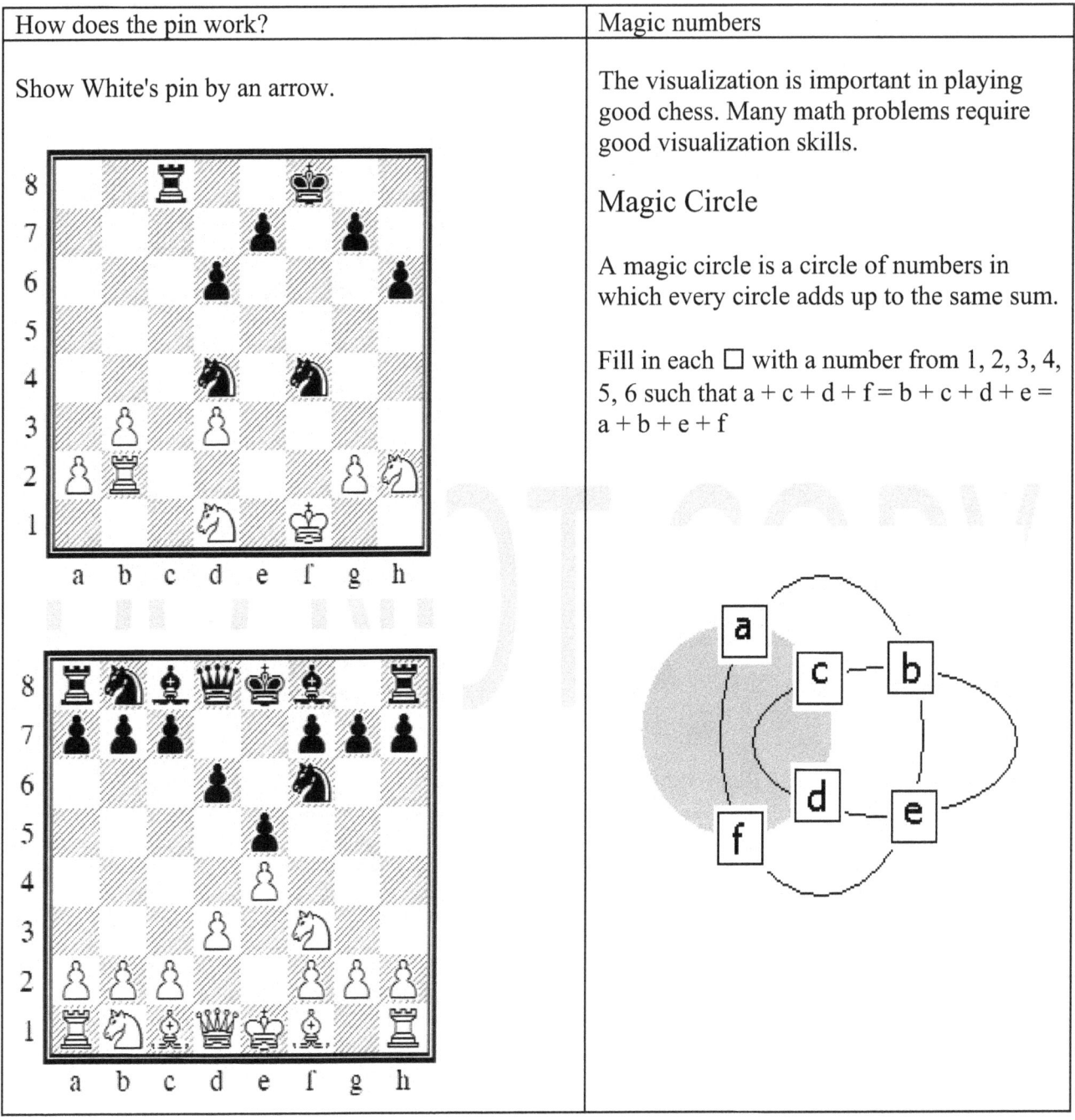

Using a pin to win a piece

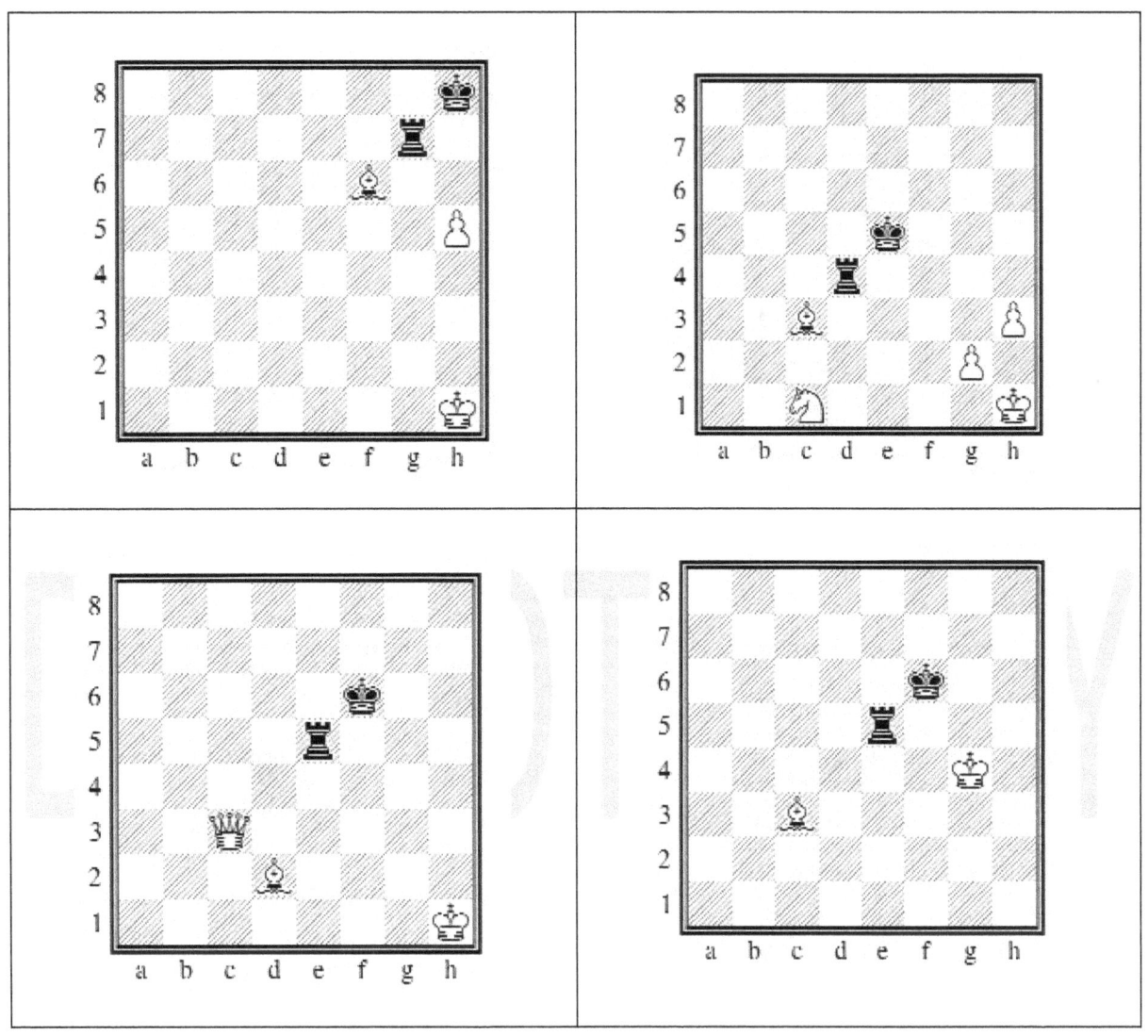

Use a pin to win a piece

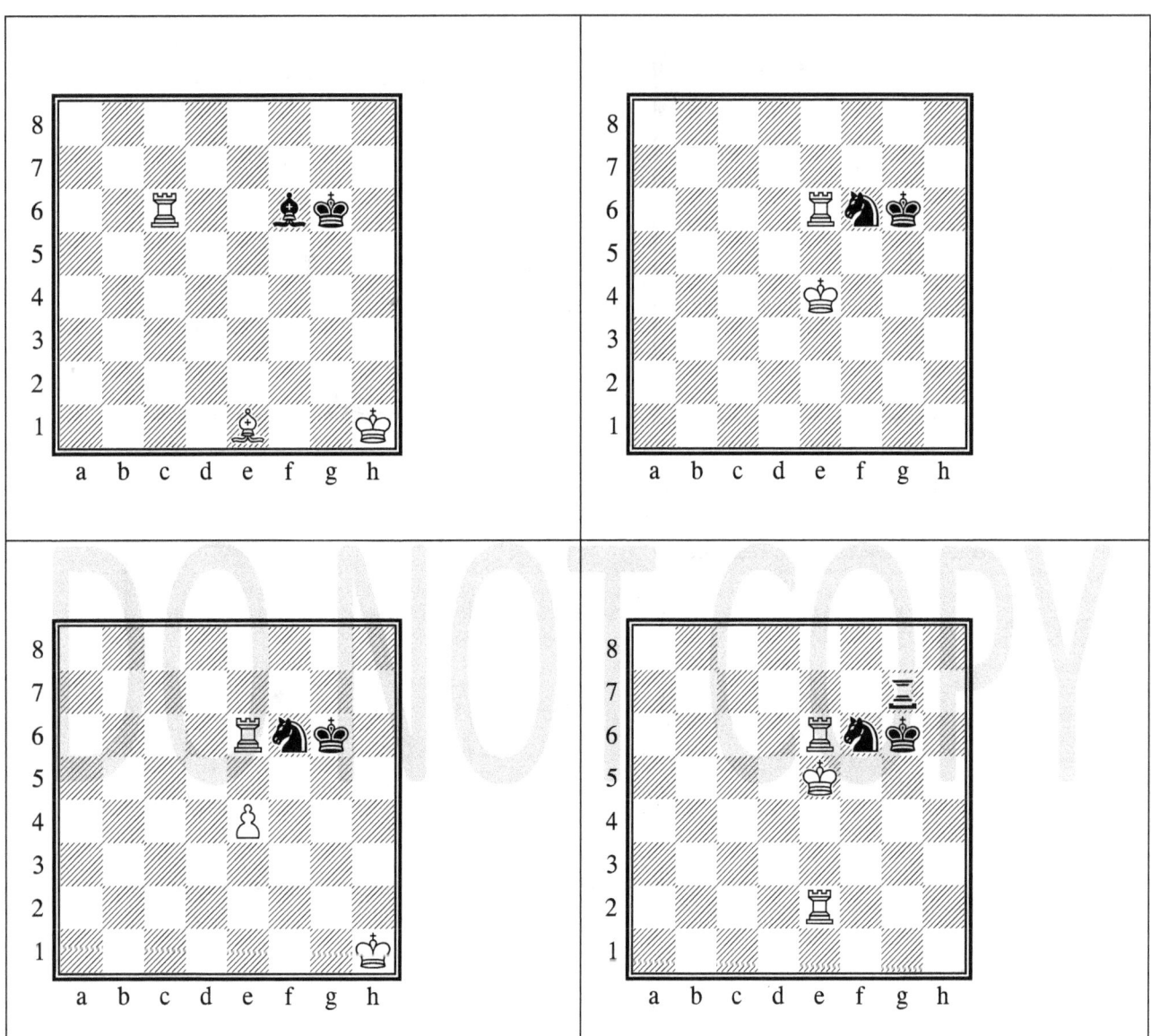

Does White's pin win?

Black to move by showing an arrow.

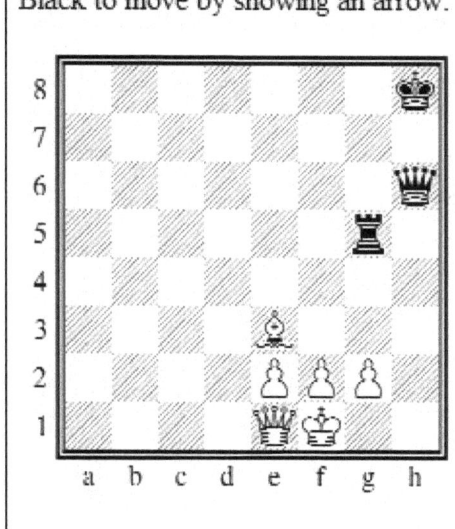

Black to move by showing an arrow.

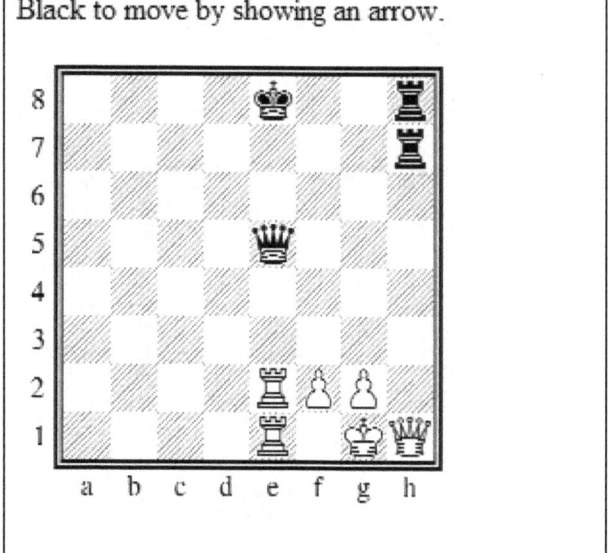

White to unpin by showing an arrow.

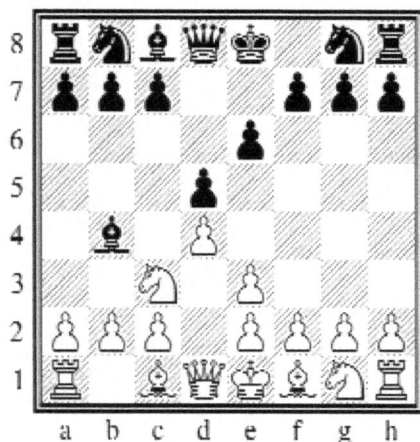

Black to unpin by showing an arrow.

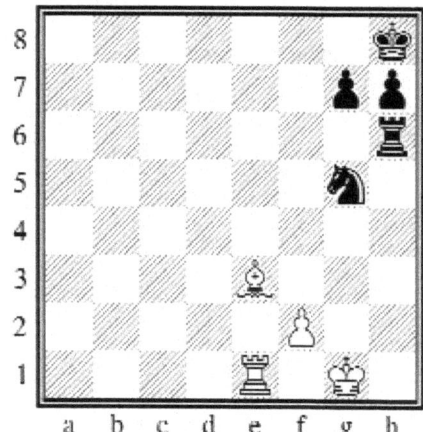

Learning Chess to Improve Math

How does the discovered check work?

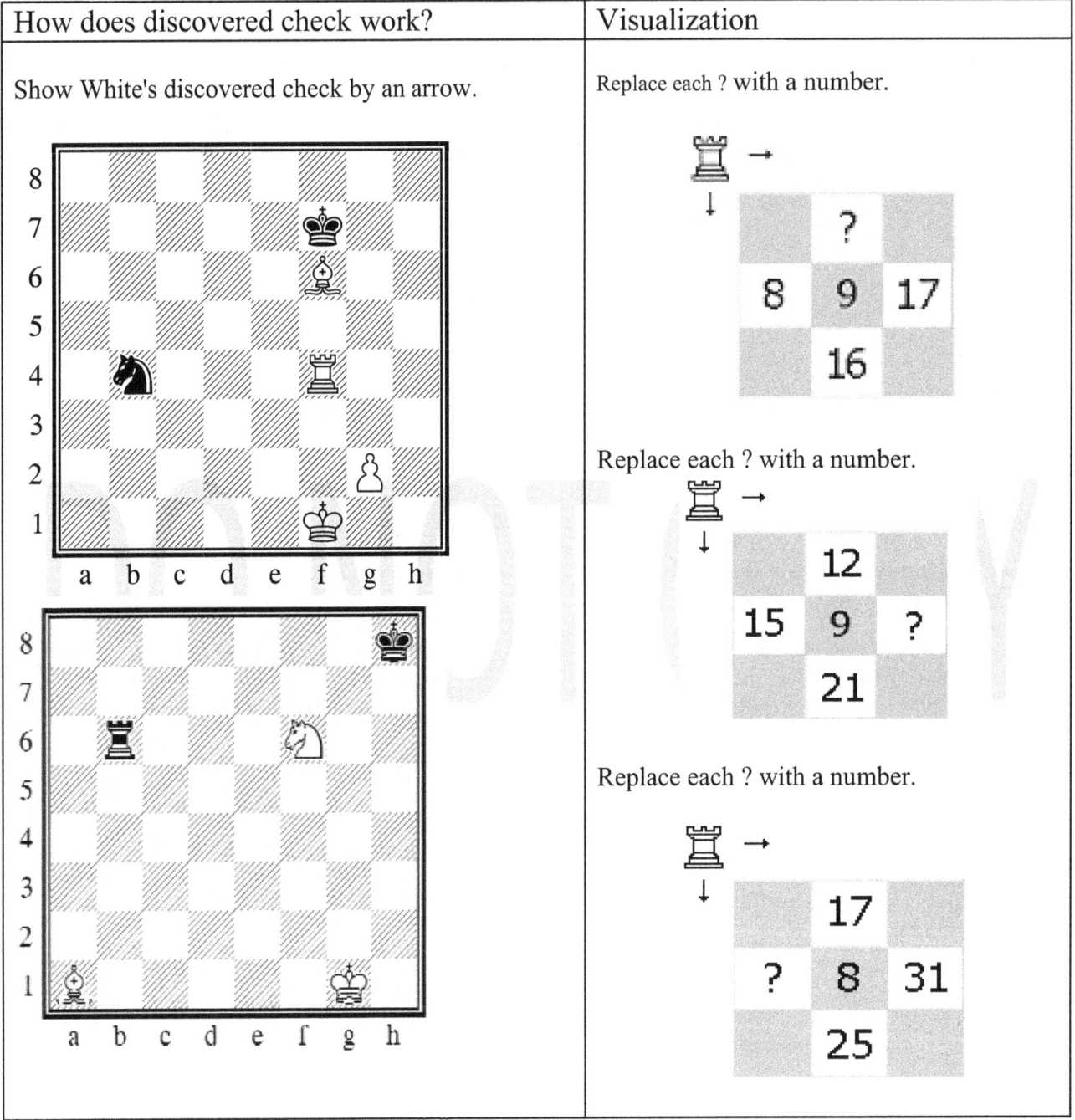

Learning Chess to Improve Math

Ho Math Chess www.homathchess.com

Frank Ho, Amanda Ho © 1995 – 2021   All rights reserved.

Student name _____ Assignment date: _____

How does the discovered check work?

How does discovered check work?	Visualization
Show White's discovered check by an arrow. 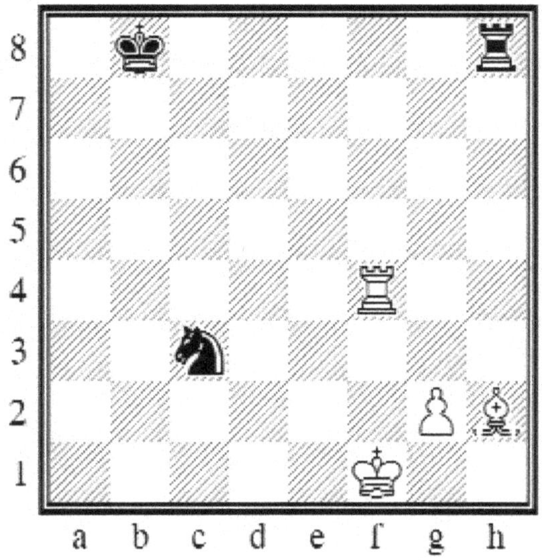 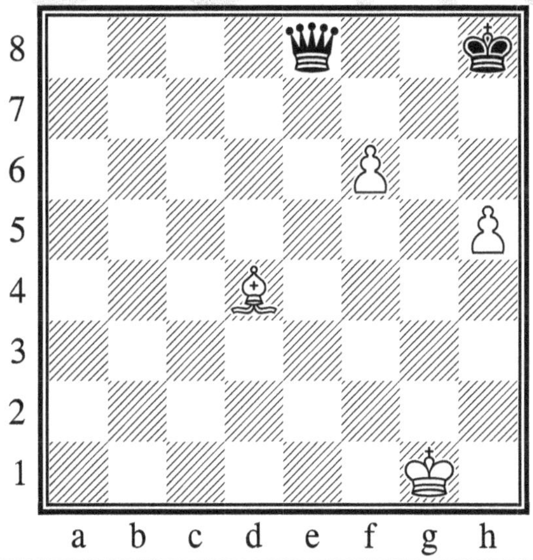	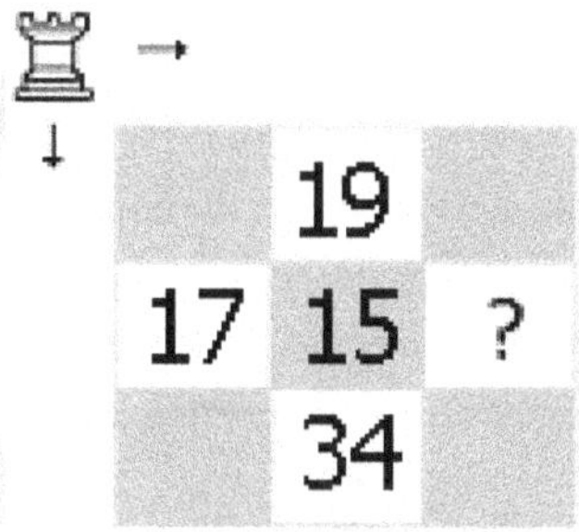 Replace each ? with a number. 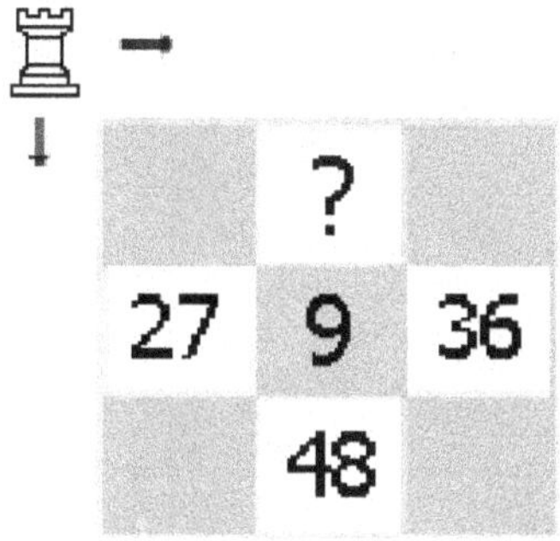 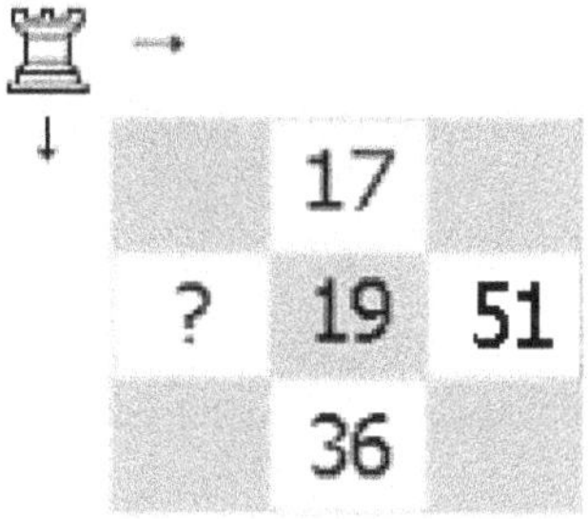

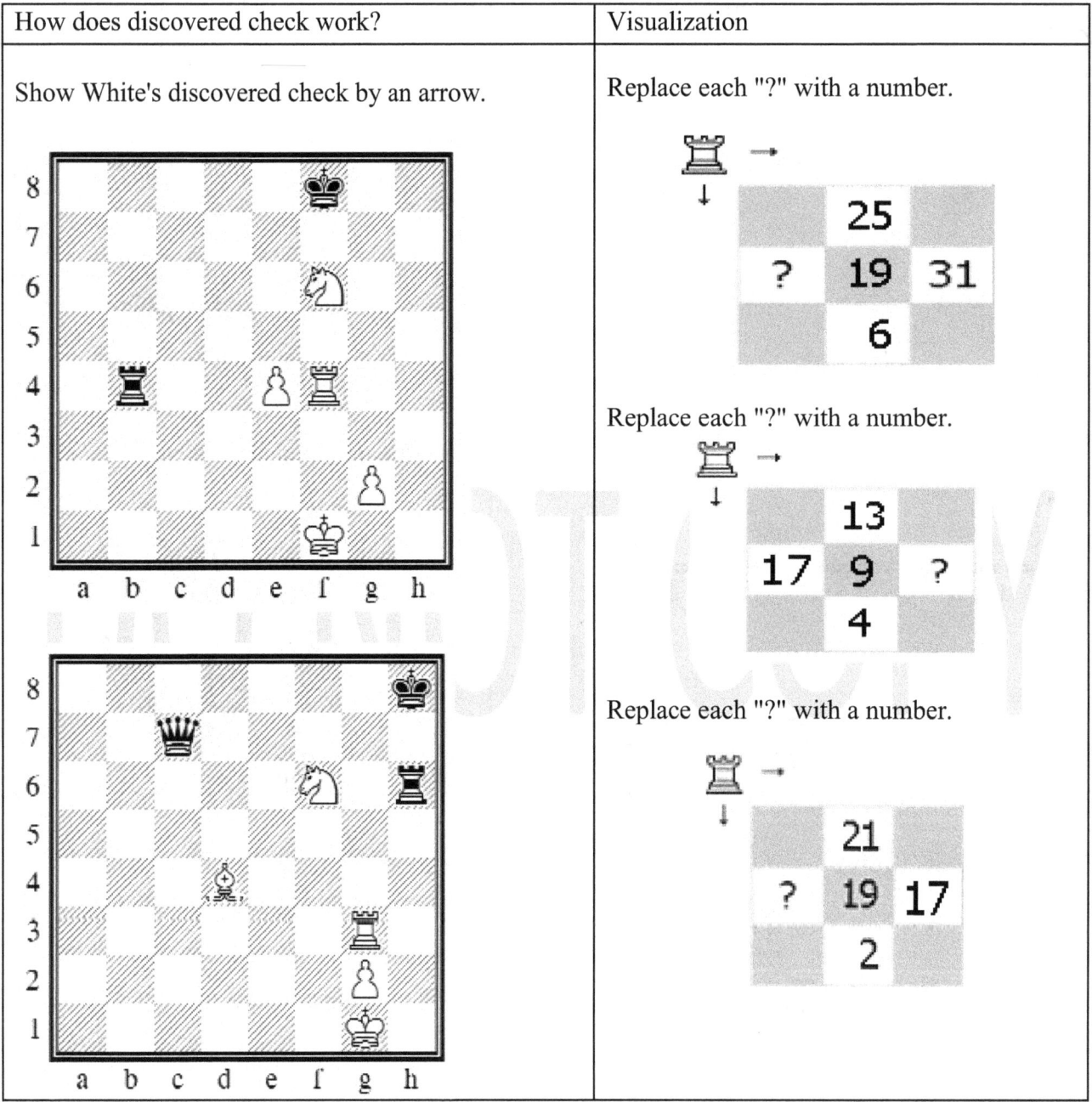

How does the discovered check work?

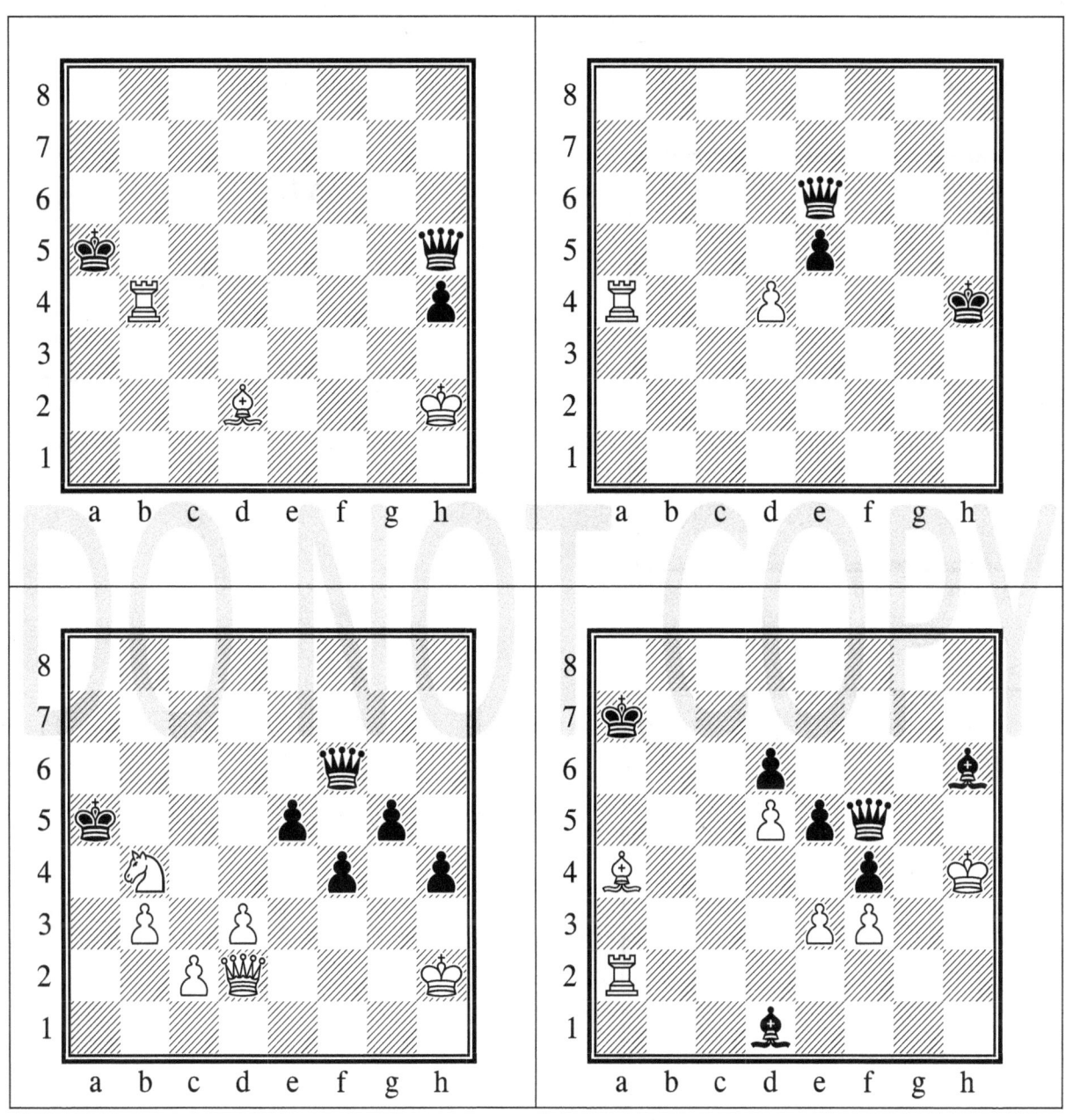

Learning Chess to Improve Math

How does the skewer work?

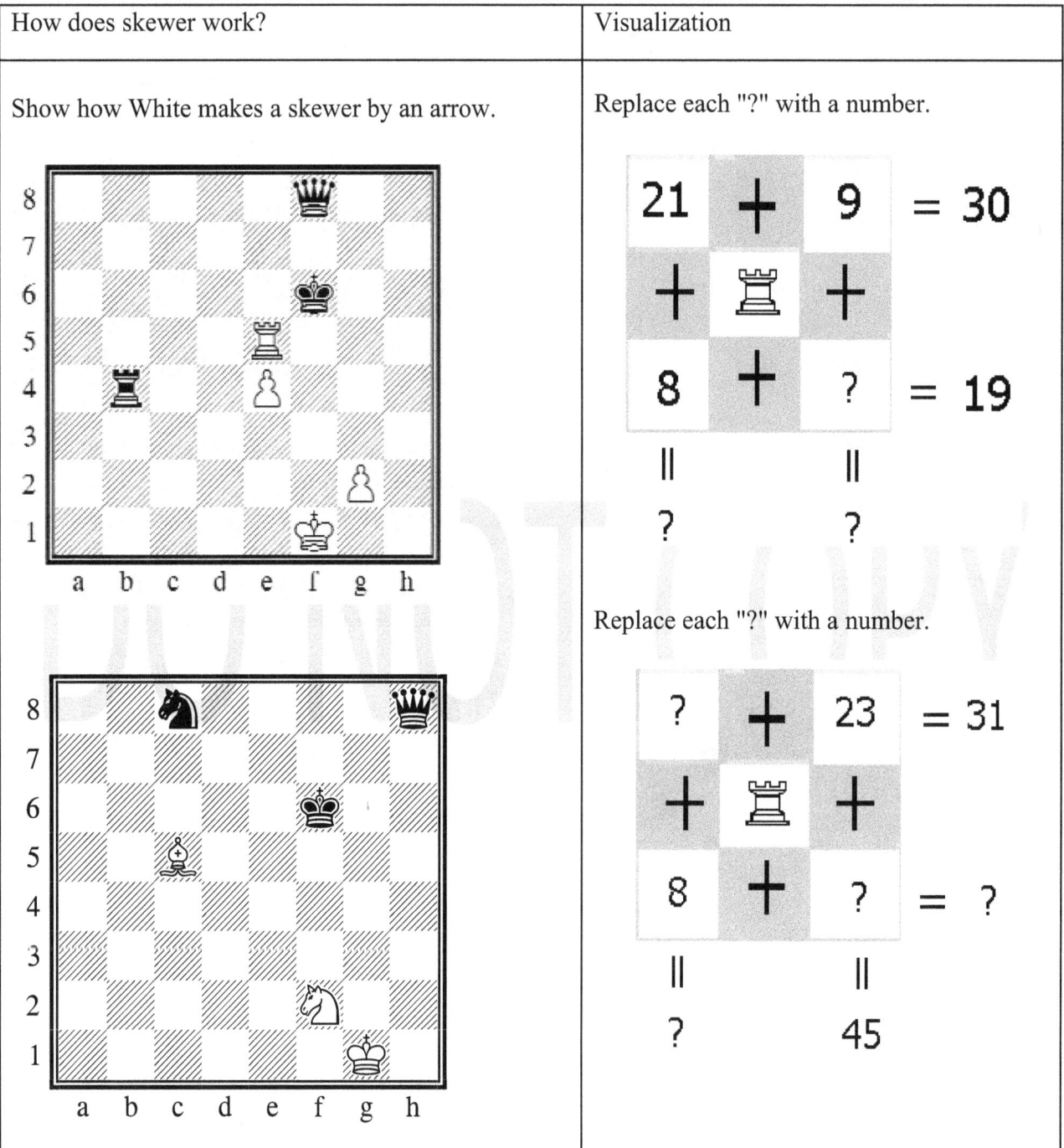

How does the skewer work?

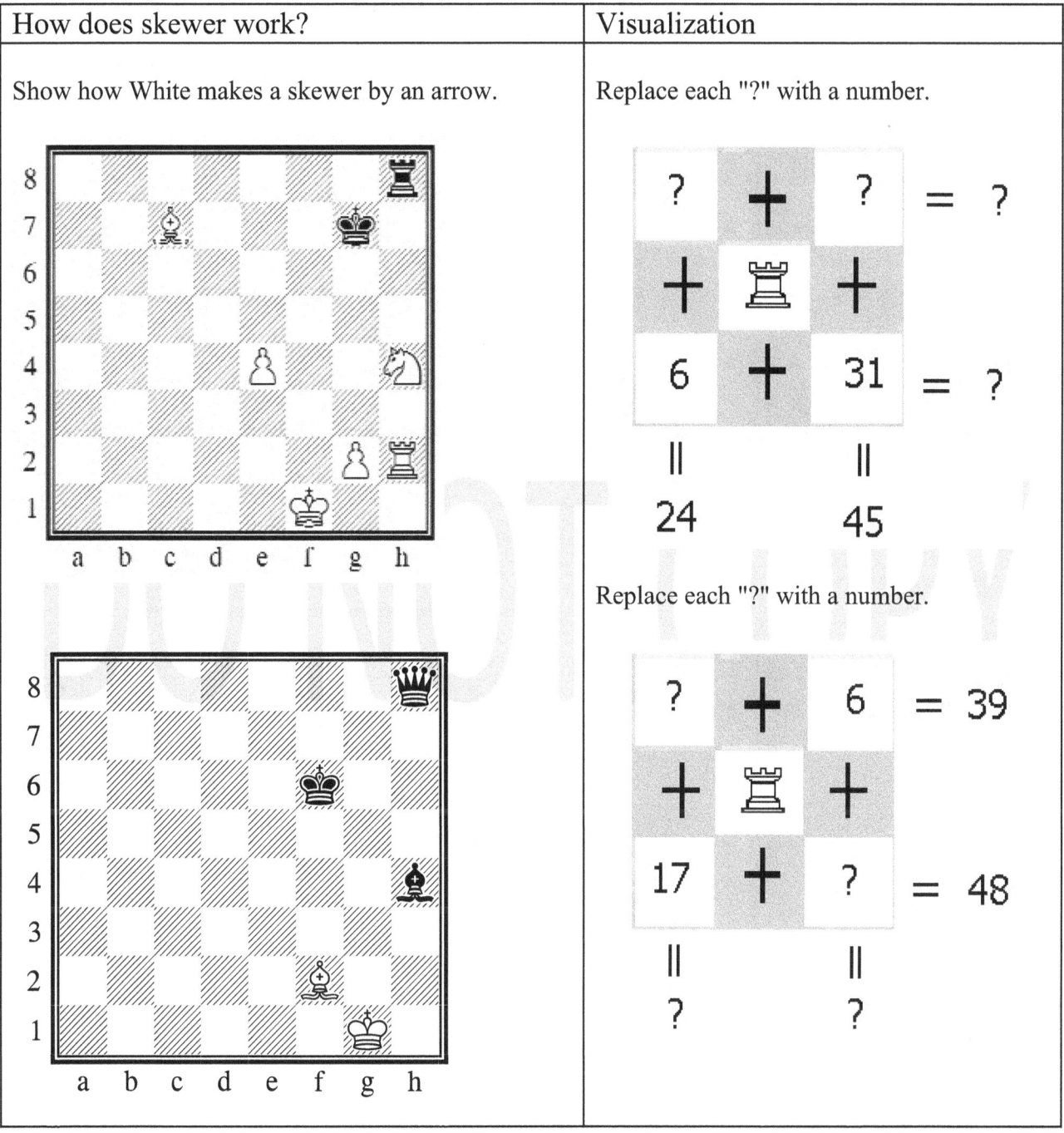

How does the skewer work?

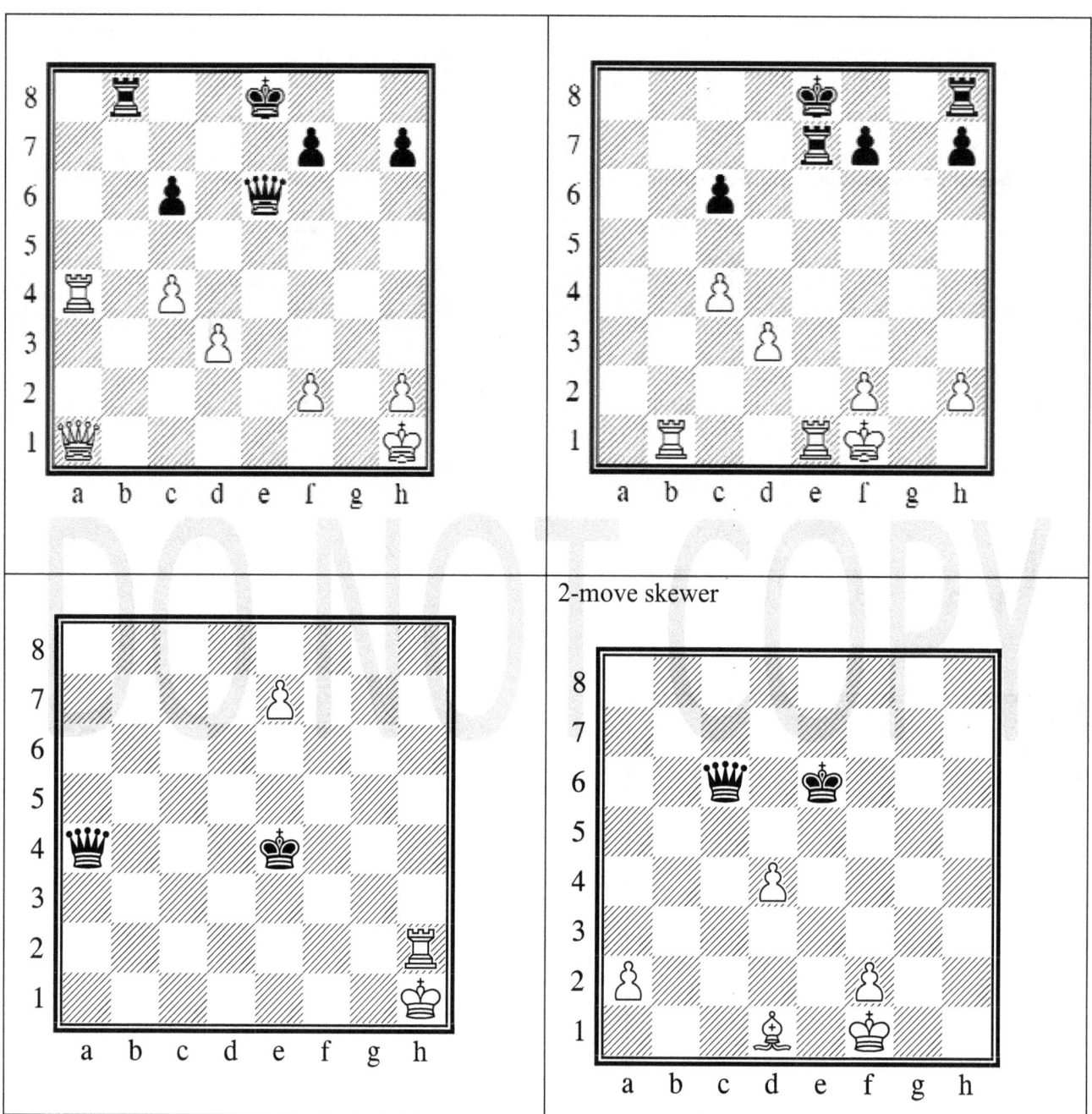

2-move skewer

Learning Chess to Improve Math 数棋谜式健脑国际象棋
Ho Math Chess 何数棋谜 www.homathchess.com
Frank Ho, Amanda Ho © 1995 – 2021   All rights reserved.

Student name _____ Assignment date:_____

Part 7 Mathematical Chess Puzzles

This part contains special puzzles that combine chess, math, and puzzles.
When creating chess and math-related problems, we try to follow the following guidelines:

1. Not to create more chess games, we found children prefer to play chess instead of more chess variants.
2. Try to create solo problems, so each child works on their own pace or worksheet without creating a feeling of competition.
3. Try not to use any other manipulatives such as chips or dominoes, trominoes, etc., if not necessary because it would seem to become an instructor's work to sort out mixed chess pieces or missing manipulatives.
4. Try to create arithmetic and chess integrated computational or logic problems instead of pure chess puzzles problems.
5. Try to integrate chess, not math, to teach some arithmetic concepts.
6. Try to create a workbook that can be used by instructors and students right off the bookshelf instead of some teaching ideas.

Student name _____ Assignment date:_____

Pattern and logic

Fill in the following ☐ with a number.

♙ ☐ ♖ ☐ ♕

Student name ______________________Assignment date:________________

Fill in the following □ with a number.

8, 6, 4, 2, ♔, □, ♘, ♖, 7, ♕,

Fill in the following □ with a number.

♘, 6, ♕, 12, □

What should replace the question mark?

RK, KT, BP, QN, ?

Pattern and logic

What should replace the question mark?

RPPRNPPNBPPBKPP?

Pattern and logic

What letter should replace the question mark?

R N B
R   K
N B ?

Pattern and logic

Find the letters that replace the question marks.

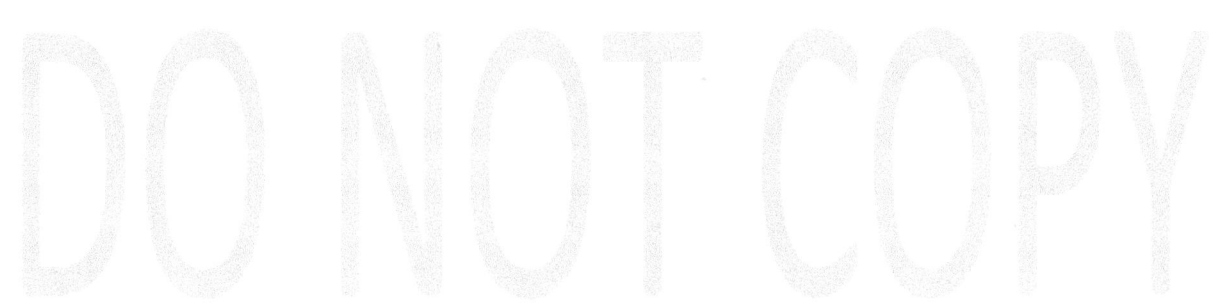

Pattern and logic

Find the next shape in the sequence.

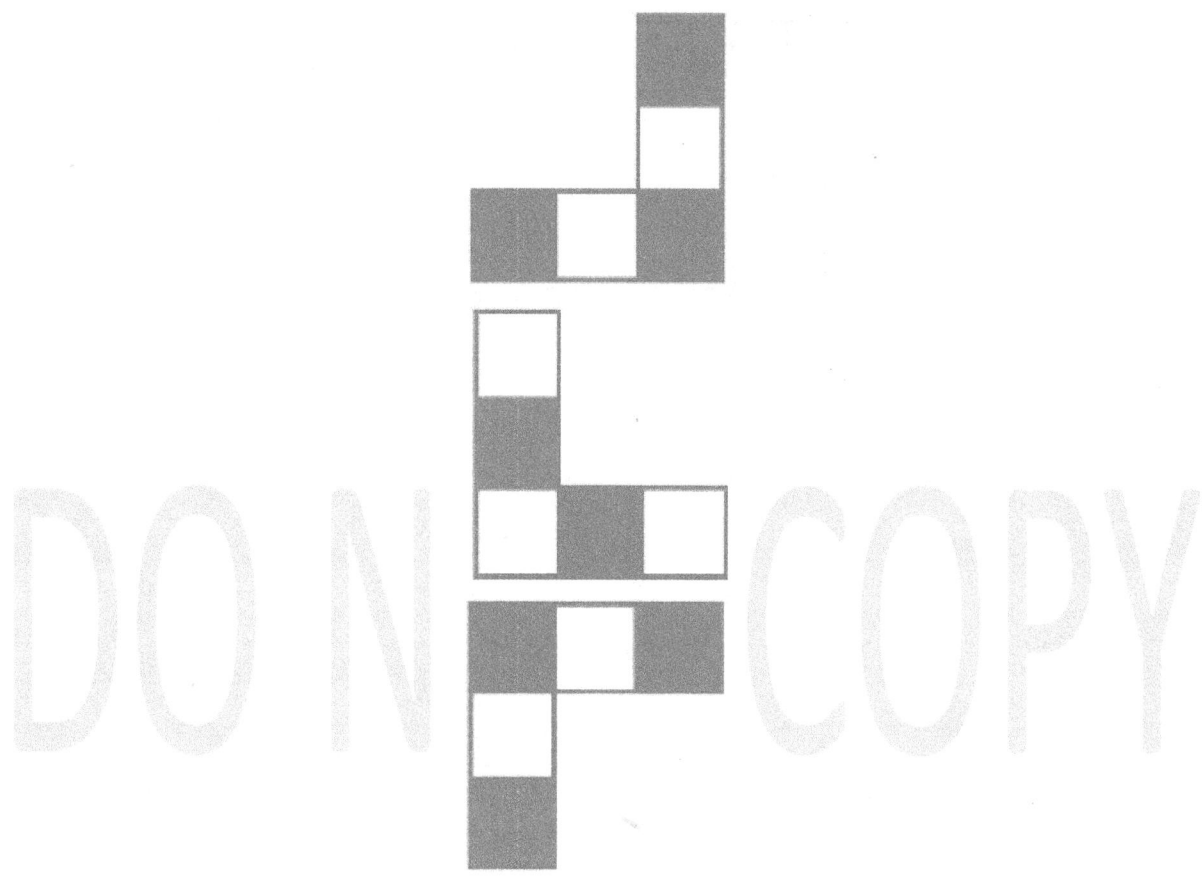

Pattern and logic

What number should replace the question mark?

Five, Three, Three, Nine, ? , Three, Three, Five

Pattern and logic

Replace the question marks with shapes.

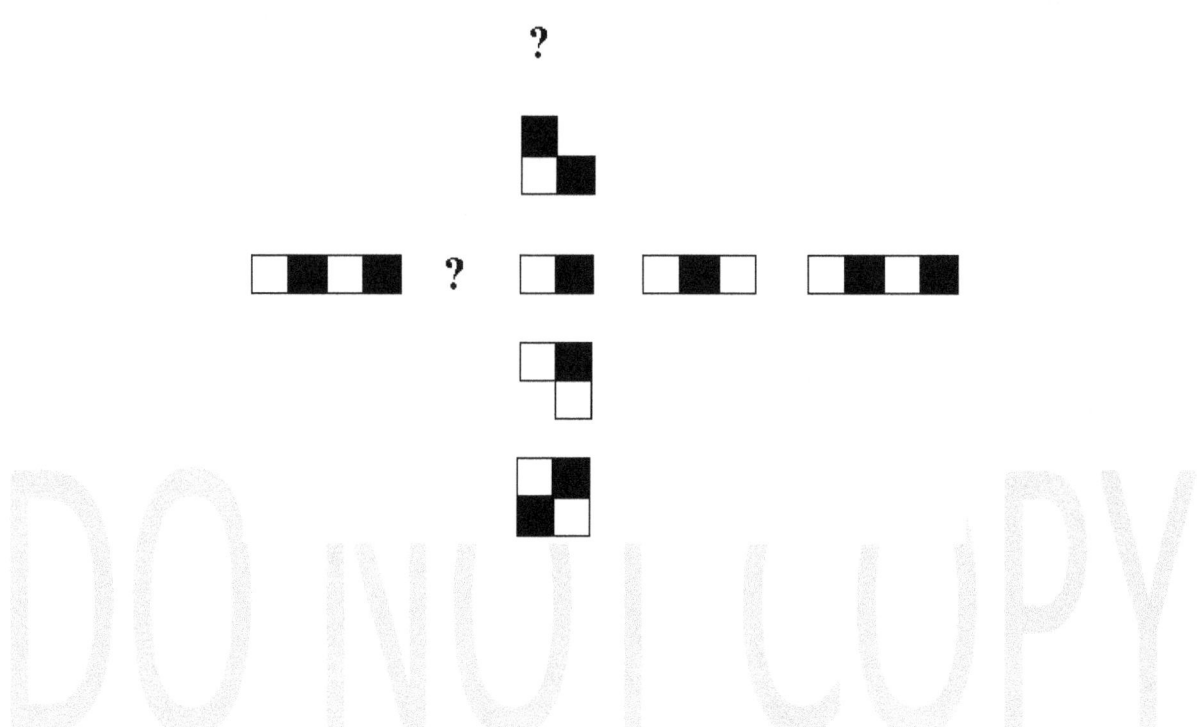

Pattern and logic

Replace the question marks with the appropriate shapes.

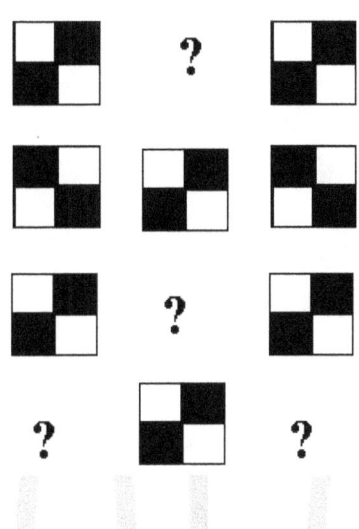

Pattern and logic

How many chess pieces does the following question mark represent?

1.

2.

3.
    ?

4.

Pattern and logic

Draw the symmetric figures along the dotted line.

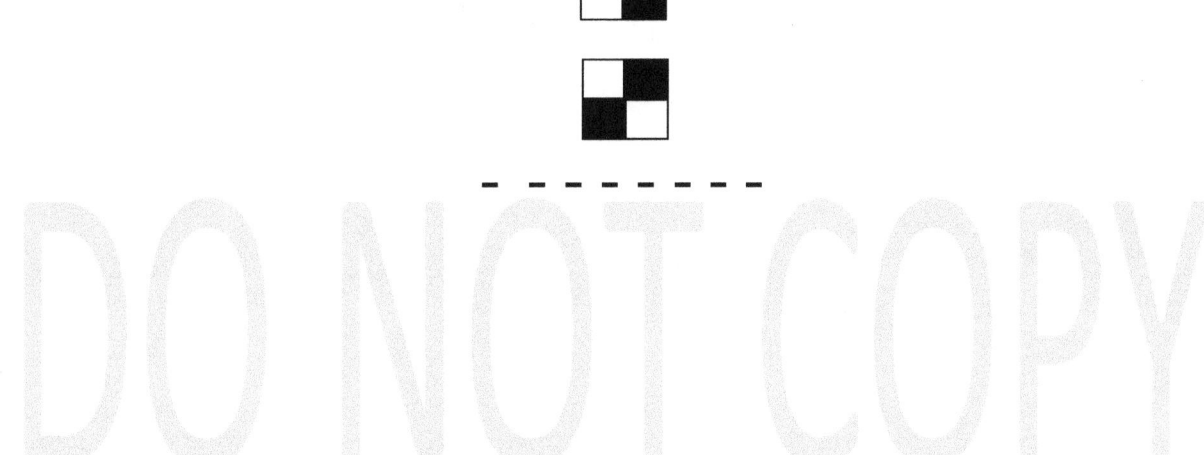

Pattern and logic

Find the chess pieces to replace the question marks.

R N B Q K B N R

R R N B Q K B N

N B ? ? B N R R

Learning Chess to Improve Math 数棋谜式健脑国际象棋
Ho Math Chess 何数棋谜 www.homathchess.com
Frank Ho, Amanda Ho © 1995 – 2021   All rights reserved.

Student name _____ Assignment date:_____

Pattern and logic

There are generally two ways of pairing chess players in a tournament: Swiss and Round Robin. The Swiss system is the winners playing against the winners and the losers playing against the losers after each round. The Round Robin system is to have everybody playing everybody else.

Andrew, Meghan, and Tricia are in the same class of Kerrisdale School, and they participated in the Canadian Grades Chess Championship using the Round Robin Pairing. Can you write all the possible pairs of these three players, and what is the highest possible point that a player could get?

Pattern and logic

Can you find the missing number to replace the question mark?

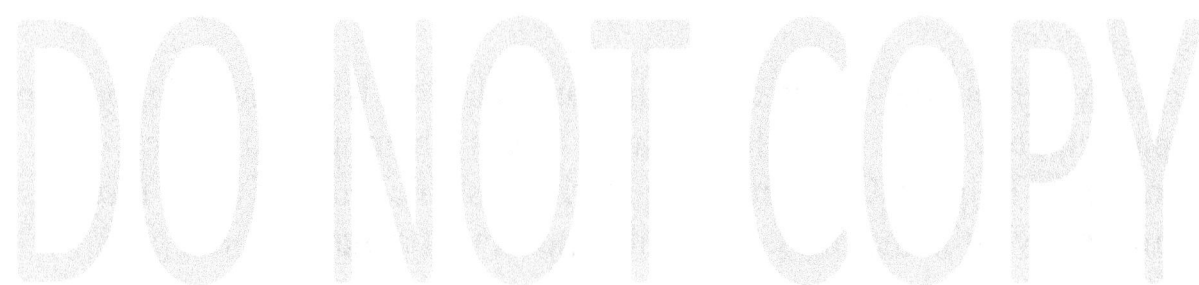

Pattern and logic

Circle the odd one in the following diagram.

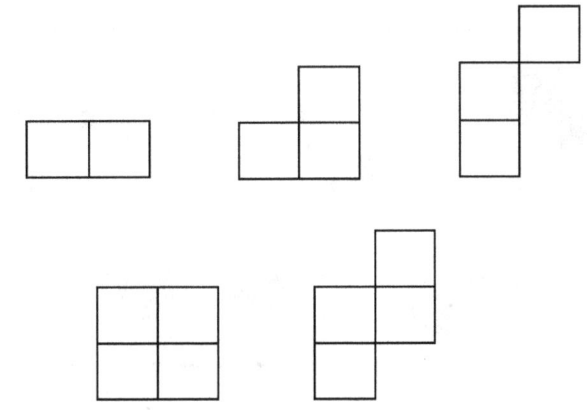

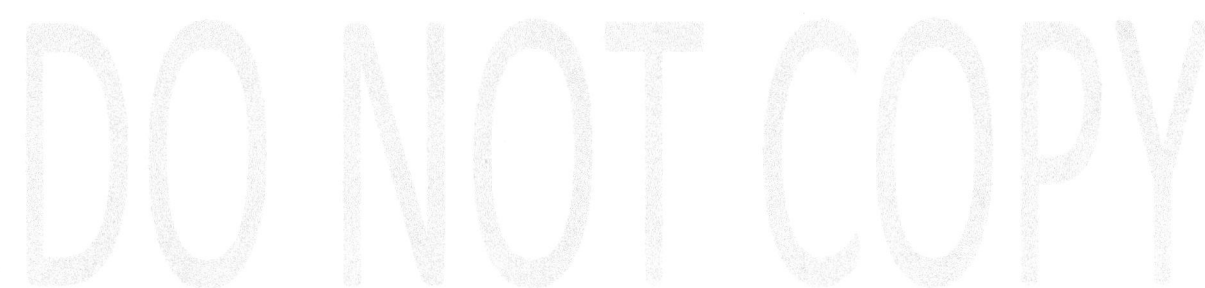

Pattern and logic

Identify the odd one in the following diagram.

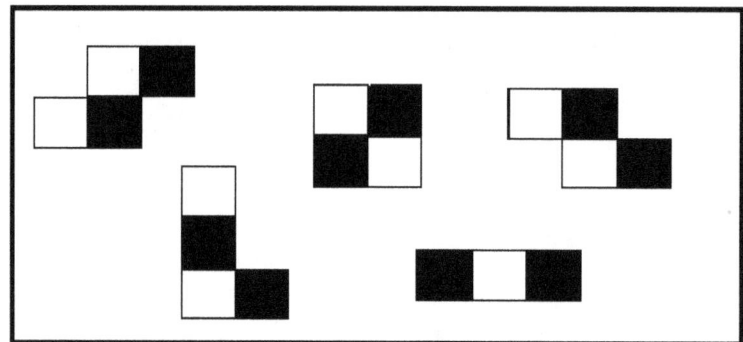

Pattern and logic

Draw the next sequence of the diagram.

 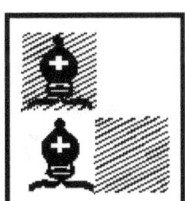 

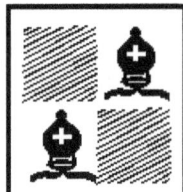 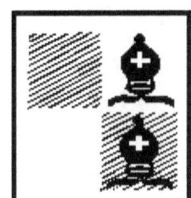 ?

Pattern and logic

Draw the next sequence of the diagram in the direction pattern of |, −, \, /.

    ?

Pattern and logic

Find all sixteen L-shaped figures (connected by four side-to-side squares) by drawing an L on each diagram.

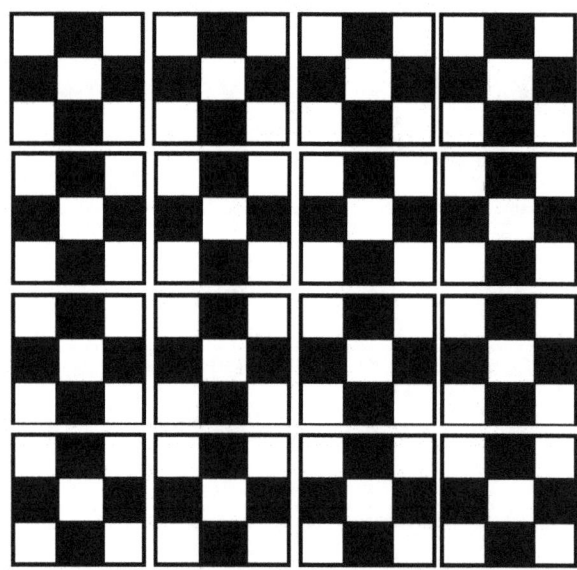

Pattern and logic

Find all twenty L-shaped figures (connected by side-to-side squares with three whites and 2 blacks) by drawing an L on each diagram.

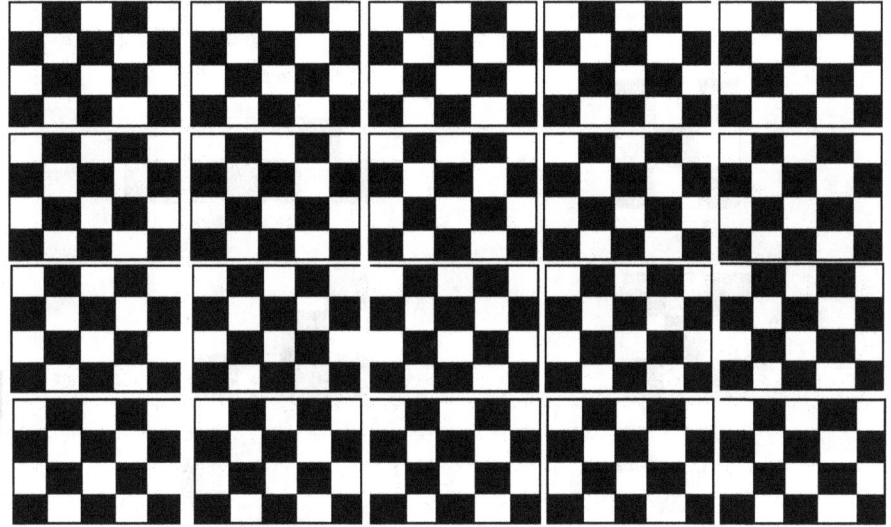

Pattern and logic

Find the odd one.

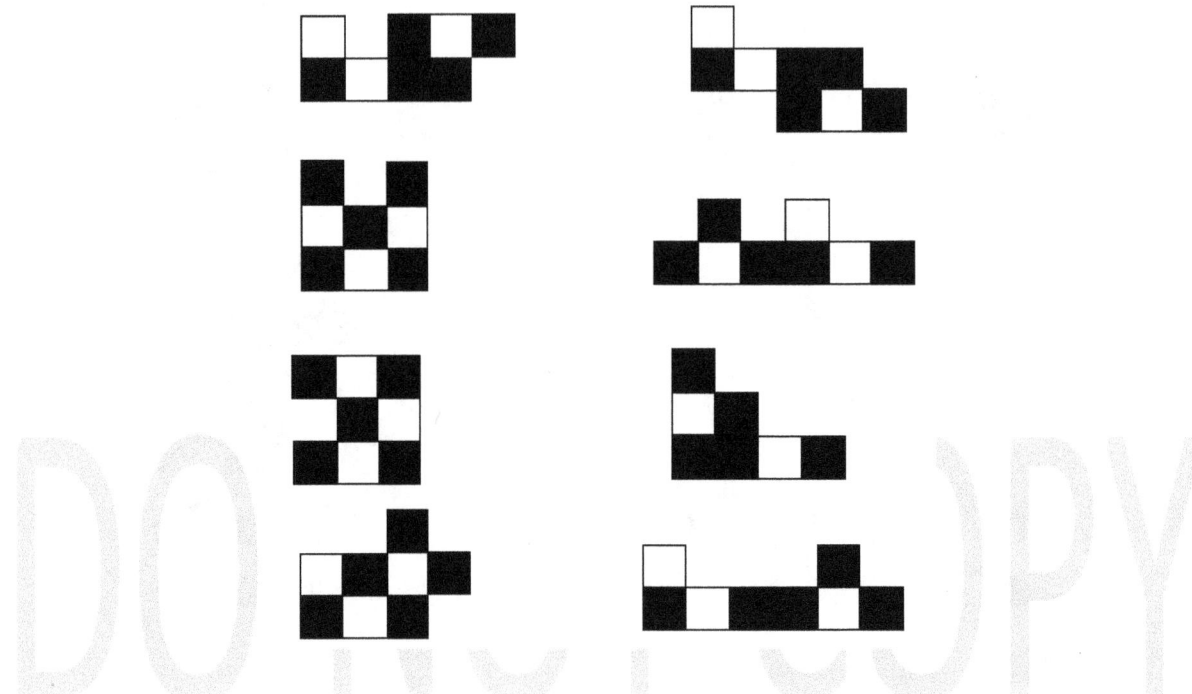

Pattern and logic

Find a number to replace the question mark.

    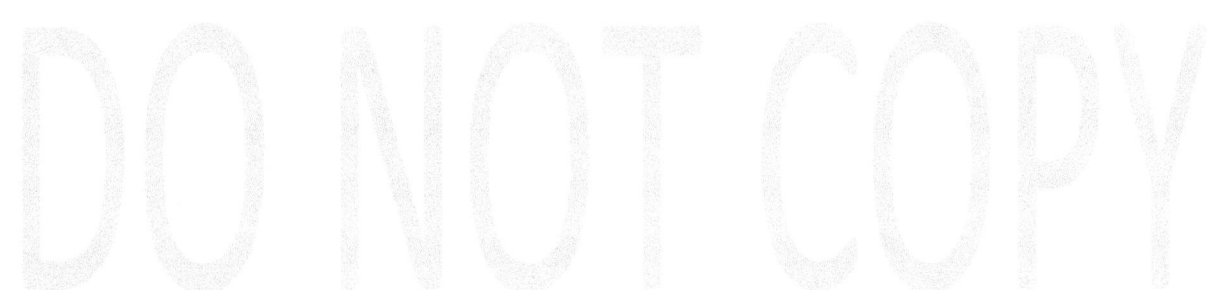

Pattern and logic

The following nets, when folded as a cube, will have the top and bottom as black and all other sides white.

Shade the following nets, so when folded, they will have the top and the bottom as black.

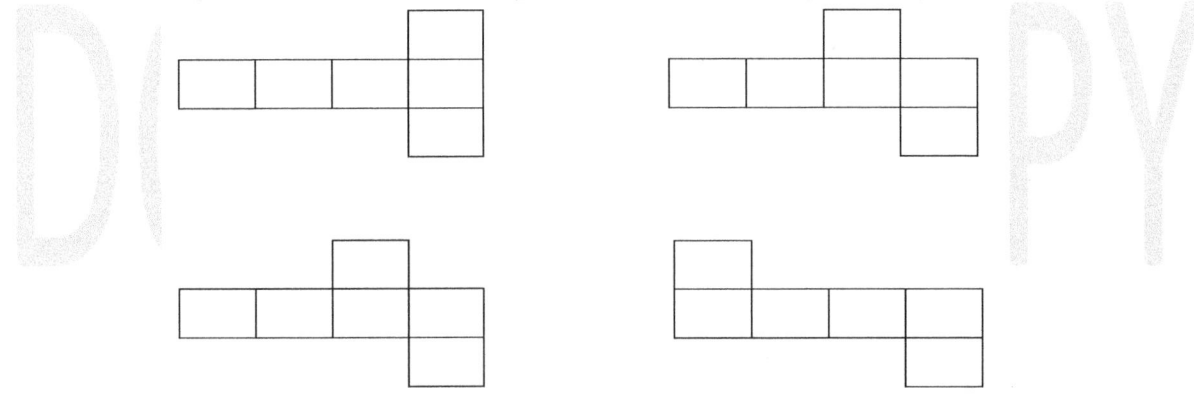

Pattern and Logic

Observe the following pattern of chessboards and complete the blank chessboard.

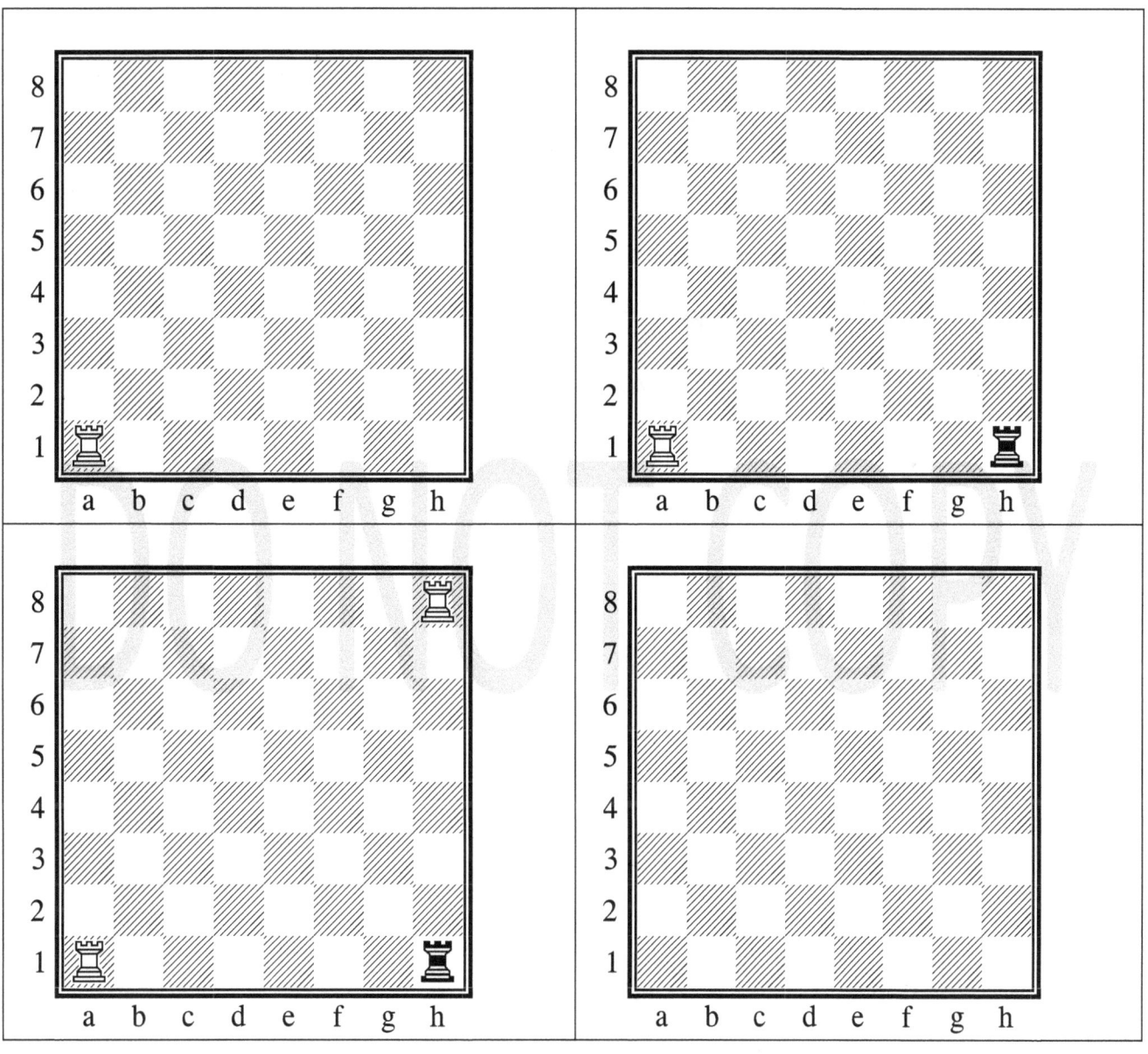

Pattern and Logic

Observe the following pattern of chess diagram and draw a chess piece in each ☐.

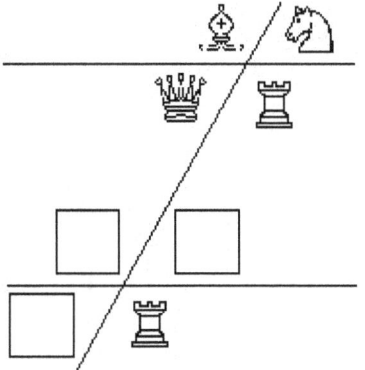

Student name ____________________Assignment date:______________

Pattern and Logic

Fill in the following □ with a number.

5, ♖♖, 5♖♖, □♖♖

Pattern and Logic

Fill in the following ☐ with a number.

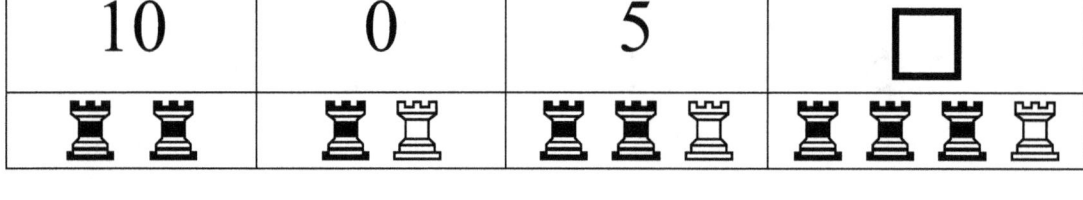

Pattern and Logic

Find the sum of points in the following chess expression.

♞ + ♝ = ☐

♞ + ♝ + ♞ + ♝ = ☐

♞ + ♝ + ♞ + ♝ + ♞ + ♝ + ♞ = ☐

♞ + ♝ + ♞ + ♝ + ♞ + ♝ + ♞ + ♝ + ♞ + ♝ = ☐

♞ + ♝ + ♞ + ♝ + ♞ + ♝ + ♞ + ♝ + ♞ + ♝ + ♞ + ♝ = ☐

Student name ______________________Assignment date:________________

Pattern and Logic

Fill in _______________ with chess pieces.

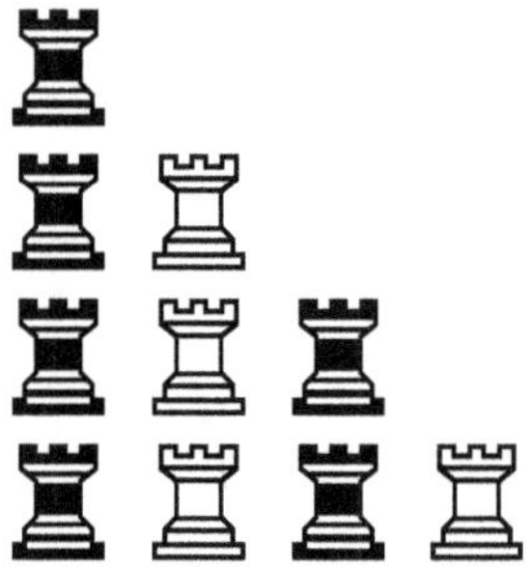

____

Pattern and Logic

Fill in the following ☐ with a number.

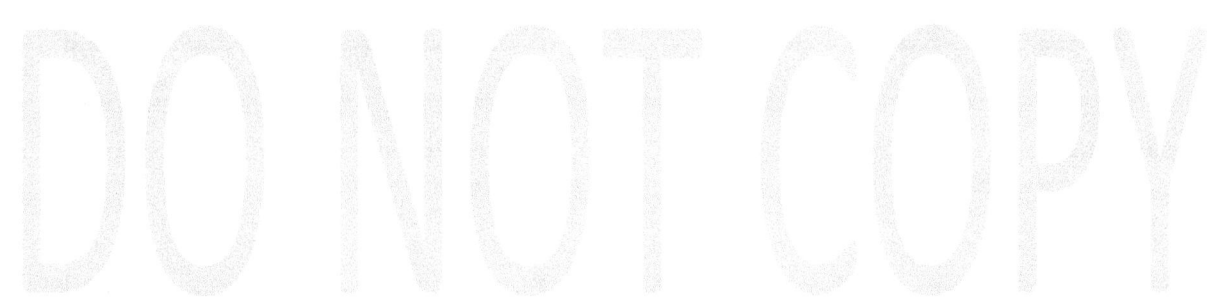

Learning Chess to Improve Math 数棋谜式健脑国际象棋

Ho Math Chess 何数棋谜 www.homathchess.com

Frank Ho, Amanda Ho © 1995 – 2021   All rights reserved.

Student name _____ Assignment date:_____

Pattern and Logic

Observe the following chessboards pattern and draw the chess piece on the blank chessboard.

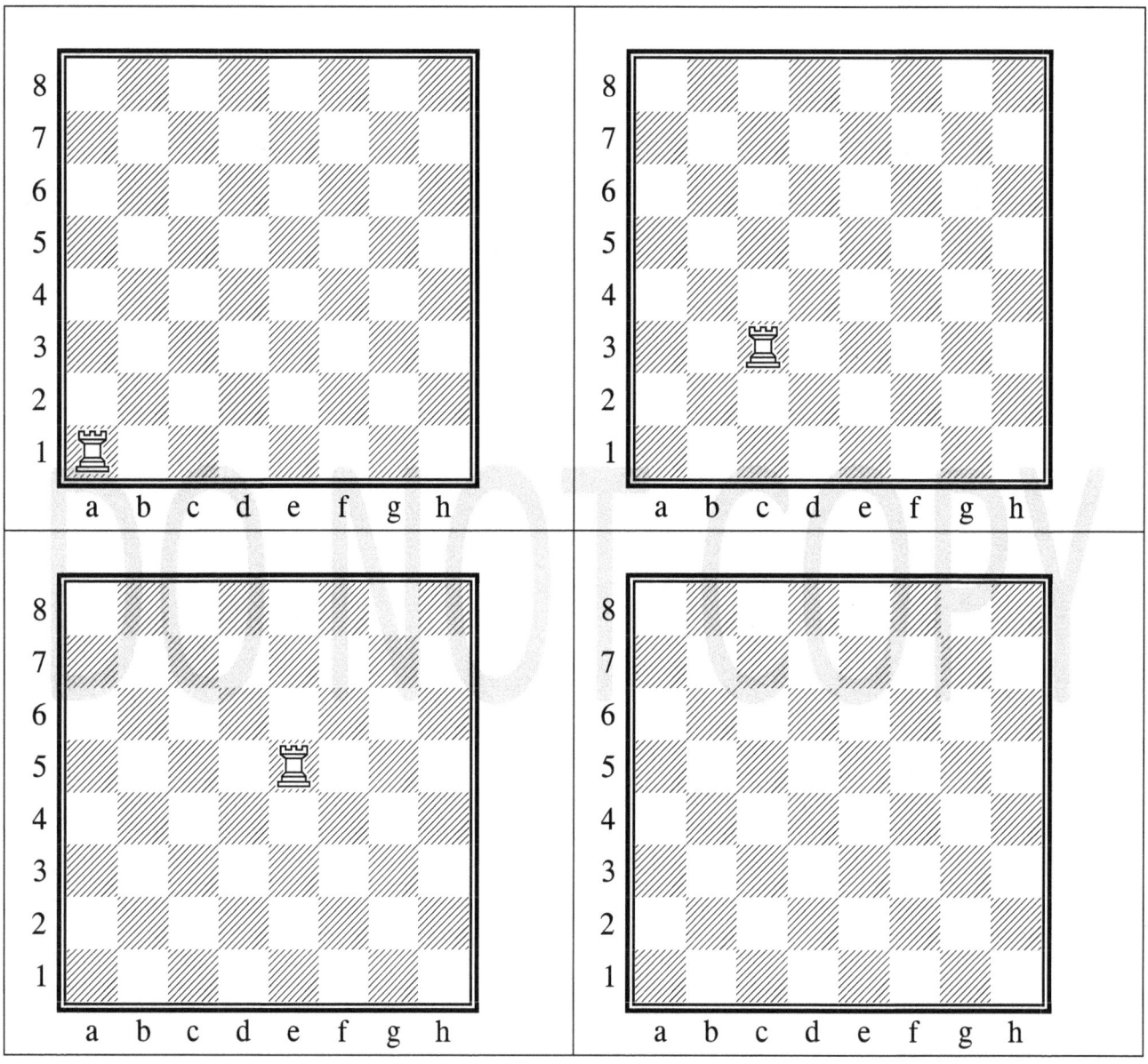

Pattern and Logic

If the following pattern continues

then what is the 18th chess piece? ___black pawn___

If the following pattern continues

then what is the 28th chess piece? ___white pawn___

Pattern and Logic

Fill in ▢ with an answer.

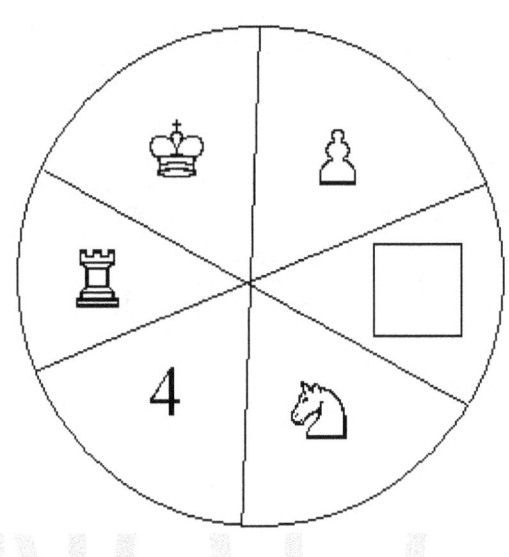

Pattern and Logic

Observe the following pattern and draw the chess pieces in the last blank squares.

Pattern and Logic

Observe the following pattern and draw the chess piece in the ☐.

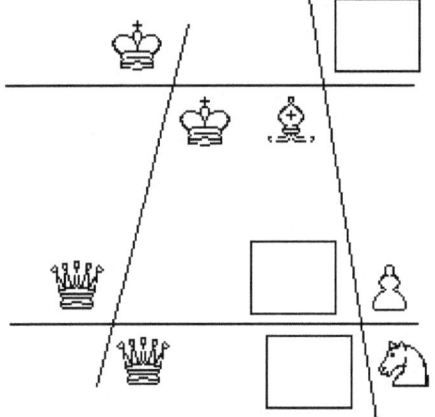

Pattern and Logic

Observe the following pattern and draw the chess piece in the ☐.

Pattern and Logic

Observe the following pattern and draw the chess pieces in the ☐.

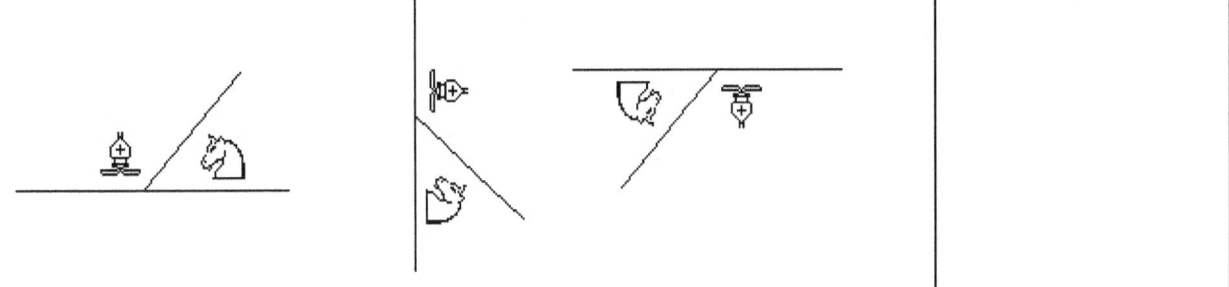

Pattern and Logic

Observe the following pattern and draw the chess piece in the ☐.

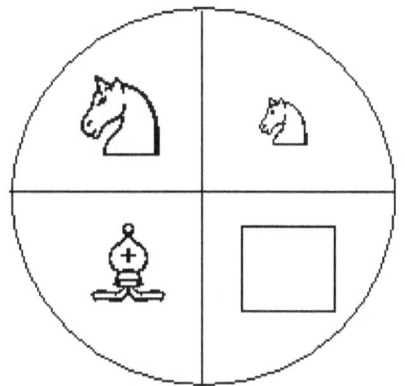

Pattern and Logic

Observe the following pattern and draw the chess piece in the ☐.
(Hint: Think how each chess piece moves.)

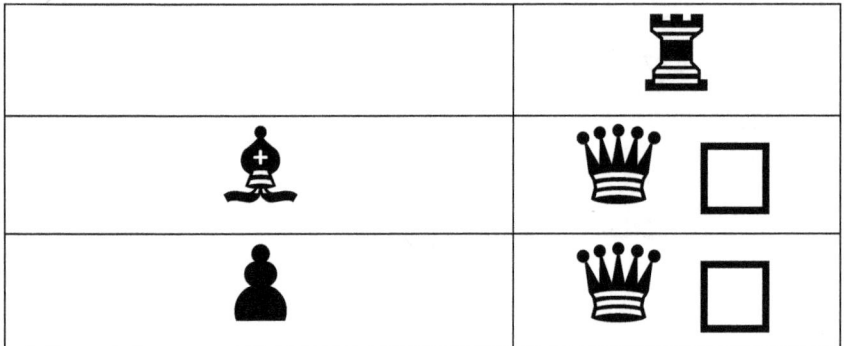

Pattern and Logic

Jonathan plays white, and Amanda copies Jonathan's move. Find Amanda's next move? Answer (in chess notation): _____

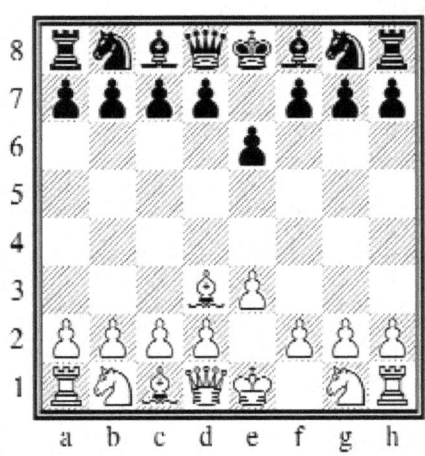

Jonathan plays white, and Amanda copies Jonathan's move. Find Amanda's next move? Answer (in chess notation): _____

Pattern and Logic

Fill in each ☐ with an answer.

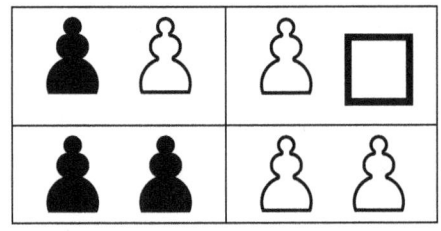

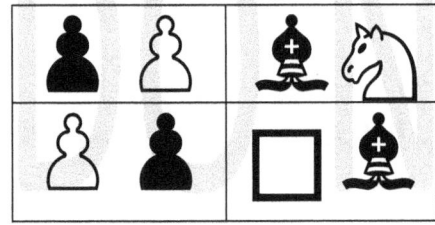

Pattern and Logic

Look at the pattern of the following chess pieces and find what chess piece is in the 33rd position? Answer _____

Pattern and Logic

Look at the pattern of the following chess pieces and find what chess piece is in the 33rd position? Answer _____

Pattern and Logic

Draw one pawn in each circle in the following diagram. What is the minimum number of the pawn(s) in the following diagram?

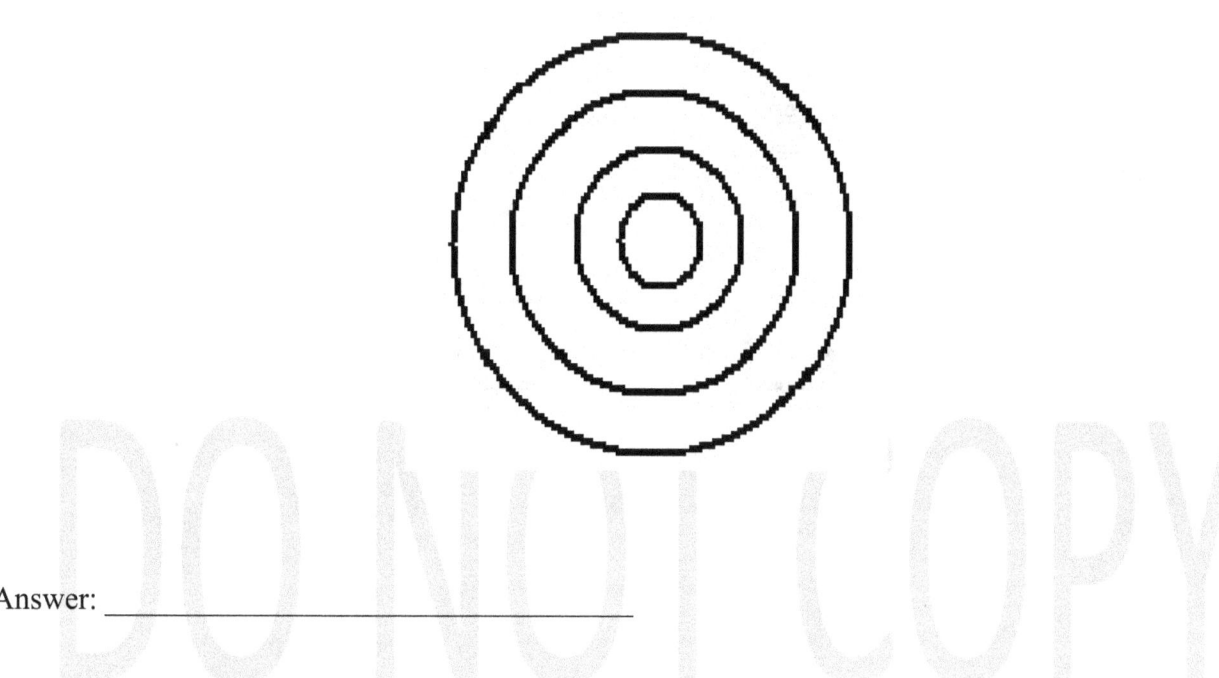

Answer: _____

Pattern and Logic

Fill in each ☐ with an answer.

♙	2
♗	4
♖	6
7	8
☐	☐

Pattern and Logic

Fill in each ☐ with an answer.

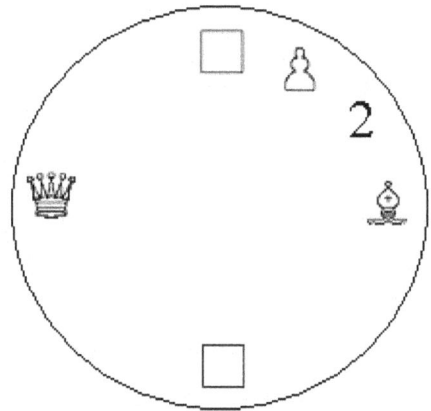

Fill in each ☐ with an answer.

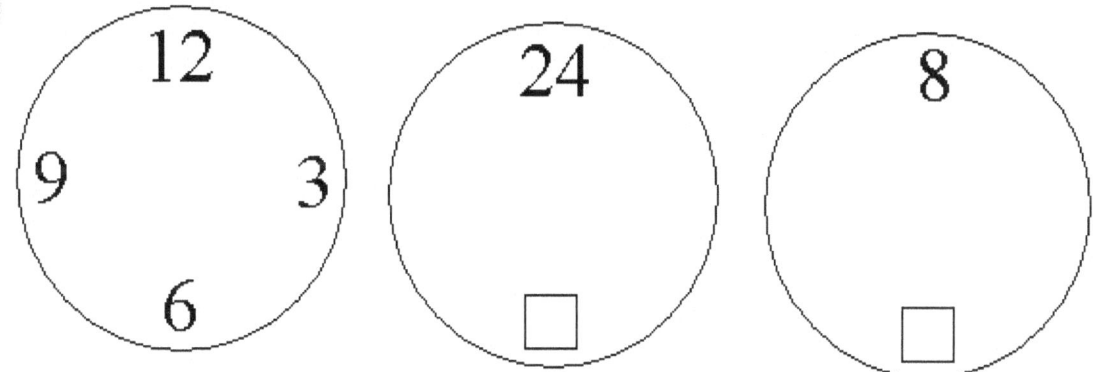

Pattern and Logic

Fill in each ☐ with an answer.

Fill in each ☐ with an answer.

Pattern and Logic

Fill in each ☐ with an answer.

Pattern and Logic

Fill in each ☐ with an answer.

Pattern and relation (Tabulation)

5, 10, 15, ☐, ☐, ☐, ☐, ☐, ☐, ☐, ☐

Number of ♜	Points
1	5
2	10
☐	☐
☐	☐
☐	☐
6	☐
☐	35

Pattern and relation (Tabulation)

9, 18, 27, ☐, ☐, ☐, ☐, ☐, ☐, ☐, ☐

Number of ♛	Points
1	9
2	18
☐	☐
☐	☐
☐	☐
☐	☐
☐	63

Pattern and relation (Tabulation in $ax + by + \ldots = c,$ where a, b, c are constant.**)**

You have three chess pieces. Your total points are 7.

What are three possible chess pieces (do not include king)?

Answer 1: _____

Answer 2: _____

Answer 3: _____

Answer 4: _____

Learning Chess to Improve Math   数棋谜式健脑国际象棋

Ho Math Chess   何数棋谜   www.homathchess.com

Frank Ho, Amanda Ho © 1995 – 2021   All rights reserved.

Student name _____ Assignment date:_____

Pattern and relation (Tabulation in $ax + by + \ldots = c$, where a, b, c are constant.)

Fill in a different number of chess pieces to come up with each total.

Number of ♖	♖ Points	Number Of ♘	♘ Points	Total points
1	5	1	3	8 ($1 \times 5 + 1 \times 3 = 8$)
☐	5	☐	3	11
☐	5	☐	3	13

Fill in a different number of chess pieces to come up with each total.

Number of ♙	Number of ♘	Number of ♖	Total points	
1	1	1	9	
3	2	0	9	
0	3	0	9	
☐1	☐3	☐3	10	
☐5	☐0	☐1	10	
☐0	☐2	☐1	11	
☐2	☐3	☐0	12	
☐1	☐0	☐2	13	
☐4	☐0	☐3	14	
☐0	☐0	☐3	15	

Path and geometry

Draw the lines of symmetry for the 8 by 8 chessboard.

Path and geometry

Make the ♖ visit each square once and only once starting at a1 and come back to a1. How many different ways can you come up with?

Path and geometry

Replace ? with a diagram following the pattern.

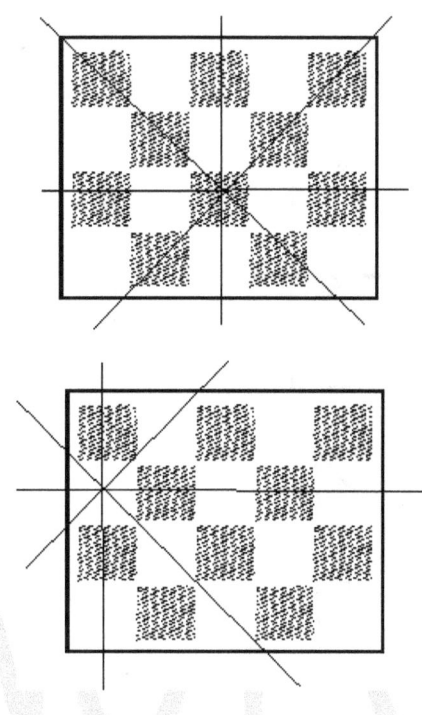

?

Path and geometry

Circle the chess piece(s) that reflect(s) each corresponding diagram.

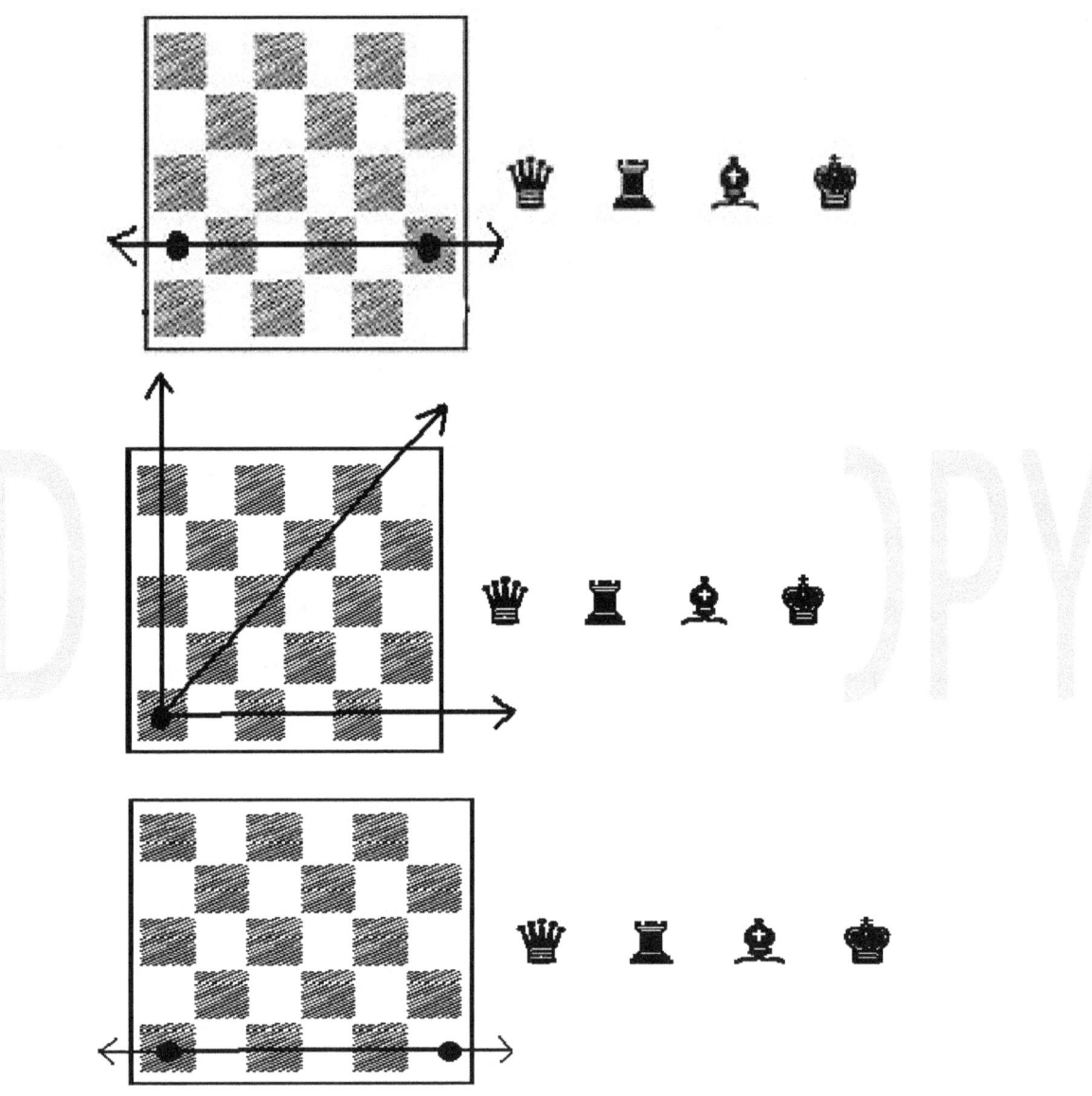

Path and geometry

How many ways can you take the  at h1 to a8? ( is only allowed to move either left or up.)

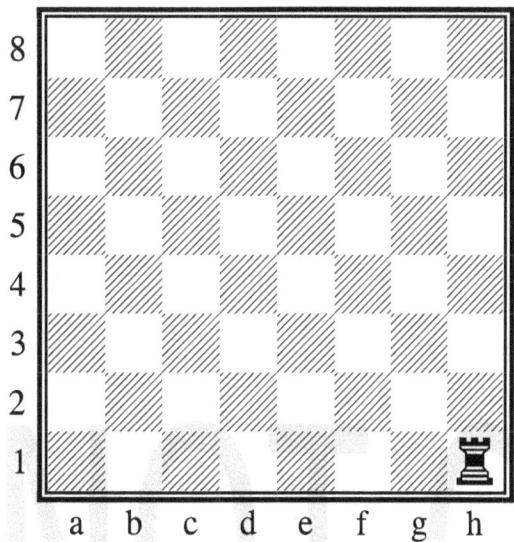

Path and geometry

What is the largest number of right angles that can be created by the path of a rook when travelling all squares once and only once.

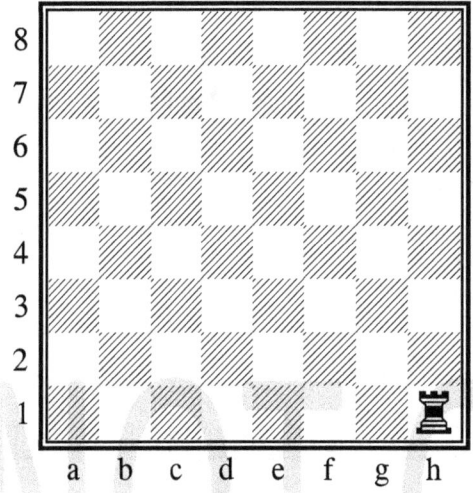

Learning Chess to Improve Math   数棋谜式健脑国际象棋
Ho Math Chess   何数棋谜   www.homathchess.com
Frank Ho, Amanda Ho © 1995 − 2021   All rights reserved.

Student name _____ Assignment date:_____

Path and geometry

Max Wang and Wendy Cheung are playing chess, and you do not see their opening moves until the first two moves between them are completed, as shown in the following chess diagram.

Can you use chess notation to write down all the possible combinations of the first two possible opening moves sequence resulting in the following chess diagram? All pawns advanced two squares in the first move.

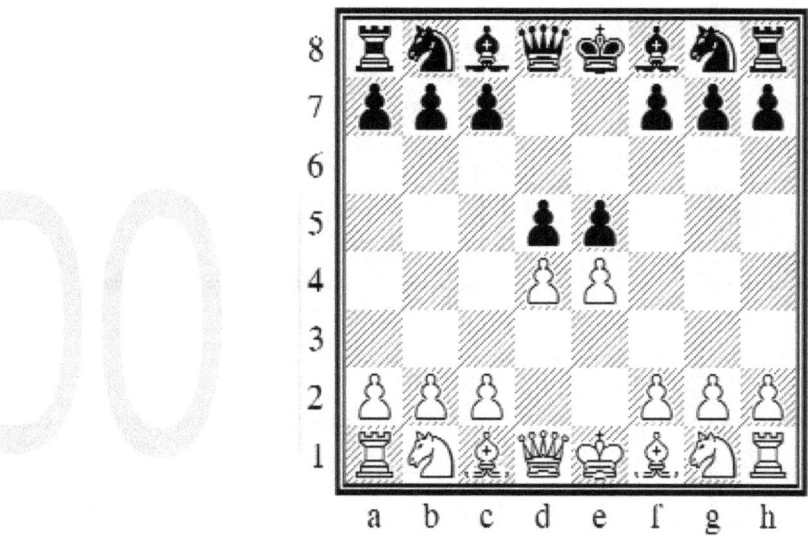

W	B	W	B
d4			
	e5		
e4			
	e5		

Path and geometry

Bishop (b4) and knight (a1) are required to move their occupying squares to meet at the same square. If a knight moves the first show, there are four ways that a knight can meet a bishop in one and a half moves for each meet-up?

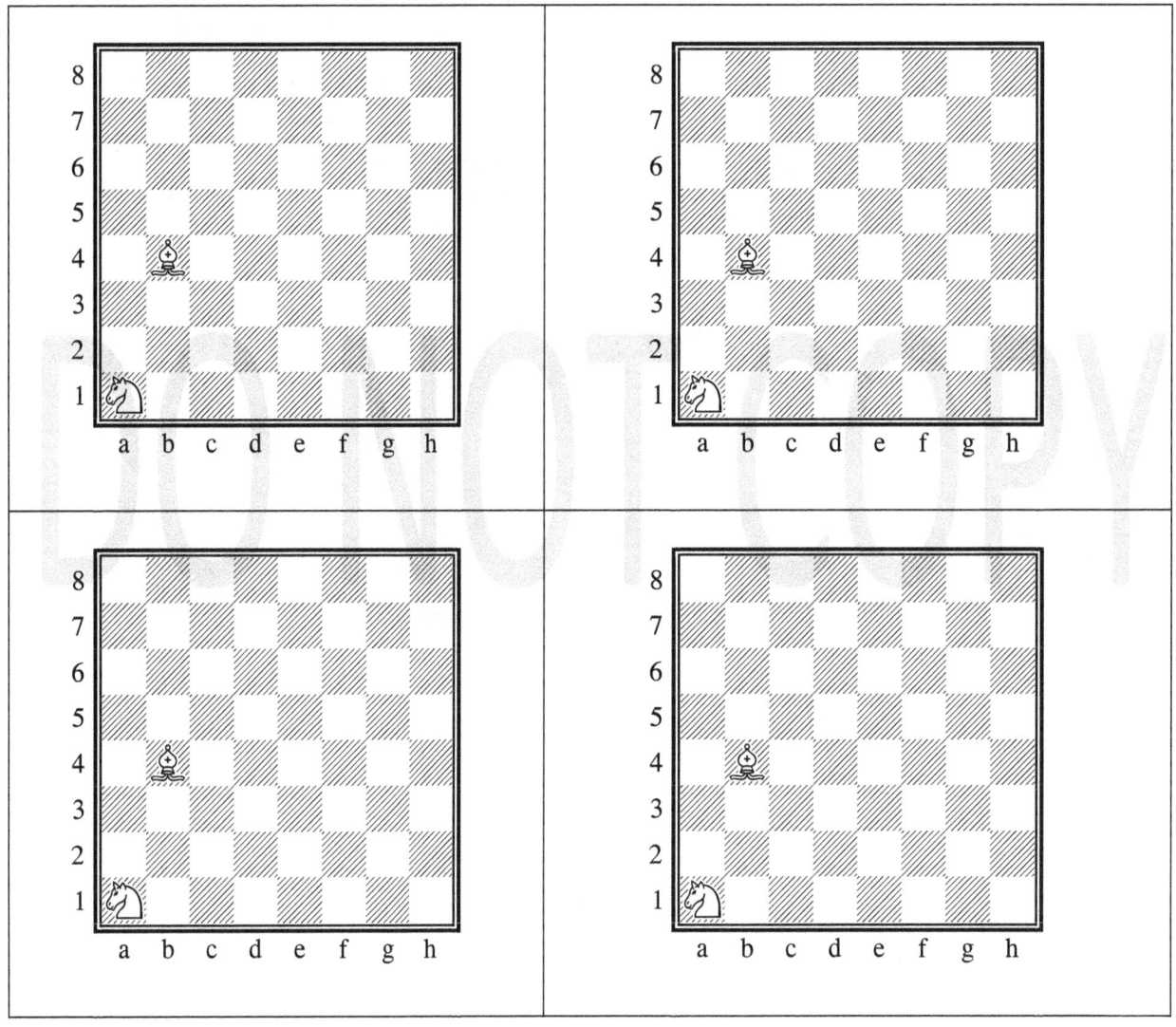

Chess Pieces and geometry

♖	no diagonal lines
♗	no horizontal or vertical lines
?	no diagonal, horizontal, vertical lines

Learning Chess to Improve Math 数棋谜式健脑国际象棋
Ho Math Chess 何数棋谜 www.homathchess.com
Frank Ho, Amanda Ho © 1995 – 2021   All rights reserved.

Student name _____ Assignment date:_____

Chess and geometry

Filling in **with** a chess piece	Geometric shapes
 ♙ (pawn)	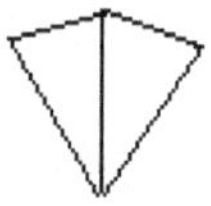 kite
 ♜ (rook)	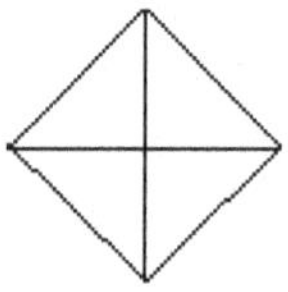 rhombus with diagonals
 ☐ (square)	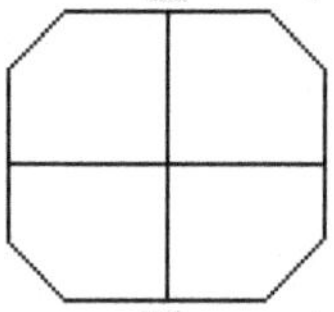 octagon with cross
 ♗ (bishop)	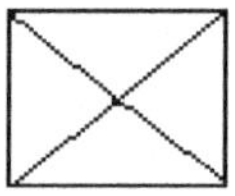 square with X

Chess and geometry

Replacing ☐ by a chess piece	Geometric shapes
♙	kite
♖	rhombus (with diagonals)
⬛ (square)	right triangle
♗	rectangle with diagonals

Logic

Can you find the chess piece that replaces the question mark?
Also, insert the proper labels to replace the numbers.
  Hint: It has something to do with English spelling.

	3	4
1	knight	King rook
2	?	queen pawn

Logic

Replace question marks with chess moves.

	Black	White
Queen d5	?	?
Knight c3	None	?
Squares controlled by both pieces	?	?

Logic

Can you find letters to replace the question marks?

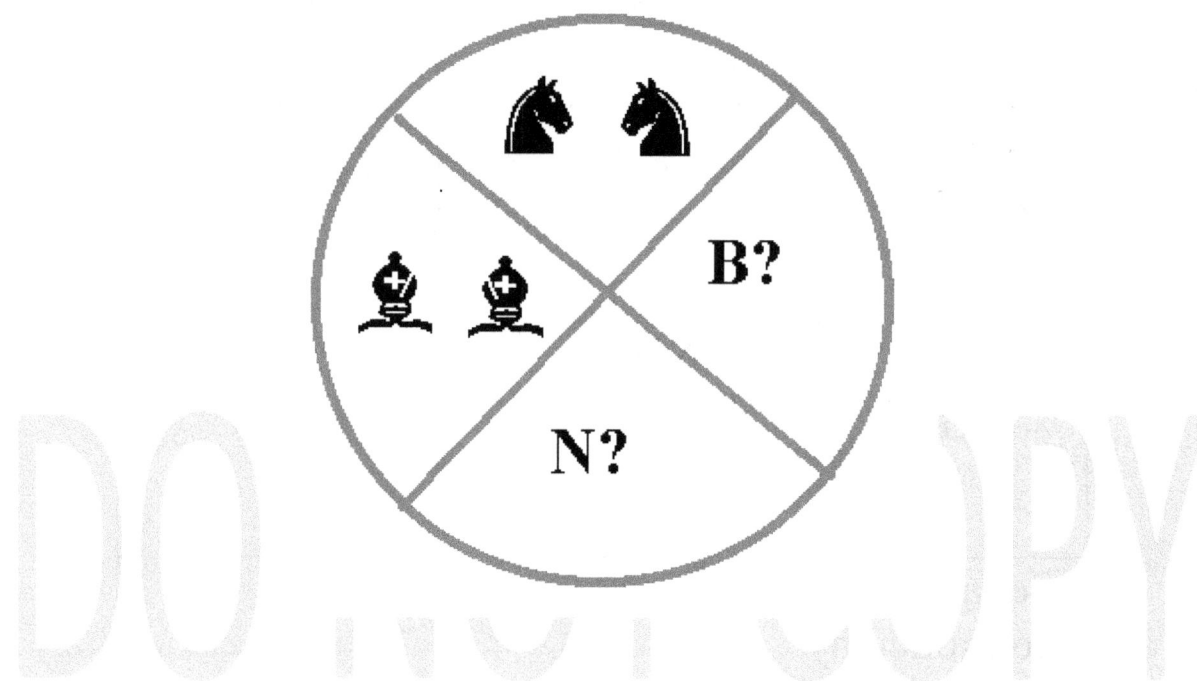

Logic

Can you find the answer to the question mark in the following diagram?

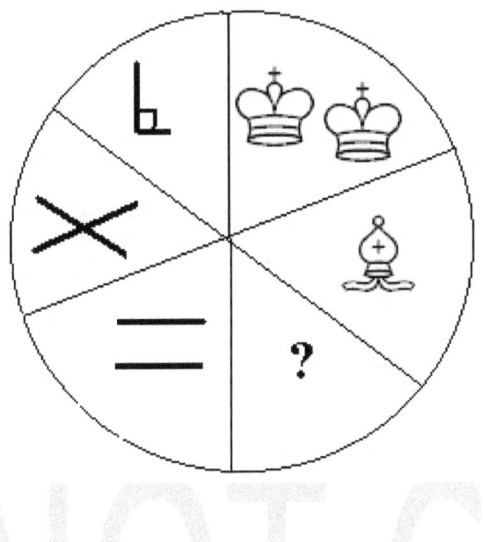

Logic

Can you find the answer to the question mark in the following diagram?

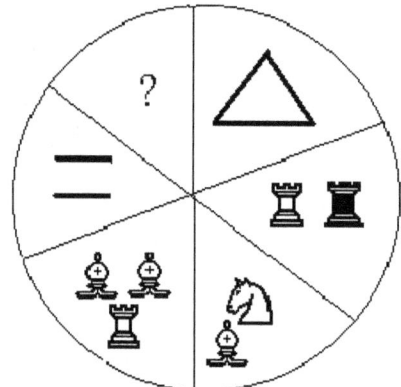

Logic

Can you find the answer to the question mark in the following diagram?

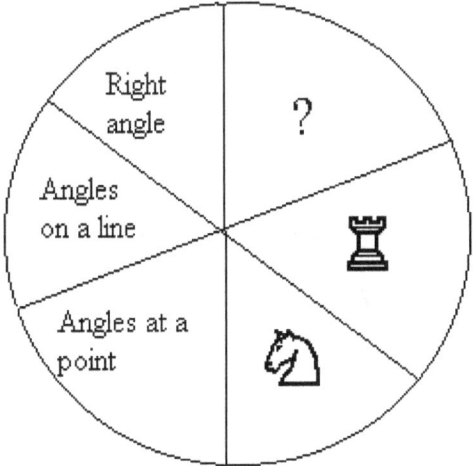

Logic

Please put the chess pieces into the squares according to the following logic:

White (moving up):

(1) 2 white pawns are on the bottom.
(2) Rook is on the left.
(3) The black king is only being checked by the knight.
(4) Bishop is on the white square.

Black (moving down):

(1) King is on the top.
(2) Knight is attacking the rook.
(3) The centre square is empty.
(4) Pawn is on the white square and on the bottom.

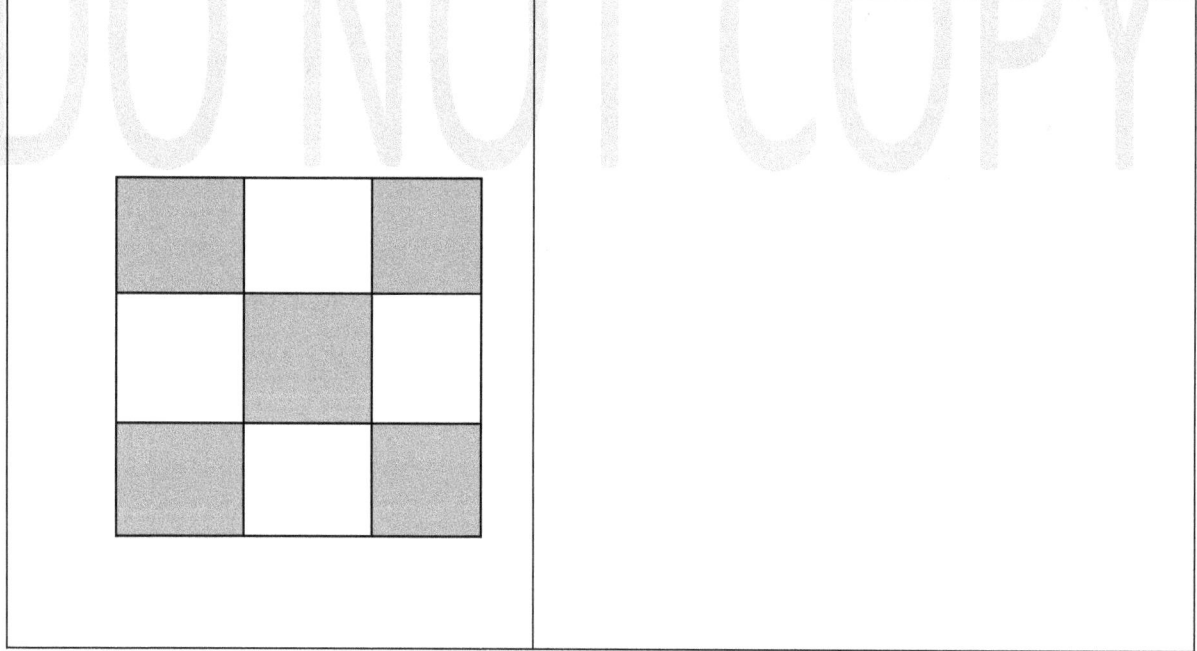

Learning Chess to Improve Math

Ho Math Chess   www.homathchess.com

Frank Ho, Amanda Ho © 1995 – 2021   All rights reserved.

Student name _____ Assignment date: _____

Tree diagram

Complete the following tree diagram starting at Nb2
(knight moves right and up only.)

Nb2 -- c4

     -- d6

     -- e5

    -- d3

				destination	path
Nb2	c4	d6	e8		1
					2
					3
					4
					5
					6
					7
					8

Probability

Out of all knight's possible paths, what is the probability that the knight will move on to the square h8? Knight is allowed to move to the right and up only.

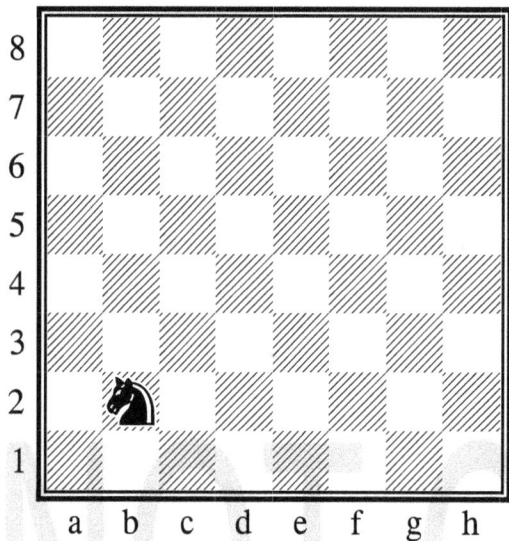

				destination	path
Nb2	c4	d6	e8		1
					2
					3
					4
					5
					6
					7
					8

Ho Math Chess

Learning Chess to Improve Math

Frank Ho, Amanda Ho © 1995 – 2021   All rights reserved.

Student name _____ Assignment date: _____

Fraction

Express the Knight's available moves, shown below, as a fraction of its possible moves when unblocked.

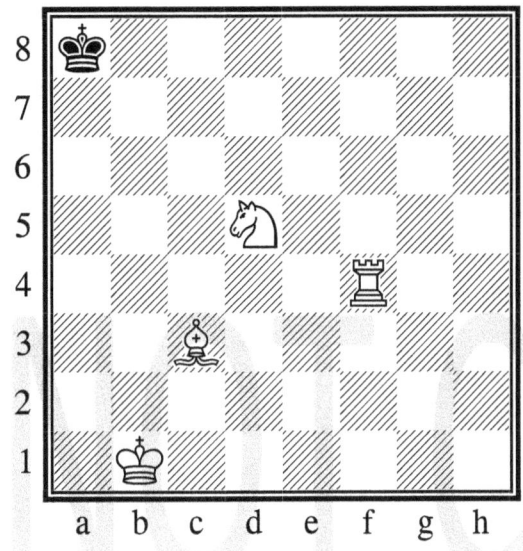

Answer: _____

Fraction

Express the Queen's available moves, shown below, as a fraction of its possible moves when unblocked.

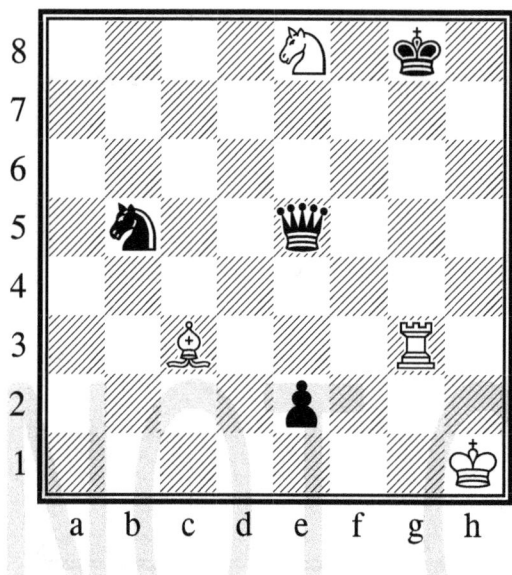

Answer: _____

Venn diagram

The following Venn diagram shows the results of a chess diagram.

What squares are controlled by both the rook and the bishop?

Answer this question by shading the area on the Venn diagram.

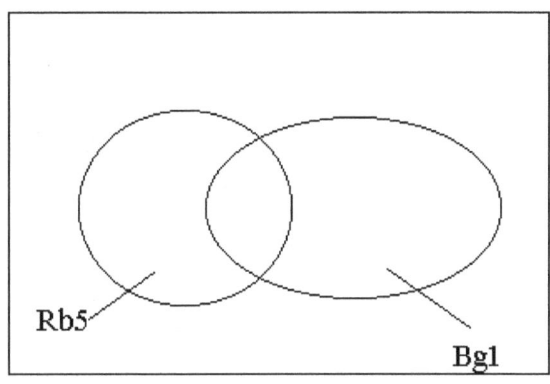

Venn diagram

The following Venn diagram shows the results of a chess diagram.

What squares are controlled either by the rook or the bishop or both? Answer this question by shading the area on the following Venn diagram.

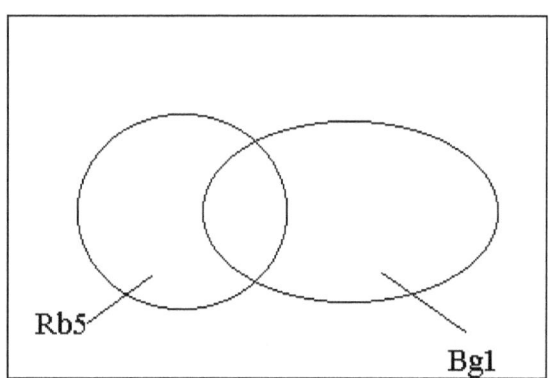

Venn diagram

The following Venn diagram shows the results of using a chessboard.

a. What squares are controlled by both a rook and a bishop? Please write answers in algebraic notations.

b. What squares are controlled by the rook? Please write answers in algebraic notations.

c. What squares are controlled by the bishop? Please write answers in algebraic notations.

d. What squares are not controlled by the rook or the bishop? Answer this question by shading the area on the following Venn diagram.

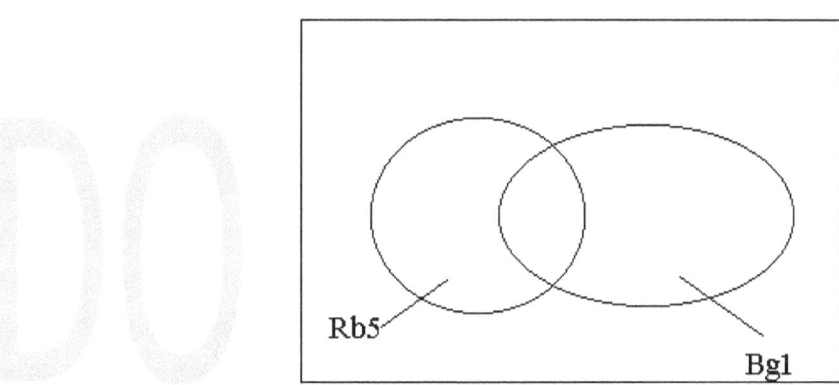

Probability

What is the probability of the following two pieces meeting together?

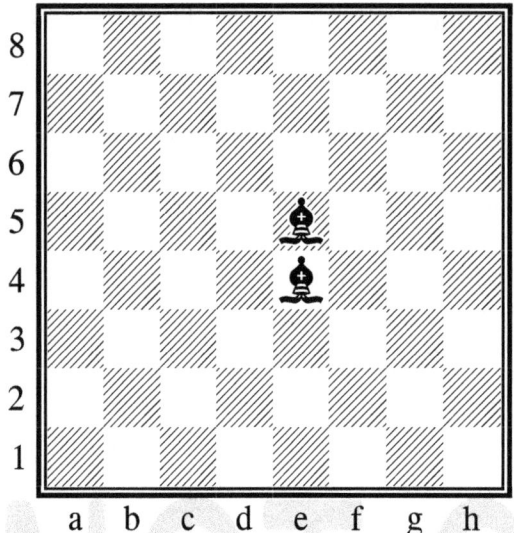

Answer: _____

Probability

What is the probability of the following two pieces meeting at c5 in one move?

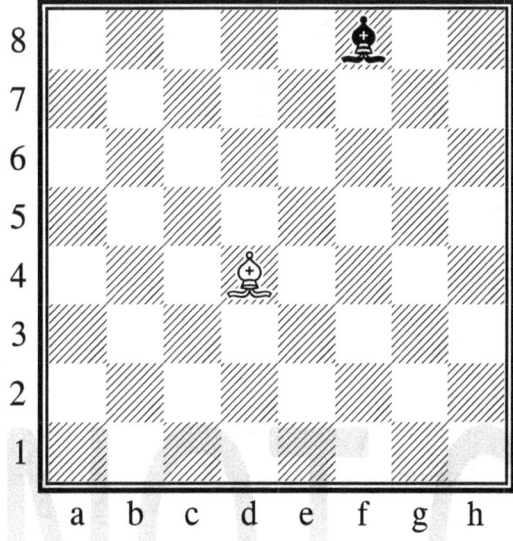

Answer: _____

Palindrome

Examine the chess pieces on the chessboard, regardless of their colours, how many palindromes can you find?

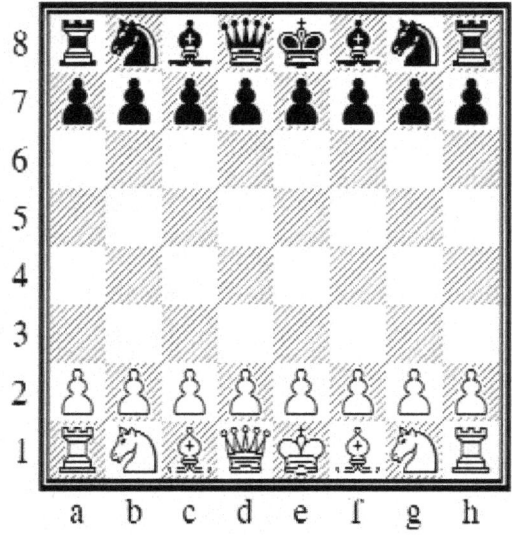

Learning Chess to Improve Math 数棋谜式健脑国际象棋

 Math Chess   何数棋谜   www.homathchess.com

Frank Ho, Amanda Ho © 1995 – 2021   All rights reserved.

Student name _____ Assignment date:_____

Chess and computations integrated problems

Replace the question marks with numerals using the following values of chess pieces and alphabets.

(The values of chess pieces are defined as follows: **Q**ueen = 9, **R**ook = 5, **K**ing = 0, **B**ishop = 3, **K**night = 3, **P**awn = 1.)

K	**P**awn	A	**B**ishop	C	**R**ook	D
0	1	2	3	?	5	?

```
        Q                R ?
    +   P            +   R P
    -------          ---------
      ? K              ? K R


      B P              R ? Q
    + Q C            - B C D
    -------          ---------
      ? A R            ? R B


      ? D              B B
    + P R            × P A
    ---------        ---------
      A P              B ? ?
```

Chess math

Can you find the missing number?

Chess math

After analyzing a chess diagram, a player made the following new value system for chess pieces. Can you find numbers to replace the question marks?

Values: Rook = 6, Knight = 5, Queen = 10, King = 3, Bishop = 3, Pawn = 1

R	R	R	18
N	N	R	16
Q	Q	N	25
K	K	Q	16
R	P	B	10
B	B	P	7
33	28	31	

Making mathematical sentences true

Fill in the following ☐ with equality and operators sign.

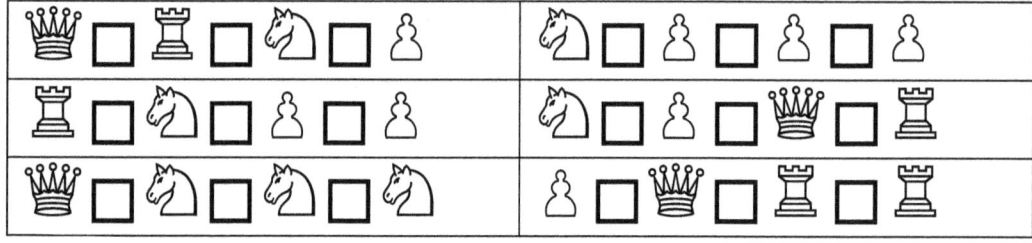

Learning Chess to Improve Math

Ho Math Chess www.homathchess.com

Frank Ho, Amanda Ho © 1995 – 2021   All rights reserved.

Student name _____   Assignment date:_____

Computation using chess pieces values

Fill in the following □ with a number.

Pawn = □, ♙ + 2 = □	King = □, ♔ + 2 = □
Pawn = □, ♙ + 4 = □	King = □, ♔ + □ = 3
Pawn = □, ♙ + □ = 2	King = □, ♔ + □ = 4
Pawn = □, □ + ♙ + ♙ = 8	King = □, ♔ + □ = 9
Pawn = □, ♙ + 9 = 10	King = □, □ + ♔ = 8
Rook = □, ♖ + □ = 7	Knight = □, ♘ + 2 = 5
Rook = □, ♖ + □ = 9	Knight = □, ♘ + □ = 8
Rook = □, ♖ + ♖ = □	Knight = □, ♘ + □ = 9
Rook = □, □ + ♖ = 7	Knight = □, ♘ + □ = 5
Rook = □, ♖ + □ = 10	Knight = □, □ + ♘ = 4
Bishop = □, ♗ + □ = 7	Queen = □, ♕ + 2 = 11
Bishop = □, ♗ + □ = 9	Queen = □, ♕ + □ = 18
Bishop = □, ♗ + ♗ = □	Queen = □, ♕ + □ = 12
Bishop = □, □ + ♗ = 7	Queen = □, ♕ + □ = 14
Bishop = □, ♗ + □ = 10	Queen = □, □ + ♕ = 13

Making ten

Fill in the following □ with a chess piece.	Fill in the following □ with a number.	
♙	9	10
♖	□	10
♕	□	10
□ or □	7	10

♛ + d

♛ + d or d + ♛

| ♛ + 1 | ♛ + 2 | ♛ + 3 | ♛ + 4 | ♛ + 5 |

| ♛ + 6 | ♛ + 7 | ♛ + 8 | 9 + ♛ | ♛ + 7 |

| ♛ + 9 | 6 + ♛ | ♛ + 7 | ♛ + ♛ | ♛ + 9 |

| ♛ + 8 | ♛ + 1 | 5 + ♛ | ♛ + 3 | ♛ + 4 |

| 9 + ♛ | ♛ + 6 | 2 + ♛ | ♛ + 5 | ♛ + 7 |

Reversed calculation of 5

Fill in the following ☐ with a non-zero number

5	=	1	+	♠	+	♠	=	1	+	☐	+	☐
5	=	♠	+	1	+	♠	=	☐	+	1	+	☐
5	=	♠	+	♠	+	1	=	☐	+	☐	+	1
5	=	2	+	♠	+	♥	=	2	+	☐	+	☐
5	=	♠	+	2	+	♥	=	☐	+	2	+	☐
5	=	♠	+	♥	+	2	=	☐	+	☐	+	2
5	=	3	+	♣	+	♣	=	3	+	☐	+	☐
5	=	♣	+	3	+	♣	=	☐	+	3	+	☐
5	=	♣	+	♣	+	3	=	☐	+	☐	+	3

Doubling

Doubling using variables

Learning Chess to Improve Math

Multiplication

Rook row:
- 5, 15, 75
- 5, ☐, 80
- 5, ☐, 600

Queen row:
- ☐, ☐, 99
- ☐, ☐, 108
- ☐, ☐, 135

Knight row:
- ☐, ☐, 75
- ☐, ☐, 105
- ☐, ☐, 135

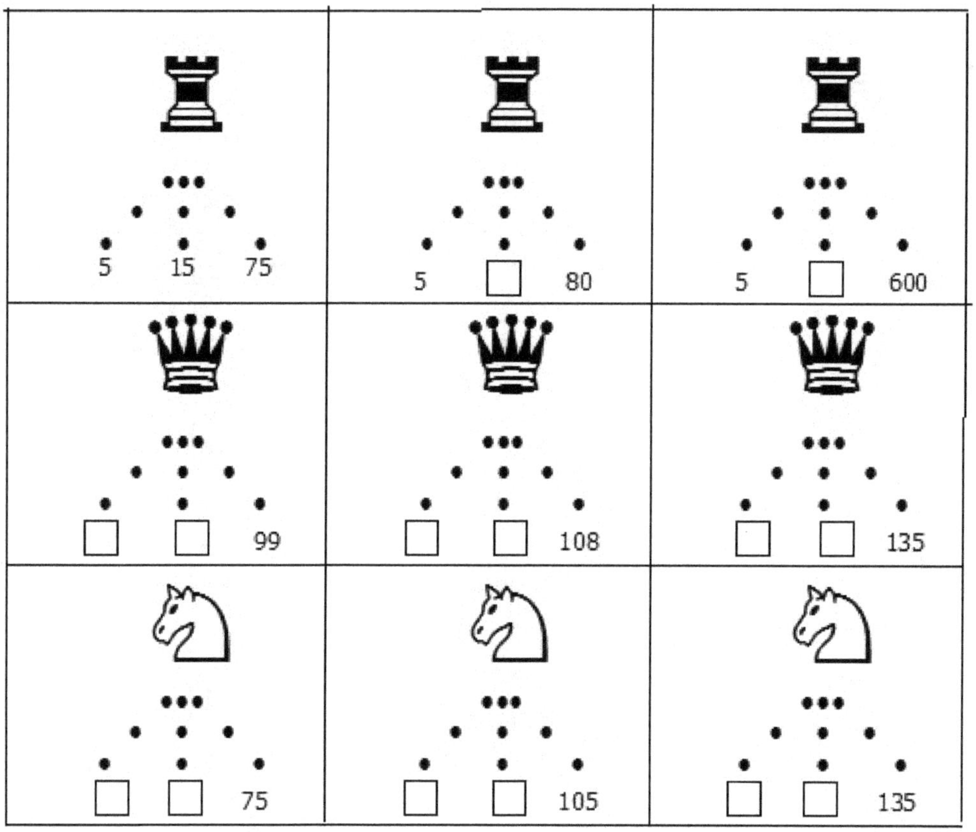

Multiplication

Puzzle 1:
- $\bigcirc = 18 \times 4 = \bigcirc_{72}$
- $18 \times \text{(Rook)} \times 4$
- $\bigcirc = \bigcirc \times \bigcirc = \bigcirc_{80}$
- Column sums: 90, 76

Multiplication box: 76 × 90

Puzzle 2:
- $\bigcirc = 21 \times 6 = \bigcirc_{126}$
- $21 \times \text{(Rook)} \times 6$
- $\bigcirc = \bigcirc \times \bigcirc = \bigcirc_{91}$
- Column sums: 147, 78

Multiplication box: 147 × 78

Student name ______________________ Assignment date: ________________

Multiplication

	○ ‖		○ ‖	
○ =	19	×	○	= 95
	×	♜	×	
○ =	○	×	15	=75
	‖ 95		‖ 75	

			9	5
		×	7	5

	138 ‖		91 ‖	
161 =	○	×	7	= ○
	×	♜	×	
○ =	6	×	13	= ○
	‖ ○		‖ ○	

		1	3	8
	×		9	1

Multiplication

96 × 72

143 × 98

Student name ____________________Assignment date:______________

Multiplication and addition

	○ +		5 +	
9 +	6	×	8	= ○
	×	♜	×	
○ +	9	×	○	= 106
	‖ □ 96		‖ 93	

			9	6
		×	9	3

	○ +		5 +	
○ +	6	×	11	=
	×	♜	×	
14 +	9	×	○	=
	‖ 108		‖ 83	

		1	0	8
	×		8	3

Student name ______________________Assignment date:_______________

Multiplication and addition

	17 +		15 +	
18 +	9	×	7	= ○
	×	♜	×	
27 +	9	×	○	=
	‖ ○		‖ ○	

			9	8
		×	8	1

	○ +		5 +	
41 +	6	×	○	=
	×	♜	×	
35 +	7	×	○	=
	‖ 101		‖ 80	

		1	0	1
	×		8	3

Multiplication and subtraction

	117 −	115 −	
118 −	9	×	7	= ○
	×	♖	×	
217 −	9	×	8	= ○
	□ ○		□ ○	

		1	9	8
	×		8	1

	109 −	105 −	
108 −	9	×	6	= ○
	×	♖	×	
207 −	6	×	8	= ○
	= ○		= ○	

		1	3	1
	×		8	9

Multiplication and subtraction

	117−	115−	
118 −	9 ×	7	= ◯
	× ♜	×	
217 −	9 ×	8	= ◯
	‖ ◯	‖ ◯	

		1	9	8
×			8	1

	109−	105−	
108 −	9 ×	6	= ◯
	× ♜	×	
207 −	6 ×	8	= ◯
	‖ ◯	‖ ◯	

		1	3	1
×			8	9

Multiplication and subtraction

	111 −		101 −	
○−	9	×	6	=
	×	♜	×	
○−	7	×	8	=
	‖ ○		‖ ○	

$$\begin{array}{r} 308 \\ \times\ 81 \\ \hline \end{array}$$

	202 −		201 −	
○−	9	×	5	=
	×	♜	×	
○−	6	×	8	=
	‖ ○		‖ ○	

$$\begin{array}{r} 409 \\ \times\ 80 \\ \hline \end{array}$$

Student name ______________________Assignment date:_______________

Equation

Add one chess piece into□ so both players have equal points.

♛ = ♖ + ♘ + □

♜ = ♗ + □ + □

♞ = □ + □ + □

♞ + ♝ = ♙ + □

♜ + ♜ = ♕ + □

♜ + ♛ = ♖ + ♖ + □ + □

♜ + ♜ + ♚ + ♛ = ♙ + ♔ + ♖ + ♖ + □ + □

♟ + ♟ + ♟ = □

♟ + ♟ + ♟ + ♟ + ♟ = □

Arrangement

In the first rank a, how many different ways can Ra1 move? _____

In the following diagrams, how many different ways can Bc4 move? _____

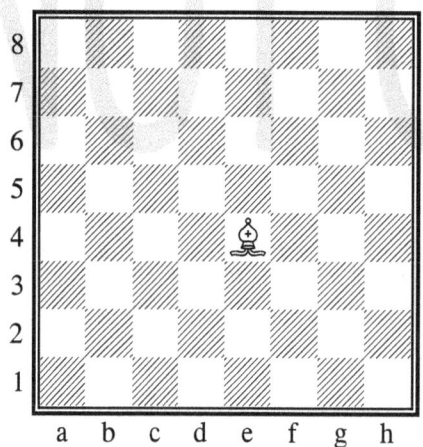

Arrangement

Write only the first letter of the chess piece in the following ☐ such that 2 kings are separated by 1 piece, 2 bishops are separated by 2 pieces, 2 queens are separated by 3 pieces.

Q	B	K	Q	B	K

Write only the first letter of the chess piece in the following ☐ such that 2 kings are together, 2 pawns are separated by 1 piece, 2 bishops are separated by 2 pieces, 2 rooks are separated by 3 pieces.

R	B	P	K	K	R	P	B

Arrangement

Write only the first letter of the chess piece in the following ☐ such that 2 kings are together, 2 pawns are separated by 1 piece, 2 bishops are separated by 2 pieces, 2 rooks are separated by 3 pieces, 2 queens are separated by 4 pieces.

K	K	Q	P	R	P	B	Q	R	B

Arrangement

How many different arrangements are there to have ♙♘♖ placed on the white squares? Draw one chess piece in each ☐.

You can use numbers 1, 2, and 3 to represent chess pieces.
123, 132, 213, 231, 312, 321

Arrangement

Put the following chess pieces in the following table so that three pieces placed horizontally are the same in one way, and two pieces placed one above the other are different in two ways.

Use letters K_w, K_b, Q_w, Q_b, B_w, B_b to fill in the table.

Student name ______________________ Assignment date: ________________

Magic square

Replace the following □ with a number such that all rows, columns, and the two main diagonals must sum to the same number.

4	♛	□
♞	♜	7
8	♟	□

If then Equation

Fill in the following ☐ with a chess algebraic notation.

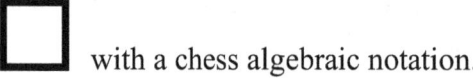

If ♖ + 2 = a7 and ♖ − 1 = a4

then ♖ − 2 = ☐.

If ♖ + ♖ + ♖ = 3♖
then ♖ + ♖ + ♖ - ♖ = ☐

Fill in ☐ with a number.

If ♗ = ♙♙♙

Then ♗♗ = ☐ ♙

If then Equation

Fill in the following ☐ with a number.

If 3 ♖ 2 = 5 then 3 ♗ 2 = ☐.

Counting Paths

If the rook is restricted to move from A to B in the direction of only moving down or toward the right, how many different ways can the rook move? Answer _____.

The following diagrams are to be used to find out the number of different ways. (Note the number of ways is less than the number of diagrams drawn below.)

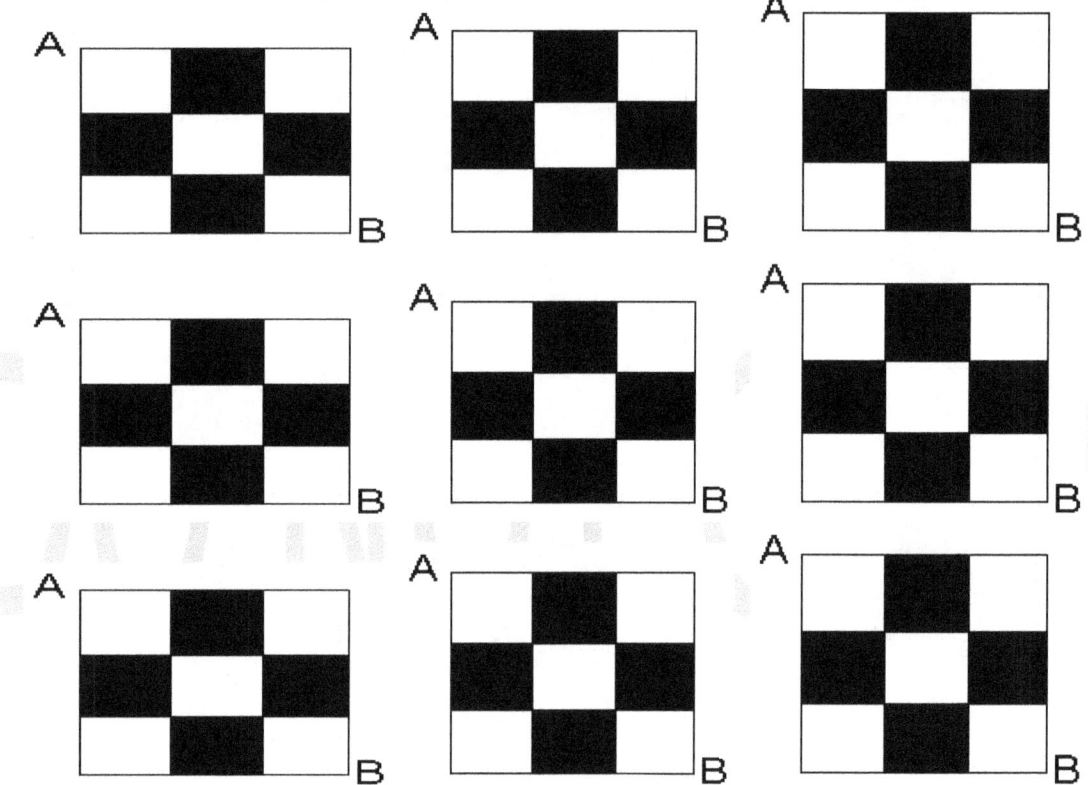

Counting Paths

How many short paths for ♗ to travel from e4 to f1?

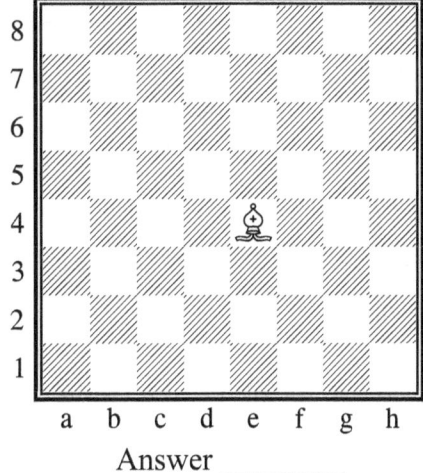

Answer _____

Learning Chess to Improve Math

Ho Math Chess — www.homathchess.com

Frank Ho, Amanda Ho © 1995 – 2021   All rights reserved.

Student name _____ Assignment date:_____

Part 8 Chess and Math Connection

Math and Chess Contests

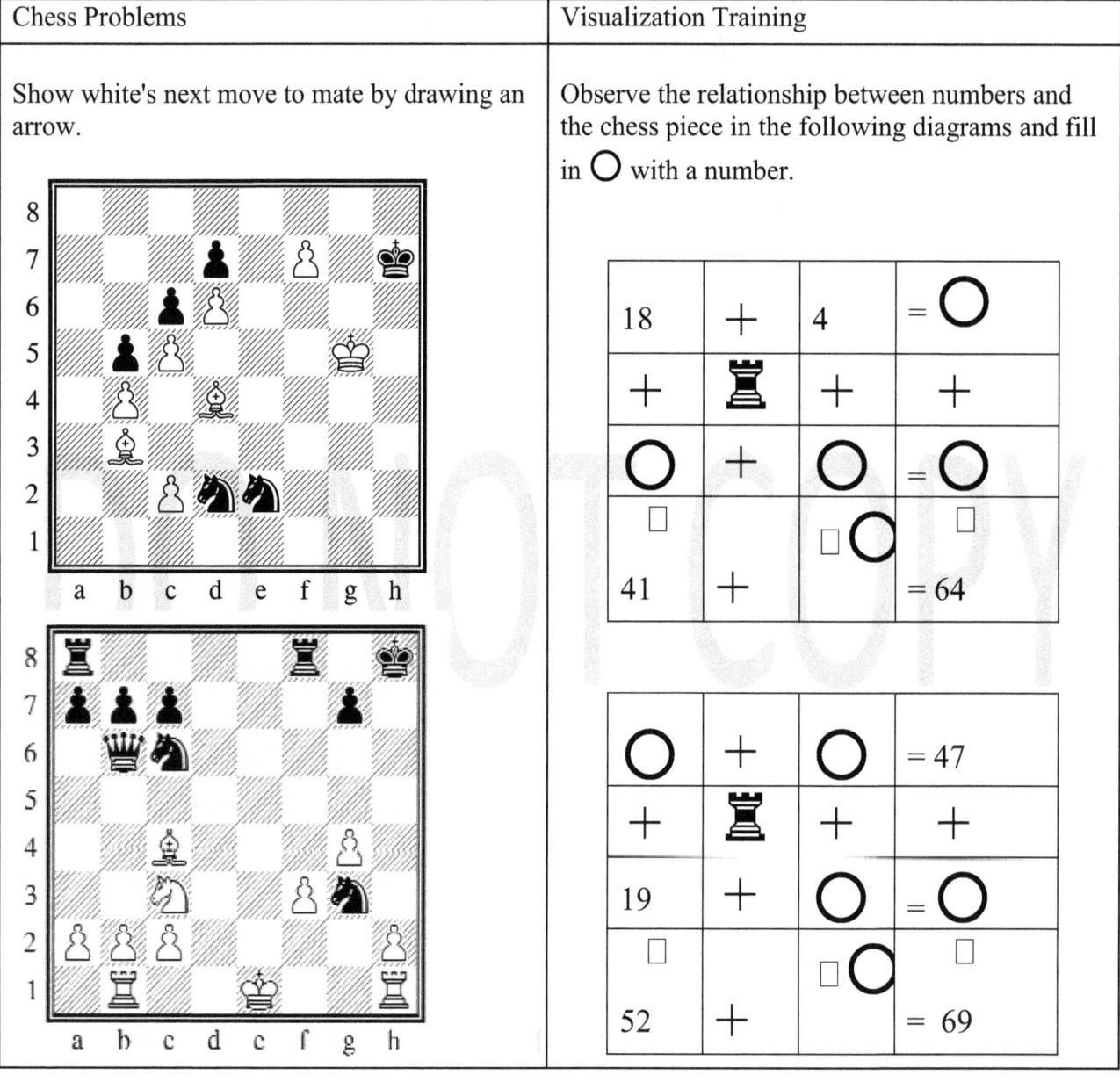

Learning Chess to Improve Math

Ho Math Chess www.homathchess.com

Frank Ho, Amanda Ho © 1995 – 2021   All rights reserved.

Student name _____ Assignment date: _____

Chess Problems

Show how white makes a skewer by drawing an arrow.

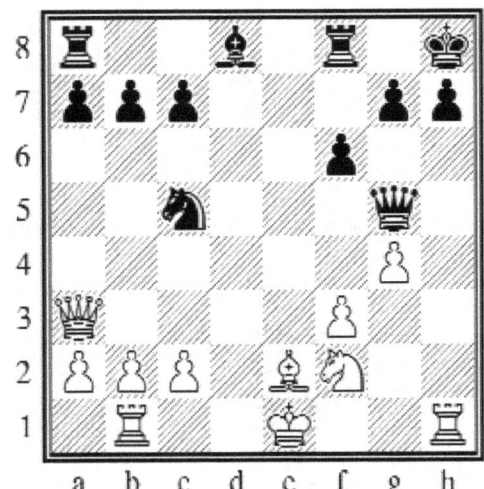

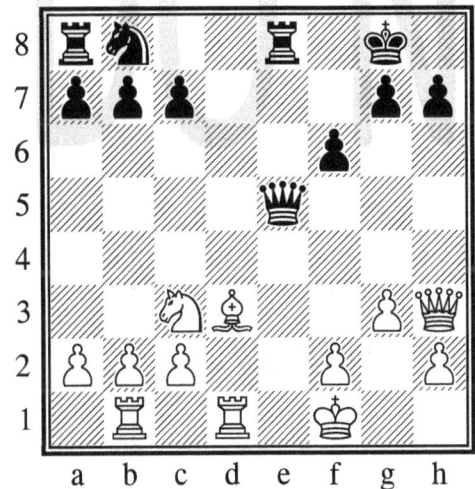

Visualization Training

Observe the relationship between numbers and the chess piece in the following diagrams and fill in ◯ with a number.

18	—	4	= ◯
—	♜	—	—
◯	—	◯	= ◯
☐	☐	☐	
9	—	◯	= 8

22	—	◯	= ◯
—	♜	—	—
◯	—	1	= ◯
☐	☐	☐	
14	—	◯	= 6

Learning Chess to Improve Math

数棋谜式健脑国际象棋

 Math Chess 何数棋谜 www.homathchess.com

Frank Ho, Amanda Ho © 1995 – 2021   All rights reserved.

Student name _____ Assignment date:_____

Chess Problems

Show white's next move to win material using a pin.

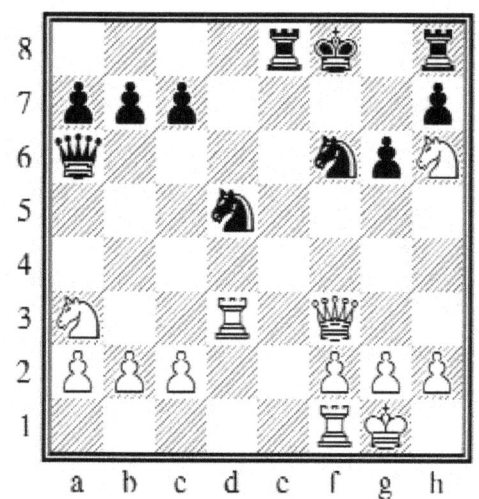

Show white's next move to discover double attacks.

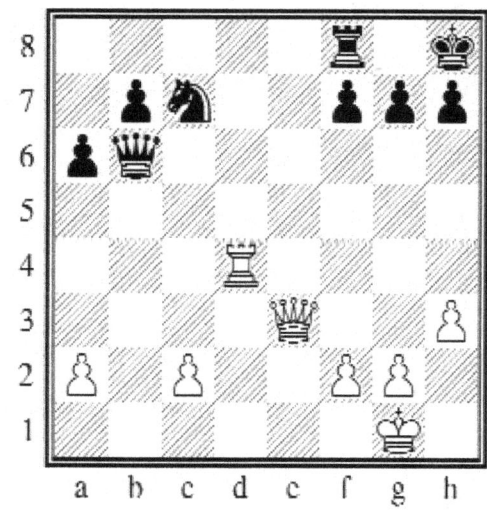

Visualization Training

Observe the relation between numbers and chess pieces in the following diagrams and fill in ○ with a number.

♙	♟	0
♙♙	♟	1
♘	♞♞	−3
♖♖♖	♜♜	○
♕♕	♛♛♛	○

Knight's tour

Examine the left diagram and replace the following question mark with an answer.

start	slide	stop
Ne4	(+2, +1)	Ng5
Ng5	(-1, +2)	Nf7
Ne4	(-2, -1)	?
Nf7	(+1, -2)	?
Ne4	(-1, -2)	?

If ♛ ÷ ♝ = ↔

Then what is ♚ ÷ ↓ = ?

Learning Chess to Improve Math 数棋谜式健脑国际象棋
Ho Math Chess 何数棋谜 www.homathchess.com
Frank Ho, Amanda Ho © 1995 – 2021   All rights reserved.

Student name _____ Assignment date:_____

Chess Symbol

A new Chess Symbol is defined as follows:

Chess figurines	Chess symbols
King	∻ (Opposition)
Rook	+
Knight	L
Bishop	×
Queen	✳
Pawn	↓

Logic Training

Observe the chess symbols on the left and fill in each ○ with a number in the following equation.

If + + + = 10

then ∻ + + = ○

```
        +   ✳
    +   +   ∻
   ─────────────
        ○ ∻ ✳
```

5 1

Use the above Chess Symbol table; find the answer for the following pattern:

Z, ∻, O, ↓, T, L, T, ×, F, +, ____, ✳

Use the above Chess Symbol table; find the answers for the following pattern:

0, ∻, 1, ↓, ___, L, 3, ×, 5, +, ___, ✳

Learning Chess to Improve Math   数棋谜式健脑国际象棋

 Math Chess   何数棋谜   www.homathchess.com

Frank Ho, Amanda Ho © 1995 – 2021   All rights reserved.

Student name _____ Assignment date: _____

Chess Problems

Show white's next best move by an arrow. (30 points)

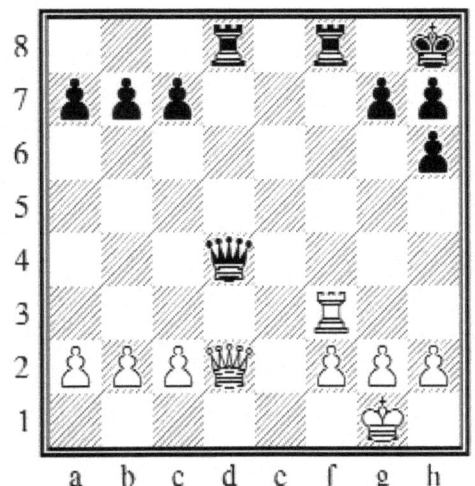

White to checkmate in 2 moves. Show white's moves by arrows. (40 points)

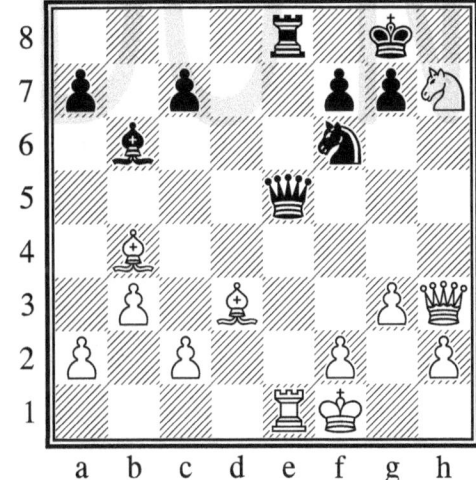

Pattern and Relation

In the following diagram, observe the relation between numbers and chess pieces and fill each ○ with a number. (10 points)

1	♙	2
2	♞	5
3	♜	8
4	○	11
5	♛	○

In the following diagram, observe the relation between numbers and fill in each ○ with a number. (20 points)

1	4	9	61
52	63	94	46
18	001	○	○

Appendix A Connection of Magic Chess and Math Puzzles

Frank Ho, M.Sc.

Founder of Ho Math Chess

www.homathchess.com

Vancouver, BC, Canada

Originally written in April 2005

Edited on August 2015

| Learning Chess to Improve Math 数棋谜式健脑国际象棋 |
| Ho Math Chess 何数棋谜 www.homathchess.com |
| Frank Ho, Amanda Ho © 1995 – 2021   All rights reserved. |

Student name _____ Assignment date:_____

Ho math Chess has published a series of basic number facts workbooks. These workbooks are an innovative idea of learning math using chess and puzzles to enrich math problem-solving ability. These workbooks are created with many features, including the following characteristics.

Hands-on
Chess provides ample hands-on opportunities. However, one has to move chess pieces to get a game going physically.

Multi-concept
Math puzzles worksheets are designed to learn division while doing multiplication and learning subtraction while doing addition.

Multi-direction
Chess is a multi-direction game. As a result, some worksheets are designed so that the operation is no longer just a linear fashion from left to right. Instead, the direction could be from bottom to top, left to right, and diagonally or even crossed.

Multi-sensory
The learning of chess involves eyes, hands, and brain coordination. The math pattern puzzle trains visualization.

This paper provides information on why using Ho Math Chess' workbooks would improve a student's math problem-solving ability. The information is provided by extracting sample problems from the workbook and then gives a corresponding math concept learned by doing the sample problems.
This one-on-one table style comparison gives concrete evidence on what math concepts are learned after working on the math puzzles that are included in the workbook.

| Learning Chess to Improve Math | 数棋谜式健脑国际象棋 |
| Ho Math Chess 何数棋谜 www.homathchess.com |
| Frank Ho, Amanda Ho © 1995 – 2021   All rights reserved. |

Student name _____ Assignment date:_____

How was math integrated into our chess workbook?

Today's updated chess workbook reflects the magic relationship between mathematics and chess and how chess could be used in improving mathematics ability.

I did not want to create a workbook, which is just a collection of chess puzzles, nor did I want to create a workbook, which was a collection of brain-teasing math puzzles. The problems in my workbook I envisioned to create must have the following characteristics:

- Must have some logical connection between chess and math problems.
- Students could learn chess and improve their math ability at the same time.
- Problems created must be innovative and interesting.
- Only basic chess is required to solve math problems.
- Elementary students from grade 1 and above could solve these problems.

Learning expectations

People always wonder what the relationship between chess and math is and how many math concepts in my workbook are children learning? What are the expected learning outcomes? My workbook is not designed to prepare children for the chess tournament, nor is it written to prepare for a math contest. It is designed to lead children into the wonderful world of learning chess and, at the same time to introduce some math concepts using chess as a learning tool. It is written with the idea to show children that math is not just doing drills and boring math computations day in and day out. It is offered as an alternative and supplemental learning resource for math education but not to replace the school math curriculum. The expected chess-learning outcome stops at the tactical level and can be easily seen from the table of contents of the workbook.

In this article, I would like to give some examples of problems taken out of some of my workbooks to outline expected learning outcomes of math concepts incorporated in these workbooks, demonstrating how chess and math could be integrated to benefit children in improving their mathematics ability.

Chess knowledge required

The chess knowledge required to do the mathematical puzzles is listed as follows:

- How to move the chess pieces, and how to write moves in algebraic notation.
- The values of chess pieces.
- How to castle.

Addition

Math Puzzle Samples	Expected Math Learning Outcomes	Chess Knowledge Required
Fill in each □. ┌ + ♕ + ┐ 1 + 3 ↓ 2 ↓ □ □ □	▪ Adding numbers ▪ Making tens ▪ Substituting unknown variable ▪ Multi-direction operation	▪ Value of chess pieces
♖ + ♞ + x = 45 + ♖ + ♞ $x =$ _____	▪ Cancellation ▪ Equation ▪ Substituting unknown variable ▪ Multi-concept learning	▪ Value of chess pieces
Replace each ? with a number. |	17	
?	9	3
	8			▪ Adding numbers ▪ Multi-direction operation	▪ Rook move
♕ + 1 + 8 + 2 + ♕ + 1 + ♕ + 1 + 8 + 2 + ♕ + 1 + 8 + 2 = ?	▪ Adding numbers ▪ Making tens ▪ Substituting unknown variable	▪ Value of chess pieces

Addition

Math Puzzle Samples	Expected Math Learning Outcomes	Chess Knowledge Required
Replace each ? with a number. 14 □ 12 □ 8 □ ? □ 6	▪ Adding numbers ▪ Multi-direction operation	▪ Bishop move
♖ + ♙ = □ + ♖ + ♔ = □ + _____ □ □	▪ Addition ▪ Comparison ▪ Multi-direction operation ▪ Substituting unknown variable	▪ Value of chess pieces
$6 + ♖ = 6 + 4 + \Box = \Box = 6 + \Box + ♙$ $\lfloor 10 \rfloor \quad \lfloor 10 \rfloor$ $\overset{6}{+♖}$ (4 + ♙)	▪ Addition ▪ Comparison ▪ Multi-direction operation ▪ Substituting variable	▪ Value of chess pieces
If ♖ + ♖ = □, then 6 + ♖ must be □. If ♖ + ♖ = □, then ♖ + 6 must be □.	▪ Addition ▪ Comparison ▪ Multi-direction operation Substituting variable	▪ Value of chess pieces

Learning Chess to Improve Math

Frank Ho, Amanda Ho © 1995 – 2021   All rights reserved.

Ho Math Chess   www.homathchess.com

Student name _____ Assignment date: _____

Subtraction

Math Puzzle Samples	Expected Math Learning Outcomes	Chess Knowledge Required
♕ + 8 ―― □ − ♕ = □	▪ Subtracting numbers ▪ Substituting unknown variable ▪ Multi-direction operation ▪ Multi-concept learning	▪ Value of chess pieces
□ □ ―― − ♟ + ♟ 8 8	▪ Subtracting numbers ▪ Substituting unknown variable ▪ Bottom-up operation and then top-down operation ▪ Multi-concept learning	▪ Value of chess pieces

DO NOT COPY

Mixed operations (addition and subtraction)

□ + ♛ = □ + 8 = 11 = 7 + □
− ♜
─────
□ − ♜ = □ = 11 − □
=   =
♛   11
□   □
2   ♜

Subtraction

Math Puzzle Samples	Expected Math Learning Outcomes	Chess Knowledge Required
♖ + ♘ + x = 63 + ♖ x = _____	<ul><li>Subtracting numbers</li><li>Substituting unknown variable</li><li>Multi-direction operation</li><li>Multi-concept learning</li></ul>	<ul><li>Value of chess pieces</li></ul>
1 1 ← ← ← − ♖ ─────── ☐ + ♖ = ☐ ↑ Check	<ul><li>Subtracting numbers</li><li>Substituting unknown variable</li><li>Multi-direction operation</li><li>Multi-concept learning</li></ul>	<ul><li>Value of chess pieces</li></ul>
♖ + 2 = ☐ + ♖ + ♔ = ☐ + ─── ─── ☐ ☐	<ul><li>Subtracting numbers</li><li>Substituting unknown variable</li><li>Multi-direction operation</li><li>Multi-concept learning</li></ul>	<ul><li>Value of chess pieces</li></ul>

Learning Chess to Improve Math 数棋谜式健脑国际象棋
Ho Math Chess 何数棋谜 www.homathchess.com
Frank Ho, Amanda Ho © 1995 – 2021   All rights reserved.

Student name _____ Assignment date:_____

Multiplication

Math Puzzle Samples	Expected Math Learning Outcomes	Chess Knowledge Required
$\dfrac{\text{♖}}{\text{♖}} = \dfrac{2}{2}$	<ul><li>Cross multiplication</li><li>Substituting unknown variable</li><li>Multi-direction operation</li></ul>	<ul><li>Value of chess pieces</li></ul>
$1 \times 6\text{♙} \times 7 = \square$	<ul><li>Multiplication</li><li>Substituting unknown variable</li></ul>	<ul><li>Value of chess pieces</li></ul>

Student name _____ Assignment date:_____

Cross Multiplication

Expected learning outcomes: multiplication, addition, subtraction, Substituting unknown variable

Chess knowledge required: Chess pieces values

♟ = □
24 = □

□ × □ + □ × □ = 10

Mixed operations

The following is an example of a multi-concept learning multi-direction operation.
Expected learning outcomes: multiplication and division

$$\frac{20}{\square \times} = 4 \qquad \underset{4}{\overset{\text{♖}}{\times}} \qquad \frac{20}{\square \times} = \text{♖}$$

$$4 \times \square = \boxed{\square} = \square \times \text{♖}$$

$$\underset{\square}{\overset{4}{\times}}$$

$$4 \overline{)20} \qquad \text{♖} \overline{)20}$$

$$4 \overline{)20} \qquad \text{♖} \overline{)20}$$
$$\times \square \qquad \qquad \times \square$$

Student name _____ **Assignment date:** _____

Mixed Operations

The following is an example of multi-concept learning with the multi-direction operation.
Expected learning outcomes: addition, subtraction, multiplication, and division

$16 \times \square$	$\square - 10$ $\parallel$ $= 48 =$ $\parallel$ 6 $\times$ $\square$	$\square \div \bishop$ $\times \square$ $4 \overline{)48}$
$\times \square$ $16 \overline{)48}$		
$2 \overline{)48}$ $\times$ $\square$	$\square \div \bishop = \square$ $\parallel$ 8 $+$ $\square$	$6 \overline{)48}$

Division

Math Puzzle Samples	Expected Math Learning Outcomes	Chess Knowledge Required
♛ × ☐ ――――― $18 \div 2 = \square$	<ul><li>Multiplication</li><li>Division</li><li>Substituting unknown variable</li><li>Multi-direction operation</li></ul>	<ul><li>Value of chess pieces</li></ul>
$(3♛ \div 3) + (2♜ \div 5)$ $= 27 \div 3 + 10 \div 5$ $= 9 + 2$ $= 11$	<ul><li>Multiplication</li><li>Division</li><li>Substituting unknown variable</li><li>Multi-direction operation</li></ul>	<ul><li>Value of chess pieces</li></ul>
♞) 180018	<ul><li>Division</li><li>Substituting unknown variable</li></ul>	<ul><li>Value of chess pieces</li></ul>

Learning Chess to Improve Math

Fraction

One would think that chess perhaps has nothing to do with fractional numbers since all moves are all in whole numbers. So why is the queen the most powerful piece of chess, and why do we usually move chess pieces toward the middle? They all have something to do with the ratio a/b, where *b* is the 64 squares, and *a* is the squares under control.

Math Puzzle Samples	Expected Math Learning Outcomes	Chess Knowledge Required
$\frac{3♘}{3} + \frac{4♘}{4} = ♘ + ♘ = 3 + 3 = 6$	<ul><li>Fraction</li><li>Logic comparison</li><li>Substituting unknown variable</li><li>Multi-direction operation</li></ul>	<ul><li>Value of chess pieces</li></ul>
$\frac{3♘}{2} = 4\frac{1}{2}$	<ul><li>Convert improper to mixed fraction</li></ul>	<ul><li>Value of chess pieces</li></ul>
$\frac{2}{♖} + \frac{1}{♖} = \frac{2+1}{♖} =$	<ul><li>Adding fractions</li></ul>	<ul><li>Value of chess pieces</li></ul>

Learning Chess to Improve Math 数棋谜式健脑国际象棋
Ho Math Chess 何数棋谜 www.homathchess.com
Frank Ho, Amanda Ho © 1995 – 2021   All rights reserved.
Student name _____Assignment date:_____

Integer

Math Puzzle Samples	Expected Math Learning Outcomes	Chess Knowledge Required
♛ + ♕ = 0	<ul><li>Adding negative number</li><li>Substituting unknown variable</li><li>Multi-direction operation</li></ul>	<ul><li>Value of chess pieces</li></ul>

Exponent

Math Puzzle Samples	Expected Math Learning Outcomes	Chess Knowledge Required
♛ ♛ = 9^2	<ul><li>Exponents</li><li>Substituting unknown variable</li><li>Multi-direction operation</li></ul>	<ul><li>Value of chess pieces</li></ul>

Radical

Math Puzzle Samples	Expected Math Learning Outcomes	Chess Knowledge Required
$\sqrt{♜\,♜}$ = ♜ = 5	<ul><li>Radicals</li><li>Substituting unknown variable</li><li>Multi-direction operation</li></ul>	<ul><li>Value of chess pieces</li></ul>

Learning Chess to Improve Math 数棋谜式健脑国际象棋

Ho Math Chess 何数棋谜 www.homathchess.com

Frank Ho, Amanda Ho © 1995 – 2021   All rights reserved.

Student name _____ Assignment date:_____

Logic

Math Puzzle Samples	Expected Math Learning Outcomes	Chess Knowledge Required
♖ × 3 ☐ ♖ × 4	<ul><li>Logic comparison</li><li>Substituting unknown variable</li><li>Multi-direction operation</li></ul>	<ul><li>Value of chess pieces</li></ul>
$x + 8 - 2 = $ ♕ What is x? _3_	<ul><li>Logic comparison</li><li>Substituting unknown variable</li><li>Multi-direction operation</li><li>Equation</li></ul>	<ul><li>Value of chess pieces</li></ul>

Equation

Math Puzzle Samples	Expected Math Learning Outcomes	Chess Knowledge Required
♖ + x = 63 + ♖ x = ____	<ul><li>Equation</li><li>Substituting unknown variable</li><li>Multi-direction operation</li></ul>	<ul><li>Value of chess pieces</li></ul>

Learning Chess to Improve Math 数棋谜式健脑国际象棋
Ho Math Chess 何数棋谜 www.homathchess.com
Frank Ho, Amanda Ho © 1995 – 2021   All rights reserved.

Student name _____ Assignment date:_____

Visualization

Chess Puzzle Samples	Expected Math Learning Outcomes	Chess Knowledge Required
Write chess notations for the following chess pieces whose positions are in the diagram.	If the rook is at a1 and is free to make moves along file *a* and rank 1, what has to be considered before moving? The most important is to see any opponent's pieces that could intersect with the rook. Thinking in math way would be to see what y is when x = 1 and what would be x when y = 1. Thus, we will be looking for intersections. The idea of coordinates would be easier for chess players to learn if they already have acquired the practical experience of "intersections" coming from different chess pieces. The chess notation is entirely transferable to the concept of math coordinates and vice versa.	- Value of chess pieces - Chess piece's move - The ranks and files are related to coordinates.

Visualization

Math Puzzle Samples	Expected Math Learning Outcomes	Chess Knowledge Required
How many different sizes of squares are there on the following 4 by 4 square?	- Counting squares	- Chessboard
Replace each "?" with a number. [4x4 grid with knight in center; values: ? 14 / ? 21 / ? 28 / 42 ?]	- Counting - Multiplication - Multi-direction operation	- Chess pieces moves

Visualization

Chess Puzzle Samples	Expected Math Learning Outcomes	Chess Knowledge Required
Place the lowest number of white pawns (using the letter P) so that the squares numbered are attacked as many times as indicated numbers on the squares. 									 |---|---|---|---|---|---|---|---| | | 1 | 1 | 1 | 1 | 1 | 1 | 1 |
									▪ Visualization	▪ Chess pieces moves

Set

Chess Puzzle Samples	Expected Math Learning Outcomes	Chess Knowledge Required
Cross mark (X) the squares where both chess pieces can move to (intersect). [Chessboard diagram: Black knight on c6, white queen on f1]	Set Find the elements that exist in both sets. ∩ means "intersect". {A, B, C} ∩ {A,B}= _____ {1, 2, 3} ∩ {2, 3, 4, 5} = _____ {A, B, C} ∩ {A,B}= _____	▪ Value of chess pieces

Cancellation

Chess Puzzle Samples	Expected Math Learning Outcomes	Chess Knowledge Required
The way to see which side has more points is not to add up all the total points of chess pieces on each side. Instead, find out which side has more points by the cancellation. For example, cancel pawn with pawn and the same chess piece (or the same number of points) of each side.	The idea of one-to-one cancellation of chess pieces left on the board is similar to the subtraction property of the equation. Evaluate the following. $$\frac{1}{2} \times \frac{2}{4} \times \frac{4}{6} \times \frac{6}{8} \times \frac{8}{10} \times \frac{10}{12}$$ Do not multiply numbers together first. Instead, cancel numbers whenever you can by having a pair of numerator and denominator divided by the same number.	- Value of chess pieces

Learning Chess to Improve Math 数棋谜式健脑国际象棋
Ho Math Chess 何数棋谜 www.homathchess.com
Frank Ho, Amanda Ho © 1995 – 2021   All rights reserved.

Student name _____ Assignment date:_____

Pattern

Chess Puzzle Samples	Expected Math Learning Outcomes	Chess Knowledge Required
Observe the following pattern of a chess diagram and draw a chess piece in each box.	▪ Geometry	▪ Value of chess pieces
	▪ Data management	▪ Value of chess pieces

Student name _____ Assignment date: _____

Arrangement

Chess Puzzle Samples	Expected Math Learning Outcomes	Chess knowledge required
In the first rank a, how many different ways can Ra1 move? _____	▪ Data management	▪ Chess pieces moves

Geometry

The chessboard and chess pieces themselves are geometry. The chessboard is symmetric in terms of its main diagonals. The chessboard is made of 4 identical small boards divided by one horizontal line and one vertical line going through the centre. The setup positions of chess pieces are symmetric between black and white — the chess pieces setup positions on either side are palindrome except for the king and queen.

The following uses chess moves to match shapes. Rook's move is a slide motion (left/right, up/down) in geometry. The between moves of rook before reaching the destination is using the concept of communicative property. For example, before Ra1 to Rh1, Rook could move from a1 to c1 (4 squares), then from c1 to h1 (3 squares) or from a1 to d1 (3 squares), then from d1 to h1 (4 squares). The complication is that the player has to watch what would happen if the different choices were made, which is much more complicated than adding 3 + 4 = 4 + 3 = 7.

Filling in with a chess piece	Geometric shapes
♙ (Pawn)	kite
♖ (Rook)	rhombus with diagonals
☐ (Square)	octagon with cross
♗ (Bishop)	square with diagonals

/ Learning Chess to Improve Math 数棋谜式健脑国际象棋
Ho Math Chess 何数棋谜 www.homathchess.com
Frank Ho, Amanda Ho © 1995 – 2021   All rights reserved.

Student name _____ Assignment date:_____

Geometry

Chess Puzzle Samples	Expected Math Learning Outcomes	Chess knowledge required
Find the answer to replace the question mark.	▪ Geometry	▪ Chess pieces moves

Learning Chess to Improve Math

If then equation

Chess Puzzle Samples	Expected Math Learning Outcomes	Chess knowledge required
You are filling in the following ☐ with a number. If 3 ♖ 2 = 5 then 3 ♗ 2 = ☐.	• Data management	• Chess pieces moves

Pattern and relation (Tabulation in $ax + by + \ldots = c$, where a, b, c are constant.)

Fill in a different number of chess pieces to come up with each total.

Number of ♖	♖ Points	Number of ♘	♘ Points	Total points
1	5	1	3	8 (1 × 5 + 1 × 3 = 8)
☐	5	☐	3	11
☐	5	☐	3	13
☐	5	☐	3	16

Counting paths

Chess Puzzle Samples	Expected Math Learning Outcomes	Chess knowledge required
How many short paths for ♗ to travel from e4 to f1? 8 7 6 5 4 3 2 1 a b c d e f g h	▪ Data management	▪ Chess pieces moves

Venn diagram

Chess Puzzle Samples	Expected Math Learning Outcomes	Chess knowledge required
The following Venn diagram shows the results of a chess diagram. What squares are only controlled by the rook and the bishop? Answer this question by shading the area on the Venn diagram. 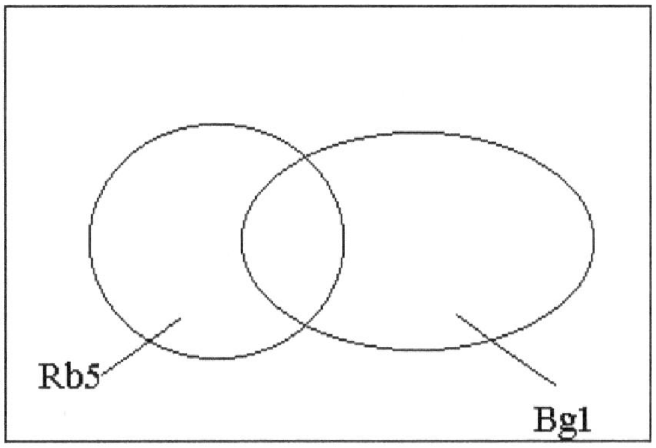 Rb5 Bg1	▪ Venn diagram	▪ Chess pieces moves

Learning Chess to Improve Math	数棋谜式健脑国际象棋
Ho Math Chess	何数棋谜 www.homathchess.com
Frank Ho, Amanda Ho © 1995 – 2021	All rights reserved.

Student name _____ Assignment date:_____

Probability

Chess Puzzle Samples	Expected Math Learning Outcomes	Chess knowledge required
What is the probability of the following two pieces meeting together? (Chess board diagram: black bishop on c4, white bishop on e5)	• Probability	• Chess pieces moves

Page 343 of 349

Learning Chess to Improve Math 数棋谜式健脑国际象棋
Ho Math Chess 何数棋谜 www.homathchess.com
Frank Ho, Amanda Ho © 1995 – 2021   All rights reserved.

Student name _____ Assignment date:_____

Tree structure

The calculations of different paths and also the opponent's possible responses are complicated. The deeper the player could calculate the paths, the higher the possibility of playing better is. The calculation of path requires logical thinking, which is very similar to using a factor tree to find out the prime factors of 64, but chess is more complicated in a way. The opponent's moves also have to be thought in advance.

Chess Puzzle Samples	Expected Math Learning Outcomes	Chess knowledge required
Complete the following tree diagram starting at Nb2 **(knight moves right and up only.)** Nb2 -- c4 -- d6 -- e5 -- d3	• Tree structure Find the product of primes of 32. 32 ↙ ↘ 2 16 ↙ ↘ 2 8 ↙ ↘ 2 4 ↙ ↘ 2 2	• Chess pieces moves

Learning Chess to Improve Math   数棋谜式健脑国际象棋
Ho Math Chess   何数棋谜   www.homathchess.com
Frank Ho, Amanda Ho © 1995 – 2021   All rights reserved.

Student name _____ Assignment date:_____

A free Paper Set of Ho Math Chess

Want to have a free (almost) Ho Math Chess set? It takes about 10 minutes to complete a DIY chess set.

You can use the following link to print the chess pieces and the chessboard.
https://1drv.ms/u/s!AnVFh_KY480OgtJsze8k6ipl9GeaCQ

Chess pieces

Print the following Ho Math Chess set (on a colour printer is preferred), then cut each piece in squared shape and paste them on pieces of corrugated papers, foams, or bottle caps.

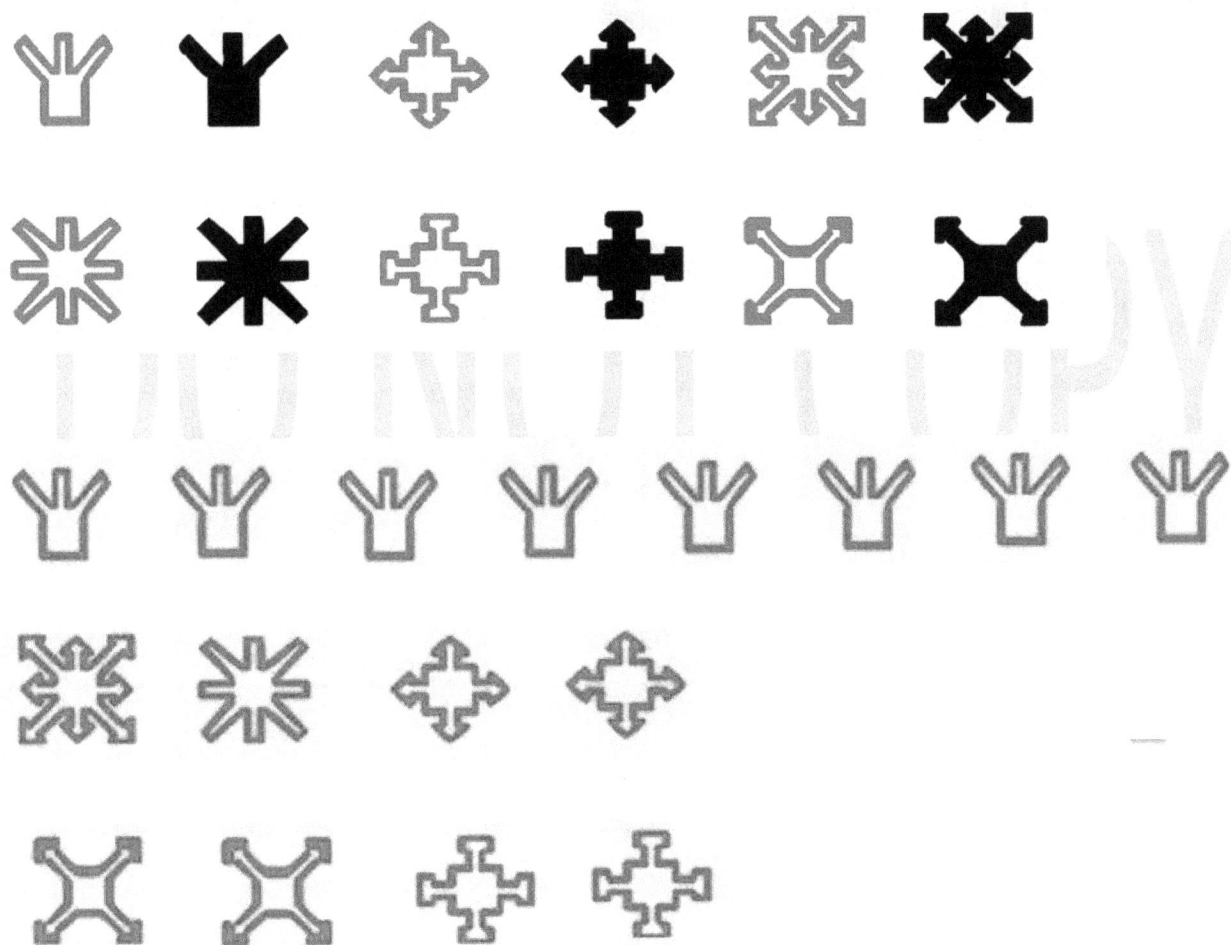

Learning Chess to Improve Math   数棋谜式健脑国际象棋
Ho Math Chess   何数棋谜   www.homathchess.com
Frank Ho, Amanda Ho © 1995 – 2021   All rights reserved.

Student name _____ Assignment date:_____

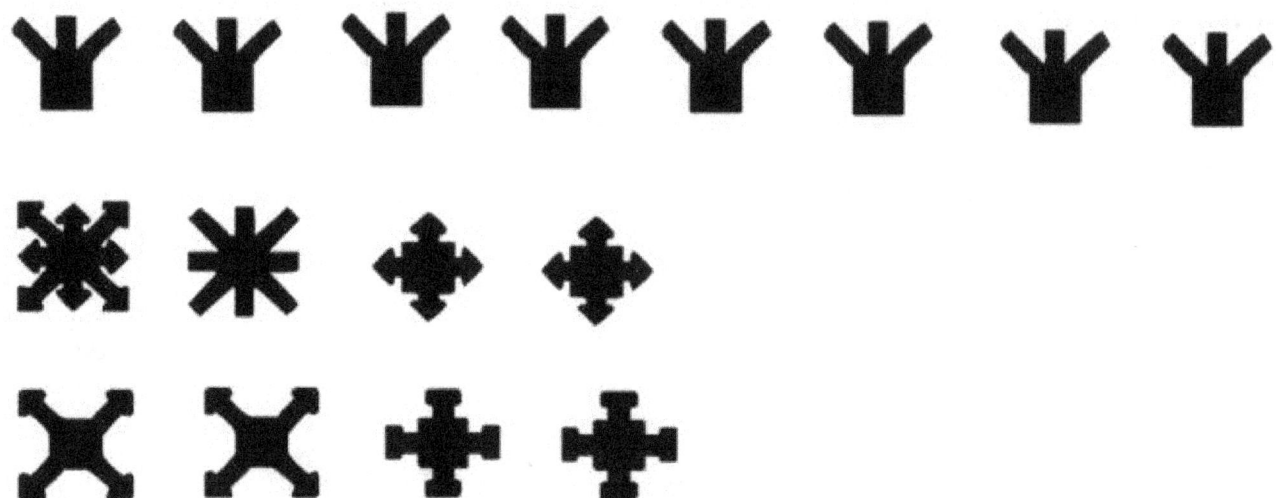

Chessboard

Learning Chess to Improve Math 数棋谜式健脑国际象棋
Ho Math Chess 何数棋谜 **www.homathchess.com**
Frank Ho, Amanda Ho © 1995 – 2021 All rights reserved.

Student name _____ Assignment date:_____

| Learning Chess to Improve Math   数棋谜式健脑国际象棋 |
| Ho Math Chess 何数棋谜 www.homathchess.com |
| Frank Ho, Amanda Ho © 1995 – 2021   All rights reserved. |
| Student name _____ Assignment date:_____ |

Introducing Ho Math Chess in Chinese 介紹何数棋谜

介紹何数棋谜

何数棋谜 = 奥数棋谜 + 思唯腦力開發
英文教材，中英双语教学

什麼是何数棋谜?

上百篇科學論文已發表國際象棋可以提高兒童問題解答能力. 並且訓練他們的專心及耐力. 所以我們已經知道下國際象棋對兒童有好處. 但是因為國際象棋與計算能力並無直接關係, 所以如何讓兒童能在一個歡樂的環境下也能利用下棋來提高數學的計算呢? 何老師首創並發明有版权的幾何棋藝符號並利用此符號發明了世界第一的獨特結合數學与棋谜教材. 何数棋谜讓兒童能利用幾何棋藝符號進行邏輯推理及數字的運算. 棋藝與算術的綜合題含蓋了整數, 幾何, 集合, 抽象數, 對比異同, 函數, 座標, 多空間圖形資料, 及規則性數字分析. 並且把棋藝的趣味性和數學的知識性結合在一起.

何数棋谜如何幫助兒童腦力思唯的開發?

很簡單的一個道理就是讓學生自願地同時去用左右腦. 何数棋谜棋谜式数学即是專为当達到此目的而研發的教法及教材.

訓練右腦
何数棋谜首創獨一無二的融合數學與棋谜的独特趣味寓教於樂教材, 利用國際象棋訓練右腦的座標, 空間分析及圖形及表的處理.

訓練左腦
何数棋谜發明了整合棋子與數學的圖形語言, 讓兒童能利用抽象棋子符號圖形訓練左腦進行邏輯推理及數字的收集以創造題目並進行數字的運算.

國際象棋與算術的綜合題含蓋了整數, 幾何, 集合, 抽象數, 對比異同, 函數, 多空間圖形資料. 所以枯燥無味的計算題變成了謎題, 學生需要通過更多的思考. 能讓腦去思考愈多則腦力也愈開發. 處里訊息, 分析資料才能發掘出題目. 做這些謎題式數學時可以訓練學生比較會專心及有耐心.

何数棋谜教学結果有科研報告嗎?

　数棋谜融合數學與國際象棋的教學理論已在 BC 省數學教師刊物上發表. 科研報告已經證實何数棋谜教學法不但可以提高兒童數學解題及思維能力, 還可以開發兒童的腦力, 及分析問題的能力並且增加兒童學習的耐力, 學生的探索創造精神及求知欲. 判斷力, 及自信心等, 啓發思維訓練機警靈巧及加強手腦眼的靈活運用.

| Learning Chess to Improve Math 数棋谜式健脑国际象棋 |
| Ho Math Chess 何数棋谜 www.homathchess.com |
| Frank Ho, Amanda Ho © 1995 – 2021   All rights reserved. |

Student name _____ Assignment date:_____

Introducing Ho Math Chess™

Ho Math Chess™ = math + puzzles + chess

After teaching his son chess, Frank Ho, a Canadian math teacher intrigued by the relationships between math and chess, started **Ho Math Chess™** in 1995. His long-term devotion to research has led his son to become a FIDE chess master and Frank's publications of over 20 math workbooks. Today **Ho Math Chess™** is the world's largest and the only franchised scholastic math, chess and puzzles specialty learning centre worldwide. In addition, **Ho Math Chess™** is a leading research organization in math, chess, and puzzles integrated teaching methodology.

Hundreds of articles already published showing chess benefits children and that math puzzles are a very good way of improving brainpower. So, by integrating chess and mathematical chess puzzles, the learning effect is more significant.

Parents send their children to **Ho Math Chess™** because they like **Ho Math Chess™** teaching philosophy – offering children problem-solving questions in a variety of formats. The questions could be pure chess, chess puzzles or mathematical chess puzzles like logic, pattern, tree structure, Venn diagram, probability and many more math concepts.

Ho Math Chess™ has developed a series of unique and high-quality math, chess, and puzzles integrated workbooks. In addition, **Ho Math Chess™** produced the world's first workbook **Learning Chess, to Improve Math.** This workbook is not only for learning chess but also for enriching math ability. This sets **Ho Math Chess** apart from other math learning centres, chess clubs, or chess classes.

The teaching method at **Ho Math Chess™** is to use math, chess, and puzzles integrated workbooks to teach children fun math. The purposes of **Ho Math Chess™** teaching method and workbooks are to:

- Improve math marks.
- Develop problem-solving and critical thinking skills.
- Improve logic thinking ability.
- Boost brainpower.

Testimonials, sample worksheets, reports, and franchise information can be found at www.homathchess.com.

More information about **Ho Math Chess™** can also be found in the following publications:

1. Why Buy a **Ho Math Chess™** Learning Centre Franchise: A Unique Learning Centre?
2. **Ho Math Chess™** Sudoku Puzzles Sample Worksheets
3. Introduction to **Ho Math Chess™** and its Founder Frank Ho

The above publications can be purchased from www.amazon.com.

www.ingramcontent.com/pod-product-compliance
Lightning Source LLC
Chambersburg PA
CBHW081125170426
43197CB00017B/2753